PRAISE FOR *THE DYING CITIZEN*

"Victor Davis Hanson's book is not a complaint nor a polemic but rather a fine-grained diagnosis of a very serious disease. Its symptoms are all around us: the fragmentation of America's national identity by the assertion of not merely separate but separatist identities with the vehement support of the most privileged of all Americans. May this brilliant diagnosis lead us to a cure."

—Edward N. Luttwak,
author of *The Rise of China vs. the Logic of Strategy*

"The great glory of the democratic revolution of the eighteenth and nineteenth centuries was extending the blessings of citizenship to anyone and everyone who embraced the principles and responsibilities of self-governing nations. As Victor Davis Hanson explains, by subtle degrees we're reversing course, through a deliberate attempt to dilute and eventually erase national identity, sovereignty, borders, and the meaningful content of citizenship itself. But if everyone is a 'citizen of everywhere,' it means they are citizens of nowhere, with the return of autocratic rule the final result. The hour is late, and we have Hanson to thank for this capacious account of what we need to recover."

—Steven F. Hayward, author of *Patriotism Is Not Enough*

"This is not a drill—this is the real thing. If you don't believe that the survival of the American republic hangs in the balance, you must read Victor Davis Hanson's relentless exposition of the facts. America's free citizenry is at imminent risk of defeat at the hands of an unelected Deep State allied to a globalist elite that flouts American law with impunity and plans to jettison the Constitution. Even if you think you're informed and alarmed about these trends, Hanson's brilliant presentation will leave you much better prepared to address these dangers. Get this book into the hands of everyone you know."

—David Goldman, deputy editor of *Asia Times*
and author of *You Will Be Assimilated*

"Once again Victor Davis Hanson has written a masterly account of a great public affairs crisis. He has given a learned history of the concept and indispensability in a democracy of responsible citizenship; has perceptively chronicled how it has been undermined in the US; how Donald Trump in his sometimes frantic way tried to revive it, and of the tense but not unhopeful current prospects. This book is a concise masterpiece that all serious citizens should read."

—Conrad Black

"This is a book about an ongoing and threatening change of 'regime,' which means a change not only in how we are governed but also in how we live. To understand such a thing requires perspective: Victor Hanson is deeply educated in the classics, where knowledge of regimes was first developed. It also requires a close observation of what is happening today, about which he writes insightfully and in profusion. In this book, Hanson demonstrates yet again his command across time and for our time. This book and he are a treasure."

—Larry P. Arnn, president of Hillsdale College

"As I write, Victor Davis Hanson's book *The Dying Citizen* is still a couple of months from publication. But here is a prediction: it will instantly be seen for what it is, one of the most important and insightful books of the early 2020s. Hanson is that rarest of authors: a man of immense erudition who also commands a penetrating and sympathetic understanding of the practical side of life. Political freedom, Hanson shows, is inextricable from the life of citizenship. And citizenship is not a given. It is an achievement, an achievement, moreover, that must be tended to survive. Most of history unfolded without citizens, only subjects, serfs, slaves, and sycophants. And just as there were ages before citizenship, so we can see from our own experience that citizenship can decay and fail. Should it fail—should citizenship give way to any of the utopian alternatives on offer—then our political freedom will go with it, a casualty of those good intentions that always seem to line the road to perdition. Among much else, then, *The Dying Citizen* is an impassioned cri de coeur, an admonition, a startling tocsin in the night. Victor Hanson has written a number of good and informative books. *The Dying Citizen* is without a doubt his magnum opus."

—Roger Kimball, editor and publisher of *The New Criterion*

THE
DYING
CITIZEN

ALSO BY VICTOR DAVIS HANSON

Warfare and Agriculture in Classical Greece

The Western Way of War

Hoplites (editor)

The Other Greeks

Fields Without Dreams

Who Killed Homer? (with John Heath)

The Wars of the Ancient Greeks

The Soul of Battle

The Land Was Everything

Bonfire of the Humanities
(with John Heath and Bruce Thornton)

An Autumn of War

Carnage and Culture

Between War and Peace

Mexifornia

Ripples of Battle

A War Like No Other

The Immigration Solution
(with Heather MacDonald and Steven Malanga)

Makers of Ancient Strategy (editor)

The Father of Us All

The End of Sparta: A Novel

The Savior Generals

The Second World Wars

The Case for Trump

THE DYING CITIZEN

How Progressive Elites,
Tribalism, and Globalization
Are Destroying the Idea of America

VICTOR DAVIS HANSON

BASIC BOOKS
New York

Basic Books
Hachette Book Group
1290 Avenue of the Americas, New York, NY 10104
www.basicbooks.com

Printed in the United States of America

First Edition: October 2021

Published by Basic Books, an imprint of Perseus Books, LLC, a subsidiary of Hachette Book Group, Inc. The Basic Books name and logo is a trademark of the Hachette Book Group.

The Hachette Speakers Bureau provides a wide range of authors for speaking events. To find out more, go to www.hachettespeakersbureau.com or call (866) 376-6591.

The publisher is not responsible for websites (or their content) that are not owned by the publisher.

Print book interior design by Jeff Williams

Library of Congress Cataloging-in-Publication Data
Names: Hanson, Victor Davis, author.
Title: The dying citizen : how progressive elites, tribalism, and globalization are
    destroying the idea of America / Victor Davis Hanson.
Description: First Edition | New York, N.Y. : Basic Books, 2021. | Includes
    bibliographical references and index.
Identifiers: LCCN 2021012459 | ISBN 9781541647534 (hardcover) | ISBN
    9781541647541 (ebook)
Subjects: LCSH: Citizenship—United States. | Citizenship—United States—History. |
    Elite (Social sciences)—United States. | World citizenship. | United States—Politics
    and government.
Classification: LCC JK1759 . H228 2021 | DDC 323.60973—dc23
LC record available at https://lccn.loc.gov/2021012459

ISBNs: 978-1-5416-4753-4 (hardcover), 978-1-5416-4754-1 (ebook)

LSC-C

Printing 1, 2021

ACKNOWLEDGMENTS

I thank my wife, Jennifer, for reading the manuscript, as well as my colleague and friend Bruce Thornton of the Hoover Institution. I owe continued thanks to Glen Harley and Lynn Chu of Writers' Representatives. For over three decades, I have relied on their principled literary representation and friendship.

Lara Heimert, publisher of Basic Books, once again read the entire manuscript, and I owe her a debt of gratitude for needed syntheses, clarifications, and economies of expression and organization. In addition, I wish to thank again Roger Labrie of Basic Books for greatly improving the manuscript with his meticulous general editing. This is the third book we have worked on at Basic, and his common sense and good judgment are deeply appreciated. The remaining errors in the book are mine alone. I also thank Jennifer Kelland for a superb job of copyediting, and again I am responsible for any errors that remain.

My research assistant at Hoover, Dr. David Berkey, likewise read the manuscript. Along with John Magruder, he helped proof the endnotes, in addition to checking and reformatting the text during various stages of editing. John compiled a bibliography of all works cited that can be accessed at victorhanson.com. My assistant, Megan Ring of the Hoover

Institution, ensured that I kept on schedule and met various deadlines, including those well beyond the scope of the book.

I thank supporters of the Hoover Institution, Stanford University, and others for allowing me time to write this book, especially Martin Anderson, Beatrice and Jim Bennet, Will Edwards, Roger and Susan Hertog, Lew Davies, Jim Jameson, John and Carole Harris, Mary Myers Kauppila, Rebekah, Jennifer, and Robert Mercer, Roger and Martha Mertz, Jeremiah Milbank, Tom and Diane Smith, Richard F. and Karen Spencer, Victor Trione, and Kay Woods.

For Jennifer

CONTENTS

PRE– AND POST–
AMERICAN CITIZENS

Citizenship is what makes a republic; monarchies can get
along without it. What keeps a republic on its legs is good
citizenship.

—MARK TWAIN, 1906

Today only a little more than half of the world's seven billion
people are citizens of fully consensual governments enjoying
constitutionally protected freedoms. They are almost all Western—or
at least they reside in nations that have become "westernized." These
realities explain why millions from North Africa risk drowning in the
Mediterranean to reach Europe and why millions more uproot from
Mexico and Latin America to cross the southern border of the United
States. Call their exodus from their homelands a desperate quest for
greater income, freedom, or security—or simply for a chance to be an
unfamiliar citizen somewhere else rather than a certain serf, noncitizen,
or subject at home.

Of the world's rare true democracies, only about twenty-two have
been in existence for a half century or more. Lamentably, the number of

democracies is now shrinking, not growing—ironic when so many people are now leaving what is ascendant to reach what is vanishing. Perhaps that depressing fact is a reminder that it is not an easy thing for people to govern themselves, much less to protect and exercise their inherited freedoms. Citizenship, after all, is not an entitlement; it requires work. Yet too many citizens of republics, ancient and modern, come to believe that they deserve rights without assuming responsibilities—and they don't worry how or why or from whom they inherited their privileges.[1]

Yet for the lucky global residents of constitutional states, citizenship has translated into shared freedoms beyond superficial appearance. It is a quality more fundamental than a common religion and collective geography. Citizens are not mere residents, prone to receiving more than giving. They are not tribal people who band together by appearance or blood ties. They are not peasants under the control of the rich. Nor is their first allegiance to an abstract worldwide commonwealth.

Eighteenth-century German political philosopher of the Enlightenment Immanuel Kant perhaps best summed up all the exceptional entitlements that he hoped one day could define a Western citizen—at least in his own rosy expectation of an idealized European to come. Kant saw the citizen alone as enjoying "lawful freedom, the attribute of obeying no other law than that to which he has given his consent." In other words, a king or dictator could not force his will upon those who never elected him. Kant added that citizens should be assured of "civil *equality*" under the law. They should not recognize "among the *people* any superior with the moral capacity to bind him as a matter of right in a way that he could not in turn bind the other." The state cannot treat the rich, the better born, or the well-connected any better than it does the poor, the peasant, and the obscure. Finally, Kant cited "the attribute of civil *independence*." The goal of a citizen was to "owe his existence and preservation to his own rights and powers as a member of the commonwealth, not to the choice of another among the people." The citizen does not have to thank anyone for his rights. They are innate and properly his own.

These eighteenth-century visions of philosophers like Kant were not realized throughout Europe until the early 1990s when parliamentary democracies replaced the last dying communist regimes of Eastern Europe—more than two centuries after the foundation of American democracy. Their creators did not always keep—or even fully grasp—the promises of Western citizenship. Yet only under consensual governments was there at least *a chance* that citizenship would eventually fully match its ideals with reality.[2]

A free, legally equal, and politically independent citizenry, when translated to the modern American experience, means that citizens of the United States should not follow any laws other than those authorized by their own elected representatives. Unelected regulators can issue edicts galore, but they should not necessarily have the force of law. No college administrator should decide on Monday that the First Amendment no longer applies on his campus. No mayor can claim on Tuesday that federal immigration law no longer exists in her city.

No one American deserves greater deference under the law than any other—not on the basis of race, class, gender, birth, or money; not on the basis of historic claims to justify contemporary advantage. Police and prosecutors arrest and charge lawbreakers, but not, like the pigs in *Animal Farm*, some lawbreakers more than others.

No senator or president bestows anything on an American, because he is a servant, not a master, of the people. American citizens believe that they do not owe privileges such as freedom and consensual governance to any particular political party or Democratic or Republican leader. American citizens, bearing natural and inalienable rights bestowed by a supreme deity, are accountable only to themselves.

Citizens differ from visitors, aliens, and residents passing through who are not rooted inside borders where a constitution and its laws reign supreme. For citizenship to work, the vast majority of residents must be citizens. But to become citizens, residents must be invited in on the condition of giving up their own past loyalties for those of their new hosts.

Citizenship is synonymous with our freedoms and their protection by law and custom, which transcend individual governments and transient leaders of the day. Barack Obama was still the president of those who were not fond of him, just as voters who loathed Donald Trump had no president but Trump. Neither president could nullify the Constitution or our freedoms—unless citizens themselves allowed him to do so.

In return for our rights to pick our own leaders and make our own laws, we are asked to obey America's statutes. We must honor the traditions and customs of our country. As Americans we cherish the memory of those who bequeathed to us such an exceptional nation, and we contribute our time, money, and, if need be, safety and lives on our country's behalf.

We must always ask ourselves whether as citizens we have earned what those who died at Shiloh or in the Meuse-Argonne gave us. Refusing to kneel during the national anthem or to salute the Stars and Stripes is not illegal, but it is not sustainable for the nation's privileged to sit in disgust for a flag that their betters raised under fire on Iwo Jima for others not yet born. Sometimes citizens can do as much harm to their commonwealth by violating custom and tradition as by breaking laws.

In practical terms, the US Constitution guarantees citizens security under a republic whose officials they alone choose and that assures them liberties. What exactly are these privileges? Everything from free speech, due process, and habeas corpus to the right to own and bear arms, to stand trial before a jury of one's peers, and to vote without restrictions as to race, religion, and sex. America, then, is only as good as the citizens of any era who choose to preserve and to nourish it for one more generation. Republics are so often lost not over centuries but within a single decade.[3]

So far, so good. This is the idea of citizenship as it was intended and should be.

But history is not static; nor does a people always progress linearly to an improved state. Civilizations experience descents, detours, and regressions—and abrupt implosions. So citizenship can wax and wane—and abruptly vanish. History also is mostly the story of noncitizenship. In the monumental civilizations of the preindustrial world, from the Babylonians and Egyptians to the Mayans and Aztecs of the New World, no residents of the sovereign soil of a monarchy, theocracy, or autocracy enjoyed any inalienable rights. Elected representatives did not decide their fates. They enjoyed no protection by a corpus of laws, much less by independent courts. It would be hard to imagine the career of a Socrates, Sophocles, or Cicero in any of these empires, just as today most Americans would find life in China, Cuba, Iran, or Russia stifling, if not dangerous. Instead, order and law came down from on high from authoritarian hereditary, tribal, or religious rulers. The disobedient were crushed, the obsequious promoted. The code of survival demanded subservience to one's superiors and haughtiness to those deemed inferiors. The harshness of the law hinged on the relative cruelty of a particular dynast. Consensual governments did not create or ratify the ancient Babylonian law code of Hammurabi (ca. 1750 BC) and the legal edicts of Darius I of Persia (ca. 500 BC).

Usually the succession of authoritarian rulers ignored popular will—a concept that itself did not formally exist. Rulers came to power by hereditary successions, coups, revolutions, civil wars, assassinations, religious revelations, and palace intrigues—as they so often do even today outside the westernized world. Nonviolent political change was rare and usually entailed succession of rulers by children or immediate relatives.

Voting, if it existed at all, was not transparent, sacrosanct, or widespread. It still is not for over three billion people today. Even in so-called democracies, "voting" often operates under implied or direct coercion, usually in rigged and scripted elections. A sign of democratic sclerosis is a loss of confidence in the integrity of voting—to the point that it becomes seen as a futile exercise rather than a bulwark of citizenship.

In most regimes of the past, there was one set of laws for the rich, priests, autocrats, and aristocrats and quite another for those without money, high religious or political office, or noble birth and lineage. Or those who gained power by election often sabotaged subsequent elections on the theory of "one election, one time."

Again, citizenship came quite late to civilization. To appreciate what we Americans enjoy, we should pause to remember the long road from antiquity to our own Constitution. Consensual government did not appear until about twenty-seven hundred years ago, most prominently in Athens, twenty-five hundred years after the beginning of large urban settlements in the Near East. In much of ancient Greece, by the early seventh century BC, property-owning citizens, or *politai*, enjoyed voting rights in the consensual governments of some fifteen hundred Greek city-states (*poleis*).

At first, a minority of the residents formed broad-based oligarchies. These governments privileged about half the resident male population, mostly those who owned small farms. The landless poor were seen as without enough material investments in society to offer sound judgment—or worse, their impoverishment was deemed proof of their moral or ethical inadequacies. Sometimes such restrictive governments slowly evolved into more direct democracies in the latter fifth and fourth centuries BC, when most of the free male resident population voted and a majority vote of the assembly often decided governance.[4]

Once established in the early West, citizenship unleashed, as the conservative philosopher Plato lamented, a rapid evolutionary process. The trajectory always bent toward greater inclusion. So, in such self-reflective societies, the lack of full citizenship accorded to the poor in oligarchies and to slaves and women in democracies was a source of constant discussion, praise, criticism, and argumentation. What so bothered Plato and other reactionary critics of democracy was that the impulse toward inclusivity always grew without logical bounds once a society had institutionalized equality and freedom within consensual governments. Among his bleaker notions—one seemingly supported by long periods of postdemocratic history—was that an always radical-izing democracy would eventually lead to chaos and then a swing back to tyranny.

For a time, the Greek city-state became more inclusive without succumbing to anarchy. It is certainly no accident that in democratic Athens the heroes (and tragic titles as well) of most of Euripides's plays were women—Alcestis, Andromache, Andromeda, Antigone, Hecuba, Helen, Iphigeneia, and Medea. Tragedians apparently explored the idea that when some women were stronger or more moral than some men, and yet all were treated as political and cultural inferiors, then the logic of the polis did not hold. Nor is it odd that the crusty comic drama-tist Aristophanes voiced the superior wisdom and morality of war-torn Athens through his feminist character Lysistrata, not the senior male apparat of Athenian democracy that started and conducted the conflict. Apparently in the mind of the dramatist, when the male leadership of the city-state could not win or end a devastating war, then perhaps marginalized others could.

Long before the British and American abolitionists, Alkidamas, the fourth-century BC Elaean orator and Athenian resident, reminded Greece of its contradictions between *eleutheria* (freedom) and *douleia* (slavery): "Nature," Alkidamas railed, "has made no man a slave." That declaration was no idle talking point. It would become a rallying cry that later resonated with the great Theban democratic liberator Epami-nondas, who freed the Messenian helots from their indentured service to Sparta—a feat that made him preeminent among the most illus-trious Greeks of the classical age. In sum, the nature of consensual government at its origins was constant self-critique and reassessment. When such perpetual introspection ceases, so does citizenship.[5]

By twenty-first-century standards, many today would call early Greek constitutional governments ethnocentric, nativist, and sexist. But compared to what exactly in the contemporary ancient world? Some twenty-five hundred years ago, the Greeks were remarkably enlightened and liberal by the then current standards of tribal northern Europe

7

or in comparison with powerful dynastic civilizations in Egypt, Persia, the Near East, India, and China. There the mass of residents remained either tribesmen, serfs, subjects, or slaves without individual rights.[6]

By the late fifth century BC, an increasing number of native-born resident males enjoyed citizenship in most Greek city-states. They alone could decide whether to grant particular residents such privileges by decree. They had the right to speak freely in the assembly, where speech was usually far more unfettered than on contemporary American campuses. As citizens, they passed on property to their chosen female or male heirs. They stood trial in criminal and civil cases before juries of their peers. They enjoyed a sovereign country with clearly defined borders. They cherished the privilege to vote on matters of war and peace and to serve their city-state in its phalanx armies—and, in exchange, they expected the state to allow them to protect their families and farms.

Citizens of the Greek city-state also reflected the empowerment of the middle class. The *mesoi* (middle ones) of the city-states were neither noble by birth nor condemned to poverty by either circumstance or lack of inheritance. "Middleness" (*to meson*) in thought and practice at the very beginning of the West was an innate ideal of citizenship. Much of Aristotle's *Politics* is a historical and contemporary analysis of consensual governments of classical Greece. So, unsurprisingly, it praises middle citizens as the glue that held the entire state together, without the hubris shown the lower classes characteristic of the rich and powerful. In his encomium about the *mesoi*, Aristotle wrote,

> A city ought to be composed, as far as possible, of equals and similars; and these are generally the middle classes. Wherefore the city which is composed of middle-class citizens is necessarily best governed; they are, as we say, the natural elements of a state. And this is the class of citizens which is most secure in a state, for they do not, like the poor, covet their goods. . . . Thus it is manifest that the best political community is formed by citizens of the middle class,

and that those states are likely to be well-administered, in which the middle class is large, and larger if possible than both the other classes, or at any rate than either singly; for the addition of the middle class turns the scale, and prevents either of the extremes from being dominant. Great then is the good fortune of a state in which the citizens have a moderate and sufficient property.[7]

Aristotle envisions the middle class not just as morally superior to the elite but also as more stable and reliable than the poor. And a city-state governed by the middle classes is superior not just to oligarchies but also to tribal peoples, often nomadic and without permanent settlements, who define their political existence by precivilizational ties of blood and marriage.

Citizenship, then, explains the Greek achievement of drawing on the talents and energy of a much-empowered resident and middle-class population. Why and how, after all, did such a numerically small number of people in such a small space as Greece nonetheless create the foundations of Western philosophy, politics, literature, history, and science? Once protected by laws, rather than by the transitory goodwill and patronage of aristocrats and autocrats, in a practical sense the citizen has far more legal and economic latitude to paint, write, build, farm, create, discover, or litigate. There is no need for either a religious fundamentalist or an unproductive political commissar to "correct" and repress inquiry and expression, vital to the material progress, security, prosperity, and freedom of the polis. The Athenian tragedian Aeschylus, in the final play of his *Oresteia* trilogy (458 BC), resolved the vendetta of the House of Atreus with the mythical establishment of the historical Areopagus court and, in the process, depicted the civilizing effects of law on society. If not worried about being arbitrarily jailed, killed, deprived of his property and inheritance, or told where and how to live, a citizen is more likely to exploit his own talents—and often create wealth for his commonwealth. And a free state that does not employ armies of unproductive snoops, spies, and politically correct commissars does not have its most daring and innovative minds crippled or its economy hobbled by costly hordes of unproductive trimmers.

Traditionally, philosophical supporters of the middle classes have argued that a majority of moderate property holders both encourages self-reliance, responsibility, and social stability, which are lacking in the poor, and curbs the ability of all-powerful, special interests to exercise inordinate influence on the state. In our age of deprecating "brick and mortar," we sometimes forget that perhaps the main impetus of ancient constitutional government was the protection of widescale property holding. Edmund Burke, drawing on the classical tradition, saw the right to property as synonymous with constitutionalism: "I hope we shall never be so totally lost to all sense of the duties imposed upon us by the law of social union, as, upon any pretext of public service, to confiscate the goods of a single unoffending citizen."

Republican Rome expanded on the Greek idea of the citizen (*civis*) in a variety of ways. The Romans codified many rights and delineated the citizen's responsibilities. In time, those privileges and obligations became institutionalized systematically under Roman imperial and universal law—including everything from habeas corpus to a sophisticated and comprehensive digest of criminal and civil statutes and courts. Nowhere in the ancient world could women or slaves vote—despite a millennium of criticism in classical literature of such systematic discrimination as hypocritical and its rules and protocols as impractical. Most importantly, though, Roman republicanism sought to ameliorate the perceived volatility and abuses inherent in radical, and especially Athenian, democracy. Rome was more influenced by the more parochial constitution of Sparta, whose dual legislative assemblies (the Apella and Gerousia), two chief executives (parallel lines of hereditary kings), and judicial auditors (the ephors) provided checks and balances on the use of power.[8]

The subsequent postclassical idea of Western constitutional citizenship ebbed and flowed through periods of retrenchment, oppression, and authoritarianism. Nevertheless, it slowly evolved through the

Middle Ages, Renaissance, Reformation, and Enlightenment toward an ever-greater array of rights and forevermore inclusion of the formerly dispossessed. The idea of equality under the law was inherently dynamic—despite preindustrial poverty ensuring a physical drudgery that curtailed political opportunities, while bearing and raising children remained a dangerous and life-consuming chore.[9]

By the twenty-first century, the Western idea of citizenship, after twenty-five hundred years of evolution, neared its logical fruition with the full emancipation of the poor, women, and minority populations after the long-ago abolition of serfdom, indentured peasantry, and chattel slavery. Yet, despite progressive legal efforts to extend all the rights of full citizenship to newly arrived illegal immigrants, to felons, and to teenagers not yet eighteen years old, in a practical sense the privileges of Western citizenship are, in fact, diluting. Just as there was no constitutional government before 700 BC, so there is no rule that there must be democracies and republics in the twenty-first century.

Failure can occur at any time and results more often from what we, rather than others, do to ourselves—affluence and leisure often prove more dangerous to citizenship than poverty and drudgery. In this context, one oddity of current American democratic culture is the strange habit of faulting the present-day United States for its past purportedly illiberal generations. The farther we progress from our origins, both chronologically and materially, the more we blame our founders for being less and less as anointed as we see ourselves. It is as if, when unhappy with the opulent present, we look to the impoverished past to blame our unhappiness on the dead, who faced daunting natural obstacles, rather than the living, who so often don't.

Indeed, the more political and social disparities disappear, the more they become emphasized and exaggerated—and the more the state takes responsibility for ensuring parity. Is that because the closer we arrive to full racial, ethnic, class, gender, and religious equality, the more we are damned for nearing but not quite achieving our utopian ideals? As the state ensures "equality" of opportunity, it is blamed for failing to provide "equity," or equality of result. Or do we equate technological progress with fated and commensurate advances in changing human nature? A culture whose citizens can monitor the world with iPhones surely cannot tolerate Neanderthals who are still biased or tribal.

Amid this desire to ensure equality of result through the use of government power, Americans currently feel that something is being lost in their daily lives. They often describe their frustrations as an attack on their very rights as citizens. In a December 2019 Harris Poll/Purple Project survey, for example, a vast majority of Americans surveyed— some 92 percent—believed that their rights were "under siege." More specifically, the poll found that Americans are most concerned that their freedom of speech (48 percent), right to bear arms (47 percent), and right to equal justice (41 percent) are at risk.[10]

Earlier surveys had revealed similar discontent, especially over the decline of local autonomy in comparison with the growth of the federal government, the erosion of popular sovereignty, and fears of an expanding federal government. A 2018 Pew Research Center poll revealed, "Two-thirds of those surveyed (67%) have a favorable opinion of their local government, compared with only 35% for the federal government." A Greek statesman of the ancient city-state might interpret such discontent as the inherent result of a government's becoming too large and powerful.[11]

Yet, while Americans sense that their constitutional rights are in jeopardy, they are not always aware of what exactly they are losing. That confusion is understandable given the erosion in civic education in our schools. In a 2017 poll taken by the University of Pennsylvania's Annenberg Public Policy Center, most Americans appeared ignorant of the fundamentals of the US Constitution. Thirty-seven percent could not name a single right protected by the First Amendment. Only one out of four Americans could name all three branches of government. One in three could not name any branch of government.

In a 2018 survey conducted by the Woodrow Wilson National Fellowship Foundation, almost 75 percent of those polled were not able to identify the thirteen original colonies. Over half had no idea whom the United States fought in World War II. Less than 25 percent knew why colonists had fought the Revolutionary War. Twelve percent thought Dwight D. Eisenhower commanded troops in the Civil War.

It is harder to lament the potential loss of constitutional freedoms when majorities of Americans willingly do not know what they are. When left-wing protesters began toppling statues in June 2020 to denounce supposed icons of racism, their target list of hallowed memorials included those commemorating the Union enforcer of Reconstruction, General Ulysses S. Grant, heroic African American veterans of the Civil War, and renowned martyred abolitionist Hans Christian Heg. Apparently the young iconoclasts learned little about the Civil War in either high school or college but a great deal about the supposed unwarranted privilege of anyone who had earned commemoration from a supposedly racist society. Sometimes American popular ignorance manifests itself by reality mimicking art. Just as the ignorant mob in Shakespeare's *Julius Caesar* mistakenly and unapologetically murdered Cinna the poet rather than Cinna the tyrannicide, so in February 2019 protesters torched the statue of World War II major general William C. Lee, apparently confusing his memorial with that of Confederate general Robert E. Lee.[12]

Citizenship in the United States is now being pulled in *two* different and often antithetical directions, from below and above, spontaneously and yet by design, through both ignorance of and intimacy with the Constitution.

Many Americans do not know or worry much about the consequences of radical demographic, cultural, or political influences for the status of citizenship. They are indifferent to millions of immigrants of uncertain status, veritable resident strangers in their midst. Similarly, many recent immigrants and many of the native born, for example, often have little idea of how American citizenship differs from simple residency or tribal grouping. Many arrivals believe that moving to and residing in the United States without legal sanction should nonetheless guarantee them all the benefits of American citizenship. Meanwhile, far too many citizens see no need to learn about the history and traditions of the United States or the civic responsibility of being an American. The contention that their country is irrevocably flawed becomes a justification for intellectual laziness and an unwillingness to learn about America's supposedly dark origins and customs. When nearly four in ten Americans have no notion of their rights under the First Amendment, it is easy to curb them.

On the other hand, some elites believe that they know the Constitution all too well and therefore believe it in dire need of radical deletions and alterations to fit the times. They envision an always improving, changing, and evolving Constitution that should serve as a global model for a vast, ecumenical brotherhood, requiring a global administrative state to monitor and enforce its ambitious idealism. Out of this chaos, some Americans prefer to be rebranded as "citizens of the world." Oddly, that tired idea dates back to Socratic utopianism and has never offered any credible blueprint for a workable transnational state.[13]

So what toxic forces and pernicious ideas have brought American citizenship—a 233-year-old idea able to transcend the conditions of its birth and accept women and those of races and ethnicities different from the majority culture fully into the political commonwealth—to the brink?

I have grouped the first three chapters together under the heading "Precitizens." The notion of precitizenry reflects ancient economic, political, and ethnic ideas and customs that were once thought antithetical to the modern democratic state. Yet, in organic fashion, they are reappearing and threaten to overwhelm the American commonwealth.

In Chapter 1, "Peasants," I review the ancient argument that to be self-governing, citizens must be economically autonomous. The Greeks defined self-sufficiency as *autarkeia*, a type of freedom from economic and thus political dependency on either the private wealthy or the state. The majority of the population cannot exercise and protect its rights of unfettered speech and behavior without the *material* security that only economic self-reliance and autonomy of the middle class ensure. Yet today the modern suburban everyman is becoming a nostalgic ideal rather than a vibrant reality. Indeed, the American middle class has lost economic ground for nearly a half century through mounting household debt, static wages, and record student-loan burdens. Without a middle class, society becomes bifurcated. It splinters into one of modern masters and peasants. In that situation, the function of government is not to ensure liberty but to subsidize the poor to avoid revolution and to exempt the wealthy, who reciprocate by enriching and empowering the governing classes.

Chapter 2, "Residents," argues that states must privilege citizens over mere residents. Citizens live within delineated and established borders. They share a common history. Their sacred physical space allows them to pursue their constitutional rights without interference from abroad. Living on common and exclusive ground encourages shared values, assimilation, and integration and defines national character. Yet we now live in an increasingly borderless world, where the notion of anyone more blessed at birth than another is seen as unfair—as if, in an age of affordable and rapid travel, an accident of birth should not deprive any of the planet's eight billion people from entering and living in the United States. Citizenship, however, is not indestructible. The more it is stretched to include everyone, the less the likelihood it can protect anyone.

Chapter 3, "Tribes," reminds us why all citizens should give up their own ethnic, racial, and tribal *primary* identities. Only through such a brutal bargain of assimilation can they sustain a common culture in a century in which superficial racial and tribal differences, the fuel for many of history's wars, are becoming no longer incidental but recalibrated as essential to the American character. In the absence of a collective civic sense of self, the inclusive idea of an American citizen wanes and fragments. Until the late twentieth century, the country suffered only sporadic episodes of blood and soil exclusivity and instead, usually through intermarriage and assimilation, made the idea of racial or ethnic purity inert. Once any nation goes tribal, however, eventually even those without easily identifiable ethnic ancestries or tribal affinities seek to reconstruct or invent them, if for no other reason than to protect themselves from the inevitable violence and factionalism on the horizon. Once a man owes more loyalty to his first cousin than to a fellow citizen, a constitutional republic cannot exist.

The three chapters of the second half of the book, under the heading "Postcitizens," focus on the even greater dangers to citizenship posed by a relatively small American elite. These "postmodernists" know all too well the history of their nation. They feel the United States should conform to a European and cosmopolitan ethos rather than pride itself in being "exceptional." They are well versed in the Constitution and therefore write eloquently about how it should be modified and its essence irrevocably changed to birth a truly direct equality-of-result democracy. Larger government and a more commanding administrative state should guarantee a mandated "equity." These elites believe that human nature has evolved since 1788, and the Constitution must catch up. In other words, it is now time to move beyond classical citizenship to accommodate a much different American and a now global community.

Chapter 4, "Unelected," chronicles how an unelected federal bureaucracy has absorbed much of the power of the US Congress, yearly creating more laws and regulations than the House and Senate together could debate, pass, and send to the president for signing. The permanent bureaucracy has overwhelmed even the office of the presidency. That all-powerful office often lacks sufficient knowledge to control the permanent legions deeply embedded within the state. Elected officials come and go. They proverbially rant about the "deep state." But the bureaucracy outlasts all, knows best, and so grows and breeds, often at the expense of the citizen. We are reaching a point similar to the rise of a fictive robotic terminator that destroys its too human creators, as the bureaucratic elite believes that it can and should preempt any elected official who deems it dangerous. If the citizen cannot elect officials to audit, control, or remove the unelected, then he has lost his sovereign power.

"Evolutionaries," the subject of Chapter 5, are the unapologetic grand architects of dismantling constitutional citizenship, inordinately represented by political activists, media grandees, the legal profession, and academics. As progressives, they feel Americans are currently stymied by an eighteenth-century constitutional albatross strung around their necks, one far too redolent of old, white, male, Christian values that supposedly have no relevance today. They accuse the Founders of lacking our modern wisdom, today's enlightened education, and the benefits of a constantly improving, innate human nature. The evolutionaries are not shy in explaining why the Constitution, along with centuries-old traditions that followed from it, are now either inert or obstructive or both. We must formally scrap and replace many such fossilized concepts and even founding documents, they insist, from the Electoral College to the Second Amendment to the Senate filibuster to a nine-person Supreme Court to two senators for every state. If perceived as impediments to progress, then by all means the current calcified rules can be changed or eliminated altogether, in a trajectory toward a 51 percent, majority-vote-rules nation, without sufficient constitutional and long-accustomed guardrails.

A final Chapter 6, "Globalists," explains the current fad that Americans are transitioning into citizens of the world. An ancient but unworkable idea of cosmopolitanism has reemerged, now driven by privileged utopians empowered by twenty-first-century global travel, finance, and communications. In the cynical sense, they rarely suffer from the real consequences of their own impractical ideas, given that their American-generated power, wealth, and influence largely exempt them from their edicts, which fall so hard on the middle and lower classes—be it overregulating the economy in pursuit of environmental agendas or sacrificing the interests of American workers to foreign commercial and trade predation. On the one hand, they are cynical critics of American exceptionalism and nationalism. On the other, they wish to extend American-style democracy and liberal tolerance across the globe—but without much thought about where such singular ideas arose or why so much of the world has always resisted them. Globalism's chief characteristic, however, is more mundane. Its architects focus on the distant and anonymous abroad, less so on concrete Americans nearby—as if theorizing about such misdemeanors as the use of plastic bags or natural gas use abroad can compensate for the failure to address the felonies of American homelessness, eroding wages, drug epidemics, and crushing student debt in their midst. In the end, globalization may not westernize the planet so much as internationalize America.

In sum, I wish to explain why everything that we once thought was so strong, so familiar, and so reassuring about America has been dissipating for some time. The year 2020, in the manner of other revolutionary years, such as 1848, 1917, and 1968, has peeled away that veneer of complacency and self-satisfaction. Contemporary events have reminded Americans that their citizenship is fragile and teetering on the abyss—and yet the calamities can also teach, indeed energize, them to rebuild and recover what they have lost.

Part 1

PRECITIZENS

Chapter One

PEASANTS

———————

There are three groups of people. There are the rich who
are never satisfied because their wealth is never enough for
them—these citizens are totally useless for the city. Then
there are the poor who, because their daily bread is never
enough, are dangerous because they are deceived by the
tongues of crooked politicians and by their own envy and
so they aim the arrows of their hatred towards the rich.
And then, between these two, there is a third. This one is
between them. It's there to keep the order, it's there to keep
the city safe.

—EURIPIDES, *Suppliants*

The English word "peasant" comes from the Old Anglo-French
word *paisant*, derived from the Latin *pagus* (rural district). "Peasant" originally denoted a subservient rural resident or laborer of inferior
rank.

It is understandable why the word has been rarely used in American
English—other than as a condescending putdown akin to "rustic" or
"boor." After all, Americans had millions of arable acres on their frontier.

The government for over seventy years of serial Homestead Acts (1862–1930) believed in granting such free land to those who would work and improve it—and thus become a stable, independent, and responsible middle class. So when "peasant" is used today in the American context, we must think away the anachronistic images of peasantry as stooped farmworkers burdened by rents and shares to absentee landowners.

Instead, for purposes of comparison, focus on the larger economic landscape of the medieval European peasants. Theirs was a world in which much of the population was dependent on an overclass of lords, barons, and bishops for its sustenance (and that is often true to this day in parts of Asia, Africa, and Latin America). They had little hope of upward mobility or even autonomy. Peasants then were like neither independent American agrarians nor autonomous yeomen.

The modern use of the word identifies the erosion of the middle class into an indebted and less independent underclass. The current reality is that millions of Americans, through debt, joblessness, and declining wages, are now becoming our own updated urban and suburban versions of the rural European peasantry of the past.

The idea that, without a middle class, there can be little participatory democracy, social tranquility, or cultural stability is not new. It is a poignant lesson from our shared past. The so-called middle ones (*mesoi*) of ancient Greece, referred to in the introduction, emerged out of the Greek Dark Age (ca. 1150–800 BC) as viable farmers of small orchards, vineyards, and grain fields. Legal citizenship, in its beginning, reflected the growing desires of these small yeomen farmers to protect and pass on to their children their property. Land ownership was the perceived font of all their rights and autonomy. Citizenship would have been impossible without this *prior* material security and independence.

The agrarians (*georgoi*) of many Greek city-states were the near majority of the resident population. They also owned and bore their own weapons. By intent their military-grade arms and armor *transcended* the need for personal safety or hunting. Quite logically, the first citizens of the West soon determined the very conditions under which their city-state's militias marched as hoplite infantry in the phalanx to defend their polis. This revolutionary right of the citizens to bear *top-grade arms*—currently the most controversial amendment of America's Bill of Rights—and to determine when, where, and against whom they would fight was also synonymous with citizenship at the very beginning of the West.

Perhaps most importantly, the new middling citizens assumed that as self-sufficient producers of food, they enjoyed economic independence from both the urban rich and poor. In the Greek philosopher Aristotle's analyses, once armed, moderate property holders became the majority in the city-state. Only then did consensual government for the first time become possible.[1]

A chauvinistic cult of "middleness" propaganda proclaimed the *mesoi* morally superior by their singular virtue of working physically while taking on the burden of self-government. Drudgery in service to others was the predictable lot of the poor, idleness, the cargo of the rich. But hard work for oneself was enshrined as the supposed superior middle way. Families responsible for their own futures would be the best guardians of the democratic state. As the Greek poet Phokylides (mid-sixth century BC) put it, "Much good is there to the middle ones: I would wish to be midmost in a city."

The Greeks' attitude toward the rich was not one of mere resentment or envy but rather a chauvinism that the wealthy, like the poor, possessed neither the requisite skills and weaponry nor the people's trust to anchor the polis. The poor could not afford the armor of hoplite infantrymen; the rich were perched on ponies. The middle ones alone were infantrymen, the armored spearmen of the phalanx—and the voices of when and when not to go to war. Too much land made one indolent. Yet no land ensured poverty and its twin, jealousy. On average, about ten acres—of olives, vines, and grain—ensured economic and political self-sufficiency. The cult of middleness spread throughout the more than fifteen hundred Greek city-states and later became the foundational assumption of the agrarian Roman Republic.[2]

There were plenty of indentured servants and helots in a few of the more backward Greek city-states. Chattel slaves—their status based on unlucky birth or the bad luck of wartime capture rather than race— were found in most. Nonetheless, an idea was born of both freedom and equality among the citizens whose natural evolutionary logic was always toward ever greater egalitarianism and inclusivity. Among the poleis of fifth-century BC Greece, the ancient idea of a "peasant"—a rustic permanently tied to the land as a renter or sharecropper without political rights and freedom—was thus superseded.

In the serf's place arose the new notion of a citizen. He soon coined an iconic name: *politês*, or "city-state person." *Polis* and *politês* were later to spawn an entire array of English constitutional terms such as "politics," "politician," "political," "policy," and "police." Contrary to popular assumption, there is simply no word for "peasant" in the classi- cal Greek vocabulary of the city-state. But there are plenty of such terms in ancient Greek pre-polis and atypical regions, such as the indentured *helotai* of Sparta and the *penestai* of Thessaly.[3]

Again, the classical traditions of the Roman Republic followed Hellenic precedent. Small agrarian Italian soldiers, the famed legion- aries of Rome, became the foundation of a republic to ensure political rights predicated on their economic viability and martial prowess—a paradigm found nowhere else in the Mediterranean. The Roman *civis* (cf. "civil," "civic," "civilization," etc.), or citizen, was the beneficiary of rights codified in an extensive body of law.

Legal protection for the *civis* against arbitrary arrest, confiscation, or taxation ensured the value of citizenship. Indeed, later, throughout the Roman-controlled Mediterranean, echoed the republican-era boast *civis Romanus sum*—"I am a Roman citizen." The speaker, if he was so fortu- nate as to live inside the boundaries of Rome's growing dominions, was entitled to rights that transcended those of both transient foreigners and mere permanent residents within Roman lands. Empowerment was again the key: give a citizen equality under the law, freedom, and economic viability, and his talents will bloom and enrich the state at large.[4]

In the second and third centuries AD, the Italian middle that had built the republic gradually over a millennium largely vanished. Rome increasingly became an empire of two classes, rich and poor, without much of a viable voting middle in between or indeed any national voting at all. The world's first experiment with globalization (in this case, the Mare Nostrum, the Roman Mediterranean) eventually hollowed out the Roman agrarian and middle classes.

Sending landowning agrarian legionaries far abroad to conquer new territory (our version of "optional overseas wars") in turn supplied foreign slaves for the consolidation of Italian agriculture in their absence. Agrarianism, remember, was thought to be the backbone of the pre-industrial middle class. The independence of the small farmer and his need to combine brain and muscle to produce food were considered to offer vital traits for self-governance, from pragmatism to individualism. Unfortunately, the once agrarian legions gradually either became mercenary or were manned by those without a stake in Roman society. To keep ruling, the elite relied on sending public largess to the army and to the poor, the stereotypical "bread and circuses" (*panem et circenses*) of the poet Juvenal, who caricatured the urban and often idle masses kept afloat by the combinations of state-subsidized food and free entertainment.

Yet, even after the collapse of the classical world in the latter fifth century AD and the transitory disappearance of a vestigial middle class, the idea of Western broad-based citizenship never quite died. Instead it reemerged in various manifestations throughout Europe over the next millennium and a half. The sometimes waxing, sometimes waning agrarian classes sought to create a constitutional state to protect and reflect their own interests. Unlike the landless poor, they did not want redistributions of someone else's land and money. In contrast to the wealthy, they did not see government mainly as an auxiliary to maintain privileges of birth or as an adornment to express influence and power.[5]

This reappearing European ideal of an independent middle class, originally agrarian, rather than a subservient peasantry became the American ideal, at least until recently. All politicians still praise the middle class, but few recently have sought or found ways to preserve it in a radically changing globalized world. The result is the emergence of a new American peasantry, of millions of Americans who own little or no property. The new majority has scant, if any, savings. Fifty-eight percent of Americans have less than $1,000 in the bank. A missed paycheck renders them destitute, completely unable to service sizable debt. Most of what they buy, from cars to electronic appurtenances, they charge on credit cards. The average charge card indebtedness is over $8,000 per household and over $2,000 per individual—paid through monthly installments at average annual interest rates of between 15 and 19 percent, at a time when most home mortgages are usually below 4 percent.

Such short-term debt is often roughly commensurate with the payments and share-cropping arrangements that premodern peasants once entered into with lords and made it impossible for the serf to exercise political independence or hope for upward mobility. The chief contemporary difference, of course, is that the modern American peasant is the beneficiary of a sophisticated technological society that allows him instant communications, advanced health care, televised and computer-driven entertainment, inexpensive food, and a social welfare state. These material blessings often mask an otherwise shrinking middle class without confidence that it is in control of its own destiny.

A fifth of America receives direct government public assistance. Well over half the country depends on some sort of state subsidy or government transfer money, explaining why about 60 percent of Americans collect more payments from the government than they pay out in various federal income taxes, in various health care entitlements, tax credits and exemptions, federally backed student and commercial loans, housing supplementals, food subsidies, disability and unemployment assistance, and legal help.

Such social insulation, along with science fueled by free market capitalism, has succeeded in ending starvation, dying in one's thirties and forties, and, for the most part, chronic malnourishment, as well as ensured access to a wealth of material appurtenances. But otherwise, twenty-first-century American "peasants"—currently perhaps about 46 percent of the population—usually die with a net worth of less than $10,000, both receiving and bequeathing little, if any, inheritance.

Drive on El Camino Real on the perimeter of Stanford University's elite campus and witness hundreds living in curbside trailers in the manner of the poor of Cairo, or visit the side streets near the Google headquarters in nearby Mountain View where thousands live in their cars, or walk among the homeless on tony University Avenue in Palo Alto. Then juxtapose their lifestyles with estates in nearby Woodside, Atherton, or Portola Valley and the Mercedes Benzes and BMWs of those in their earlier twenties parked in the student lots at Stanford University.

The natural historical referent for this dichotomy is certainly not the booming middle classes emerging following World War II. Instead the image is one of the manors and keeps of medieval Europe amid peasant huts outside the walls. For all practical purposes, it is almost impossible for young families to buy a home anywhere in California's five-hundred-mile progressive coastal corridor from San Diego to Berkeley or in the greater Portland and Seattle areas. The same is largely true in the metropolitan and suburban areas from Boston to Washington, DC. Whatever this bifurcated new culture is—and it is new and different from that of a half century ago—it is not so conducive anymore to classical citizenship.[6]

Even those of the middle class who can be thrifty, who save some of their income and develop modest passbook savings accounts, are now targeted by institutionalized cheap interest. The result of massive and chronic trillion-dollar annual budget deficits—the national debt is now near $30 trillion—and the zero interest rates of the often jittery Federal Reserve is the destruction of any interest income on savings accounts. The modest, middle-class citizen saver thus faces daunting options just to preserve the value of his money. He can engage in risky real estate speculation or invest in a booming stock market, fueled not by business performance, per se, but often by those who have nowhere else to park their money. So middle-class families, to be safe, often keep their modest savings in passbook accounts or buy federal bonds, where interest payouts below 1 percent do not cover the erosion in value of their principal due to annual inflation.[7]

American citizenship always differed even from the Western tradition found in the Europe of the last three centuries. The founding of America saw an entire array of newly expanded rights, responsibilities, and privileges for the vast majority of the resident population. This late-eighteenth-century new birth of citizenship arose in part because of an almost limitless supply of land, in part because colonial America lacked many of the European mainland's traditions of class distinctions, primogeniture, peasantry, and serfdom, in part because of the parliamentary traditions that Britain had implanted in North America, and in part because of the protections of the Constitution of the newly formed United States. America would soon become the freest and most egalitarian society in the history of civilization.[8]

At the beginning of the American experiment, there were, of course, still indentured servants sent to North America. Far more numerous were the African American slaves owned and exploited by Americans. But by the dawn of the nineteenth century, chattel slavery was confined mostly to wealthy plantations in the South and border states, while there still remained a multitude of statutory ways of discriminating against minority, non-northern-European free populations.

The point is not that late-eighteenth-century America was perfect at birth or could even approach what we now enshrine as twenty-first-century moral values. Rather, the new United States was unlike, or rather superior to, most contemporary nations. Indeed, almost alone of governments, America had hit upon a mechanism that would allow constant self-criticism, legal amendments to its founding documents, and moral improvement. Such change came without the necessity of collective suicide or permanent revolution—and yet within the boundaries of constitutional absolutes that transcended time and space.

Most other systems of the age in Asia, Africa, and Latin America that had allowed and profited from chattel slavery were authoritarian in nature. No one in such regimes was a free citizen. As a result, legitimate voices of opposition to slavery were far fewer and far more impotent. From the moment of the American founding, however, the new government confronted mounting pressure, predominately Christian, to match its ideals with the grim reality of its tolerance for chattel slavery and the denial of full voting rights to over half the resident population. This religious and abolitionist zeal dated back over a century in the colonies and had been formalized in the 1688 Pennsylvania "Germantown Quaker Petition Against Slavery."

Nowhere does the US Constitution mention racial exclusivity. The only oblique reference to it is the infamous "three-fifths clause"—the result of a demand by northern states that southern slave owners *not* be rewarded for the hypocrisy of counting their chattel slaves as full citizens, which would earn southern states greater representation in the House of Representatives. In such a bankrupt logic, slaves in the South would not be treated as free native-born Americans entitled to full protections under the Constitution; yet they would earn their masters greater political clout. The heated compromise to hold the proposed tenuous union together was to grant southern states only partial population representation for their slaves—a conciliation with those who had opposed all such concessions.[9]

The egalitarian chauvinism of the early American agrarian, in spirit, survived the nineteenth-century shift of populations to the cities during the Industrial Revolution. The ancient value of middleness was manifested as the emerging middle-class blue-collar worker and, in the latter twentieth century, as the archetypal suburban, two-car-garage family. As long as the farm, then the factory, then the office offered social stability and upward mobility to the citizen, the American idea of empowered political citizenship remained viable. When it would or could not, then citizenship was imperiled.[10]

These new American concepts of expanding the pool of citizens were antithetical to the age-old peasant notion of a "limited good." Free market capitalism was not a zero-sum proposition: someone could succeed without an exact counterpart failing. The American model was instead originally to own and farm a plot of ground—the more agrarians, the better for all. Over 90 percent of American colonists were self-sufficient small farmers. As the nation urbanized and industrialized, the original notion of property ownership and rights and the autonomy that a small farm had afforded were best updated by home ownership, inexpensive access to college or vocational training, and a steady well-paying job. Hollywood and popular culture enshrined the middle-class ideal, iconized in films as diverse as Frank Capra's *Mr. Smith Goes to Washington* and *Mr. Deeds Goes to Town*, John Ford's *The Grapes of Wrath*, and George Stevens's Western *Shane*.[11]

The trend of middle-class economic stagnation, at a time when the United States as a whole became ever wealthier, was of long-term duration, not a sudden occurrence. The middle class over the half century following 1970 was losing the ability to buy homes—even as, or in part because, houses became far larger and more livable. Far more rarely could the middle classes meet the family budget sacrifices needed to service growing mortgage debt. In the last fifty years of the twentieth century, for example, the ratio of collective mortgage debt to other family loan obligations rose from 20 to 73 percent. The ratio of household mortgage debt to household assets rose from 15 to 41 percent.

Middle-class Americans still wanted to own their homes. But increasingly they lacked the wherewithal to buy them and turned to ever-larger mortgages—if they could get them. As house costs rose, middle-class income did not increase commensurately, and financing became either unavailable or too costly. In the early twentieth century nearly half of

Americans owned their own homes. That healthy percentage grew to 60 percent in the 1950s and nearly reached an incredible 70 percent in 2004. Yet just twelve years later, by 2016 home ownership had dipped back to 63 percent of Americans—the lowest percentage in nearly fifty years. The likely causes were in part record student debt, spiraling costs in urban areas that had shut an entire generation of youth out of the housing market, and the aftershocks of the 2008 housing collapse and subprime mortgage scandal, which resulted in foreclosures and discouraged subsequent mortgage lending to first-time buyers.[12]

The economic, social, and political desirability of owning a home has increasingly sentenced the average American family to stifling mortgage payments and a lifetime of debt. In just the twenty-year period between 1985 and 2005, monthly housing costs as a percentage of household budgets increased 128 percent. If small farms had created the stability of the original American population, postwar home ownership had seen it continue. But in the latter twentieth century, both were fading from the American landscape.

In the 1940s, the average appraised value of an American home was under $3,000. Yet sixty years later, in 2000, the average cost in adjusted dollars had soared to $119,600. Currently, the average American home sells for about $200,000—roughly $170,000 more than the average 1940 cost, adjusted for inflation.

Of course, both remodeled and new homes are usually bigger and better equipped than their earlier counterparts—but not to the degree that their real costs should have increased tenfold. The surge in costs was largely a result of new government codes and zoning regulations, increased land prices, new builders' and legal fees, steep property taxes, environmental regulations, and developers' reluctance to invest in less remunerative starter homes. Federal loan programs such as those sponsored by the Federal Housing Authority and the Veterans Administration, along with rising incomes, for a time helped to grow the home-owning middle class in the postwar period. But they could not keep up with the inflationary pressures on home pricing. In some sense, the new regulations and obstacles to home ownership were birthed by legislators, regulators, and bureaucrats who already owned homes.

More recent and far more costly federal programs run by the Department of Housing and Urban Development—$50 billion spent in 2014 alone—in a cost-to-benefit analysis have proved mostly unsuccessful in ensuring adequate home ownership, either for the poor through housing subsidies or in mortgage guarantees for the lower middle classes. Despite these massive government outlays, the costs of home ownership have climbed more rapidly. The social desirability of owning a home became institutionalized, but as real incomes began to stagnate, Americans grew more indebted and angry at the idea of becoming indentured in order to remain middle class.[13]

Nicholas Eberstadt, an American Enterprise Institute economist, summed up well the relationship between declining middling-class income and eroding home ownership:

> The numbers are shocking. Nearly three in eight American homes today are rentals. Most are too near a hand-to-mouth existence. In 2019, half of all renters had a net worth of under $6,000. Over half of renting seniors had less than $7,000 to their name. Nearly half of all female-headed renter families had less than $2,000 in net worth. . . . Moreover, whether renters or homeowners, the lower half in America saw its mean net worth fall between 1989 and 2019—by a sixth or even more, depending on which measure of inflation one prefers.

Workers' wages had also risen dramatically throughout much of the twentieth century in steady fashion, at least until slowing in the 1960s. The increases reflected the postwar era in which, for three decades, the United States had a near monopoly on supplying consumer goods to much of the war-torn world in Europe and Asia. Yet, between 1980 and 2017, wages noticeably began to stagnate, at least for the majority of the middle class. The cause was in part lethargic productivity and in part the ascendance of the exporting colossuses of Germany, Japan, the so-called Asian Tigers, and China. Unsurprisingly, then, whereas 70 percent of American families had relied on one income earner in 1960, sixty years later only 30 percent could.[14]

In terms of college costs, the story of middle-class erosion is similar, or perhaps even worse. In 1987–1988 students who enrolled in *public* four-year higher education institutions on average paid $3,190 for tuition adjusted to 2017 dollars. Yet in 2017–2018, three decades later, the average cost for tuition had soared to $9,970—a real increase of some 213 percent.

Mostly progressive private colleges and universities stepped up their real tuition costs by 129 percent over this same three-decade period. The huge increases were largely a result of administrative bloat, non-academic auxiliary programs, gender and diversity regulations, and compliance costs. In addition, faculty teaching loads were reduced. Luxury enhancements on campus appeared. The array of nonteaching, in loco parentis, and therapeutic services grew—all at a time of increasingly static wages for recent graduates with increasingly noncompetitive degrees and skills.

In other words, too often the universities saw themselves no longer as teachers of the inductive method and the elements of foundational knowledge. Instead, they were activists. They became intent on shaping young minds to adopt a politicized agenda, whether defined as unquestioned embrace of climate change activism, identity politics, or redistributive economics. Deductivism—picking and choosing examples to conform to a preconceived result—was a recalibration that proved far more costly, and ultimately toxic, for the student than the prior commitment to traditional education that had emphasized a set body of knowledge, an inductive method of accessing it, and the training of an inquisitive mind.

No wonder current aggregate student debt now exceeds $1.6 trillion—ironic when the collective endowments of US colleges and universities exceed $600 billion, with average returns on such principal of over 8 percent per annum. It was almost as if the more those in higher education overtly railed against the inequities and oppressions of modern capitalist American society, the more their institutions became hypercapitalist at the expense of increasingly indebted students and the federal government that backstops their loan debts.

Unfortunately, the faculty and administration showed no inclination to halt spiraling tuition costs, to increase teaching loads, to cut administrative bloat in efforts to ease middle-class students' indebtedness, and to prepare them with skills that would lead to good jobs and quick repayment of student debt. Instead, the concrete declining lot of students remained in sharp contrast to the abstract radicalism of academics. Faculty who are full-time and tenured teach fewer large introductory courses than was true forty years ago, correct fewer undergraduate assignments, and are surrounded by ever more campus facilitators who do not teach at all—a new ethos subsidized by student loan debt.

Faculty activists may have pushed more-relevant studies/courses (gender, race, class, environmental, peace, etc.). But such foci were among the least likely majors and minors to ensure well-paying jobs upon graduation that might service student debt. In addition, over-extended colleges increasingly began to rely on part-time, poorly paid lecturers, without tenure and often lacking full benefits. In an ironic sense, the most progressive institution in America became the most medieval, often institutionalizing its own version of sweatshop, seasonal instructional labor to subsidize an overclass of relatively few. In 1969, 80 percent of faculty at American colleges were full-time and tenured or tenure-track. Today half are nontenured. A third of them work only part-time.[15]

There are real consequences for middle-class workers when their wages ossify, the costs of college or vocational schooling for their children soar, and they go into lifelong debt to own a home or to school their children. Upward mobility erodes. Worry mounts over slipping from the middle class into impoverishment. There is almost no margin of error for the middle-class family when faced with a death, illness, or divorce or when the country sinks into recession, is hit by financial panic—or goes into a national lockdown in fear of a new pandemic.

The most prominent symptoms of economic ossification for younger generations—and of concern for the country at large—are radical disruptions in the usual middle-class patterns that encourage traditional citizenship and national cohesion: marriage, child rearing, and home ownership. All are increasingly being delayed until the late twenties—or never envisioned at all by a new urban caste. Many see child rearing and even marriage as bothersome abstractions. Social justifications for the diminishment of these traditionally more conservative institutions follow from the economic realities that make them more difficult.[16]

From 1950 to 2019 the average age of first marriage soared for males from about twenty-three to thirty and for females from twenty-two to twenty-nine. The average age for the first childbirth for women likewise spiked even more dramatically to nearly twenty-seven—that marked a radical increase from the median of about twenty-one just fifty years ago in the early 1970s. For the first time in American history, in 2015 there were only 62.5 births per one thousand women—a number that has subsequently dipped below 60. Many states reported more deaths than births. These realities are beginning to bother both liberals and conservatives.[17]

Despite massive immigration of the last half century, with immigrants traditionally more prone to have large families, the national median family size has shrunk dramatically. The 1960s average of 2.3 children per family has declined to a current 1.9. That figure is well below the 2.1 percent rate necessary to maintain current population size. When we speak of a "dying citizen," we can take that phrasing quite literally: Americans are not reproducing themselves and are starting to follow European models of slow-motion demographic suicide.[18]

Most American middle-class families can easily sense the radical changes in demographics, cultural norms, and student debt that have occurred over just two to three generations. My two late parents (both born between 1921 and 1922) had four children (born between 1949 and 1953). One daughter died in her first year. We three surviving boys, in turn, sired collectively five children (born between 1981 and 1985). Our five have so far had four children (born between 2011 and 2019). I and my siblings, then, had fewer children at a later age than my parents. Our children began smaller families even at older ages than did we.

In terms of higher education, the three of us had graduated with degrees from the University of California (UC), Santa Cruz, by 1975—the closest UC campus to our farm, at a time when there were few administrators, ample faculty teaching loads, spartan student dorms, nonexistent recreation centers, *and small fees without the full cost of tuition*. The latter was not instituted at UC campuses until 1975. All of us had summer and school-time jobs. All graduated with *no* long-term student debt.

As far as housing went, to save money on dorms and boarding, my parents purchased in 1972 a small eleven-hundred-square-foot house in Santa Cruz near the campus for $26,000 ($23 per square foot). The purchase required a separate loan for a small down payment of about $4,000 and a $170 monthly payment on the first thirty-year mortgage—a cost at the time mostly covered by three of us taking on two additional renters. The house in 1972 had a rental value of about $200 per month. In today's dollars that 1972 rental rate would be roughly $1,250. In fact, the current monthly rental value of the house is about $3,500 to $4,000—beyond the means of most middle-class households, not to mention students.

Nearly a half century later, I still own the same tiny house, in which my daughter and her husband and children now live. In 2020 inflation-adjusted dollars, it should be worth roughly $160,000 according to its 1972 cost. But its current saleable value in the inflated Santa Cruz real estate market of 2020 is nearly $1 million. The price per square foot for such a near-campus residence went up in my lifetime from an inflation-adjusted $143 in 1972 to a current value of over $900. Purchasing such a small "starter" home is impossible for nearly any family.

These general trends of smaller families, later and fewer marriages, more expensive tuition and housing, and greater debt burdens hold for the middle classes of the postindustrial affluent West in general. Of course, costs and lifestyles vary in the United States by race, region, education, and actual income. These trends reflect changing cultural attitudes as well as increased education and job opportunities for women.

Yet, again, these shared developments are indicative of an undeniable era of middle-class economic insecurity and uncertainty—and fall inordinately on those whose real wages stagnated or whose jobs were lost over the last half century of globalization and outsourcing. Millions of young people now believe that they cannot buy a home, pay off their student loans, get married, or begin to raise a family of two or three children by their mid-twenties. Accordingly they have been taught in college or otherwise come to believe that such past but unattainable norms are somehow either illiberal or unsustainable. They perhaps logically make the necessary political adjustments or cultural exegeses to mask the reality of their own pessimistic economic expectations and existing financial realities. All of the above is a fair stereotype of thousands of young people in Antifa-inspired demonstrations who hit the streets to commit acts of violence in spring 2020.[19]

The ascendance of conservative outsider Donald Trump and socialist Bernie Sanders in 2016 is a testament to dissatisfaction with the establishments of both the Democratic and Republican parties. These populist outsiders accused both conservative and liberal elites of indifference or outright hostility to the traditional concerns of the middle classes, whether by, respectively, favoring the rich or strangling the citizen through larger and grasping government. The common denominator between the antithetical Sanders and Trump was that both believed youth did not have the same opportunities as their forebearers. Both alleged that the "system"—respectively, either the greedy oligarchy or the swampy government—had thwarted opportunity.

How can the new sophisticated urban dweller, or the college educated, or the renter with a big-screen television and smart phone possibly be compared to what we have called precitizens—mere residents before the rise of Western citizenship—given their distaste for the large families of the traditional peasant and their supposed cosmopolitanism so at odds with agrarian parochialism?

The current comparison of modern America to the age of precitizenship is largely cultural and economic. By the twenty-first century, some American youth often advanced a new environmental credo or social ethos that having few if any children helped to "save the planet." One child, or indeed childlessness altogether, ostensibly expanded the career opportunities of women and ensured more disposable family income for leisure, travel, and recreation.

Alternatively, others claimed that the increasingly scorched planet was inconducive to bringing up children. Thus the moral choice was not to inflict the pathologies of modern Western life on yet another innocent generation. For example, first-term representative Alexandria Ocasio-Cortez (D-NY), the influential congressional voice of youthful progressives, announced that her generation questioned whether having any children at all was wise or ethical—given her prognosis of an environmental Armageddon in little more than a decade: "There's scientific consensus that the lives of children are going to be very difficult. And it does lead young people to have a legitimate question: Is it OK to still have children? We had time when I was born, but—ticktock— nothing got done. As the youngest member of Congress, I wish we didn't have 12 years. It's our lungs that are going to get choked with wildfire smoke." In fact, in 2019, when Ocasio-Cortez talked of increasingly intolerable conditions, the United States had decreased its carbon emissions to the lowest level since 1992.[20]

Not only was childbearing thought to be dooming the next generation to early climate-change deaths, but young people espousing this perspective, especially from an urban and university context, saw traditional families of five, six, or seven as somehow hogging resources to the detriment of the earth at large. These ideas that traditionally larger families of the past now either deny young women the ability to find full spiritual fulfillment or harm the planet have only further discouraged fertility.

These demographic developments were not just singularly American or even contemporary Western idiosyncrasies. They were, again, Western cultural phenomena with an ancient pedigree. Indeed, alarm over childlessness dated back to the various crises of the increasingly affluent late Roman Republic and early empire. Decreased fertility most famously frightened the emperor Augustus. He relentlessly railed over falling populations, declining marriage and fertility, increased urbanization, and accompanying loss of "traditional values" in the Italian countryside where large families had worked small plots that provided the famed manpower of the Roman Republic.

In reductionist terms, by the first century AD, a far wealthier city of Rome of roughly one million residents had become fully aware— at least in the view of poets such as Horace and Ovid, satirists like Petronius and Juvenal, the historians Livy and Tacitus, and biographers such as Suetonius and Plutarch—of the strange paradox of material progress accompanied by moral regress. This irony was often marked in literature by the perceived virtual end of the viability of the traditional Italian rural middle class and customary Roman family. The ancients often believed that as the landless urban population grew, child raising became seen increasingly as less important, too costly, or simply an optional expense that impinged on the satisfaction of the appetites.[21]

Popular culture and politics also can put a human face on these dreary demographic statistics, one of acceptable prolonged adolescence and government dependence. Today's American peasants, especially those in our major cities, may be better fed, better educated, better housed, and better connected with the world than the world's poor of the past or present. They are clearly better clothed than their nineteenth-century counterparts. They certainly would not accept that they are peasants at all—especially those with bachelor's degrees, familiarity with an array of sophisticated technological gadgetry, and refined urban tastes. None raise chickens or grow their own grain. Only a few have gardens. A minority of debt-ridden youth work at backbreaking, physically exhausting jobs requiring hours of manual labor. Obesity and diabetes, not malnutrition and tuberculosis, more likely threaten young people. They don't quite see their landlords as hereditary aristocrats or their loans as the obligations of serfdom.

Nevertheless, in terms of their perceived ability to marry, raise children, own a home, and plot an autonomous course to have control of their own financial destinies—the fundamentals of traditional middle-class citizenship—contemporary peasants are not so unlike their rural predecessors. Few millennials today would see personal fulfillment and responsible citizenship defined as raising families in a stable society. They are hardly analogous to Tellus, the model Athenian of Herodotus's *Histories*. The historian says he died secure since he "had good and noble children, and he saw all his children and grandchildren surviving him."[22]

Government has adjusted to the new norms, if not itself fueled them. Popular culture and contemporary politics have more or less institutionalized an ascendant model of citizenship quite unlike that once seen as based on the autonomous family—at least in terms of the middle-class college educated.

Take the example of a popular political ad of 2010 designed to sell the Affordable Care Act to the general public. The poster boy for the campaign was *not* analogous to the *American Gothic* married couple. The iconic advocate became known as "Pajama Boy." As the Obamacare promoter, a young man in thick, black retro-rimmed glasses was supposed to win our empathy. He appeared confident and self-aware. Yet he was wearing black-and-red-plaid children's-style pajamas, sipping from a mug, with an all-knowing expression of seasoned certainty on his face.

The visual was accompanied by text urging, "Wear pajamas. Drink hot chocolate. Talk about getting health insurance. #Get Talking." What a strange mix of immaturity and adulthood. The ad was an inadvertent confirmation of philosophical warnings from Juvenal to Tocqueville about the connection between government subsidies and the creation of perpetual puerility and dependency. His snark "get talking" suggested a strained adult confidence betrayed by the pajamas of his prolonged adolescence.

The point, then, is that our elites who sought to sell Obamacare apparently think they best do just that by focusing on a new sort of young ascendant American. They envision the novel American archetype now as a single, urban youth. He is a new hip postcitizen who in truth is an age-old precitizen. He is presumably well educated and glib but dependent on government subsidies and suffering arrested development. He is not shy and feels entitled to lecture others purportedly less informed about how to approach government. Of course, ironically, the elite, who so often espouse such values for others, are themselves more likely than the underclass to have opportunities to marry, raise children, and earn the income to purchase homes and provide advantages for their own children.[23]

Two years later, the Barack Obama reelection campaign of 2012 sought to amplify its omnipresent government resonance. This time it focused on another new citizen demographic—young, unmarried urban women, of the same generation and culture as Ethan Krupp, the real-life Pajama Boy. It ran an interactive web ad, "The Life of Julia." The promotion narrated the attractions of government dependency, now more expansively defined as the liberation of an everywoman blessed with cradle-to-grave government reliance.

Julia is proudly and perennially a ward of the state. The subtext is that in today's economy, she is apparently unable to become autonomous and independent without federal help. In other words, the new American model is strangely medieval: Julia is assumed to be dependent on the Washington bureaucracy to sustain her.

We are told that Julia got through high school and college. But such success was only thanks to prior Head Start programs and federally backed student loans. There is no mention that at the time of the ad, students were collectively well over $1 trillion in debt and often without marketable college degrees.[24]

In 2012, we are additionally advised, the Small Business Administration and the Lilly Ledbetter Fair Pay Act (and certainly not a booming private sector short of labor) mostly enabled Julia to find work. Though unmarried, Julia has one child—but no health care worries thanks to the Obamacare effort to collectivize medicine. There is no mention that the absence of a two-parent household puts enormous strain on child raising, not to mention child development itself. Did the father of her child contribute to the latter's livelihood? In her retirement years, only Social Security and Medicare allow Julia to find security, comfort, and the time and wherewithal to volunteer for a communal urban garden— apparently a hobby rather than a critical food source.

Julia shows no awareness that the Social Security system is headed for financial catastrophe, given the increased longevity of recipients and expanded benefits, coupled with the shrinking base of contributors in an America of declining fertility. Again, the expectation is that an American worker in her sixties will not have had opportunity either to accumulate much savings or to fund a sustainable individual retirement account. Both of the Obama administration's pessimistic assumptions were mostly right.

Yet, through the metaphors of "Pajama Boy" and the "Life of Julia," the government was reflecting the assumptions of soft despotism and its twin: the transformation of the free and autonomous citizen into a dependent peasant. Ironically, Alexis de Tocqueville warned of just such a loss of autonomy in democracies about 185 years ago in his classic *Democracy in America*:

> Above this race of men stands an immense and tutelary power, which takes upon itself alone to secure their gratifications, and to watch over their fate. That power is absolute, minute, regular, provident, and mild. It would be like the authority of a parent, if, like

that authority, its object was to prepare men for manhood; but it seeks on the contrary to keep them in perpetual childhood: it is well content that the people should rejoice, provided they think of nothing but rejoicing. For their happiness such a government willingly labors, but it chooses to be the sole agent and the only arbiter of that happiness: it provides for their security, foresees and supplies their necessities, facilitates their pleasures, manages their principal concerns, directs their industry, regulates the descent of property, and subdivides their inheritances—what remains, but to spare them all the care of thinking and all the trouble of living?[25]

From these public relations campaigns, we were to assume that youth were credentialed, but not educated, at least in the sense of being able to think for themselves without tutelage from a government program. They clearly would not become risk takers who threw off their government training wheels to ride off into the autonomous unknown. In terms of their respective dependencies, the fictive Pajama Boy and Julia were both dependent upon the state, although supposedly happily so. Or at least they were assumed to have few options other than a government-subsidized prolonged adolescence—Tocqueville's "permanent childhood"—without the traditional maturing experiences that had once forged the middle class.

Finally, Julia and Pajama Boy were high-profile reflections of the government dependence of the college educated. But the real collapse of the middle class arose among those, both white and black, without college degrees and no longer able to find high-paying blue-collar jobs. American sociologist Andrew Cherlin once called the stunning decline in wages of non-college-educated workers between 1975 and 2010 "the fall of the working-class family," noting the cultural catastrophe that accompanied it: a decline in marriage and a sharp rise in child rearing by single, unmarried women.[26]

Joel Kotkin, an astute social critic of California's many paradoxes, has dubbed the new elite the "clerisy"—a term also popularized in our era by Fred Siegel, a pioneer observer of the contradictions inherent in elite progressives' championing of policies that hurt the poor and middle classes. Samuel Taylor Coleridge (1772–1834), the British Romantic poet, essayist, and literary critic, originally coined the term to describe a new group of enlightened intellectuals and learned professionals— those who had the curiosity, means, and skill to read for pleasure. For Coleridge, these free thinkers were gratefully more akin to the curious scholars of the medieval clergy than to the staid religious bureaucracy of the contemporary church. The new clerisy was not an independent new middle class but rather emulated the privileges and influence of the High Church clergy, albeit usually substituting their own god Reason for a belief in the Christian God.[27]

The medieval-like bifurcation of America has a number of causes. Many blame the most recent stagnation of the middle classes on globalized trade that privileged bicoastal, degreed elites in finance, investment, high tech, law, media, academia, and entertainment. Their work transcended national boundaries. It relied on offshoring, outsourcing, and indifference to asymmetrical trade with China, the European Union, Japan, and South Korea. Automation and computerization certainly both replaced and also depreciated the value of muscular labor, especially in manufacturing and assembly jobs.

Other, far earlier force multipliers contributed to the erosion of the old muscular American middle classes. The bureaucratic and administrative state overregulated commerce and choked economic growth and start-up businesses. Such a near command economy reflected the interests of a largely well-to-do affluent class that had profited enormously from globalized marketing—and regulating and monitoring all that from Washington. Those still dependent upon, but entirely removed from, the smelly processes of production—energy generation, manufacturing, smelting, mining, logging, and farming—sought to dictate how others would operate to their own sole satisfaction.

The growing gulf between concrete challenges to producers and workers and the more abstract agendas of legislatures, bureaucracies, and the courts often meant that the poor were given greater subsidies, the agendas of the wealthy often permitted exemptions for themselves, and middle-class workers either lost jobs or competitive wages, lacking the influence of the rich and the sympathies accorded the poor. Scholars such as the sociologist and political scientist Charles Murray long ago argued that ever-rising government entitlements eroded initiative by providing guaranteed sustenance, yet with little hope of upward mobility. Joel Kotkin saw the new clerisy as primarily comprising those with secure, high-paying jobs, predicated on degrees and certification, "such as teaching, consulting, law, the medical field, and the civil service." While these modern clerics may number perhaps only 10 to 15 percent of the population, they exercise enormous influence and clout given their predominance in the regulatory state, education, the media, and the law.

The subtext of such an indictment is also that the certification of a JD, MBA, MD, or PhD does not necessarily equate to inculcation with superior morality, a traditional liberal arts education, common sense, or, much less, increased awareness about the effects of globalization on the less credentialed. Many four-year degrees of the clerisy are more like alphabetic cattle brands that reflect herd status and provide entrée rather than proof of learning.[28]

Elites assumed that the rules of the new economy were set in stone and thus not subject to change. Americans were to shrug that there would no longer be many well-paying American manufacturing or assembly jobs. They were to accept asymmetrical free trade as either fair and advantageous or, if conceded as unfair and injurious, beyond remedy. Of course, few pointed out that sympathetic journalists, academics, and corporate analysts offered most news accounts and analyses of globalization and the new economy. They were precisely those who had largely benefited from globalization with huge increases in their clients, audiences, and consumers.

President Obama in 2016 critiqued candidate Trump's plan for an economic renaissance centered on a reindustrialized Midwest: "Well, how exactly are you going to do that? What exactly are you going to do? There's no answer to it. . . . He [Trump] just says, 'Well, I'm going to negotiate a better deal.' Well, what, how exactly are you going to negotiate that? What magic wand do you have? Usually the answer is, he doesn't have an answer." Obama merely reflected a bipartisan consensus that the benefits of globalization were a given and need not be debated. He further reminded America that such blue-collar jobs were "just not going to come back."

But why could they not come back? What law dictated they were lost forever in the United States but not elsewhere in the world? Were American workers dumber or lazier than their overseas competitors, their factories less efficient, their energy costlier, their infrastructure less conducive to mass production? Seventy-five years ago, during World War II, did the Franklin Roosevelt administration outsource the production of B-24 bombers to cheaper labor sites in Mexico, because the making of one larger bomber per hour at Willow Run, Michigan, was deemed too slow or too expensive?[29]

Nobel laureate economist Paul Krugman, shortly after the 2016 election, similarly laughed at the idea that America would ever again need widescale manufacturing or assembly labor: "Nothing policy can do will bring back those lost jobs. The service sector is the future of work; but nobody wants to hear it." No one wanted "to hear it" because implicit in Krugman's bleak prognosis was the notion that "service jobs" pay far less with far fewer benefits than the lost industrial and manufacturing work. Krugman, like many liberal and conservative economists, at once largely discounted any notion that there might be disadvantages to importing vast quantities of Chinese-made foodstuffs and pharmaceuticals. Nor did he cite any strategic dangers from outsourcing the assembly of computer appurtenances. Apparently he saw little advantage to ensuring that Americans produce the overwhelming majority of their food, energy, weapons, medicines, and building materials—such as that they themselves would then adjudicate the daily availability and safety of such critical stuffs.

Esteemed Harvard economist Larry Summers similarly charged that Trump's boast as a candidate that he would achieve 3 percent economic growth was the stuff of those who believe in "tooth fairies and ludicrous supply-side economics." Such quotes in defense of the status quo from traditional politicians and economists could be multiplied. But their importance lies in their reflection of the clerisy's belief that the stagnant and declining wages of the middle class were, by 2016, both inevitable and permanent—and by implication perhaps tolerable in the future. By further inference, the erosion of middle-class jobs was often blamed on those who did not recalibrate their skills to facilitate a global economy— rather than on the decisions of corporate officials, investors, and government policy makers. The latter advanced lots of reasons to shut down assembly plants in the United States rather than seek innovative ways to salvage profitable businesses that employed fellow Americans.

As far as faulting the losers of globalization, Summers himself at one point felt any resulting inequality simply reflected merit-based reality and purportedly remarked, "One of the challenges in our society is that the truth is a kind of disequalizer. One of the reasons that inequality has probably gone up in our society is that people are being treated closer to the way that they're supposed to be treated."[30]

A number of popular landmark studies over the last four decades— most notably those of Fred Siegel, Joel Kotkin, social critic of popular culture and values Christopher Lasch, Charles Murray, sociologist Robert Nisbet, and political scientist Kevin Philips—all warned of the costs to the nation when middle-class viability is lost. Many earlier on had focused on the cultural ramifications of such economic erosion— from the opioid crises and rises in premature deaths and suicides to the destruction of the nuclear family. Familial erosion was particularly prevalent among the white working classes of the deindustrialized interior of America and the inlands of otherwise affluent coastal states.

Such pathologies reflected a decade of inert wages, increasing labor-nonparticipation rates, ossified economic growth, and stubborn unemployment. Soon, however, a genre of social disparagement grew around the "losers" in the new economy. It was as if social pathologies drove out American industry rather than that the flight of industry abroad catalyzed familial erosion.

Republicans, for example, for much of the twenty-first century ignored the vestigial middle classes on the theory that the blinkered did not understand the immutable laws of laissez-faire capitalism and the primacy of absolutely unfettered free trade over fair commerce. Their support for open borders to ensure cheap foreign labor was considered a pillar of economic rationalism, even if massive illegal immigration drove down the wages of the shrinking American middles classes. "An act of love" is what 2016 Republican primary candidate Jeb Bush called illegal immigration. Libertarian Kevin Williamson, in more passionate fashion, noted that the damage to the fading blue-collar white middle class was mostly self-inflicted:

> The truth about these dysfunctional, downscale communities is that they deserve to die. Economically, they are negative assets. Morally, they are indefensible. . . . The white American underclass is in thrall to a vicious, selfish culture whose main products are misery and used heroin needles. Donald Trump's speeches make them feel good. So does OxyContin. What they need isn't analgesics, literal or political. They need real opportunity, which means that they need real change, which means that they need U-Haul.[31]

Oddly, there *has* been a shortage of U-Haul moving equipment. But the dearth of available rentals reflects a one-way exodus from blue– Electoral College, clerisy states whose taxes, regulations, steep costs, monolithic politics, and poor services and schools drove out the upper and middle classes eager to find antitheses to their home states rather than the lower middle classes and poor, who did not have the means so easily to relocate. In some sense, the asymmetrical migration to a Dallas or Boise suggests a preference for traditional stability rather than the supposedly sophisticated chaos of San Francisco or Los Angeles.

Fred Siegel pointed out how the longshoreman philosopher Eric Hoffer some seventy years ago could see the future contours of a working class regulated, controlled, and yet ridiculed by a new intellectual and bureaucratic elite.[32]

> "The masses are on the way out," he wrote. "The [elites] are finally catching up with us. We can hear the swish of leather as the saddles are heaved on our backs. The intellectuals, and the young, booted and spurred, feel themselves born to ride us." Hoffer foresaw the New Class would try to govern the working people much as the colonial officials governed the natives. "They are," he wrote, "an army of scribes clamoring for a society in which planning, regulation, and supervision are paramount and the prerogative of the educated."[33]

The philosophical theories and economic tenets of elites were no doubt based on logical premises, but often they guided public policy with little concern about their effects on real people. "Creative destruction"—which Joseph Schumpeter called "the central fact about capitalism"—is inherent and necessary in a free market. The constant creation and dismantling of businesses to meet rapidly changing consumer tastes, government policies, and national security and natural resource realities certainly are requisites of economic growth and flexibility in adapting to rapid global change. But often the domestic destruction of American businesses after the 1970s was hardly "creative," given that free markets and trade were not always entirely "free." Firms did not always implode because daring competitors, inventors, or visionaries had found a more efficient system, a more useful product, or a cheaper gadget to render inferior the status quo and to benefit society at large.

Instead, the destruction was also a predictable result of unfettered, but otherwise unfair, trade predicated on political or cultural, but not always economic, rationales or on government interference and irrational regulation. Often mercantile actors, the Chinese especially, systematically violated international agreements. They stole patents and copyrights. They appropriated technologies, manipulated currencies, and dumped product on the market temporarily at below cost to win market share—and thereby made themselves only ostensibly more competitive and immune from Schumpeter's laws of capitalism. China's Communist Party government was appeased on the deductive premise that such indulgence would make the Chinese rich and thus either prompt them to reciprocate such magnanimity or embrace consensual government.

In mirror-image fashion, increasingly Democrats grew tired of their prior support for so-called lunch-bucket issues of blue-collar unionization, reciprocal trade, low taxes, and secure borders. Perhaps their weariness with the old middle classes was symptomatic of new identity politics agendas and the allure of changing voting demographics, in which race supposedly displaced class concerns.

The new progressive orthodoxy was that a changing electorate had turned Democrats into the party of multiculturalism, open borders, immigration law nonenforcement, and an array of race and gender issues. Their old, but now declining, constituencies of the industrialized Midwest were insufficiently "woke" to such progressive issues. They could safely be ignored, given their own pathologies, declining numbers, supposedly waning economic and political clout—and apparently lack of a viable political alternative home. This Democratic near political abandonment of the white working classes, coupled with traditional Republican attention to corporate concerns, left a political void. Not until 2015, it seems, did Donald Trump, oddly almost alone among both parties, sense the Electoral College political possibilities of that lost constituency.

It was no accident that national Democratic leaders such as Barack Obama, Hillary Clinton, and Joe Biden now employed the vocabulary of working-class disparagement, speaking of "clingers" to their religion and guns, illiberal "deplorables" and "irredeemables," the losing bottom class of "dregs" to be shunned for their supposed cultural and racial insensitivities. Only the earthquake election of 2016 for a while questioned the assumption that the white working classes had become both politically inert and economically unsalvageable, as did near-record peacetime employment and steady economic growth between 2017 and early 2020.

Nowhere does such a dystopian future of two classes without a middle in between seem more ominous than in twenty-first-century California. As such, the state is an icon of the premodern and postmodern forces that are extinguishing citizenship, a warning to the country of things to come. California has become the progressive dream for the nation's future and the middle-class nightmare of the present. During the 2020 presidential primaries, Democratic candidate Mike Bloomberg gushed of the electorally rich golden state, "I think that California can serve as a great example for the rest of this country," as "something the rest of the country looks up to. California has been a leader in an awful lot of things."

Bloomberg curiously did not define "things," much less the ironic implications of his modifier "awful." Nor did he quantify "leader." In fact, the state was among the nation's leaders in terms of high taxes, the highest poverty rates, the largest number of welfare residents, both in absolute and relative numbers, the greatest number of homeless people, among the steepest gasoline and electricity prices, the largest number of illegal aliens, the greatest number of outmigrants, among the worst schools and roads, and the greatest ratios of inequality.[34]

The multibillionaire Bloomberg in 2020 no doubt admired California because of its radical green energy policies that put off-limits the state's cheap and easily available gas and oil supplies and instead promoted expensive but often unreliable solar and wind renewables—ensuring a supposedly carbon-neutral lifestyle for those with incomes who could afford it. Yet such green agendas and the taxes that accompanied them led to among the highest fuel and power costs in the nation.

That proved a collective disaster when one remembers that over a fifth of California residents lived below the poverty line.[35]

Sometimes the elite green gospel has proved catastrophic—especially for the middle classes. In August and September 2020, high winds, lightning strikes, and scorching temperatures caused hundreds of forest fires throughout California. Past "more natural" policies had discouraged controlled burning, removal of brush from forest floors, cattle grazing on hillsides of dead undergrowth, and the logging of tens of millions of dead trees lost during recent droughts. Even the emasculated timber industry might have managed if it had been permitted to hire thousands to harvest the dead trees of the last six years, thus providing jobs, timber, and forest safety. Instead, the summer perfect storm created a sort of green napalm—a combustible fuel of unharvested timber that would turn a traditional wildfire into an uncontrollable inferno, burn over four million acres, and send one hundred million metric tons of carbon emissions into the air. Due to the tremendous temperatures created by the infernos, eerie pyrocumulus clouds for weeks dotted the Sierra Nevada skyline, in apocalyptical fashion emulating the mushroom clouds that billow up after nuclear blasts.

The ensuing smoke clouds soon covered much of the state and overwhelmed the efficacy of public and private solar farms, which in turn led to rolling scheduled power outages. And the power crisis had been made worse by the voluntary state shutdown of clean-burning natural gas and nuclear power plants—all exacerbated by near-record temperatures in some areas of the state reaching 110 degrees. The poor resident, without power for hours on end, sometimes had to choose between baking indoors without the electricity to run air conditioning and venturing outside to breathe hot, smoke-laden air. The choices were even worse for many of the middle class who lived in the foothills and mountains, tens of thousands of whom were evacuated, often with complete loss of their property.

The state had also shorted roads and bridges in favor of a soon-to-be disastrous high-speed rail project. It was cancelled after its first phase suffered multi-billion-dollar cost overruns—at a time when the nearby and parallel chief north-south freeway, the 99, remained in decrepit shape and by most metrics was the most dangerous major thoroughfare in the nation. Had billions of dollars, wasted on utopian transit dreams, been first invested in expanding and repairing the calcified California freeway system, the lives of millions of daily middle-class commuters might have been far safer and less taxing. California also encouraged an open southern border and established hundreds of sanctuary city jurisdictions while welcoming in millions of abject poor with few of the skills necessary to prosper in a sophisticated postmodern society. Over a quarter of all California's immigrants—who themselves constitute over one-quarter of the state's current resident population—entered and remained in the state without legal sanction.[36]

Again, few of these outcomes affected the very wealthy classes that had supported the policies and laws leading to these crises and had the resources to ensure their consequences fell on others. The Bay Area, until recently a bastion of opposition to charter schools and school choice, witnessed an epidemic of expensive new and enlarged private academies as the per capita wealth of the rich soared. Meanwhile, the public schools increasingly enrolled the impoverished children of immigrants from Central America and Mexico.[37]

What did the beleaguered and shrinking middle class say in opposition to all of these state policies and socioeconomic trends? For the most part, little. Again, it preferred to leave the state in order to survive. In the twenty-five years between 1991 and 2016, California lost 423,700 manufacturing jobs, even as top-paying high-tech opportunities boomed in Silicon Valley. Otherwise, 80 percent of all the jobs created in California in the last decade paid less than the medium income. Quite logically, then, in high-tech, wealthy San Francisco, inequality still grew amid the general high-tech largess. Joel Kotkin and Michael Toplansky have emphasized the paradoxes: "According to a recent study by the California Budget Center, San Francisco ranks first in California for economic inequality; average income of the top 1% of households in the city averages $3.6 million, 44 times the average income of the bottom 99%, which stands at $81,094."[38]

The state currently has a top marginal income tax rate of 13.3 percent—until recent increases in New York, the highest in the nation. Only about 150,000 households in a state of forty million people now pay nearly half the total annual state income tax. Forty percent of state residents pay zero state income tax. This asymmetry is the result of millions of upper-middle-class professionals leaving the state, huge influxes of poor immigrants, and the multimillionaire class finding creative ways not to define the enormous returns on their investments as highly taxed annual income.

Indeed, the state's golden geese continue to fly from California at a rapid clip—at least five million in the single decade between 2004 and 2013, or at a rate of almost ten thousand a week. The rates of departure have only increased. Some census estimates suggest that seven hundred thousand fled California in 2018 alone, at a rate of over two thousand per day. The usual complaints of the departing are exorbitant taxes on the middle class, poor schools and infrastructure, high crime, costly fuel and food, and astronomical housing costs. In many state-by-state rankings of the "business climate" (categorized by regulations and taxes), California now rates in the bottom tiers. It is usually judged dead last in terms of the cost of doing business. Translated, that means that small-business operators relocated to more business-friendly states (for example, seventy thousand Californians on average have left for Texas alone each year of the last decade, and the rate is climbing to over eighty thousand per year), as did retirees on fixed incomes and young people shut out of the high-priced coastal housing market.[39]

Oddly the state rarely lamented the loss of its once thriving middle classes. The inference is that many of the evacuees were conservatives, so their departure only further ensured a monopoly of progressive elected officials. Or as Silicon Valley activist Shankar Singam put it, "If everyone in the middle class is leaving, that's actually a good thing. We need these spots opened up for the new wave of immigrants to come up."

California for over a century had drawn in millions of immigrants from other states. Newcomers flocked to its Mediterranean climate, singular scenic geography, one-thousand-mile coastline, marquee public and private universities, reputation for top-flight public schools, brilliantly designed water transference system of lakes and dams, superb transportation system, affordable housing, and competent state government. Yet, currently, some polls suggest that over 50 percent of the resident California population would like to leave as well.[40]

On arrival to no- or low-tax states like Florida, Idaho, Montana, Nevada, Texas, and Utah, some of California's expatriates tend to wish to recreate the conditions from which they fled. Others will adapt to the more conservative cultures of their new homes. The net political effect of California out-migration on the nation remains a matter of controversy. In some strange matrix, California increasingly became the promised land for impoverished immigrants, many of them arriving illegally, even as it alienated its own middle class. In reductionist terms, arrivals still saw California in decline as far preferable to Mexico and Central America, even as departees saw it as less attractive than a once comparatively unattractive Boise, Idaho, Nashville, Tennessee, or Dallas, Texas.

Or put another way, under the ideology of open borders, as long as people in Central America or southern Mexico deem California preferable, it will draw newcomers, many of them entering the United States illegally. And as long as the state is seen as far less attractive than a dozen or so other states, millions of California residents will continue to leave. The state's population may remain largely the same, but it will likely become a poorer, more culturally and economically bifurcated, and ultimately more medieval place.[41]

More specifically, California recently voted to raise its gas taxes by 40 percent and by July 1, 2020, had the highest gas taxes in the United States—with still further gas tax rises scheduled over the next ten years. Yet even as more revenue arrived in state coffers, the more residents were warned of an increasing shortfall in funding for road construction and repair.

Indeed, California has the ninth-highest combined state and local sales taxes in the country—taxes that hit the poor and middle classes especially hard. In spring 2019, California slapped an additional regressive state sales tax on goods that residents buy online from out-of-state sellers. Such high taxes may have brought California a temporary budget surplus of more than $20 billion at the end of 2019. Yet, by May 2020, during the first months of the national COVID-19 quarantine, California had exhausted its reserves and piled up the largest budget deficits in the country. Due to its decisions to be the first state to lock down and one of the last to open up and to pay out generous subsidies to residents, California, by early May 2020, faced somewhere between a $60 billion and $100 billion annual shortfall, as talk increased of higher top rates on income and a possible new state estate tax.[42]

In any discussion of the transformation of the middle class into our modern version of traditional peasantry, California is of foremost importance. It is the largest state in the union. Since its founding that state has billed itself, usually correctly so, as the trendsetter for the nation, where America's contemporary popular ideas, values, and practices, both good and bad, originate. California's marquee universities, such as Stanford, UC Berkeley, UCLA, the California Institute of Technology (Caltech), and the University of Southern California, along with other UC satellite campuses and the huge twenty-three-campus California State University system, encapsulate all the contradictions of modern academia and staggering student debt. The state is home to the nation's largest population of illegal immigrants and homeless people. And the growing national divergence of wealth and poverty is most evident in Silicon Valley, with over $6 trillion in market-capitalized companies, a now globalized Hollywood, and the haves of Los Angeles and San Francisco.

Moreover, California can be found near the bottom of national rankings for schools and infrastructure. San Francisco ranks first among America's largest cities in property crimes per capita. The massive concrete ruins of the state's quarter-built and now either cancelled or postponed multi-billion-dollar high-speed rail system are already collecting graffiti. Aside from the Southern California Diamond Valley Lake and dam project of 2003, the state has not built a single major reservoir in nearly four decades—since construction was completed on the New Melones Dam in 1979. Since that time, the state has doubled its population and become even more dependent than ever on the massive water transfers of the now ossified California Water Project, federal Central Valley Project, and Colorado River allotments. As in the case of California's neglected freeways, had the state simply used its initial $10 billion high-speed rail allocation on building three major dams critical to the California Water Project, Californians might have had another eight to ten million acre-feet of critical water storage to ride out the next drought.

In any case, the new orthodoxy that dams and reservoirs are scars upon the natural landscape, with deleterious effects on rivers and streams, still does not change the reality that thirty million Californians live in naturally desert conditions. They simply cannot either work or live without vast importations of water from the northern third of the state and the Sierra Nevada mountain range.[43]

California also restricts long-ago contracted water allotments to Central Valley agriculture on the theory that ever greater percentages of stored Sierra Nevada and Northern California water should be freed to flow through the tributaries of the Sacramento and San Joaquin Rivers to the sea, as in the pristine glory days of the nineteenth century. Yet green engineers are selective in their repugnance for the vast water transfers of the California Water Project and Central Valley Project that once dammed rivers and sent water from sparsely populated areas of high rainfall and snowfall to the densely populated and intensively farmed arid areas of the state.

When state regulatory and environmental policies do not encourage middle-class viability and access to affordable housing, electric power, gasoline, and infrastructure, society descends into a binary of haves and have-nots. Progressive California ranks as the third-highest state in the nation in terms of inequality, according to the so-called Gini coefficient that measures purported levels of income and capital wealth disequilibrium. Nearly half of the nation's homeless live in California—a state that professes to have the most progressive policies concerning the poor. About one-third of all Americans on public assistance reside in California. Approximately one-fifth of the state's population lives below the poverty line, largely as a result of massive illegal immigration from the poorest regions of southern Mexico and Central America, which lowers wages and increases social entitlement costs. About one-third of Californians are now enrolled in Medi-Cal, the state's health care program for low-income residents. Many of the latter are illegal residents, who suffer inordinately from diabetes and kidney complications requiring dialysis.

California's social programs are magnets that draw in the indigent from all over the world, who arrive in search of generous health, educational, legal, nutritional, and housing subsidies. Some 27 percent of the state's current residents were not born in the United States. Some 5.5 million Californian immigrants were estimated to be eligible to vote in 2020.[44]

What is the ideological rationale behind such state policies that so taxed the middle classes, giving them in return such poor state services, and drove so many Californians out of their state? Why did citizens make such poor choices in self-governance? In simple terms, the wealthy were not harmed by higher taxes, which they either avoided or found tolerable. And they usually had the clout, money, and influence to mitigate the concrete consequences of their own ideologies. Likewise, many of the poor, who paid little if any state income tax and received generous entitlements, felt California was far more generous than either other states or their foreign places of birth. Few of these exemptions and enticements applied to the middle class.

California also became "prepolitical" in the sense that there are no real Left/Right or Democratic/Republican formal political tensions in the state. It is the nation's first large twenty-first-century experiment in single-party rule, a situation analogous to the role of the Democratic Party in the pre–Civil Rights South. Dissidents have little formal political remedy. In January 2020, not a single Republican held statewide elective office. There were Democratic supermajorities in both houses of the legislature. Democrats held forty-six of fifty-three congressional seats.

Again, in California a historical model is at work of the wealthy medieval keep, primarily among the coastal elite in such iconic enclaves as La Jolla, Malibu, Montecito, Carmel, Pebble Beach, Menlo Park, Atherton, Pacific Heights, Sausalito, and Napa. Great fortunes and privilege surround global cultural and commercial brand names such as Apple, Caltech, eBay, Facebook, Gap, Google, Hewlett-Packard, Hollywood, Intel, Netflix, Oracle, Stanford, Walt Disney, Wells Fargo, and hundreds more that anchor a five-hundred-mile-long affluent California coastal belt.

In the most productive and richest agricultural state, radical farming changes, from the vibrant agrarianism of California's first century to its polarized second, also contribute to medievalism. In my own environs of southern Fresno County, almost all the small forty- to two-hundred-acre family farms of my youth have vanished. They have become the tesserae of vast corporate mosaics. Most megafarms are many thousands of acres, the conglomerations of brilliant family farmers who had the vision and the will to take the advice of their lenders long ago to "go big or go broke." Thus arose vertically integrated farms, incorporating packers, processors, truckers, shippers, brokers, and merchandisers rather than just farmers dependent on a chain of mercurial middlemen well beyond their control.

The iconic old clapboard farmhouses of the region, once owned by a rich diversity of first- and second-generation agrarian Americans of Armenian, Basque, Dutch, Greek, Italian, Mexican, Portuguese, and Scandinavian ancestry, are now often the homes of mostly impoverished Mexican nationals, many without legal residence. The small farmers of the twentieth century left, squeezed by the conglomeration of corporate farms and agribusiness and disheartened by the increasing crime rates, soaring taxes, and failing schools and medical services that could not accommodate the newly arrived and impoverished.

Many of us who grew up on these small farms were "free-range." That is, in our preteen years from ages six to twelve, we roamed freely and unsupervised throughout the vineyards and orchards of our neighboring family farms, watched over by the rural community. To allow children to do so now, in a climate of gangs, untethered fighting dogs, trash piles of abandoned appliances and furniture among trees and vines, and random crime, would be fairly classified as child endangerment—and negligent parenting warranting the intervention of a county child services social worker.[45]

The state-run Medi-Cal program pays for half of all births in California, and 30 percent of Medi-Cal births are to mothers with undocumented immigration status. The San Ysidro border crossing between Tijuana, Mexico, and San Diego is the world's busiest. Some seventy million people cross on foot and in cars into and out of California each year. The presence of millions without English and without diplomas helps explain much of the alarming poverty in California. Many of the poorest concentrate away from the coast, in the eastern environs of Southern California, some of the coastal foothill communities, and the state's vast Central Valley.[46]

The effect of so many immigrant poor has certainly transformed California into not so much two different states as two different worlds: a highly sophisticated, highly regulated, and uniform coastal gentry juxtaposed with an impoverished interior of largely immigrant and first-generation Californians with little ability or desire to adhere to California's labyrinth of rules and regulations. Well over half of all immigrant households in California receive some sort of public assistance, which can include health care, food, housing, transportation, education, and legal subsidies. California's trifecta economic model and one-party governance may become the model of most states: impoverish or drive out the middle class, import the poor from abroad, enable staggering levels of global wealth concentrated in the hands of the few—and see one party fuel such medievalism.

In the next chapter, we will see that Americans are reverting to pre-citizenship not just because of the squeezing of the middle class and its transformation into a modern version of peasantry but, in addition, due to the conflation between residency and citizenship. One's mere physical presence within the borders of the United States is becoming synonymous with the privilege of being an American citizen. As we shall learn, massive and illegal immigration has proved a disaster for the idea of American citizenship by lowering wages, straining government services, undermining the sanctity of the law, energizing tribalism, fueling identity politics, fostering racialism, and importing massive poverty—even as it is deliberately conflated with mostly welcome legal immigration and praised loudest by an elite that knows, and wishes to know, almost nothing about it.

Chapter Two

RESIDENTS

I voted numerous times when I was a senator to
spend money to build a barrier to try to prevent illegal
immigrants from coming in. And I do think that you
have to control your borders.

—HILLARY CLINTON,
campaign stop, November 9, 2015

A resident of America should be easily distinguished from a citizen by the etymologies of the respective two nouns. "Resident" derives from the Latin *residere*, "to sit down or settle." It denotes the concrete fact of living in a particular place. In contrast, "citizen" entails a quality, a privilege of enjoying particular rights predicated on responsibilities—and not necessarily on location at any given time.

An American resident can be a citizen or subject of any foreign nation who just happens to be living within the boundaries of the United States. US citizens, however, are entitled to constitutional protections wherever they go—to the extent possible given the constraints of their hosts. Most specifically, citizenship ensures the right to a US passport and, with it, to leave and return to America whenever one wishes.

In the past, the distinction between the two statuses was comprehensive and important. It once involved everything from voting, holding elected office, serving in all ranks of the military, and eligibility for state assistance. Today, those differences have virtually collapsed, as we shall see, to little more than eligibility to hold most elected offices and the residual permission of legal entry and exit. And that latter privilege of free transit by default is now likewise eroding. Recent US censuses have not asked respondents whether they are even citizens of the United States.

The fusion of residency and citizenship is fairly new. America was founded on an implicit, tough quid pro quo. Immigrants, originally mostly from Europe, were welcomed into the vast, underpopulated America of the nineteenth and twentieth centuries. Labor was scarce. Land was plentiful. Resources were abundant. The country needed people. It offered newcomers freedom and opportunity unknown in both the Old World and Latin America.

Soon diverse populations flocked to American shores through a chain of massive, often bloc immigrations—from western and eastern Europe and, by the late nineteenth century, often from Asia and Latin America. The arriving immigrant was implicitly expected to surrender his prior identity and adopt a new American one. National identity, though a source of pride to an individual, would not permanently define him. Instead the immigrant was measured by shared human characteristics well beyond his superficial appearance or religious creed.

The so-called white population of the United States, like all majority populations in the history of civilization, saw immigration through the lens of its own tribal self-interest. But the inherent logic of the US Declaration of Independence and the Constitution, which saw all men as created equal, constrained such narrowmindedness. Both founding documents inevitably and eventually guaranteed immigrants the full rights of their hosts. The immigrant citizen, who might appear superficially different from the Founders, understood that the idea of

America meant the nation strived to be always better than it was, which was already far better than the alternatives elsewhere.

Call it chauvinism or arrogance, but Americans somehow squared the circle of accepting their shortcomings while assuming the choices elsewhere were always worse. Likewise, the immigrant arrived thinking that America would be better than what he left. And to the extent it was not, he was determined to help his new fellow citizens to ensure that it became so.

The prescient Founders had emphasized unity and homogeneity. They rightly feared that numerous and independent American nation-states might resemble the multiplicity of European nations and thus incur the lethal European habit of constant warring on the North American continent. They also worried equally about factions and unassimilated interests that might foment the sort of unrest that had traditionally likewise fueled European internal civil religious and ethnic discord and outright war—especially if multiplied by obvious geographic divisions that might lend themselves to separation from the Union.

The answer to all these fears of dissolution and factionalism was a large nation governed by checks and balances, encompassing ethnicities within common borders as they all eventually assimilated and disappeared into a common Americanism. The immigrant, then, was to adopt English as his primary spoken language as well as the responsibilities that accompanied the gift of citizenship. He accepted the Constitution, both in fact and spirit. In lieu of blood and soil, it was to be his unifying, guiding political doctrine.

Native customs and traditions, while tolerated in civil society, within two or three generations were forgotten, to be replaced by American versions often quite alien to those of the immigrant's birthplace. The ideal was that a citizen was to be defined by his values, not just by his birth and not at all by his creed or color.

So the mid-nineteenth-century essayist and philosopher Ralph Waldo Emerson waxed about the novel American citizen in a now often-caricatured display of supposed naïveté if not cultural chauvinism: "The energy of Irish, Germans, Swedes, Poles, and Cossacks, and all the European tribes—of the Africans, and of the Polynesians—will construct a new race, a new religion, a new state, a new literature, which will be as vigorous as the new Europe which came out of the smelting-pot of the Dark Ages, or that which earlier emerged from the Pelasgic and Etruscan barbarism."[1]

In the most brutal of bargains, America and the immigrant took risks. Both usually won. America, eager for manpower in a vast and underpopulated country, wagered that its diverse new immigrants, for the most part poor and often without capital, would find common ties and alliances in their new common American identity—as they would "melt" into the majority rather quickly within two or three generations.

Newcomers from so many different tribes and races would not permanently separate into permanent enclaves, revert to tribal infighting, or undermine the unity of their adopted nation. Instead, the diverse languages, customs, races, classes, and religions of immigrants would wane in varying degrees. More practically, the multifaceted tribalism of the majority would vastly outnumber the would-be tribalism of any one minority. In other words, adopting the new American majority culture, language, and tenets of citizenship became the only protection against the bullying and chauvinism of any one tribe against another. In counterintuitive fashion, the presence of so many different arriving ethnic and religious groups enhanced Americanism as the only common bond amid such chaos of keeping the common peace.

The original vast citizen majority of white Christians of northern European descent, often grudgingly and with reluctance, over some two hundred years was forced to extend the promise of their once exclusive citizenship to those who did not look or necessarily practice religion like the nation's Founders. After all, the ideas of the Founders did not simply reflect the ethnic chauvinism of white Protestant Anglo-Americans, the majority of the new country. Rather, they were transcendent, drawing and expanding upon ideas absorbed over centuries from the growth of

a multiethnic Rome, a multiracial Christianity, the European Enlightenment and Reformation, and the traditions of British parliamentary
republicanism.

At first, in the early nineteenth century, most newcomers—largely
western and northern Europeans with the initial exception of the
Irish—were welcomed. Their race and ethnicity were still mostly akin
to the original European settler population and the current majority of American citizens—despite vast cultural differences among the
European arrivals, and despite the bondage of millions of slaves and
institutionalized racism against African American freedmen and Native
Americans. On the ever-expanding frontier, the federal government
had not yet the desire or power to surveille the vast borders of the
early-nineteenth-century nation. Much less could it often distinguish
between legal and unlawful immigration.

In such a void, the frontier and remote locales were more or less
porous. Boundary folk often welcomed in any foreigner they could.
Most Americans were too busy to worry about suspicious newcomers
in such empty landscapes. The country was soon enriched by immigrants' diverse foods, fashions, literatures, music, and arts—as long as
the nation's core values, traditions, and laws were kept sacrosanct.

By the mid- and late nineteenth century, as the United States expanded
in the aftermath of the Civil War, a number of nascent immigration and
citizenship laws were passed. Supreme Court rulings began institutionalizing the legal differences between citizens and mere residents. As a
result, there gradually emerged a comprehensive system of legal immigration. Borders solidified, and security concerns increased. Rules and
protocols were established for granting newcomers either citizenship or
legal residency. Many of these statutes were certainly exclusionary in
the sense of discouraging massive immigration from any one particular
place—and, in racialist fashion, especially from non-northern and non-
western European countries.[2]

America always took a risk that the peoples of the world could recom-
bine inside the United States and eventually integrate, intermarry, and

assimilate. There was also an implicit challenge that the original Native American population, African American descendants of slaves, immigrants from south of the border, and eastern and southern Europeans and Asians would be subject to varying degrees of greater discrimination, hatred, segregation, and second-class citizenship from the large, majority-European assimilated population.[3]

Nonetheless, there still loomed innately within the nation's founding documents the promise of something even better. Indeed, the intrinsic American assumption was that the Old World's poor were largely a product not of native lack of talent but of a stultifying class system erroneously equating natural merit with the circumstances of birth. Once freed of that straitjacket, the world's immigrating poor would form their own aristocracy of merit in America.

By the first decade of the twenty-first century, Americans were all mostly equal under the law in both fact and theory, despite massive immigration since the 1860s of a sort quite different from in the past and notwithstanding the timeless imperfections of human nature. So most American immigrants throughout the early and mid-twentieth century prospered. They learned English and became legal citizens. They fought in America's wars, paid taxes, voted, and held elective offices. By the third generation most were indistinguishable from sixth- or seventh-generation Americans.

Eventually, in this tough exchange, ideologies, customs, and politics were no longer predicated on original place of birth. The grandchildren of neither former mayor of New York City Rudy Giuliani nor of the late New York governor Mario Cuomo can speak Italian. The Italian names Rudy and Mario or Giuliani and Cuomo are no guide to either's politics. Ethnicity became increasingly irrelevant once America absorbed and integrated the immigrants' descendants.

Nor were whites guaranteed economic supremacy by virtue of sharing an ethnic or racial heritage with the country's Founding Fathers. By the twenty-first century the number of ethnic Americans who were not of European ancestry but were, on average, wealthier than so-called white Americans was astonishing. By most metrics of median household income, Asian Americans (e.g., Japanese, Indians, Chinese, South Koreans, etc.) made far more per year on average than did so-called European Americans.[4]

Nor did America quite fragment into a balkanized European state. It had survived the Civil War. It dismantled Jim Crow in the South. It finally embraced universal civil rights that made race increasingly irrelevant legally—at least until recently. The United States took up the challenge of matching the idealism of its founding principles with the reality of equality under the law and of opportunity. Thereby America became the most powerful nation in the history of civilization and now the world's oldest functioning constitutional republic. Unlike the United States, most nations have not been founded on the implicit principle that its newly arriving citizens are the stuff of future greatness. America assumed that immigrants' past unhappiness and indeed second-class citizenship in their places of birth were due to the failings of their homelands rather than to their own inability to succeed.

In turn, any immigrants who dreamed that they could remain perpetually Japanese, Swedish, or Mexican in such a huge expanse of America were soon sorely disappointed. To their own children and certainly their grandchildren, the immigrants' original languages, homes, and very manners soon became foreign. The trajectory of the brutal bargain in some decades slowed or accelerated. Its speed and ease often unfortunately hinged on the particular race or religion of the immigrant.

Proximity to borders mattered too. Those who could go back and forth across the southern border faced greater challenges of Americanization than those more distant for whom a nineteenth-century sailing passage across the rough Atlantic or a long steamship trip from Tokyo marked a clean break from the past. Distance, premodern travel and transport, two oceans, and the huge size of the United States all made America a point of no return.

Numbers were critical. When yearly immigrants came in the tens, rather than the hundreds, of thousands, integration proved far easier.

The surrounded immigrant accommodated to the majority culture and language rather than vice versa. In contrast, wave immigration made rapid assimilation far more problematic. Mass migrations of eastern Europeans, Jews, and Italians during the "Great Wave" between 1880 and 1924, in the manner of the earlier massive influx of 1.5 million Irish between 1845 and 1855, cast doubts on the efficacy of the melting pot.

Eventually frantic calls arose for immigration restrictions—reflecting nativist fears that nonwestern, non-Protestant, and non–northern European newcomers would not integrate and might establish foreign customs, religions, and ideas contrary to the values and traditions of the majority of Americans. Late-nineteenth-century progressive notions of eugenics added a pseudoscientific patina to restrictionism, spiking fears of domestic racial superiority and purity suddenly under threat from supposedly less advanced races abroad.[5]

There were certainly always quirks and paradoxes. Often the more the assimilation, the more the immigrant's psychological resistance—or sometimes sincere, if not pathetic and strained, ethnic chauvinism—at least superficially and for a brief period. I did not speak the Swedish of my paternal grandfather. Yet, as a concession, my father insisted that we drive used (and often unreliable) early-1960s-model Volvos, bought Electrolux vacuum cleaners, and ate Swedish rye crackers—symbolic anachronisms bewildering to us youths.

Yet, under the changing conditions of late-twentieth-century immigration, identity politics, and salad-bowl separatism, which encourages ethnicities to retain their tribal identifications, sometimes the assimilated third generation was more likely to resurrect a lost ethnic pedigree than was the first generation, which had wished to discard it. Some grandchildren of immigrants still adopt hyphenated names or the use of accentuation to highlight or emphasize an otherwise naturally eroding non-American identity. In my rural neighborhood, during the decades of ethnic reassertion following the 1960s, a few suddenly re-Latinized their names. Peters became Pedros and Lindas became Herlindas, often to solidify careers predicated on their assumed unique resonance with new waves of immigrants from south of the border and to fill institutions' de facto diversity quotas.

Nonetheless, as long as immigration was measured, legal, and diverse, Mexican immigrants, for example, more or less followed the paradigm of mostly poorer Italian and Catholic immigrants of the late nineteenth and early twentieth centuries: arriving impoverished, experiencing greater initial difficulty in assimilation than some other European groups, and by the third generation mostly achieving economic parity and cultural and social integration within the American mainstream.

What currently threatens to change historic patterns of Mexican and Latin American integration, assimilation, and intermarriage is not sudden white racism. The challenge ahead is simply the huge numbers of impoverished aliens without high school diplomas who have recently crossed the border illegally and, upon arrival, are encouraged to emphasize their otherness by a mostly white progressive elite.[6]

To take a recent example, during the 2019 Democratic presidential primary debates, candidate Julián Castro, a non-Spanish-speaking third-generation American with a Stanford University degree, on the debate stage insisted on trilling his *r*'s and using Spanish pronunciations of the usual buzzwords of the identity politics vocabulary. His was an apparent effort to exude ethnic authenticity and thereby appeal to supposedly less assimilated voters or to distance himself from the assumed pathologies of the majority culture of which he was otherwise so much a part.

The principles of equality under the law inherent in the Constitution ensured that the citizen of five generations had no more rights as an American than the recently arrived legal immigrant and naturalized citizen. Or as ex-president Theodore Roosevelt put it brutally in a famous 1919 letter to Richard Hurd, president of the American Defense Society, "In the first place, we should insist that if the immigrant who comes here in good faith becomes an American and assimilates himself to us, he shall be treated on an exact equality with everyone else, for it is an outrage to discriminate against any such man because of creed, or birthplace, or origin. But this is predicated upon the person's becoming in every facet an American, and nothing but an American."[7]

The ancient idea of gratitude once also permeated the entire American ideal of immigration. As difficult as America could be for destitute refugees and untrained and impoverished immigrants with little English fluency, most newcomers became strong defenders of their new country. Most accepted that it treated them far better, both materially and spiritually, than did the homelands they had forsaken. To think otherwise for the immigrant was incoherent: if America was no better than Ireland, Denmark, Japan, or Armenia, why then come at all? Or why stay when things were more backward, unfair, or impoverished than the place one had left? More practically, it was felt unwise to move to a new home and present upon arrival grievances against the host and his hospitality.

I once asked a neighbor from southern Mexico why exactly had he left his birthplace some twenty years earlier to come to the Central Valley of California. I expected the usual answer of immigrants that he was poor and America was rich. But instead his reply astounded me. I remember it as something like the following: "Dignity. Dignity. Here even strangers call me Mr. Rojas—the doctor, the sheriff, everyone calls me mister. Not like in Mexico where señor depends on who you are." In short, he summarized brilliantly how and why the melting pot had worked. He had transmogrified from a mere resident of Mexico, a subject without innate, constitutionally protected freedoms, into a naturalized US citizen who was thankful that he was now an equal to all other American citizens and treated accordingly.

If the melting pot and the granting of legal citizenship to legal immigrants had worked so well to form and enhance the American nation, why then have so many interests sought to replace the successful paradigm with alternatives that have no historical record of harmonizing a multiracial nation? To understand sudden and radical changes in government policy, a Roman might ask, *Cui bono?* Who benefits?

The first radical change came with the Immigration and Naturalization Act of 1965, also less formally known as the Hart-Celler Act. The legislation was born and passed in the aftermath of the assassination of John F. Kennedy and championed by his brother Senator Ted Kennedy (D-MA). It ostensibly addressed the concerns of minority populations that an earlier quota system—based on then current ethnic and racial percentages within the existing citizen population—increasingly discriminated against non-European newcomers, then the largest group of foreign nationals who wished to emigrate to the United States.

There were plenty of complexities to the new law and unforeseen consequences. Yet, in general, over the next half century, it achieved the likely intent of its Democratic sponsors of radically changing the demography of the United States. Immigrants now arrived most often from Africa, Asia, and Latin America and rarely from Europe. For the most part, they were poorer, with lesser skill sets, and more dependent on the emerging entitlements of the newly announced Great Society programs of the 1960s. They often arrived illegally, and the majority became natural constituents of the Democratic Party. Or as Pulitzer Prize–winning liberal historian Theodore White later conceded of the politicized Hart-Celler Act, it was "revolutionary and probably the most thoughtless of the many acts of the Great Society."[8]

White saw that the law eliminated most meritocratic criteria based on education and acquired skill levels. Instead, immigration was fast-tracked for family unification and, more informally, proximity to the borders. The new rules resulted in much larger rates of admission on the basis of ties to naturalized American citizens and legal residents.

The act also abolished most ideas of a national-origins quota, as it limited considerations of national origin or ancestry in the formulation of immigration policy—*or rather, it recalibrated them by race and ethnicity*. In other words, the law did not specifically privilege those without high school diplomas over neurosurgeons, but it certainly had the effect of favoring admission of far more of the former than of the latter.

The Democrats had sponsored the bill, signed by Lyndon Johnson, on assurances to their own racialist Southern Democrat colleagues that neither the numbers nor the origins of immigrants would change all that much. But they almost immediately did just that—as measured immigration from an increasingly affluent and demographically static Europe and the British Commonwealth of Nations all but ceased. In 2017, only about 7 percent of yearly legal immigrants claimed prior citizenship in Europe, with the vast majority coming from Africa (11 percent), Asia (38 percent), and Mexico or Central and South America (44 percent).[9]

Legal immigration prior to 1960 had still mostly mirrored the current demographics of the United States—70 percent from Europe and Canada. But more than a half century later, by 2016, nearly 90 percent of new arrivals were non-Canadian or of non-European ancestry and without native English fluency. Immigrants and the non–native born, as a percentage of the US population, soared during this period from less than 10 percent of the population to over 13 percent.[10]

The next radical change came mostly from both Democratic and Republican pressures on the Ronald Reagan administration. The 1986 Immigration Reform and Control Act, known better as the Simpson-Mazzoli Act, was a bipartisan effort intended not so much as a compromise as a gifting of concessions to a wide variety of special interests all unhappy with then existing immigration enforcement.

Traditional conservatives were, in theory, assured that employers would be required to authenticate their workers' immigration status and would soon be fined if caught hiring illegal aliens. Corporate interests, especially agribusiness, received sweeping amnesties for their workers who had arrived before 1982 and were without criminal records. Liberal concerns pushed for even more amnesties. And President Reagan followed up the legislation with an executive order extending the 1986 amnesties to children under eighteen of those who had received legal status the year before.

Ethnic lobbyists quietly delighted that immigration enforcement both at the border and within the United States was increasingly inert, given that authentication was in part transferred to employers—who collected legal documentation from laborers that was often impossible to verify. As a practical matter, employers were not so eager to reject workers' suspicious documentation and lacked the ability to verify immigration forms anyway.

At the same time, immigration officers all but disappeared from the interior of the United States and were relegated to the southern border corridor now swamped with influxes of immigrants. Immigrants assumed that the old proactive border patrol had transmogrified into an administrative agency or that reaching the United States through an unsecure border was tantamount to eventual legal residency or citizenship, given the new American precedent of mass rolling amnesties. And over the next quarter century following Simpson-Mazzoli, the number of illegal aliens soared from five million to over eleven million to perhaps nearly twenty million today—as likely reformists no doubt expected, despite their denials of such cynicism.[11]

In America, quiet revolutions occur most often when both Right and Left collude in a tacit agreement to change the system for their own particular interests—even if they concede that their respective conservative and liberal agendas seem antithetical. So it has been during the last half century with nonenforcement of immigration law and the conflation of citizenship and mere residency.

The politics of illegal immigration into America over the last fifty years is, in truth, not complicated at all. Simply put, corporate America wanted cheap imported labor without the bother of unionization. Hand in glove with business, the progressive Left agreed with virtual open borders. Progressives assumed either that massive influxes from an impoverished Mexico and Central America would eventually lead to a politically useful new demography or that the United States should use its resources to help the foreign poor by inviting them to enter America.

Pulitzer Prize–winning journalist Jerry Kammer recently dedicated an entire book to the unlikely bedfellows who enabled illegal immigration: "Corporations cited the authority of free-market libertarians who argued that the market—that is, supply and demand–governed wages—should trump border enforcement. Apparently, the implicit logic was that when millions crossed illegally and their unskilled labor crashed wages, then only tens of thousands would keep coming: Problem solved."[12]

The Left offered an array of its own rationales for illegal immigration, from the race-based La Raza (the race)–inspired myth that "the borders crossed us, we didn't cross the borders" to "diversity is our strength"—as if no government had a right to disrupt historical migrations with artificial borders. Or was the rationale that Mexico had some claim on California because of the earlier, tiny nineteenth-century presence of a few thousand Mexican citizens in a vast unpopulated region? The pre-1840s Mexican skeleton government had seized upper California from the Spanish, who in turn had appropriated the region from Native Americans. The latter often grabbed sections of it from each other.[13]

The immigration law lobby is so large because many ethnic groups, politicians, and corporate chiefs have a stake in open borders. Ethnic groups enjoy more political clout with the arrival of immigrants. Employers push for labor markets jammed with eager job seekers. Businesses profit from the increased demand for everything from groceries to housing to automobiles to prisons. Libertarians and cosmopolitans delight in the idea of no borders. Humanitarians take moral satisfaction in embracing illegal immigrants. Far from acknowledging that there are legitimate reasons to oppose those who come illegally and in large numbers, many warmhearted liberals regard it as an opportunity to demonstrate their commitment to diversity and inclusion.

So long as the numbers of resident illegal aliens were considered manageable—under ten million or so from the 1970s through the 1990s—and their citizen children did not yet vote, both Republicans and Democrats could still deplore the flagrant violation of federal immigration law rhetorically while doing little about it. This schizophrenia of damning while empowering unlawful entries was emblematized by President Bill Clinton's warning about illegal immigration—to bipartisan thunderous applause—in his 1995 State of the Union address to Congress:

> All Americans, not only in the States most heavily affected but in every place in this country, are rightly disturbed by the large numbers of illegal aliens entering our country.
>
> The jobs they hold might otherwise be held by citizens or legal immigrants. The public services they use impose burdens on our taxpayers.
>
> That's why our administration has moved aggressively to secure our borders more by hiring a record number of new border guards, by deporting twice as many criminal aliens as ever before, by cracking down on illegal hiring, by barring welfare benefits to illegal aliens. . . .
>
> We are a nation of immigrants. But we are also a nation of laws. It is wrong and ultimately self-defeating for a nation of immigrants to permit the kind of abuse of our immigration laws we have seen in recent years, and we must do more to stop it.

Clinton at the time was not voicing a liberal or Democratic position on illegal immigration; rather he was reflecting a bipartisan consensus that illegal and legal immigration should not be conflated. And in general, Clinton had argued that illegal immigration was deleterious for the country. During the first term of the Barack Obama administration (2009–2012), the official Democratic position had not changed that much from Clinton's even two decades later.

Or rather, the rhetoric still had not quite caught up with radical growth in the number of illegal aliens residing on American soil and their children's accession to voting age. The advantages to liberal politicians of millions of new impoverished arrivals apparently were now once again becoming undeniable. Thus began an even more radical change in the politics of illegality. Yet, even as late as 2013, Barack Obama, in his own State of the Union, at least signaled a willingness to secure the now open border: "Real reform means strong border security, and we can build on the progress my administration has already made—putting more boots on the Southern border than at any time in our history and reducing illegal crossings to their lowest levels in 40 years."

Such a boast by 2020 would have earned Obama the charge of racism and xenophobia. Nonetheless, despite changing demography and often politicized polls, the public—including immigrants—remain opposed to *illegal* immigration. American citizens of Mexican origin often resent unlawful invasion into either Mexico or the United States from Central America. Americans especially found offensive the exemption of foreign nationals from federal law, when the citizens themselves are not exempt.

Mostly Democratic but some Republican politicians and the media soon squared the circle of public discontent and political utility in predictable ways. One tactic was to conflate illegal with legal immigration in polling questions in an attempt to downplay public opposition. Rarely asked whether they opposed "illegal" immigration, voters were usually just polled about "immigration" in general, which they typically took to mean traditional legal, measured, meritocratic, and diverse immigration. They were asked not whether they supported a border wall but rather whether they supported a wall along the *entire* two-thousand-mile border—some of it inaccessible and without need of a barrier.

The new phrase "comprehensive immigration reform" also contributed to euphemistic obfuscation of the issue—political scientist Peter Skerry rightly relabeled it "comprehensive immigration confusion." The word "comprehensive" seemed to emphasize border enforcement. But in fact it referred to legal amnesties for illegal entrants and residents and continued "comprehensive" nonenforcement of immigration law.[14]

In Orwellian fashion, language continues to be reinvented to reflect the political massaging of illegal immigration. The key to understanding the entire immigration controversy is to remember the sustained attempt to remove the critical adjective "illegal" from any of the many nouns that follow. The linguistic effort aimed to culturally recalibrate an unlawful act as something either legal or even admirable—without appealing to the will of the people through congressional action or state plebiscites. "Illegal alien" was initially euphemized as "illegal immigrant" to avoid any suggestion that the status of the illegal arrival was in some way different from that of an American (cf. Latin *alienus*, "foreigner"). Soon "illegal" also became taboo, and so "undocumented" replaced it, as if "undocumented immigrants" were simply virtual Americans who arrived without bringing along their legal papers. Finally, the adjective "undocumented" itself was sometimes dropped, as if there were to be no distinction between legal or illegal "immigrants." But even the noun "immigrant" was sometimes considered too judgmental, given its prefix's supposed implicit bias of dividing migrants (those who move from one place to another) into categories of entrants (immigrants) and departees (emigrants). So finally "migrants" alone is now beginning to gain currency. Soon the phrase "illegal alien" will likely be taboo and banned from formal discourse—despite its use by diverse federal agencies and the US Supreme Court.[15]

Again, the changing situation on the ground explained the linguistic gymnastics. The illegal immigrant community grew exponentially to nearly twenty million in the twenty-first century. Second-generation citizen children of unlawful residents began to organize politically. They voted, often understandably supporting agendas that had allowed their parents to enter the United States illegally and reside without worrying about the legal consequences. Suddenly both parties realized that the politics of illegal immigration had permanently changed.

The Democrats subtly shed their past vocal opposition—especially now that their union labor base was eroding. Openly supporting defiance of federal law, they hoped to flip southwestern red states blue with new monolithic Latino and identity politics voters. Soon over 550 sanctuary jurisdictions arose to protect those illegal immigrants formerly subject to federal arrest and apprehension.[16]

The Republicans, for the most part in fear, muted their resistance to illegal immigration—although in 2012, for example, they might have made class inroads with the old Democratic white, Latino, and black working classes, whose wages were being driven down by imported cheap labor. As the number of illegal immigrants grew, Republicans grew terrified both of accusations of racism, xenophobia, and nativism and of refusal by big-donor employers, eager for inexpensive labor, to contribute to Republican campaigns.

Almost everyone who had once railed against illegal immigration now either supported or tolerated it. They assumed most US citizens, who still opposed illegal immigration, did not regard it as a high-priority issue or could be shamed into silence by insinuations of illiberality and intolerance. When economic data revealed that illegal immigration had cost the country hundreds of billions of dollars—namely, that despite a variety of complex federal eligibility regulations, each illegal immigrant required far more in social services than he paid in taxes—the messengers of such unwelcome facts were attacked as heretics and worse. Once state assistance was allowed for noncitizens, the rate of naturalization fell—apparently because residents saw few further advantages in becoming citizens once state support was guaranteed.[17]

Vestigial distinctions between citizens and residents will likely continue to disappear. For example, 2020 presidential primary candidate Pete Buttigieg, speaking in Spanish, assured illegal immigrants who came to the United States before adulthood that their residence was tantamount to citizenship: "We can say to a Dreamer, lying awake at night, questioning if this country is her own . . . this country is your country too." During the 2019 Democratic primary debates, almost all the candidates agreed that they would ensure comprehensive health coverage to illegal aliens, a privilege that not all American citizens enjoy but as taxpayers would apparently fund.[18]

Buttigieg was reflecting a growing trend in the Congress and the courts to blur the distinctions between citizens and noncitizens, in the fashion well underway in the European Union. Naturalization rates flattened as illegal residency soared. The holders of green cards saw few advantages in becoming citizens when, by court ruling, citizenship was no longer a prerequisite to receive welfare.[19]

A final quirk in the illegal immigration debate: if open-border advocates could not ensure amnesty and citizenship for illegals, then the value of citizenship could be diminished altogether. A sort of compromise citizenship could be reformulated in which noncitizens would gain what citizens lost, as the more entitlement services were stressed, the less citizens could expect prior levels of service. The more non-English immigrants sometimes overwhelmed schools and public services, the fewer resources would be available to citizens. And the more there were calls for fewer requirements for legal identification for voting, the more citizens doubted the value of their own ballots.

The ultimate caricature of the fusion between temporary residency and citizenship came in early 2021. Citizens of Mexico, reportedly in the "thousands," flocked to American border states—*encouraged by Mexican health officials*—to become vaccinated ahead of millions of American citizens. Thousands also crossed into the United States without COVID-19 testing at a time when many Americans were still in lockdown and the federal government was considering travel restrictions to and from Florida but not across the southern border. As one celebrity Mexican television host, Juan Origel, said of the ease of jumping ahead of citizens in the vaccination line and receiving shots without any legal reactions from US authorities, "I've known lots of Mexicans, thousands, who have gone to get the vaccine in the U.S. And nothing happened."

Throughout history, when residency and citizenship have become indistinguishable, then citizenship has either eroded or come to mean nothing. We should remember that the word "utopia" derives from the Greek *ou topos* (a no place), not *eu topos* (a good place). When residents and citizens are equally Americans, then the place called America itself in a sense no longer exists and becomes a fantasy, a no place—or even a dystopia.[20]

How and why did immigration descend into an often illegal and chaotic process? How did residency become conflated with citizenship? How did illegal immigration contribute to the tribalism of the salad bowl? How did millions of newcomers arrive illegally, expecting to become exempt from elements of their hosts' own immigration laws?

Start with the host, America itself. The university and even popular culture now often caricature assimilation as "cultural appropriation" by a host that is supposedly inauthentic, as well as racist and nativist. In other words, as one sociologist put it, "With a failure of American culture to acknowledge its mythological identity, dominant American culture whitewashes immigrant cultural identity to force assimilation." Translated that incoherence means when immigrants choose to come to America, whether legally or not, they have no obligation to assume a "mythological" identity at the expense of what they just left behind but chose to reject by leaving their homelands. Assimilation is ridiculed as an abject impediment to what we are now becoming—quite opposite to the observations of J. Hector St. John de Crèvecoeur, who at the nation's founding remarked that an American is a unique person "who, leaving behind him all his ancient prejudices and manners, receives new ones from the new mode of life he has embraced, the new government he obeys, and the new rank he holds."[21]

What followed from American immigration reform movements of the 1960s was not always just optimism and collective confidence in overcoming a history of racialist biases in immigration. Instead growing cultural renunciations of the American past eventually arose and, with them, a new effort to redefine America itself. As a frequent result, immigrants who arrived in the belief that at last they had reached a fair and just country were disabused by the media and universities of their supposed naïveté.

In universities and the media and among the Left, the image of the United States gradually transmogrified from a flawed but otherwise best hope for the immigrant into a largely racist society. It could only partially do penance to redeem itself by taking in millions of non-Western immigrants, legal or not. And it would encourage them to retain their former primary identities, voice new complaints against their supposedly illiberal hosts, and, indeed, help transform the United States into something more akin to the homeland they had abandoned. Accordingly, immigration enforcement itself became constructed as a sort of racist act perpetuated against immigrants whose only crime was being of nonwhite ancestry and breaking minor federal laws in entering and residing in a foreign country without legal permission.[22]

So this late-twentieth- and twenty-first-century project was to "diversify" America in order to remold its political traditions along more progressive lines. Immigration now became an unapologetic political weapon of transformation by the Left. It worried little about the paradox of claiming the country was flawed by racism while inviting nonwhite foreigners to enter such a dreadful place. Given the millions who crossed the border without legality or background checks, citizenship would by necessity be modulated to accommodate new immigrants, many without much knowledge of English or of the United States' history, traditions, or constitutional definition of citizenship. Few dared to object that people had risked their lives to reach America from Mexico and Central America precisely because they no longer wished to live under the paradigms of their birthplaces, which had resulted in autocratic government, poverty, few freedoms, and less security—not because they intended to replicate them on their arrival in America. Yet, if the host is unwilling to acclimatize the guest to the customs and conditions of his own house, how can the guest be entirely faulted?

What catalysts had led to millions crossing the southern border? In essence, Latin America and especially Mexico did not reach the long-promised economic parity with Canada and the United States—from income opportunities to health care to basic safety and security. Corrupt and violent socialist and right-wing authoritarian governments, often hand in glove with drug cartels and gangs, destroyed or crippled the already statist and inert economies of Latin America. That stasis only created more asymmetry between North and South, in a way not true of the Canadian-American northern border.

Central American and Mexican elites also encouraged their impoverished to trek northward legally if possible, illegally if necessary. And they did so for a variety of reasons, ranging from eliminating internal dissidents, discriminating against indigenous people, and reducing social welfare and health care costs to envisioning expatriates as sources of generous remittances and valuable lobbying and diplomatic levers. There is currently much concern about both Russian and Chinese interference in US election campaigns. Yet, by any fair standard, one could argue that the Mexican government's policy of deliberately encouraging mass immigration to the United States, under illegal auspices, has been far more influential in its long-term effects of changing the electorate and swaying elections.[23]

A few in the American establishment originally assumed that an open American border might provide a needed safety valve and thereby ward off communist revolutions in Mexico and Central America. Also helpful to the Mexican government's policy of encouraging illegal immigration into the United States were the views of some Mexican citizens that the American Southwest still properly belonged to Mexico. For example, in a controversial 2002 Zogby poll, 58 percent of polled Mexican citizens felt that "the territory of the United States Southwest rightfully belongs to Mexico."

It is unclear how American citizens should interpret such two-decade-old polls, given that a large majority of Mexicans (65 percent) polled in 2017 held an unfavorable view of America. But if you dislike the United States, why go there illegally? Because it rightfully belongs to Mexico and its immigration law therefore does not exist? If America did belong to Mexico, why would the would-be emigrant flee Mexico only to travel more deeply into Mexico or what rightfully should once again become Mexico?[24]

In real numbers, by 2019 almost fifty million American residents had not been born in the United States. Perhaps nearly 40 percent of that number resided here illegally. The majority of them arrived from Central America and Mexico. Some recent estimates peg the non-native population as even larger, given the inability to ascertain accurately the number of foreign-born residents who are here illegally.

If there had been any past institutionalized bias in US immigration policy, the Hart-Celler Act certainly ended much of it—while creating a new nondiversity bias of its own. Immigration became less calibrated by the ethnic percentages of the US population and instead dominated by Latin Americans and to a lesser degree Asians—in numbers never envisioned even by the bill's progressive sponsors, often in reality weighted as much to illegal as to legal entry. Few nations in history have been deemed racist as they, by design, opened their borders to people of origins other than those of roughly 80 to 90 percent of their population—as the nation's demographics again by design radically changed. The immigration reformers of the 1960s may have thought that by ending ethnic quotas and emphasizing skill sets, they were democratizing immigration policy. But in fact, immigration increasingly began to become less diverse and more illegal, often with less regard for education and skills and more predicated on family considerations, domestic special interests, and closeness to the border.[25]

In other words, in the last half century and by legislative intent, many immigrants have arrived from war-torn and impoverished countries. They came in huge numbers, without a great deal of diversity and in frequent need of US state services. But for the sponsors of the new immigration rules, the new wave of immigrants also certainly represented a continuance of the spirit of the civil rights era. Millions of non-European newcomers would swell the numbers of Americans who might harbor, or soon be taught to embrace, the culture of victimization of the Left and thus lend support to the expansion of programs to achieve rapid parity with the income levels of American citizens.[26]

A recent Yale/MIT joint study of illegal immigration from 1990 to 2016 concluded that the commonly cited, yet static, figure of eleven million illegal aliens currently in the United States is inaccurate. Commentators have recited this number—unchanged—for at least thirty years. The authors found there are more likely almost twice that many residents in the United States illegally, largely immune from legal consequences. After 2017, that figure was believed to be declining due to self-deportation. But it is still the highest number of illegal aliens in the nation's history—a population larger than that of the nation of Chile. Currently we host both the largest absolute number of people not born in the United States and nearly this group's highest percentage of the population in our history.

Ironically, in the age of computerized records and high-tech communications, we are likely far less confident about the real numbers of non-native-born US residents than we were a hundred years ago in the precomputer age. Then immigration was mostly legal and recorded. Today we are only confident about the number of yearly legal entrants—a little more than one million—with no real notion of how many more arrive illegally, although guesses often put the influx at somewhere over a half million. The Department of Homeland Security reported that the US Border Patrol apprehended four hundred thousand illegal entrants in 2018, a number generally felt to be smaller than that of those who successfully entered the United States illegally. Children born to perhaps twenty-two million illegal aliens living in the United States were de jure American citizens at birth. They are, of course, not counted as immigrants given their birth on US soil.[27]

Statistics and anecdotes about illegal immigration are often selectively collated and sometimes warped to reflect either the need to minimize or to puff up the numbers of entering illegal aliens. After all, in a huge population of twenty million residing illegally in the United States, it is easy to find antithetical data or empirical observations in support of the idea that illegal immigration, coupled with massive nonmeritocratic legal immigration, enhances or endangers America, or both, or neither.

Business interests came to support open borders for cheap entry-level labor at the same time that ethnic activists and progressive politicians became intent on shifting voter demographics. The open southern border was a prime culprit behind the wage stagnation of the last thirty years. Such downward pressures trapped millions of Americans in the lower class and prevented them from ascending to the now hollowed-out middle classes.[28]

Again, in public polls, Americans don't support *illegal* immigration. This holds true even when many poll questions are warped to conflate legal immigration with illegal immigration—or to goad respondents to assess extreme views and positions, such as the call for immediate deportation of *all* illegal aliens. In general, Americans oppose the common use of social services by those not residing legally inside the United States, including granting in-state tuition discounts for illegal aliens and entitlements such as Medicare "for all." They especially reject any extension of citizenship rights like voting to the noncitizen. For example, in a 2018 Hill/HarrisX poll, over 70 percent of Americans opposed the idea of granting voting rights to both illegal immigrants and legal noncitizen residents.[29]

A 2019 Gallup survey cited immigration as the key political issue of the day. A far higher percentage thought current levels of immigration of all kinds were too high than thought they were too low. Aside from particular grievances, the public has a general sense that illegal immigration has made their own citizenship less exceptional. Few can identify the vestigial differences between citizenship and legal or illegal residence anymore. In theory, *only a few distinctions still remain of many*: the right to vote (currently under question), the right to hold office (currently a topic of controversy), and the right to hold a US passport (whose prior exclusivity in adjudicating leaving and reentering the country easily and at will has waned).[30]

For many American citizens, their own history, Constitution, and institutions are as foreign to them as they are to most immigrants. No wonder most who enter the United States do so on the theory that more freedom and more prosperity will be available to them here, but without wondering why that would be so, as a result of our past history and present circumstances.[31]

But how exactly do these various changes in laws and attitudes, as well as numbers, suggest that *illegal* immigration endangers the broader concept of citizenship? They do so in a number of ways.

First, consider again the 560 jurisdictions that proclaim themselves sanctuaries for illegal immigrants. "Sanctuary" is another Orwellian euphemism. These states, counties, and cities nullify federal immigration laws and discourage immigration authorities from deporting illegal aliens arrested in their jurisdictions for a variety of crimes. What or whom, then, does a "sanctuary" actually protect? The citizen per se or those residing illegally and without invitation in the country of their host? A far more accurate term for these jurisdictions would be "federal nullification zones" of the sort that spread in 1860 throughout the South and would eventually spark a Civil War. Or perhaps they could be called "areas of unequal application of federal law."[32]

Most American citizens cannot pick which federal statutes they choose to obey. Equality under the law is the foundation of constitutional citizenship. Some conservatives too could choose to ignore large swathes of laws and regulations, such as federal handgun registration, elements of the endangered species act, or the inland waterways codes. Such nullification would no doubt be popular in some cities and counties. Yet there are not 550 such nullification cities in the fashion of sanctuary cities.

The Second Amendment sanctuary counties in Virginia that have emerged to defy promised state crackdowns on the ability of Virginians to purchase and own particular weapons have understandably created a firestorm. The Left, otherwise an ironic and staunch supporter of local nullification of federal laws, grew furious over these counties' defiance of new state gun laws. As of early 2020, well over one hundred Virginia cities and counties had declared themselves exempt from proposed state restrictions on firearms.

Yet these nullification zones argued that they were *not* nullifications at all of federal law but rather confirmations of it. Whereas prior regional and local sanctuary jurisdictions that sought to override federal immigration laws by local statutes were likely unapologetically unconstitutional, Virginia's cities and counties argued that they were upholding the Constitution by defending it from illegal efforts by the state of Virginia to circumvent and override both the Bill of Rights and a long history of federal court cases. If some citizens with impunity pick and choose which federal laws to obey, then why should other citizens obey any state laws with which they disagree?[33]

Second, the status of illegal immigrants is by nature different from that of legal immigrants. "Legal illegality" makes a mockery of a would-be citizen's dutiful attempt to follow the letter of the law of his soon-to-be adopted country. In contrast, many illegal immigrants violate a number of state and federal laws: first, by entering the United States illegally; second, by continuing to reside inside the United States illegally; and third, often by impersonating American citizens in assuming a false identity, Social Security number, or Internal Revenue Service tax identification number. In each iteration, lawbreaking often has typically been excused or contextualized—rewarding those who break immigration law and punishing those who patiently wait in line to arrive legally to United States. Why would anyone then go through a lengthy, costly, and unsure process of legal immigration when the alternative is quicker and cheaper, with a type of greater certainty?[34]

As a rule, although the education levels of illegal immigrants have recently improved and the unlawful entry into the United States is increasingly not confined to the southern border, it remains true that *legal* immigrants of any background are more likely to speak or at least quickly learn English. Temperamentally, those who seek to abide by immigration law on entry are likely, initially at least, to be more law abiding in general. They are also empirically more likely to be screened for prior criminal history, more likely to have health checks and testing at a time of the COVID-19 pandemic, more likely to be ethnically diverse, more likely to have greater skills and education, and more likely to arrive in measured numbers. As a less cohesive group arriving in smaller numbers, legal immigrants are also more likely to assimilate, integrate, and intermarry sooner and thus to become more quickly indistinguishable from American citizens.[35]

Third, the cost-to-benefit value of the citizen's access to government services is diluted though competition from millions of noncitizens. The real costs of illegal immigration are embedded deeply within politics and almost impossible to illustrate in the form of mere data, given the stakes involved and wide disagreement over the exact number of foreign nationals residing unlawfully in the United States. Nonetheless, a number of studies have tried to assess at least some of the costs to US taxpayers of the millions who enter and reside in America illegally, as offset by contributions in payroll and sales taxes paid to the government. Some studies put the direct costs of illegal immigration at well over $110 billion per year to the treasury.[36]

In the 2020 Democratic primaries, once front-runner but ultimately failed candidate Bernie Sanders, the avowed socialist, apparently won the majority of Latino votes in early primary races. A number of analysts were confused as to how a seventy-eight-year-old, northeastern, white-male, socialist candidate could appeal to Latinos, many of whom, or their parents, had fled from impoverished countries mismanaged by statist, neosocialist, or communist regimes in Cuba, Venezuela, and Central America and, in some cases, would later vote in the 2020 election in sizable numbers for Donald Trump.

The consensus explanation was that they saw Sanders's redistributionist agendas, his advocacies for an array of increased entitlements, and his belated embrace of open-border policies as preferable to both liberal and conservative alternatives. Younger voters especially—dubbed "Sandernistas"—like illegal immigrants, naturalized citizens, green-card holders, or first-generation children of immigrants, apparently liked his condemnations of establishment America as unfair and even selfish. They agreed with Sanders that the United States was an illiberal nation that had rigged the game against exploited working classes.[37]

Fourth, illegal immigration warps the census. It eventually alters the very way citizens vote in the Electoral College and are apportioned congressional representation. There were few, if any, formal sanctuary cities and counties in 1980, 1990, or 2000 because there were not then enough illegal immigrants and their offspring to comprise a potent political force in the American Southwest. Yet, by the twenty-first century, the electoral ramifications were clearer. The US census used for congressional reapportionment doesn't count only US citizens. It was estimated that at least twenty-six House seats would be reapportioned in 2020 based on census results, shifting the mostly red states more to blue, particularly in the American Southwest and in states with large cities. Counting noncitizens in congressional reapportionment diminishes the unique value of citizenship. Massive recent illegal and legal immigration may radically recalibrate the allocation of congressional seats.[38]

Fifth, illegal immigration has resulted in a spike in crime that affects the safety of American citizens, not surprising when hundreds of thousands walk into the United States without audit or criminal background checks. The vast majority of crimes committed by illegal aliens are state and local offenses, thus hard to total on a national basis. But often in matters of fraud, drug dealing, and smuggling, criminality becomes a federal matter. Currently the United States is suffering an epidemic of federal offenses committed by noncitizen residents. In fact, in 2019 it was announced that 64 percent of all arrests by all federal authorities are of noncitizens, here both legally and illegally, although they comprise just 14 to 17 percent of the US population—a figure that may even undercount noncitizen residents. In 2018, 26 percent of all federal inmates were either legal or illegal aliens.[39]

Even more disturbing, the US Immigration and Customs Enforcement Fiscal Year 2019 Enforcement and Removal Operations Report noted that there were twenty-five hundred illegal aliens charged with murder (for murders committed up to 2019). In 2018 (the latest year counted), 9,049 suspects in total were arrested in the United States for homicide. Enforcement and Removal Operations in 2019 "issued 165,487 detainers for aliens with criminal histories including more than 56,000 assaults, 14,500 sex crimes, 5,000 robberies, 2,500 homicides, and 2,500 kidnappings."[40]

These statistics represent staggering costs to citizens for law enforcement, legal fees, and prison costs associated with the tens of thousands of aliens who enter the United States illegally, then proceed to cause mayhem for their hosts. Again, citizens expect noncitizens who enter and exit their country to follow the same laws that they do. If citizens were to violate those laws, they would expect to be punished in a way that noncitizens sometimes are not.

If, in a reductionist sense, the citizen loses out in most matters of illegal immigration, who then wins out? Which special interests combine to erode federal immigration law—and why would they do that?

First, as noted, profit-minded employers want cheap labor in lieu of hiring more expensive American citizens. Their primary concern has not been whether such circumvention of federal law drives down the entry-level wages of the citizen poor. They seem even less concerned about whether citizens are asked to pick up the tab for ailing, ill, and aging noncitizen workers once employers find them not so useful and seek new replacements from south of the border.

Illegal alien labor was once largely confined to agriculture. Today, farming accounts for less than 20 percent of such work—and recent figures suggest even a much smaller percentage, as agriculture continues to be mechanized. If, in prior days, the argument for open borders was "Who will pick the vegetables on your table," today such cynicism would have to extend to "Who will cut your hair, or shingle your roof, or clean your house, or slaughter the beef for your steak, or mow your lawn?" In other words, the tasks that Americans supposedly cannot or will not do has apparently increased exponentially.[41]

Second, the Mexican and Central American governments count on about $60 billion in annual remittances from their expatriate poor—a rough figure impossible to confirm. In 2018 Mexico alone received over $33 billion in remittances from the United States. Yet the degree to which governments flagrantly ignore US law to ensure American remittances is sometimes tragicomic. In past years, Mexico has gone so far as to print comic book instructions for its own citizens on how best to enter its northern neighbor illegally. It has distributed these booklets at the border—cynically exporting its illiterate citizens by teaching them how to break US immigration law with impunity. In 2017, both legal and illegal immigrants of all nationalities sent nearly $150 billion out of the United States. Nor does the Mexican government care that scrimping and saving to send remittances means that its expatriates become more reliant on US social services. The formula serves Mexico: capital comes in, young male Mexican citizens who are otherwise potential dissidents or often recipients of Mexican state services go out.[42]

Third, American upper-middle and elite classes also help to warp US immigration law. Much of the American Southwest's professional class depends on low-paid illegal aliens to do lawn work, cook, clean, and watch children and aged parents. Or, as Democratic House member Tom Malinowski (D-NJ) put it in August 2019, "Who do you think is mowing our beautiful lawns in Somerset County? We don't usually ask, but a lot of those workers are undocumented." I consider myself a busy sixty-seven-year-old, and yet until this year, for a half century, I've found time to mow my own lawn and done my own landscaping and maintenance, despite having a one-acre yard. When a US congressman contextualizes flagrant violations of federal immigration law on the basis of convenience or assumes no one but those here illegally will do his yard work, should we laugh or cry?[43]

Fourth, yet another catalyst of illegal immigration is the self-interested professional Latino lobby in politics and academia. Activists apparently see a steady stream of impoverished Latin American nationals as a revolving, but also permanent, victimized constituency of marginalized peoples dependent on social services. They are considered critical in empowering and showcasing self-appointed minority spokespeople such as themselves. In 2019 congressman and presidential candidate Julián Castro (D-TX) advocated decriminalizing illegal entry into the United States and recalibrating this violation as a civil infraction.[44]

Ethnic chauvinism often enables illegal immigration—and often is used blatantly both to encourage ethnic solidarity and to diminish critics with charges of purported racism. Only in 2018, after decades of criticism, did the National Council of La Raza finally change its name to UnidosUS. Certainly, the prior term, *La Raza*, was, despite decades of denials, racist to the core. The Spanish noun *raza* (cf. Latin *radix*, "root" or "race") is somewhat akin to the now discarded German *Volk*. In the early twentieth century, *Volk* came to denote a common blood-and-soil German racial identity that transcended linguistic and cultural affinities: to be a real member of the *Volk*, one had to "appear" German and be of "real" German blood, in addition to speaking German, residing in Germany, and possessing German citizenship.

La Raza is just such a racialist term. It goes beyond a common language and country of origin. And it thus transcends the more neutral *pueblo* (people; Latin: *populus*) or *gente* (people; Latin: *gens*). *Raza* was deliberately reintroduced in the 1960s to promote a racially superior identity of indigenous peoples and mestizos born in the Spanish-speaking countries of the New World. That is why the National Council of La Raza once had a close affinity with the infamous racialist US student group the Movimiento Estudiantil Chicano de Aztlán (MEChA, an acronym that in Spanish means "fuse"), whose ironic motto is "La Unión Hace la Fuerza" (with unity, there is strength). Some of MEChA's various past slogans—consider the Castroite derivative "Por La Raza todo, Fuera de La Raza nada" (for the race, everything, outside the race, nothing)—finally became sources of national embarrassment and were erased from official literature.[45]

Ironically, the use of the term *La Raza* came into popular currency during the 1930s in Spain. The fascist dictatorship of Francisco Franco wished to promote a new Iberian identity that went well beyond the commonality of Spanish citizenship and fluency in the Spanish language. Franco expropriated *La Raza* to promote the racist idea that the Spanish were intrinsically a superior people by birth. He penned a crackpot novel, *Raza*, embodying fascist and racist themes of Spanish genetic and cultural superiority. *Raza* even appeared on the big screen in the form of a hokey 1942 Spanish-language movie, full of racist themes, anti-Americanism, and fashionable fascist politics.

But Franco was only channeling other, earlier contemporary fascists, most infamously Benito Mussolini, who had his own Italian version of the term, *la Razza*. In 1938 Mussolini published his *Manifesto della Razza* (The racial manifesto), which defined Italians as a superior Aryan race and excluded Italian Jews, Africans, and other supposedly less pure groups from various positions in the Italian government.[46]

Moderates in the Democratic Party have been unaware of or in denial about the unfortunate brew of racialist and ethnically driven interests that on occasion can either fuel or legitimize illegal immigration to their own political advantage. Over the last thirty years, California, New Mexico, and Colorado have flipped in most national elections from red to blue or purple states. Nevada and Arizona often do as well, and Texas may soon. Most students of electoral demography believe the transformation is in part due to open borders. Again, changing demography explains a radical transformation in the Democratic Party's past stance on illegal immigration.

In the early 2000s, influential Democratic congressional leaders such as Senators Hillary Clinton (D-NY), Harry Reid (D-NV), and Charles Schumer (D-NY), as well as House Speaker Nancy Pelosi (D-CA), were on record opposing illegal immigration. Indeed, the Democratic Party, during its 1996 convention, formalized its tough opposition to open borders and illegal immigration:

Today's Democratic Party also believes we must remain a nation of laws. We cannot tolerate illegal immigration and we must stop it. For years before Bill Clinton became President, Washington talked tough but failed to act. In 1992, our borders might as well not have existed. The border was under-patrolled, and what patrols there were, were under-equipped. Drugs flowed freely. Illegal immigration was rampant. Criminal immigrants, deported after committing crimes in America, returned the very next day to commit crimes again.

By 2016, they were all for sanctuary cities, lax border security, and an array of amnesties—in other words, they were no longer so worried about illegal immigration driving down the wages of citizens, undermining the equal application of the law, fueling the drug trade, or spiking the crime rate. What had changed was not ideology per se but the vast increase in the numbers of illegal immigrants and growing electoral clout of second-generation American citizen offspring of illegal aliens. Soon liberalized voting laws in many states required little if any identification at the polls and had greenlighted DMV automatic voter registration, massive mail-in voting, and same-day registration and voting. An embarrassed chairman of the Democratic National Committee, Thomas Perez, put his party grandees' radical flip-flops in a more honest context: "We're in a different era." And indeed, we surely are.[47]

Open borders are now becoming institutionalized as a universal right of all humans to emigrate to anywhere they choose. In other words, we are reverting to the world of the precitizen and to a prenation mindset of normalizing migrations in the West, with values and assumptions more similar to those of the seventeenth century than the twenty-first. Rome had few if any border patrollers before the eighth century BC or during and after the latter fifth century AD, when Vandals, Visigoths, Ostrogoths, and Huns freely crossed into Roman lands. But for centuries of a robust republic and resilient empire, Rome stationed legions on the borders and eventually on the Rhine and Danube and other *limites* (boundaries) that sought to control who entered its sovereign territory and when and how.

Nothing in the US Constitution guarantees any foreign national the right to enter the United States illegally—or, for that matter, even legally—much less to share all the same rights as US citizens. That entrants increasingly do suggests that citizenship, as defined by the Constitution, in some ways no longer really exists.

A sibling of open borders, tribalism, as we shall see in the next chapter, is quite antithetical to the melting pot. It recalibrates loyalties not to ideals, customs, and laws but largely to those who superficially look alike or worship the same God. In that regressive sense, tribalism is another mortal enemy of the dying citizen.

Chapter Three

TRIBES

People who think with their epidermis or their genitalia
or their clan are the problem to begin with. One does not
banish this specter by invoking it.

—CHRISTOPHER HITCHENS,
"The Perils of Identity Politics,"
Wall Street Journal, *January 18, 2008*

Tribes are usually defined as particular social divisions within a traditional society. They are made up of families, kin groups, and communities that in turn share common social, economic, religious, or blood ties. They often are ruled by a hereditary hierarchy that selects a leader or chief.

Our English word "tribe" derives from the Latin *tri-/tribus* (three/tripartite). *Tribus* referred to the ancient Roman notion that, in the age before common Roman citizenship, three ethnic groups made up the Roman state. Later Romans assumed that these earlier concrete affinities had been far stronger—and more troublesome—than current national loyalties.

Such tribal bonds were seen as at odds with the idea of a harmonious and unified Italian nation, fused from hundreds of cities and ethnicities. Rome gave us the word *natio* (nation) to reflect the revolutionary idea that the free citizens of a state did not all have to look the same or be born in the same place to enjoy the same rights or be of the same *tribus*. There was no word similar to *natio* in any ancient language.

American *multiracialism*—which envisions one inclusive and common culture of many races—wars with the very different idea of *multiculturalism*, which seeks to define the country by many, often adversarial, cultures. The current conflict of visions will likely soon determine the future of the United States. The country will remain one inhabited by millions of quite different-looking Americans, unifying and coalescing as citizens of one culture. Or it will become something quite different, something far more typical of nations abroad that are defined by either race or chaos. In the later scenario, various races, sects, and identities will feud as collectives. They will fight for ascendancy and thereby unwind the nation as it reverts to prestate status, a Hobbesian *bellum omnium contra omnes* (the war of all against all).

Will how we look become essential or remain incidental to who we are? And who exactly are we, in a nation of increasing intermarriage and assimilation, where racial purity is being accentuated at the very time it is ever more difficult to measure? No one knows the answer, only that it will likely determine the fate of the country.

Tribalism is by far the more ancient, natural, insidious, and stronger idea than nonracial citizenship. It is the default state of mankind. Its pedigree dates back to prehistory, and its vestiges were worrisome to later civilized states. Plato warned of like kind bonding with proverbial like kind: "I will tell you, Socrates, he said, what my own feeling is: Men of my age we congregate together; just as the old proverb says."[1]

Tribalism is now swiftly becoming a synonym for multiculturalism. It accepts that the strongest human affinities in a society, past and future, must arise from similar and natural racial, ethnic, religious, or clannish ties of blood among like groups. These prestate bonds properly should supersede the citizen's collective and constructed political and social allegiance to the nation-state.

At least until recently, tribalism was seen as backward, a reactionary, precivilizational notion that made it impossible for a citizen of a multi-racial nation to consider those of different appearances or religions his equal. It was the bane of constitutional government, higher education, and popular culture, undercut meritocracy, and marked the road to poverty, chaos, and violence. Few Americans wished to defend the Jim Crow South, the caste system of India, the racial laws of 1930s fascist Europe, the apartheid of South Africa, or the ethnic and religious cat-egorizations of the former Yugoslavia. Innately toxic to humankind, tribalism, fully expressed as infighting and rivalry, was understood as an anathema to any pluralistic democratic society.

Well before the birth of the United States, a variety of Hellenic historians, such as Herodotus and Thucydides, critiqued tribalism as precivilizational. In his role as an anthropologist, the historian Thu-cydides noted that before the city-state, tribal people were hopelessly nomadic and, without laws, could not become stationary:

> Migrations were of frequent occurrence, the several tribes readily abandoning their homes under the pressure of superior numbers. Without commerce, without freedom of communication either by land or sea, cultivating no more of their territory than the exigen-cies of life required, destitute of capital, never planting their land (for they could not tell when an invader might come and take it all away, and when he did come they had no walls to stop him), thinking that the necessities of daily sustenance could be supplied at one place as well as another, they cared little for shifting their habitation, and consequently neither built large cities nor attained to any other form of greatness.

Even after the onset of the polis, the historian collated the suicidal factionalism at Corcyra with the failure to suppress ancient tribal
loyalties:

> The ancient simplicity into which honor so largely entered was
> laughed down and disappeared; and society became divided into
> camps in which no man trusted his fellow. To put an end to this,
> there was neither promise to be depended upon, nor oath that
> could command respect; but all parties dwelling rather in their cal-
> culation upon the hopelessness of a permanent state of things, were
> more intent upon self-defense than capable of confidence. In this
> contest the blunter wits were most successful.[2]

The invention of politics and the rule of law initiated the slow and
fragile ascent over the normal, natural state of tribalism. Ethnicities
surrendered their primary identities and loyalties to a higher notion of
transcendent ideas, bonds, and traditions. The resulting Greek notion
of *politeia* (constitutional government) gave citizens natural rights to
elect their own officials and make their own laws despite accidents of
clan or tribal affiliation.

So Greek city-states in the eighth century BC slowly found ways for
residents to transfer loyalties away from their clans to the constitutional
oligarchies. They did this by forming artificial political jurisdictions
across ethnic groups, while framing public commemoration and art in
terms of collective interests.

These new governments of the polis demanded civic participation
of diverse groups unified in their new citizenship, in exchange for
granting them rights immune from government encroachment. At
ancient Athens, the birth of democracy followed from the Athenian
statesman Cleisthenes's successful efforts (508/7 BC) in reorganizing
ancient Attica. A region traditionally based on tribal affiliations and the
great family clans was reorganized into new geographical and political

organizations that suppressed such identities. The result was a novel collective democratic ethos.[3]

The ensuing cornerstone of Western citizenship was the equality of all those free males who qualified for rights. Such new citizens might otherwise *not* be related by blood or even aware of any common affinities other than geography, religion, language, or shared history and values. In other words, the state appropriated the legislative, judicial, executive, and military clout of tribal leaders. The latter had previously made and enforced agreements, settled arguments, and gone to war on the sole basis of helping their own clan and hurting another.

Yet tribalism is never ended. Its pull is only suspended and suppressed—at best by constitutional pluralism, at worst sometimes by dictatorial or ideological coercion. How odd that America's current progressive turn to tribalism and primary self-identification by race and gender is reactionary to the core. Our current retribalization embraces concepts seen twenty-five hundred years ago as the final obstacles to the rise of representative government and pluralism—and in the twentieth century they led to mass genocide under German fascism and Soviet totalitarianism. In other words, identity politics is at its essence precivilizational.

Women, resident aliens, teenagers, and slaves were not citizens of the emerging ancient Greek polis. But the early city-state was distinguished not by the number of those excluded from full civic participation but by the unique idea that there could be a civic role for *anyone* at all beyond the usual tight circle of aristocratic cronies, family and clan heads, or royals—the norm everywhere else in the ancient Mediterranean world, Near East, and tribal northern Europe.

In the long evolution from property-based consensual governments to Athenian democracy, by the late sixth and early fifth centuries BC, constructed political ties replaced natural blood ties in Athens and in some democracies elsewhere. Many of the most gifted of Athenian citizens—for example, Themistocles, the hero of Salamis, and the historian

Thucydides—were not citizens of pure Athenian ethnic ancestry. Instead, they reflected how intermarriage between ethnicities increased with the redefinition of Athens as a democracy that trumped prior loyalties. Earlier, in the pre-city-state age of Athens, both iconic figures would have largely remained aliens because of their checkered foreign pedigrees, which still remained objects of stubborn suspicion to many Athenians.[4]

The new antitribalist mindset redefined life as something more than just hunting, gathering, subsistence farming, and continually warring for resources. Under all those guarantees of citizenship without clan, ethnic, or racial qualifications, people flourish. Without them, they end up a pre-polis Greek backwater like the wilder regions of Acarnania or Ambracia—or, in our own day, a Somalia, Sudan, or Rwanda. A society that spends its time feuding over tribal and ethnic loyalties never has the resources to focus on its collective prosperity, freedom, accomplishments, and security and certainly cannot hire, admit to higher education, or reward and punish on the basis of merit.

In ancient terms, Germania or Caledonia, unchanging over the centuries, by definition would never produce anything similar to the Romans' habeas corpus, transnational roads such as the Via Appia and the Via Egnatia, or authors such as Tacitus and Caesar, who freely critiqued such precivilized tribes as well as their own sophisticated Rome. Tribalism, again, in civilizational terms, was an evolutionary dead end.[5]

Ethnically homogeneous countries and societies, such as the ancient Germanic tribes living beyond the Rhine or modern Japan, feel they are inherently more stable and secure than the alternative, be it late imperial Rome or contemporary America. There is certainly far less work involved in uniting citizens of disparate backgrounds when everyone looks about the same, speaks the same native language, and has lived for generations in the same place. Diversity, remember, not homogeneity, is the kindling of tribal violence.

Many largely monoracial societies have predictably created words to highlight their own racial purity—and perceived superiority. At times,

Volk in German and, as we have seen, *raza* in Spanish (and *razza* in Italian) have meant more than just shared language, residence, or culture. Those exclusionary words also exude a racial essence: all but a tiny minority of citizens are bound by similar skin, hair, and eye color or general appearance.

Even today, it would be hard for someone Japanese to be fully accepted as a Mexican citizen. Could a native-born Mexican immigrate to Japan and become embraced as a naturalized Japanese citizen? Ninety-two percent of China's population are Han Chinese. They believe that their own racial unity enhances being Chinese and are certainly not eager to expand the idea of citizenship to non-Han Chinese, such as the Muslim Uyghurs, who are often relegated to reeducation camps, frequently in the hundreds of thousands.

In one of the last speeches of his presidency, Ronald Reagan emphasized these very points: "You can go to live in France, but you cannot become a Frenchman. You can go to live in Germany or Turkey or Japan, but you cannot become a German, a Turk, or a Japanese. But anyone, from any corner of the Earth, can come to live in America and become an American." The Hungarian-born immigrant author Peter Schramm recalled how his father explained why they should make the decision to leave during the turmoil of the failed anticommunist Hungarian revolution of 1956: "Because, son. We were born Americans, but in the wrong place."[6]

Over centuries many cultures without much ethnic or racial diversity reflected their suspicion of different peoples linguistically by creating pejorative and exclusive nouns for the "other." In Hebrew and Yiddish, *goy/goyim* refers loosely to the other non-Jewish nations and peoples. *Odar* in Armenian denotes the rest of the world that is not ethnically Armenian. For Japanese, *gaijin* applies to those who by nationality, ethnicity, and race cannot become fully accepted as Japanese. In eighteenth-century Castilian Spain, *gringo* (now a common Mexican racial pejorative for Americans, especially white Americans) meant any foreign, nonnative speaker of Spanish who might just as well have been an utterly incomprehensible Greek—or gringo—somewhat in the fashion that the Cantonese *gweilo* describes the mostly light-skinned Westerners with whom Chinese meet. No equivalents of these ethnicized and racialized terms now exist in formal American English for the aggregate of non-American foreign peoples.[7]

The Balkan states were the powder kegs of twentieth-century European world wars. Their various tribes wished to change national boundaries to reflect their separate ethnicities and not share a multi-racial and pluralistic state. And given the checkered history of the region, there were lots of such competing Balkan tribes. The racially inclusive nation was a supposedly progressive idea of idealistic self-determination advanced by Woodrow Wilson during the Versailles Treaty negotiations, but one whose baleful ramifications in the real world Wilson himself did not initially appreciate or live to witness.[8]

The premise of Nazi Germany was to incorporate all the German *Volk* into one vast racially and linguistically harmonious *Reich*. In practice that meant destroying the national borders of Austria, Czecho-slovakia, France, and Poland to achieve the "natural" purity and fusion of the "master race." Through a series of immigration laws, Mexico for 150 years until 1974 had traditionally and unapologetically predi-cated its national immigration policies on the idea of admitting only "assimilable" immigrants. In theory, such exclusionism may sound understandable, but in practice it discriminated against almost anyone not of Mexican heritage.[9]

The few unusual countries, ancient and modern, that have tried to unite diverse tribes without imperial coercion have usually fared poorly. The mostly Italian Roman Republic lasted about eight hundred years. In contrast, its multiracial successor, the Roman Empire—which, after the so-called Edict of Caracalla (Constitutio Antoniniana) in AD 212, made all its increasingly diverse people equal citizens—endured little more than two (often violent) subsequent centuries. Vast, eth-nically diverse empires such as those of the Austro-Hungarians, the Ottomans, and the Soviets resorted to deadly force or rigid religious and political ideologies to exploit their populations but also to keep their bickering ethnic factions in line—and from killing each other. The United Kingdom was mostly able to keep Scotland, Wales, and Northern Ireland united after their forced conquest or absorption into England by imposing a common language, assimilating former enemies into the government, civil service, and army, and incorporating regional authors, artists, and cultures into a broader story of the English-speaking peoples.

Europe is halfheartedly trying to emulate the multiracial but once unified culture of the United States. Yet the European Union may well tear itself apart attempting to assimilate millions of disparate migrants who are reluctant to fully integrate and find few traditions of multiracialism among their new hosts. Certainly, eastern European countries such as the Czech Republic, Hungary, Poland, Romania, and Slovakia have had a different sort of historical experience with ethnic tensions and immigration than has western Europe. Eastern European countries especially currently favor border enforcement rather than the abolition of European national border controls under the protocols of the 1990 Schengen Agreement, which, in fact, was suspended for a time during the coronavirus pandemic of 2020.[10]

America, which survived a gory civil war among political and geographical factions, has become so far one of history's few exceptions. The ultimate rationale of America's unique Constitution led Americans eventually to define themselves by their shared values, not by their inconsequential appearances. Eventually, most who were willing to give up their prior identities and assume a new American persona were accepted as Americans. The United States has always cherished its universally applicable melting-pot ethos of *e pluribus unum*—of blending diverse peoples into one through assimilation, integration, and intermarriage in the manner that diverse colonies united to become one nation. What was the alternative to the melting pot in early colonial and American history? It was something akin to the imperial Spanish paradigm of colonization in Mexico, the Caribbean, and most of South

America and Latin America between 1500 and 1830. For over three centuries, non-Spanish Europeans, and non-Catholics in particular, were more or less barred from the New World Spanish colonies. In the case of North America in general, and the United States in particular, an analogous paradigm would have been if the British government, over roughly the same period, had allowed entry into areas of North America under its jurisdiction only to Protestant British subjects and the newly founded United States had continued that imperial legacy. That is, America would have de jure absolutely banned both non–English speakers and non-Protestants for much of the latter eighteenth and early nineteenth centuries.[11]

As in ancient times, contemporary tribalism in the postindustrial world is often thought to explain backwardness itself. Its many liabilities include robbing the state of talent and efficiency by ignoring merit and conferring privileges on the basis of blood or ethnic ties. Worse, there can be no political legitimacy if officeholding of any sort is predicated solely on the kin, clan, and race of one particular portion of the resident population. A multiethnic state of first-cousin privilege and tribal bias does not work; nor does constant calibration and recalibration of citizenship by racial and ethnic percentages.

In the modern United States, tribalism is increasingly at war with American citizenship and only with vigilance goes into temporary remission—resurging from its dormancy in times of laxity. In the 1950s, campus housing was segregated by race. And in the 2020s it is becoming so again. In the 1940s, English departments likely favored admissions of those with the proper skin colors. In the 2020s, they are beginning to do so again.

Senator Bernie Sanders once was proud that he fought for integrated off-campus student housing at the University of Chicago. Now, with other progressives, he supports segregated campus theme houses. Blacks have rightly complained that they were unfairly shut out of graduate schools fifty years ago. Today, the Department of English at the

University of Chicago has announced that no English majors need apply to its graduate programs unless they focus on black-related studies.[12]

Once tribalism takes hold, it is almost impossible to thwart this ancient narcotic or to prevent it from destroying the centuries-long and much harder work of establishing multiracial nationhood and citizenship. I grew up and still live in a predominately Mexican American and rather poor town in California's Central Valley. I still remember, back in 1963 at age ten, the ethnic jostling at school. The Mexican American majority in my grammar school occasionally fought with the local white minority. The majority of this minority of white students was part of the Oklahoma diaspora that had arrived in the Central Valley during the Great Depression and was so well described by novelist John Steinbeck, whose *The Grapes of Wrath* both exaggerated and incorporated some of his experiences in this area.

Each day at recess, randomly selected boys chose their weekly intramural sports teams. One day, the captain of our team, an impoverished white kid (whites then made up about 20 percent of that particular barrio school), chose a mediocre white athlete, George, over a number of far-more-skilled Mexican American baseball players. I thought our captain, Jimmy, had just ruined any chance that we could win the weekly tournament. And I told him so.

I remember still how Jimmy barked back at me, "I could give a — about Georgie, but at least he is white." When I objected that he also could neither hit nor throw and would lose us the game, he retorted, "OK, but why did those Mexican kids always choose all Mexicans instead of you?" And I remember arrogantly saying, "That's why some of them lose a lot too."

Jimmy's point, I think, was that out on the playground, beyond the doctrines of integration and assimilation within the civilized classroom, all ten-year-olds reverted to a sort of *Lord of the Flies* tribalism, but one, in this instance, based on race. Beyond the reach of our teachers, we descended to what was comfortable, safe, known, and familiar in strengthening tribal bonds of race. And tribalism became the enemy of decision-making on the basis of athletic competency and ultimately meritocracy or even collective self-interest. So nihilistic was his tribalism that Jimmy would rather lose baseball games than break presupposed ethnic or racial solidarity. In his thinking, there should be no disunity in the ranks of the small white minority, when the larger majority of Mexican American kids operated on the same tribal agendas.

In contrast, some twenty years later, I cofounded a classical language program at California State University (CSU), Fresno, mostly attended by Mexican American, Southeast Asian, black, and a few working-class white students. The aim was to offer a competitive education for poorer Americans of mostly minority backgrounds in the fundamental languages, literatures, history, and culture of the West in particular, but also in general to emphasize America's unique political and cultural heritage, which, after all, everyone in the program's classes shared.

At one point, mostly minority youth were enrolled in Greek and Roman history, introductory and advanced Greek and Latin, Greek and Latin literature in translation, classical mythology, Greek rationalism, the humanities of the Western world, Latin composition, and independent studies in ancient Greek composition and epigraphy. More advanced Greek and Latin language students also took directed reading courses in Homer, the Greek tragedians, Herodotus, Thucydides, and Xenophon, and Latin authors such as Virgil, Catullus, Horace, Cicero, Livy, and Tacitus.

I note the irony of students at a supposedly third-tier, relatively inexpensive state university receiving a first-class liberal arts education of the sort common earlier. In contrast, many of the elite, on tony and costly private campuses, often receive an increasingly therapeutic studies-based education, one that emphasizes ethnic differences. CSU Fresno otherwise was (and is) a nexus of multiculturalism. It conducts separate graduation ceremonies predicated on race and is characterized by various ethnic studies departments and a large La Raza student activist group. But the college's administration still did encourage a number of pathways for competitive education for minority youth, many of whom were not native born and did not grow up speaking English.

Students' tribal affiliations disappeared in Greek class. Being white, brown, or black meant nothing when studying Sappho or Hesiod. Homer was no more or less foreign to a Mexican American student than to me, a Swedish American professor. There was no such thing as "cultural appropriation." A tattooed gang member in class suggested that the blowhard Agamemnon never earned his street cred—and explained why with references to the text of *The Iliad*. He added in contrast that his hero Achilles had earned his "rep," not inherited it. No one cared with what particular accent a student struggled to conjugate *paideuô*. A Jewish woman in a wheelchair at eighty was often helped out of one class by a twenty-year-old Hmong student, once as both were complaining that Sophocles was far harder to translate than Euripides.

Such a common pursuit permeated well beyond the classroom. Students dated, sometimes married, but at least often befriended fellow classics students without attention to their class, race, or gender. Gradually students began to sense they shared a common ancestry, whose original racial pedigree was irrelevant but was now the logical font of their own everyday lives, be they native-born or naturalized American citizens. They understood why and how they spoke freely, voted, and demanded equal protection under the law, in a constitutionally based nation whose laws and customs were largely inherited, modified, and improved from a long Western tradition.

There grew, then, camaraderie, if not confidence and optimism, based on the awareness that all were becoming educated in the classical foundations of their civilization—language, literature, history, philosophy, art, and music—and in such an odyssey were becoming better writers, debaters, and citizens. They were proud of their achievements. The critics of such instruction were not purported white reactionaries in the agriculture or business departments, although some thought study of the classics was a waste of time for all races. Uniformly, censors belonged to ethnic studies programs. And such professors objected that their English-speaking, American-living, university-enrolled students were being culturally colonized—as they soon spoke perfect English, wrote superb English compositions, mastered foreign languages, and headed off to professional and graduate programs.[13]

How odd that, in a country in which higher education rituals once supposedly aimed to assimilate and integrate diverse citizens, an esoteric study of the ancient world for a few hours each week could prove more successful in creating civic unity than a state university's official policies on diversity and its reversion to promoting tribal precitizenship. These classes often took place in opposition to official university policy that encouraged ethnic solidarity and identification.

Yet, when the curriculum is rigorous, its demands shared without concern for superficial appearance, age, or religion, then students have less time for tribal affinities. They become united through a common, difficult challenge rather than divided by superficial ethnic chauvinism and therapeutic course work. Achievement, as measured by quantifiable skills in language, speech, history, and literature, creates a sense of confidence and pride—and also cuts a lot of tribal ties.

In most cases second-generation Mexican American and Hmong, as well as immigrant, students came to believe that through their shared status as American citizens, Homer and Aeschylus were as much part of their own cultural legacy as of any fifth-generation white American's. Most importantly, they sensed they were learning collective wisdom central to America's unity—even as their own cherished ethnic traditions and customs would gradually gravitate to the periphery and become recalibrated as a valuable adornment of such an immutable common core. And they became stewards of a precious cultural legacy about which many of their liberal professors at the university were largely clueless. Some even felt it their missionary duty as immigrants to keep alive Western and American traditions that complacent native-born Americans had long ignored.

The opposite of multiculturalism is not just equitable multiracialism. It is the rare presence of true citizenship that further diminishes the power of ethnic identification and race. The spiritual predecessors of the current multicultural critics of early America, who slander the United States as insufficiently racially aware, in some ways are the Southern secessionists who lodged the same complaints against the nonslaveholding North, Midwest, and West. They customarily reviled Northerners for occasionally claiming that ultimately transcending race was the logical assumption of the Founders and the Constitution.

Alexander H. Stephens, vice president of the Confederacy, for example, offered an infamous existential race-based criticism of the United States—whining that the country tragically was either *not* founded on race or founded *entirely* on race. Stephens, for example, felt that white supremacy should have been the theme of the founding of America. But, alas, in his judgment it was not. In his infamous "Cornerstone Speech" of March 21, 1861, Stephens contrasted the new Confederate constitution favorably with the supposedly inherently flawed US Constitution. He deeply lamented that the latter had not enshrined white supremacy:

> Those ideas, however, were fundamentally wrong. They rested upon the assumption of the equality of races. This was an error. It was a sandy foundation, and the government built upon it fell when the "storm came and the wind blew."
>
> Our new government is founded upon exactly the opposite idea; its foundations are laid, its cornerstone rests, upon the great truth that the negro is not equal to the white man; that slavery, subordination to the superior race is his natural and normal condition. This, our new government, is the first, in the history of the world, based upon this great physical, philosophical, and moral truth.

Stephens, in his fixation on race, also sought to avoid other embarrassing issues for the new Confederacy, especially fundamental and static class ossification. The sociology of the Old South was largely one of a small plantation class controlling nearly all the aggregate wealth of the region, a vast, unfree, servile black population, and an impoverished white poor who lacked the opportunities of class progression found in the North and West. In the booming cotton economy of the antebellum South, the rich had encouraged poor whites to vent their anger by loathing the black slaves of the plantations. In that way, the southern elite ignored the region's existential failure to foster a large and viable middle class of autonomous small farmers, businesspeople, professionals, and well-paid laborers.

This rich-poor bifurcation only compounded the southern moral failure of race-based slavery. The South's unwillingness or economic inability to foster a middle class should serve as a reminder that our own growing racial and ethnic tribalism is likewise not just a threat to national unity and cohesion but a diversion from our growing crisis of a failing middle class of all races.

Class commonalities unite rather than divide races. Class need not stigmatize or reward a person in perpetuity. Race, in contrast, is not nearly as contingent or ephemeral a concept as transient money or material sustenance. Fortunes can be made and lost, bringing class status changes. Money comes and goes. Millions of Americans enter and leave the coveted upper 5 percent income bracket each year; tragically, more sink into poverty. Yet one's race or ancestry, be it emphasized or downplayed, is a far stronger, more stubborn, and especially dangerous stamp. In twenty-first-century America, income is increasingly divorcing itself from race and gender, and there are record rates of intermarriage among different ethnic groups.

Yet public acceptance of set-asides and reparatory measures that trump purely meritocratic admissions and hiring assumes some fixed, indeed lifelong, tangible connections between class and race. When the wealthy children of privilege who are not white gain further advantage over the poor who are white, or, alternatively, when wealthy whites enjoy both class *and* supposed racial advantages, then the ingredients of social chaos arise.

So why has twenty-first-century American race and gender victimization supplanted doctrinaire Marxist class oppression in the culture of resistance against establishment norms? Apart from the obvious reason that there are more nonwhites than poor in the United States, poor whites are the largest impoverished ethnic group and usually larger than all other poor minority groups combined. In short, today's social justice warrior apparently would not wish to empathize with a West Virginian coal miner but prefers instead CNN anchor Don Lemon or billionaire rapper Jay-Z.

Consequently, the effort to weaken citizenship has turned in part to race, because America is a fluid and often upwardly mobile society in which it is difficult to galvanize a permanent class of the oppressed. Remember also that it was once the determination of 1960s radicals that class struggle in America could not work. They confessed that communist paradigms of exploitation did not, as hoped, galvanize the supposedly oppressed proletariat. The lower middle class was too consumerist, too upwardly mobile to join college-educated leftists on the barricades, in a fluid, free market, and growing economy of the 1960s. As a result, "cultural hegemony"—the supposed power machinations of an entrenched elite that made the rules—became the new bogeyman. And this elite cultural prison had to be dismantled via a long march of liberation through academia, the bureaucracy, the arts, business, and cultural institutions.

As a result of that recognition, some "cultural Marxists"—such as Louis Althusser ("Ideology and Ideological State Apparatuses"), Herbert Marcuse (*One-Dimensional Man*), and Saul Alinsky (*Rules for Radicals*), drawing on the work of the cultural Marxist Antonio Gramsci (*The Prison Notebooks*) and anticolonialist Frantz Fanon (*The Wretched of the Earth*)—began to focus on the elite's supposed cultural and racial power rather than its economic dominance. In its current phase of evolution, cultural hegemony came to be defined in terms of race, gender, and sexual oppression. Thus permanent and innate identity could be substituted as the cause of oppression for victim groups rather than their (too) fluid class status. This transformation of Americans into racial rather than just economic oppressors created permanent rather than transient and fluid categories of victims and victimizers that superseded common class and American commonalities. American citizens can be poor, then middle-class, then poor again and thus do not see class fragmenting citizenship in the way that racial categorization results in perpetually hyphenated Americans.

In the late-twentieth-century West, the rich and the capitalists could be rebooted as not merely exploitive and greedy citizens but also as static white, male, racist, and sexist citizens. They were guilty of constructing cultural norms for all in their own image—again, their "cultural hegemony"—solely to advance their own venal interests and long history of exploitation and discrimination. In an affluent society such as America, with a finite supply of native-born poor as a percentage of the general population, supposed victims now could be found at any income level—as long as they were not white and not male.

Affluent white liberals, who allegedly had infiltrated and compromised class-struggle movements, would have far greater trouble finding bona fides when they were, by appearance, clearly and permanently not the "other." They certainly could never leverage or paper over exploitation, since it was declared racially innate, existential, and endless. However, they could offer confessions of their "unearned privilege"— while keeping it. That way they could pay penance and join the Left in redefining or dismantling the very institutions they oversaw, most notably the administrative state, the courts, the universities, entertainment, professional sports, and religion.

So race and sex, not money, birth, and class, more determined who and what one was. There was no such thing in the radical mind as "racial upward mobility," and therefore the new exploited, rich or poor, were a far more iron-clad group of permanently oppressed than the ecumenical poor. Thus these divisions posed a far greater threat to the ideal of ecumenical citizenship.

New Marxists enlisted the former enemies of old Marxists as their powerful allies. Everyone from Mexican billionaire Carlos Slim to National Basketball Association (NBA) multimillionaire superstars no longer needed to apologize for becoming the filthy and predatory rich. They too instead had a claim on oppression, by their very unalterable identity, and thus could put their formerly caricatured ill-gotten gains to work for the new woke cause—while squaring the circle of their very real economic and social privilege. Few have noted the deleterious new role of identity politics, wealth, and the eclipse of class in the fragmentation of citizenship into tribes.

White male billionaires like Bill Gates, Mark Zuckerberg, and the heads of Goldman Sachs need only concede the unfairness of the system they had mastered for their own benefit—and then put a percentage of their billions in the service of race and sex equality—to be part of the revolution, while being granted easy exemptions for the continuance of their own fortunes, influence, privilege, and power.[14]

If old Marxism had once sought to transcend race and unite the global oppressed, in a much wealthier twenty-first-century world, new cultural and racial Marxism sought to return to ancient tribal criteria of oppression. Forgetting class and uniting by race now defined the collective conscious. Samuel Huntington, in a controversial and much criticized passage in his *Who Are We?*, describes the infamous case of Los Angeles fans, over two decades ago, booing the home US soccer team while cheering on Mexico's. His ostensible point was that a historically dangerous tribalism replaces common ties of citizenship when record numbers of illegal and nondiverse border crossings stymie the traditional forces of assimilation, integration, and intermarriage.

At a Gold Cup soccer game between Mexico and the United States in February 1998, the 91,255 fans were immersed in a "sea of red, white and green flags"; they booed when "The Star-Spangled Banner" was played; they "pelted" the US players "with debris and cups of what might have been water, beer or worse"; and they attacked with "fruit and cups of beer" a few fans who tried to raise an American flag. This game took place not in Mexico City but in Los Angeles. "Something's wrong when I can't even raise an American flag in my own country," a US fan commented, as he ducked a lemon going by his head. "Playing in Los Angeles is not a home game for the United States," a *Los Angeles Times* reporter agreed.[15]

Yet civic education in matters of race and class is a delicate enterprise. It usually fails, as we have seen in contemporary Iraq and Lebanon or in the former Soviet Union and Yugoslavia. Groups claim that their tribe's achievements have not only been ignored by the majority but are marks of superiority deserving privileged status in the society. It is a zero-sum game of winners and losers—with the prize ultimately being favoritism under the law among supposedly equal citizens.

In *Federalist Papers* No. 10, James Madison ("Publius") wrote that factionalism—in his view arising over material inequality and unequal property holding—was inevitable in a free society. The purpose of the new Constitution was not to end such divisions. In Madison's view that was impossible. Instead he sought to ensure that such strife was mitigated, attenuated, and ultimately adjudicated through legislative, executive, and judicial checks and balances. His aim, then, was to prevent one political faction from amassing enough power to lessen the freedoms of others. Our Founders were not Platonists who wanted divine powers to force citizens to be equal or even change innate human behaviors. Instead, they were Aristotelians who sought pragmatic laws and customs in order to work around innate human nature and to balance a host of competing historical realities.[16]

The US government once encouraged cohesive rituals early on, celebrating national holidays such as Christmas, Thanksgiving, Easter, and the Fourth of July—and later Labor Day and Veterans Day. Originally, showing the US flag at fairs, celebrations, and public events brought the disparate classes of a mostly European American country together. Such civic traditions later sought to do the same with far more ethnically and racially disparate citizens. If everyone could unite in feasting and enjoying fireworks during a shared commemoration, then the idea that some were better than others on the basis of how they appeared or the size of their bank accounts became ever more difficult to accept.

Now, however, most of those traditional holidays have been under assault as either racist, religiously exclusionist, or neocolonialist. Or as former quarterback and celebrity Colin Kaepernick put it about Fourth of July celebrations of the signing of the Declaration of Independence, "We reject your celebration of white supremacy & look forward to liberation for all."

The subtext of all these assaults on traditional commemoration—from holidays to statues to eponymous street names—is to redefine the past as a way of recalibrating the future. Wiping away as trivial or evil the foundations of America will obviously enable new, entirely good foundations antithetical to past bad ones to proceed. Or as Winston Smith said, quoting the Party's slogan in George Orwell's *1984*, "Who controls the past controls the future; who controls the present controls the past."[17]

American novelists such as James Fenimore Cooper, Nathaniel Hawthorne, Herman Melville, Louisa May Alcott, Harriet Beecher Stowe, Mark Twain, Jack London, Theodore Dreiser, William Faulkner, Thomas Wolfe, John Dos Passos, Edith Wharton, John Steinbeck, Harper Lee, and Ralph Ellison once all sought to write a national epic. Their goal was the proverbial "great American novel"—a term first coined in 1868 by the realist novelist John William De Forest—that would critique, sometimes harshly, but also ultimately celebrate the flawed American experience. The latter concept was to be defined by a shared language, culture, and struggle that grew out of a unique expansive geography, diverse people, and common republic.

The protagonists of such novels usually represent the archetypal American individual. He is often admittedly unpolished and uncouth. The hero is usually not romanticized but fights in an often harsh natural and human landscape. Such unruly characters seek, and often fail, to resolve many of the contradictions and unfairnesses—sometimes expressed in terms of race, sex, and class—of America by their own force of will, skepticism of conventional wisdom, or willingness to risk their persons for an unconventional, unpopular, or dangerous idea or cause.

Again, the point of examining these diverse texts was to see commonalities with, rather than differences between, fellow citizens and to remind the country that the oppressed and victimized had a right to demand that lofty promises be matched with concrete realities. The aim was to embrace a collective chauvinism that everyone was part of something historically exceptional. Plop anyone from anywhere in America, and he too could become the archetypal American hero, while not minimizing the contradictions of any great nation in terms of professed ecumenicalism and state discrimination.[18]

So heroes—political, military, scientific, cultural, social—were to be emulated: George Washington, Abraham Lincoln, Helen Keller, Susan B. Anthony, Martin Luther King Jr., Ulysses S. Grant, Booker T. Washington, John J. Pershing, Amelia Earhart, Dwight Eisenhower, Thomas Edison, Alexander Graham Bell, the Wright Brothers, Jonas Salk, and John Glenn. These pantheons were elastic as the demography of the United States changed, the poverty of racialism and sexism was exposed, immigration increased, and the melting pot incorporated into its halls of fame Frederick Douglass, George Washington Carver, Harriet Tubman, Tecumseh, Jim Thorpe, Chief Joseph, Jackie Robinson, and Cochise.

In the cinema of the 1950s and 1960s, B movies often portrayed the crushing of Indian revolts as a patriotic necessity on the path to mastering the West. But in topflight cinema of that same era, usually with larger budgets and celebrity actors, native Americans were often romanticized as tragic, admirable tribal heroes. Sometimes they were portrayed as preferable in their innate honesty to conniving and greedy white men, especially in films such as *Hombre*, *Cheyenne Autumn*, *The Naked Spur*, *Broken Arrow*, and *A Man Called Horse*. Ultimately, Hollywood transcended such positive portrayals and now offers equally stereotyped Native Americans as morally superior to almost all their white adversaries in such movies as *Dances with Wolves* and *Legends of the Fall*—and indeed as defenders of a culture far preferable to what became the present America.[19]

If originally the American heroic archetype emulated the white-male Founders, by the late twentieth century it had long abandoned this theme. The original point had been not necessarily the particular race or tribe of the hero but the illustration of the American character and values that transcended the circumstances of his birth.

Key here were a few assumptions. Given constant technological and social evolution, the standards of the present were *not* to be applied retroactively to deprecate collectively the long dead. Certainly, heroes could be good men and women, even if they were not judged perfect by the values of an ensuing and morally evolving century. Instead, some allowance was given that each evolutionary generation rests on the shoulders of a prior one, as if the present censorious age might itself one day also be judged wanting by a future one likely to be far more affluent and leisured—and of uncertain ideology. If citizens do not believe that they inherited an exceptional past, if they instead claim all the perceived good of the present as their own and all the bad the cargo of the inferior and now dead, then inevitably they fall into self-righteousness, smug ahistoricism, and hypocrisy.

The socialist Robert Nisbet once lamented that no great state can really long endure without a common effort to create unity and a collective belief that it is exceptional or at least better than the alternative: "No government can hope to achieve anything of a political, social, and economic character that rises much above the level of a written statute unless there is present a sense of veneration for that government that is but another way of expressing patriotism." In other words, a state that does not exalt common citizenship itself loses credibility. Cynical citizens see no need to heed its rules.[20]

The keys to American patriotism, I think, are two, now vanishing, values: first, gratitude for being a citizen of the United States; second, recognition that one immigrates to the United States or continues to live within its confines because one believes it to be preferable to other countries. These truths are grounded in the reality that America's uniqueness at its birth in 1776 and throughout its various constitutional reforms and amendments has logically made it the envied destination of most of the world's immigrants.

To the degree that some Americans saw history as melodrama rather than tragedy, they still once looked at the totality of the historical actor. They balanced the past person's saintly and sinful characteristics, content to honor those on the moral plus side of the ledger. Discovery of incidents of bad behavior, unfortunate speech, or conflicted loyalty did not necessarily erase an otherwise exemplary life. Few thought Martin Luther King Jr. was not a great civil rights leader because he was later found to be a serial adulterer and sometimes callous, if not downright abusive, to women in his private life or had plagiarized parts of his Boston University doctoral thesis.

George Patton Jr. is still considered a landmark general despite insinuations that he was adulterously sleeping with his niece by marriage, Jean Gordon, who later committed suicide after his death. Liberal idealist Woodrow Wilson on balance was praised by progressives as a successful president despite his inveterate racism against the nonwhite. Jimmy Carter is likely a more humane man than was Wilson and perhaps a worse president. Americans honored their heroes for their preponderance of good and allowed some leeway for the occasional bad. If Father Junipero Serra sometimes was blinkered and harsh in disciplining Native American converts, in the typical manner of eighteenth-century corporal punishment, that sin did not nullify his civilizing missions that enriched California, accomplished often at great personal danger and with enormous physical pain and difficulty.

Americans also once acknowledged that men and women of the preindustrial age spent much of their days in drudgery and discomfort to produce food, wear clean clothes, and fight off illnesses and injury—during their mostly "solitary, poor, nasty, brutish, and short" lives. There was a concession that people of the past who were more frequently sick and closer to daily starvation and who lived far shorter, more painful, and harder lives might not have the money, leisure, health, food, and security that, in theory, can accelerate moral evolution but, in historical fact, sometimes leads to moral regression.

It was harder to be a feminist in the preindustrial world, when a teenage wife might become pregnant ten times in order to deliver seven healthy babies, in order to ensure that five survived childhood diseases, in order to guarantee that three or four made it safely to adulthood—in an age without washing machines, vacuum cleaners, electricity, antiseptics, disposable diapers, infant formula, antibiotics, and vaccinations. Husbands did not resent getting off their couches to help their working spouses by carrying out the garbage and instead toiled fourteen hours in the field in hopes that nature did not destroy the family grain crop.

The Irish workers on the transcontinental railroad were racist in their attitudes toward rival Chinese laborers. But then again, they bled and died with about the same frequency as the exploited Chinese. They too had small hope of a long and healthy life. And they were likewise considered the scum of the earth by their distant grandee employers. The story of the United States was never just a simplistic psychodrama of the white versus the nonwhite; rather, it was a tale of class antagonism and often shared ordeals, the contradictions and hypocrisies of seeing race as all important, and the inherent and correcting logic of the Constitution and founding documents, which offered a sanctioned pathway out of bias to a fairer and more racially blind society. We forget that while the Founders reflected almost divine wisdom in crafting the American system of government, they were hardly themselves gods but rather men subject to all the prejudices, appetites, and pathologies of their age. White and male, they lived in a country whose citizenry was roughly 85 to 90 percent white—a demographic nearly unchanged until the latter twentieth century. Simply indicting a nation's past for its preponderance of luminaries of a particular race raises a number of logical contradictions. What nation in history has damned its illustrious heroes for being racially similar to a 90 percent majority of the contemporary population? And if one believes that in some sense America is economically, politically, militarily, and culturally the most durable and successful nation, both in history and in the contemporary world, then surely some of the credit is due to those who dreamed up this singular system of government and custom of constant self-reflection and self-criticism.[21]

Yet once-accepted political and historical arguments for a racially diverse citizenry united by a common past, shared loyalties to constitutional citizenship, and suppression of tribal loyalties and identifications are now eroding. A modern reversion to race and ethnic identification in just about everything, from politics to sports to entertainment, is replacing citizenry.

In 2019 Beto O'Rourke, a candidate in the Democratic presidential primary, agreed with Confederate vice president Alexander Stephens's notion of a fatally flawed America. But whereas Stephens at least had scoured the Constitution and failed to find in it support for his racist theories, O'Rourke simply was ignorant that such racists as Stephens had ever quite logically criticized the US Constitution for its failure to institutionalize racial supremacy. O'Rourke saw instead an entire country, North and South, founded on, and in service of, white supremacy rather than indifference to it. On the campaign trail in July 2019, O'Rourke told a crowd of mostly recent immigrants and refugees, "Here we are in Nashville, I know this from my home state, Texas, those places that formed the Confederacy, that this country was founded on white supremacy. And every single institution and structure that we have in our country still reflects the legacy of the slavery and segregation and Jim Crow and suppression, even in our democracy."[22]

Notice how O'Rourke in a nanosecond jumped from the former Confederate states of Tennessee and Texas to the entirety of "this country." His made-up history assumed that past fights over the Constitution and the Civil War had never taken place, as if nearly seven hundred thousand Americans had never died in a struggle over eliminating slavery and the traditions of resolving differences in nonviolent fashion through legislative action and national elections.

Yet, if O'Rourke were correct, why would his particular audience of immigrants have dared come to such an unattractive place? Why would not O'Rourke have advised them to leave, as soon as possible, such a toxic locale in which "every single institution and structure" was racist—in a way that perhaps Mexico, Central America, India, and China are not?

In the twenty-first century we are reversing course, a little more than a half century after the successful civil rights movement. Martin Luther King Jr.'s former dream of judging black Americans by the content of their character rather than the color of their skin has given way to "It's a black thing, you wouldn't understand" and, more recently, "Black Lives Matter."

The civil rights movement finally killed off the dangerous vestiges of the Ku Klux Klan. Yet the latter's few incoherent remnants are starting to recombobulate in the era of diversity to supposedly preserve their "white" identity by professing a right to emulate the tribal chauvinism of other racial groups. In a series of essays and books, Francis Fukuyama has warned of such unintended consequences of identity politics when all are redefining themselves according to appearance:

Perhaps the worst thing about identity politics as currently practiced by the left is that it has stimulated the rise of identity politics on the right. This is due in no small part to the left's embrace of political correctness, a social norm that prohibits people from publicly expressing their beliefs or opinions without fearing moral opprobrium. Every society has certain views that run counter to its foundational ideas of legitimacy and therefore are off-limits in public discourse. But the constant discovery of new identities and the shifting grounds for acceptable speech are hard to follow. In a society highly attuned to group dignity, new boundaries [sic] lines keep appearing, and previously acceptable ways of talking or expressing oneself become offensive.[23]

The notion that Mexican Americans of the American Southwest throughout the twentieth century were righteously fighting systematic discrimination by the majority white populations is, of course, a matter of historical record. But the demand for protected equality of opportunity has unfortunately become mixed up with racialist triumphalism, such as the National Council of La Raza (which under pressure has recently changed its name to UnidosUS) and the initial separatism of the Movimiento Estudiantil Chicano de Aztlán, or MEChA.

Such late-twentieth-century groups—many are now waning or inert—are splinter protest movements that evolved out of the radical 1960s civil rights movement. But their vestigial emphases on politically correct racial chauvinism are now mostly institutionalized among elites. Their casual identity politicking seems to ground much of their political outlook—be they the Congressional Black Caucus, or chapters of the La Raza Lawyers Association, or the common practice of conducting separate campus graduation ceremonies on the basis of race. The result is that an entire generation of youth has grown up and been educated on the now mainstreamed premise that their ethnic and/or gender identifications define who they are at the expense of their commonality as Americans.[24]

The current American unwinding is insidious and discernable in both trivial and fundamental ways. Once rare, hyphenated names and accent marks have now become popular among the bureaucratic classes in government, on campuses, and in politics and entertainment. They are intended to reveal ethnic pride and to enhance career advantages. The government's archipelago of social service agencies and the census alike track Americans' often complicated ethnic lineages. These often Byzantine rubrics are used to adjudicate racial victims in need of reparatory admissions or hiring, as courts rule that present discrimination against Peter is allowable compensation for past discrimination against Paul.

The result can become muddled. It seems now to be resolved by shrugging that America is merely bifurcated into two antithetical groups of "whites" and "nonwhites." Few calculate the reluctance of most whites to self-identify as whites, especially given their own quite diverse ethnic European heritages and their propensity often to marry the so-called nonwhite. Just as importantly, it is difficult to agree upon a definition of what "white" actually is, given that it is not necessarily aligned with superficial appearance.

The diversity industry—the network of interests that lobby for reparatory considerations in hiring and admissions on the basis of race—hinges on US citizens still envisioning a shrinking white population as the "majority." Again, "white" itself is now not always easily definable—if it ever was—given intermarriage and constructed identities. In California, those who check "white" on Orwellian racial boxes are now a minority, even as, for example, on occasion darker Armenians and Italians and lighter Latinos disagree about the category to which they belong.

Currently, however, Latinos make up the largest minority group in California, since 2014 comprising 39 percent of state residents. Only 37 percent of the population is white, with 15 percent Asian American, 6 percent African American, and smaller percentages for other groups and those of mixed race. The nomenclature of identity politics and affirmative action has not yet caught up with reality on the ground. Are Latinos now a minority/majority population or whites a majority/minority? Are reparatory set-asides now to be adjudicated by income and class rather than race or demography? Will neologisms arise such as belonging to a "privileged minority" that might encompass both whites and Asian Americans on the basis of average income?

The *New York Times* and CNN have already invented a term, "white Hispanic," to denote ostensibly anyone who either cannot be easily, if superficially, identified as Latino or must be identified solely as a hyphenated or asterisked minority due to his political incorrectness. In simpler terms, in the progressive media, when someone of mixed ancestry has done something ostensibly good, he is identified more often as a minority. But when suspected of committing a bad act—such as the shooting of Trayvon Martin by "white Hispanic" George Zimmerman, who was acquitted of second-degree murder—he is damned further by the inclusion of the adjective "white." The addition is intended to negate what would otherwise be a positive and helpful racial ancestry.

Will some working-class whites one day describe themselves as aggrieved minorities and thus demand affirmative action, encourage Viking-like names such as Ragnar or Odin, and insert umlauts and diereses into their names to hype their newfound minority European bona fides, seek segregated European American dorms, and set up Caucasian studies programs at universities, on the logic that the present generation, while not a beneficiary of past discrimination, was born into less privilege in hiring and admissions than other groups? One might object that a previously privileged population has no recourse to complaint when it finds itself in a disadvantaged minority demographic. Yet generations to come who never experienced majority status and the supposed advantages it always conveys might object that they were being discriminated against for the purported sins of the now long dead—in the Euripidean fashion of "The gods visit the sins of the fathers upon the children."[25]

Again the irony: the more we separate by race, the harder it becomes to trace our own racial heritages, much less to adjudicate the relative victim status of each. As Richard Alba recently noted in *The Great Demographic Illusion: Majority, Minority and Expanding American Mainstream*, "The rigidity of ethno-racial lines is already being challenged by a robust development that is largely unheralded: a surge in the number of young Americans who come from mixed majority-minority families and have one white parent and one nonwhite or

Hispanic parent. Today more than 10 percent of all babies born in the United States are of such mixed parentage."[26]

Perhaps Nemesis explains why, if in our racist past those with some nonwhite ancestry were condemned to be discriminated against as non-white, now those with even a measurable fraction of nonwhite ancestry are privileged to be positively distinguished as nonwhite. Efforts to pass for white once were symptoms of a racist society in which a minority of the population strove to enjoy the racialist advantages of the majority. Attempts to pass for nonwhite are now likewise indications of a racial-ist society in which a majority, occasionally and fraudulently, seeks to enjoy the advantages of the minority, mostly in terms of admissions and hiring.[27]

Many have taken DNA ancestry tests—by 2019 an estimated thirty million Americans—perhaps in part to trace lineages and categorize themselves within an ever more important racial rubric. As far as the citizen goes, he by needs seeks to find some cachet that transcends his mere citizenship—a precivilizational tribal affiliation of some sort that suggests the state and his fellow citizens who lack such ethnic fides owe him reparations and set-asides.

Obviously when we reach a point where a majority of citizens seek and obtain a measure of victim status deserving reparatory hiring or admissions, then there may not be enough victimizers to offer compen-sations: when everyone is a tribalist victim, then no one is, a sign that tribalism is beginning to replace shared citizenship. In circular fashion, citizenship is weakened by tribal identification, which in turn seeks to offer Americans the prior security and solidarity now absent in anemic citizenship.[28]

The logic of the Old South's "one-drop rule" has often been employed to assure employers or universities that one qualifies as a minority. Given our racial fixations, we may soon have to undergo computer scans of our skin colors to rank competing claims of griev-ance or simply adopt the centuries-old Mexican *sistema de castas*, a both formal and informal controversial mechanism of branding citizens on the basis of their skin color in determining their appropriate social, political, and economic status within Latin American society. We often also forget that hundreds of billions of dollars each year are invested in what can be fairly termed diversity commissars. Their duties in the workplace and on campuses are to monitor the precise racial makeup of the labor force, to adjudicate the authenticity of individual racial pedigrees, to "reeducate" the majority of the white population about its toxic insidious privilege, to ensure that curricula and communications include proper vocabulary and phraseology, and, of course, constantly to ferret out a racial microaggression or transgression that might end a career or livelihood.[29]

Nor do we say publicly that some nonwhite groups seem more comfortable with whites than with other nonwhite groups, belying the notion of a monolithic them-versus-us America defined as a binary of the privileged white population and the nonwhite underprivileged. Indeed, many whom the government would characterize as "nonwhite" or "other" on government forms themselves identify as "white." And we fail also to appreciate that the public often aligns on matters of culture and customs rather than just race or economic status. In an age when gender is no longer necessarily deemed biologically determined but can be socially constructed, it is no surprise that racial identification likewise can become a matter of individual choice and effort.[30]

Nonetheless, the more the evidence mounts that vestigial American traditions of pluralism and a common culture are not yet inert, the still more fervently are they opposed. Hollywood producers have agreed that their films will now have certain mandatory percentages of themes, actors, directors, and support staff of particular races and genders, apparently on the theory that art will now serve and advance social justice first and worry about excellence second. The old Metro-Goldwyn-Mayer motto—*ars gratis artis* (art for art's sake)—that appears at the beginning of MGM films over a roaring lion's head is now apparently passé.[31]

Barack Obama's official presidential portrait painter, Kehinde Wiley, offers a good example of how tribalism warps the arts. He self-identified as a black and gay identity politics conceptual artist. Wiley had earlier courted controversy with photoshopped paintings of inter-racial executions. In one, a black woman, sword in one hand, holds up the severed head of a white woman she has just decapitated. Wiley once described his black-on-white beheadings to the *New York Times Magazine* this way: "It's sort of a play on the 'kill whitey' thing." In fact, it was nearly impossible to find critiques of Wiley's work without reference to his race or sexual preferences. In such an increasingly common landscape, the artist understands the career advantages of identifying by tribal characteristics rather than just universal artistic themes.[32]

Multiculturalism's chief danger to American citizenship is that its growing institutional acceptability also seeps into the legal system. Particular "marginalized" groups are now to be treated unequally under the law in Orwellian accordance with doctrines of equality and fairness. Instead of earlier pseudoscientific arguments of racial superiority, the notions of reparatory justice for past collective sins, or tit-for-tat, eye-for-an-eye transgenerational payback, serve as justifications for the new tribal asymmetry. That raises the issue of the degree to which the perceived victims and victimizers of the present generation are so classified according to the sins of the past and whether ancestral bias exists similarly as such in the present. It further raises the age-old moral dilemma of whether two wrongs make a right.

Take an illustrative example from 2017, when the New York Fire Department (FDNY) removed one of its most famous members from a three-man, flag-bearing color guard that was asked to perform at a public event—due to his race. Despite his heroic service during the September 11, 2001, terrorist attacks, white firefighter Lt. Daniel McWilliams was taken off the team so that the guard could present itself to the public as having an all-black membership. FDNY's chief diversity and inclusion officer, lawyer Cecilia Loving, in her 2020 court testimony, defended her decision at a New York State Division of

Human Rights trial. Loving testified that it was permissible to remove McWilliams on the basis of his race in order to "uplift our identities and our separate ethnicities in order to instill a sense of pride and community and support for one another."

A Confederate zealot of the Old South—whose ideology was incompatible with the Declaration of Independence—could not have expressed the idea of the need for discriminatory racial pride more clearly. Nursing ancient wounds along ethnic and racial lines is a prescription for societal failure and fragments citizenship linguistically into endless categories sometimes used to justify different treatment under the law. Cecilia Loving's ruling about "separate ethnicities" essentially took the fire department back to the era before the civil rights movement. Indeed, the Supreme Court of 1896 long ago anticipated Loving's decision when it ruled in *Plessey v. Ferguson*—one of the court's most infamous decisions—that state laws against discrimination did not violate the Fourteenth Amendment if they "were separate but equal."[33]

On the website La Raza Lawyers of California ("an independent unincorporated association of Lawyers organized in 1977 to support Chicano and Latino Lawyers in California and serve as a statewide network for local affiliate La Raza Lawyers Groups"), there is a link to a 2016 *Atlantic* article, "The Problem with Calling Out Judges for Their Race," with the subtitle "Donald Trump has no legal justification for questioning Gonzalo Curiel."

In 2016 candidate Trump—improperly—suggested that, as a harsh critic of open borders and illegal immigration, he was on the receiving end of a negative civil judgment due to the supposed bias of a "Latino judge." Trump was quite rightly criticized by some for identifying Judge Curiel with his ethnic background, by more censors also for not at least referring to him as "Latino American," and by all observers for attacking the character of a sitting judge.[34]

Yet one can become confused about what constitutes politically correct and incorrect vocabulary and usage. The members of La Raza Lawyers of California (including Judge Curiel himself) self-identify as lawyers and justices precisely by their race (La Raza). Supreme Court justice Sonia Sotomayor—likewise, I think, wrongly—identified herself in a now infamous October 2001 lecture at the University of California, Berkeley, not as a Latino American, or just an American, but foremost as a Latina.

More controversially, she suggested that such a racial identity gave her superior insight into a white-male judicial counterpart: "I would hope that a wise Latina woman [*sic*] with the richness of her experiences would more often than not reach a better conclusion than a white male who hasn't lived that life." How exactly would Sotomayor know that in the twenty-first century particular individuals who happen to be white and male would not have as rich experiences as other particular Latino American females? Indeed, in one single speech, Sotomayor referred to herself simply as Latina or Latino thirty-eight times—as if she were not so much a unique individual as a representative of a collective.[35]

Once Americans embrace such ethnic chauvinism and identify by superficial appearances and ethnic fides—even on the pretext of correcting past wrongs—then embarrassing contradictions, ironies, contortions, and paradoxes are inevitable. So here we are left with the surrealism of a national figure criticized crudely as a "Mexican judge," who self-identifies as a "La Raza lawyer" and is a member of the La Raza Lawyers of California, yet objects to being identified by his ethnic background, even though "Latina" is a favorite self-appellation of a Supreme Court justice.

Yale Law School professor Amy Chua has noted where this substitution of race for class inevitably leads:

Educational prospects for poor white children are extremely bleak. Private tutors and one-thousand-dollar SAT courses are completely cost prohibitive to poor or even working-class people—and poor whites don't benefit from affirmative action. Whereas most elite colleges do special outreach for racial minorities, they rarely send scouts to the backwoods of Kentucky. Out of roughly two hundred students in the Yale Law School class of 2019, there appears to be exactly one poor white, or three, if we include students from families living just above the poverty line. Administrators have described this class as the most "diverse" in the school's history.[36]

The results of such racial contortions are predictable in such a balkanized spoils system that ignores class and fixates on race. And even the later focus results in anomalies. Asian Americans, for example, are discriminated against by race when applying to top American schools. They are seen as taking slots away from Latinos and blacks because, due to their test scores and grades, they are "overrepresented" at top universities. Their success is written off as a cultural or even genetic quirk, occasionally expressed vulgarly as Asians "study too hard" or are "naturally better in math."[37]

There is a large Punjabi immigrant farming community in my rural neighborhood. A strange experience is on occasion to hear their complaints that they are "darker" than Mexican Americans and certainly more so than Chilean and Argentinian immigrants, that they are subject to as much bias, and yet, until recently, they did not qualify for affirmative action to the same degree as do those who often arrive from Mexico and Latin America and reside illegally in Fresno County.

Racial categorization determining reparatory action may take into account that Punjabi Americans lack the historical discrimination suffered by prior generations of Mexican Americans or that the average per capita income of Indian Americans vastly exceeds that of the white majority. Or perhaps Indian immigrants are seen as from the middle and professional classes, having arrived legally, and are therefore more likely to become part of the American elite.

A Punjabi American friend also objected to me that California should be bound by Proposition 209, the so-called California Civil Rights Initiative. Indeed, the state constitutional amendment was passed by over 54 percent of California voters in 1996. The statute reads, "The state shall not discriminate against, or grant preferential treatment to, any individual or group on the basis of race, sex, color, ethnicity, or national origin in the operation of public employment, public education, or public contracting."

In fact, almost all of higher education, given its liberal faculty, students, and investments in race-based institutions, opposed Proposition 209. I added to my friend that, as a faculty member who chaired and sat on a number of hiring, awards, and admissions committees, I could tell him that the proposition was mostly ignored. Faculty were simply advised not to put in writing that race, gender, and ethnicity were still being used to weigh selections. To do so would only encourage lawsuits.

Instead, we were more or less guided by the principle that "nothing had changed." If pressed, we university employees were to act as legal scholars and plead that "federal" affirmative action guidelines superseded our state constitution—even though California's Proposition 209 was consistent with federal law and the US Constitution and with many court decisions banning overt racial discrimination. In effect, we had the power to render null and void the will of voting taxpayers who paid our salaries. In general, most California public institutions of higher learning practiced such nullification and paid little heed to 209 as they continued to weigh race and gender in their admissions and hiring policies.[38]

Since 1996, the California legislature and both state and federal courts have tried without success to overturn the constitutional amendment—despite success in some states elsewhere in upholding the validity of race-based admissions and hiring. In May 2020, the Democratic supermajorities in the California legislature promised they finally had the power and support to annul the ballot-driven 209. They apparently assumed that the liberal California electorate in November 2020 bore little semblance to that of a quarter century earlier and would easily pass the proposition. In fact, the attempt to overturn 209 was soundly defeated by mostly liberal, but apparently increasingly frightened, California voters.

In fact, the replacement measure that the legislature placed on the ballot (Proposition 16) failed miserably—in theory because Latino and Asian American groups, who together form a majority of the California population, likely felt that it would institutionally discriminate against them in favor of the state's far smaller African American minority. There is also growing realization among minorities that once the nation begins doling out preferences on the basis of tribal considerations, their own racially based arguments can be superseded by those of another tribe—the historical bane of all multitribal societies.[39]

What are the wages of these new protocols of multiculturalism and the consequences for contemporary citizenship? Of course, we are witnessing a fragmentation of common citizenship into racial categories of Americans. Hiring and admissions become battlegrounds where ethnic and racial pedigrees become primary rather than secondary considerations. The American past becomes melodrama rather than tragedy, as it gets used in the present to redefine the future of citizenship in premodern tribal terms.

No one now escapes the current epidemic of tribalism. For example, some students attending Southern California's Claremont Colleges openly demand roommates of the same race. We call these Jim Crow–like arrangements "theme houses" or "theme rooms" to disguise the reality that we are regressing to early-twentieth-century obsessions with race and segregated housing. Will a "fair housing" branch of the Department of Housing and Urban Development one day cite colleges for embracing racial segregation in their dormitories, a policy predicated on selecting boarders on the basis of race? Or as one student at the Claremont Colleges put it in her social media posting, "I don't want to live with any white folks."[40]

Racially segregated "safe spaces" are now fixtures on many college campuses. Civil rights advocates of the 1960s—as we saw earlier in the case of Bernie Sanders—would have widely damned these as condescending efforts of racists to single out supposedly fragile blacks in need of shelter and ensure they were not fully integrated into the student body.

One survey of 173 schools found that 42 percent of these institutions offered segregated residences, 46 percent offered segregated orientation programs, and 72 percent held segregated graduation ceremonies. Had they been landlords off campus, all would have been sued. Yet an Orwellian barrier of sorts prevents any use of the word "segregation" to identify voluntary "separate-but-equal" rooming assignments. It is as if the last century of civil rights battles for open, racially blind housing *never occurred.*

Women now enroll in college at a much higher rate (56 percent) than men. In the perpetual logic of disparate impact and identity politics, will there be a male effort to ensure affirmative action for college admissions and graduation rates? If the white vote ever reaches 90 percent for a particular white candidate, will that really be such a good thing, as it was considered to be when President Barack Obama was praised for capturing 95 percent of the black vote?

Are we to believe that whites were not racist when 43 percent of them voted for Obama over white candidate John McCain—a higher percentage than the 41 percent of whites who had voted four years earlier for John Kerry or the 42 percent who did in 2000 for Al Gore? Did whites then later suddenly revert to being racist in 2016 because they voted for Republican Donald Trump (58 percent) over another white candidate, Democrat Hillary Clinton (37 percent), who won a markedly smaller percentage of white supporters than did Barack Obama in 2008?

Even onetime diversity advocate Oprah Winfrey has had second thoughts about the lack of commonality in America—and where the trajectory of racial obsessions ultimately leads. She recently vowed—at least until the social chaos of spring 2020 and her about-face—to quit using the word "diversity" in preference for "inclusion." After all, a Latino American undergraduate who studies Shakespeare is not "culturally appropriating" anyone's white-European legacy but instead seeking transcendent ideas and a common humanity. African Americans who excel in physics and engineering are not "acting white" but finding the proper career pathways for their natural talents.[41]

Privileged white elites are often, if not usually, the drivers of these radical obsessions that result in racial categorization and reparatory action. Yet their verbal advocacy of multiculturalism seems at first contrary to their own careers and embrace of Western bourgeois customs and values that reflect many of the norms of common American culture now under assault. Perhaps multicultural advocacy psychologically squares the circle of still being able to enjoy the material life that accrues from some 245 years of American freedom and capitalism, while being released from the burdens of past American racism, sexism, colonialism, imperialism, and all the other isms that supposedly ensured current generations of white males their singular privilege.

Often in response to student activist criticism, college presidents will issue confessions attesting to their own "unearned" white privilege. But given such admissions, it is strange how none have thereafter resigned their "unearned" lucrative and influential billets. Similarly, when universities, in loud atonement, admit that they still practice "systemic racism," they somehow insist that the federal government must continue to grant them generous funding—despite federal laws that prohibit such entitlements to institutions that are found to be, much less admit to being, racist.[42]

This tendency to denigrate institutions that have resulted in privilege is not new. Nearly a quarter century ago, economic historian David Landes noted the larger paradox that Western economic and political paradigms—what he broadly called the invention of modernity—had enhanced the world, even as criticism of the West ("Europhobia") had grown commensurately among its blessed material beneficiaries.[43]

Rarely in this race/class/gender victimization narrative of the last decades was there much admission that such prejudices are the stuff of all humans. The US citizen is not apprised in his schools or popular culture of the common pathologies inherent in all human experience, as, for example, that Middle Eastern Muslims may have imported in aggregate as many slaves, albeit often under different circumstances and sometimes for different reasons, as did Europeans to North America—and did so for nearly a millennium longer and sometimes continue to do so in small numbers and stealthily even in the present age. Religious and class discrimination in India and Saudi Arabia today can in some cases approach the oppression of America's recent past. The contemporary Chinese prove extremely xenophobic, often in blatantly racial terms.

Yet, at least until recently, the traditions of self-criticism have worked to suppress these unfortunate and innate human tribal passions most successfully in the West and the United States. An irony follows that those who are most empirical about their past sins thereby receive the most condemnation as a result of detailing them. This innate paradox of the West is critical in understanding the current reversion to tribalism in American society. Protected Western free expression, the classical legacy of utopianism, the Puritan variant of finding salvation through confession of sin, and the upward mobility of free market economics all allow and encourage self-criticism of institutions. Yet, without much knowledge of the past and in excess, these traditions also can contribute to a sense of nihilism, self-loathing, and performance virtue-signaling, especially when historical context and contemporary cultural comparison are absent.[44]

In addition, pick-and-choose critics can silently embrace past American traditions that have led to prosperity and opportunity, while squaring that concrete acquiescence by easily and loudly condemning the easy targets of past American institutionalized racism and sexism. Are we still to enjoy electric lights, even though their polymath inventor, Thomas Alva Edison (1847–1931), also believed in racial stereotypes? Do those who have supported abortion as a societal good now not defend abortion because the founder of Planned Parenthood, Margaret Higgins Sanger (1879–1966), is increasingly condemned as a racist eugenicist? Her campaign for abortion had been in part an effort to decrease the populations of the nonwhite.[45]

This phenomenon of Western hyper-self-criticism has been named "oikophobia." It is an antonym for "xenophobia" (loathing of the "other"), from the Greek words for one's own household (*oikos*) and for loathing (*phobia*), to render "loathing of one's own culture or home." Again, the ingredients—wealth, leisure, security—are many that enable Americans to castigate their own history and culture while fragmenting into a tribal society.

As social critic Benedict Beckeld put it recently,

> Diverse interests are created that view each other as greater enemies than they do foreign threats. Since the common civilizational enemy has been successfully repulsed, it can no longer serve as an effective target for and outlet of people's sense of superiority, and human psychology generally requires an adversary for the purpose of self-identification, and so a new adversary is crafted: other people in the same civilization. Since this condition of leisure and empowerment, as well as a perception of external threats as non-existential, are the results of a society's success, success is, ironically, a prerequisite for a society's self-hatred.[46]

One odd artifact of these growing obsessions with race is that the theory of omnipotent white supremacy (which has supplanted "white privilege" as the latest narrative) and oppression, so necessary to the narrative, is often not borne out in fact. There are certainly vestigial white supremacists. But the charge that such racist ideology, known as "systemic racism," permeates all of American society is rarely demonstrated. Still, the charge is put to good use by the industry of diversity that must find ever-subtler ways of tracking down biases by employing terms like "microaggressions" and "implicit bias" that reveal by their very qualifiers a poverty of such overt pathologies.

Few yet have offered a systematic definition of systemic racism, especially in terms of how it differs from practice in other nations and societies. Could such a putative exegesis explain how it operates, say, in the NBA, by either denying full opportunities to multimillionaire and disproportionately overrepresented African Americans or, contrarily, "rigging" an industry that "systemically" excludes Asian and Latino Americans? In a close 2020 race for lieutenant governor in South Carolina, both the successful Republican candidate, Mark Robinson, and his Democratic rival, Yvonne Lewis Holley, were African American—in a state that is nearly 70 percent "white," was for over sixty years the political fiefdom of Dixiecrat Strom Thurmond, and was the first southern state to secede from the Union in December 1860. Truly white supremacist states, such as the former apartheid government of South Africa, do not elect black presidents or vice presidents as does the United States, any more than Islamic supremacist societies like Iran or Saudi Arabia would ever allow a Christian or Jew to become their head of state.[47]

Even in the anguished age of George Floyd's death at the hands of police while in custody, there has been, over the last two decades, an epidemic of hate crime hoaxes. Supposed victims of various awful oppressors come forward to suggest their own personal bouts with racial hatred reflect larger nationwide pathologies and call for reparatory measures to their own benefit. Such a phenomenon would be unnecessary in a society actually plagued by such systemically racist acts.

In the widely publicized hoaxes involving Al Sharpton and Tawana Brawley, the Duke University lacrosse team, the so-called Covington Kids, and Jussie Smollett, the supposed victims all sought to fabricate racist-driven crimes, either to escape culpability or for personal aggrandizement, on the accurate assumption of broad media and popular support. In addition to such inventions, African American professor Wilfred Reilly compiled over four hundred recent incidents of false hate crime reporting, noting,

Hate crime hoaxers are "calling attention to a problem" that is a very small part of total crimes. There is very little brutally violent racism in the modern USA. There are less than 7,000 real hate crimes reported in a typical year. Inter-racial crime is quite rare; 84% of white murder victims and 93% of Black murder victims are killed by criminals of their own race, and the person most likely to kill you is your ex-wife or husband. When violent inter-racial crimes do occur, whites are at least as likely to be the targets as are minorities. Simply put, Klansmen armed with nooses are not lurking on Chicago street corners.[48]

Once we deify multiculturalism, all else becomes subordinate. The individual's accomplishments are hijacked as the property of the tribe to whom he owes first allegiance. An incoherence of "intersectionality" is inevitable when we shed our common humanity and replace it with a host of tribal loyalties that cannot all be sorted out, much less reconciled, even by focusing on a common target of the dominant culture and the majority population.

In such a paradigm, history is rendered near meaningless. Collectivism erases individualism, as the past is reduced to a monotonous melodrama of inhuman forces in conflict. If all pioneers are deemed racists, does it matter that some trailblazers in fact were cowards and some heroes or at times a mixture of both? Can individuals act singularly apart from their race and from the use of racial division for larger political purposes? Can uninspiring black actors now get parts because of diversity quotas in the same manner that mediocre white actors used "old boy" networks to land roles for which they were unqualified?

If the Founders were simply racists, then what separated them from millions of less extraordinary British racist subjects? The reverse is true too: Were there no ignoble black civil rights leaders, no differences between an opportunistic Jesse Jackson or Al Sharpton and the iconic Martin Luther King Jr., given both were black and on the right side of the civil rights movement?

The true enemy of tribalism is individualism, which is antithetical to the idea that all who are deemed victimizers are more or less identical, and likewise their supposed victims, given all are rendered politically useful as anonymous members of a collective race or tribe. When Joe Biden in 2020 blasted an African American radio host for questioning his stance on civil rights, he inadvertently exposed the progressive emphasis on the collective rather than the individual, inherent in identity politics: "Well I tell you what," Biden fumed, "if you have a problem figuring out whether you're for me or Trump, then you ain't black." So spoke Biden, the expert on what constitutes authentic or indeed even legitimate individual African American political expression.[49]

The ultimate end of tribalism is an odious reductionism, in which all art, music, literature, and history is distilled down to the issue of race. And as we learned from twentieth-century communism, when such ideologies destroy all other considerations, opportunists and mediocrities fill the void, substituting their political purity and correctness for want of merit and competitive talent.

There are also national security considerations and dangers inherent in the growing tribalism at home. Bigotry abroad will only grow as others sense that the United States lacks the confidence in its own values to extend its self-critical principles. If the so-called white at home—supposedly by America's own admission—systematically discriminate against the nonwhite, then why would they not do so abroad as well and thus also deserve to be blanketly condemned? China long ago grasped that paradox and throughout the coronavirus pandemic showed itself to be a brilliant propagandist—and not just in the utter hypocrisy of a racist and xenophobic state cynically leveling charges of racism and xenophobia against a pluralistic constitutional republic. Rather, China rightly expected that the American media would parrot its accusations, which privately even the communist apparat in Beijing likely does not believe. If it did trust its own propaganda, Beijing certainly would not send over three hundred thousand of its best students to American universities to live in jeopardy in an inherently racist society.

Tribalism, then, can endanger the citizens' national security. During the pandemic itself, Americans were apparently either to agree with the Chinese charge or to cede leverage to Beijing in terror of being called racist again. A Chinese daily newspaper adroitly attacked legitimate American complaints that Chinese laxity had led to a deadly global pandemic with boilerplate charges of racism: "The U.S. and other Western countries' overreactions to the outbreak in China smack of a 'segregation' policy laced with extreme racism." At a time when African students and visitors were being systematically barred from entering some Chinese stores and restaurants, the *China Daily* was urging their home governments "to reject the triple Western diseases of xenophobia, ideological bias and the fear of China's rise."

Translate that propaganda and the message is that China believes American citizens are torn apart by racial factionalism. America can easily be intimidated by false charges of intolerance that ironically would realistically apply to China itself. The fact that China's communist leadership does not care about its own concrete bias and that the United States fears even the false charge of illiberality suggests to Beijing that Western democracies are without self-confidence and that its own racialist totalitarianism is rightfully ascendant.

China no doubt wonders how Americans can feel any patriotic unity or affection, the bonding agent of classical citizenship, for a country so confessedly and irredeemably racist and divided. No wonder, then, indications arose that in 2020 China was directly funding various identity politics groups within the United States, apparently on the theory that their adherence to tribalism weakened Beijing's existential rival.[50]

By any fair standard, the population, GDP, more sophisticated propaganda, and Communist Party ideology of China make it a far greater threat to American interests than Vladimir Putin's Russian kleptocracy. Both Moscow and Beijing seek to subvert US elections, buy influence with American political and corporate elites, and undermine particular candidates through social media skullduggery. Yet the nation since 2016 has been obsessed with "Russian collusion" rather than "Chinese collusion." That schizophrenia is explicable at least in part because the white, macho, and often right-wing racist Russians made a much more easily caricatured threat than the macho, left-wing, but nonwhite Chinese.

Indeed, the Chinese apparently targeted California liberal lawmakers on the theory that they might be exempt from scrutiny, given their supposed diversity credentials and a more favorable media. In any case, the media paid little attention to disclosures that the onetime head of the Senate Intelligence Committee, Senator Diane Feinstein (D-CA), had employed a Chinese spy as her personal driver for nearly twenty years or that House Intelligence Committee member Representative Eric Swalwell (D-CA) conducted a long personal relationship with a Chinese government operative. Indeed, it more often focused on false allegations from both that "Russian collusion" had compromised Donald Trump.[51]

Multiculturalism also erodes citizenship in a number of key ways beyond its hypocrisies and incoherence and the dangers of offering propaganda to American rivals and enemies. First, it perpetuates a Tower of Babel culture in which particular groups do not necessarily use a common English language or shared culture in the public square, thereby impeding the bureaucracy and commerce and adding considerable costs for translators, interpreters, and facilitators.

But the dangers often transcend just the expense and inconvenience of multilingualism. The courts are also swamped with the writs of particular groups who demand exemptions from shared customs and laws. Do particular tribes object to safety codes on the basis of their ethnic fashion or religion? Are segregated spaces reserved for only one particular ethnic or racial group in public places and universities? Are violations of the laws mitigated by cultural or racial exemptions?[52]

As a result, does one "go multicultural" or get left out and suffer the consequences? A sharply distinct multiethnic or multilingual nation might be able to deal with a binary culture, such as Canada's English-speaking majority and Francophone minority, or modern Belgium, which barely manages to accommodate a minority of French-speaking Walloons and Dutch-speaking Flemish. The civil rights era of the 1960s began at last to bring equal justice to American blacks a century after the Civil War. But when a number of ethnicities begin to identify in tribal rather than national fashion, the problems of unity expand until they implode. It is simply too difficult to adjudicate relative grievances, too hard to assess tribal purity, and too complex to allot national entitlements and preferences on the basis of a host of claimants.

Today in the United States there still exists a certain paradox about multiculturalism and identity politicism. On the one hand, Americans in the abstract voice objections to tribalism, affirmative action, and privileges handed out on the basis of race and class as contrary to the American idea of both equality under the law and merit. Indeed, nearly three-quarters of Americans consistently poll that while they support a diverse society, they are still opposed to hiring, promotions, and admissions predicated on racial considerations.[53]

On the other hand, Americans seek advantage for family and friends by emphasizing otherness if it is perceived to offer rewards. This disconnect is not unlike the effort of the progressive rich to leverage advantage through either influence, ancestry, or money in conflict with their professed egalitarian creed and their support for reparatory affirmative action as a remedy for "old boy" networking.

Universities may demand that college English faculties reflect the racial percentages of the United States, but often provosts do not apply such concern to the medical school's faculty of neurosurgeons—at least not fully yet. Take the dean proudest of diversifying his faculty: when he faces open heart surgery, he does not select his doctor on the basis of his particular ethnic background. He will not preselect a surgeon by race in an effort to do his part to support diversity. Instead, he weighs the surgeon's record of prior operations and then considers his identity largely irrelevant to his conclusions.

Passengers would not appreciate any affirmative action program that puts pilots in the cockpit with fewer hours of flying experience or less proven expertise on the theory that the flight crew was now more diverse. In fact, most passengers accept that while flight attendants are quite diverse, pilots are less so—a disconnect rarely discussed. Even the most ardent progressives make the necessary and often cynical adjustments of preferring merit-based professionals in areas that adjudicate their very health and safety.[54]

Recently "woke" professional sports are just as hypocritical as university campuses. The National Football League (NFL) is composed of roughly 70 to 75 percent African American athletes. No one sues to make professional football racially and ethnically proportionately diverse, with set-asides for Asian American tight ends or Mexican American quarterbacks. No one seems to object that the 12 to 13 percent of the population that is African American comprises roughly 75 percent of the NBA's rosters. All the players in the league, of every race, certainly enjoy the unearned and quite bankable privilege of being born with superior athletic skills—from height to innate coordination—in comparison to most Americans. Yet to demand racial proportional representation would be rightly seen as destroying meritocracy. To initiate affirmative action in professional sports could be to deny talented African American billets in favor of less talented non–African Americans—and to make the game played by the less talented less exciting.

So the emphasis on race and the arithmetic of compensatory action result in strange disconnects. African Americans make up only about 20 to 30 percent of all NFL television analysts. That percentage is still about double to triple the percentage of African Americans in the general population. While the number of black NFL head coaches and their staffs has radically declined from an approximate 20 percent of the total, it still in most years, at least until recently, matched the percentage of blacks in the general population.

Yet more recent lower numbers are often cited as proof of racism, given that the African American players comprise nearly three-quarters of the league's rosters. No one by fiat wishes to make the NFL teams "look more like America" by reserving slots for other minorities, much less upping white player participation to reflect current American demography—given that African American players are "overrepresented" at almost six times their percentage in the population. For that matter, of the thirty-two professional football franchises, there are no principal black owners, despite the owners' efforts to insist that the NFL is "diverse."

Of course, there is a logic to the idea that a league composed overwhelmingly of black players should result in more than at least 50 percent black coaches and staff, but only if one first believes that players themselves, selected by merit, should be apportioned to teams on the basis of race or to address underrepresentation, or one accepts the payback argument that the last half-century effort of affirmative action and mandated diversity requires another 350 years of compensation for slavery and Jim Crow discrimination prior to the civil rights era.

The result of racial fixation is surreal: the NBA and NFL have taken up the social activist cudgels in embracing "taking the knee" during the national anthem and lecturing the nation on the need for inclusiveness and diversity—even as the players, the owners, and often the coaches comprise the *most nondiverse racial profiles of any major American institution.*[55]

The twin pillars of the multicultural doctrine are "proportional representation" (hiring and admissions must reflect national demography) and "disparate impact" (intentional bias is automatically assumed and need not be proved for remediation). Because the former is not enforced systematically and the latter operates without proof of bias and prejudice, the result is the rise of "thought crimes" that must be addressed to ensure reparatory government action.

The nation is supposedly 65 to 70 percent "white," nearly 12 to 13 percent African American, 15 to 17 percent Latino American, and 5 to 6 percent Asian American. But such rubrics are misleading in a number of ways. African and Caribbean immigrants have sharply different cultures and histories from those of American blacks, and vice versa. "Latino" can include wealthy white Spaniards, upper-middle-class Cubans, poor immigrants from Oaxaca state, and third-generation middle-class Mexican Americans.

The same fluidity is true of "Asians," given that Filipinos, Japanese, Chinese, and Vietnamese do not necessarily see any cross-cultural affinities, given their different and often antithetical histories. In terms of class, a third-generation Japanese American is far more likely to be privileged than a recent immigrant from Cambodia, and both are likely to have a great deal of shared historical acrimony. "White" is hardly a monolithic concept unless one believes the "deplorable" and "irredeemable" Trump voter seeks innate racial solidarity with the Harvard English professor or Antifa protester.

For all practical purposes, proportional representation refers only to professions deemed overrepresented by so-called whites and occasionally Asians in blue-chip universities. It does not suggest Asians are "overrepresented" in the medical professions, even though so-called Asian doctors are almost three times as common (17 percent) as their proportion (6 percent) of the general population. By the same token, few object that African Americans occupy 21 percent of coveted federal postal service jobs, almost double their percentage in the general population.[56]

Again, examine the case of the National Football League, where racial emphases do not always prompt interleague squabbles but can affect the unity of the entire country, especially in the 2016 matter of San Francisco 49ers quarterback Colin Rand Kaepernick. Kaepernick is of mixed-race parentage. He was put up for adoption by his white mother, to be raised by a white couple named Rick and Teresa Kaepernick. Prior to his celebrity status as a protester and a diversity icon, Kaepernick's chief controversy was being cited by the league for leveling an *N*-word racial taunt at Lamarr Houston, an opposing African American player.

After being a near star for a number of years, Kaepernick was benched in 2016 following injuries and chronic poor performance as the San Francisco 49ers continued to falter. He then refused to stand for the national anthem. As a result, he quickly became the self-appointed leader of a player "take-the-knee" protest movement in response to the supposed racism of the league and indeed of the country itself.

The 2016 protests continued through 2018, before petering out in 2019. Meanwhile, Kaepernick himself garnered a number of lucrative merchandising endorsements and business opportunities. He became a multimillionaire many times over, even as he blamed punitive racism for the failure of other NFL teams to hire him as a free agent. Kaepernick kept largely quiet about the systematic racism of China, whose communist-affiliated companies engage many of his sponsors and thus provide a lucrative part of his income.

Indeed, as a result of Kaepernick's protest movements, the league's 2017 and 2018 television and radio ratings dived about 8 percent. Attendance dipped in some regions nearly 20 percent. In general, professional sports teams had suffered prior flat ratings or a decrease in fan support both because of consumers' changing entertainment preferences and a sense that professional sports had already become too brutal, too partisan, and too predictably politicized. Still, few explained why professional sports had dipped even further or questioned whether the idea of multimillionaire athletes lecturing Americans on their racist tendencies, while not standing during the national anthem, was a contributing cause.

This serial theme of paradox and irony is a trademark of identity politics. The players were never able to convince fans of their own moral shortcomings. Even less persuasive was the notion that the players had a superior ethical compass or had themselves in some way suffered the systemic discrimination that they alleged required such protests.[57]

In the end, millions of citizens perhaps tuned out their once beloved sports on the theory that tribalism had intruded into every facet of their lives, and sporting events were no longer necessarily occasions of civic unity and pride—much less an escape from divisive politics.

There are even more fundamental threats to citizenship from our elites, whose theories about diluting or recalibrating citizenship do not remain mere theories for long. Their top-down assaults on citizenship are often not even alleged to be in service to the poor, the immigrant, or the nonwhite and yet are instead nakedly self-serving. In the next chapter, we shall see how those who were rarely elected to any office now can control the lives of millions of voting citizens, combining the powers of the executive, judicial, and legislative branches to enhance agendas for America that their politics otherwise could not achieve.

Part 2

POSTCITIZENS

Chapter Four

UNELECTED

The bureaucracy, the gigantic power set into motion by
dwarfs, was thus born.

(La bureaucratie, pouvoir gigantesque mis en mouvement
par des nains, est née ainsi.)

      —HONORÉ DE BALZAC, *Les Employés*

I n the prior three chapters, we have explored how ancient, indeed
premodern, phenomena—the medieval bifurcation of society, the
prenation migrations of large populations, and the primary identification by tribal loyalties—in organic fashion have returned and conspired
to undermine American citizenship. Yet, the threats to citizenship
outlined in the following three chapters, while no less real, are certainly more contrived and deliberate, the work of a professional and
often ideologically driven elite. The first such danger is the effort of a
near-permanent caste of unelected officials, regulators, and bureaucrats
who hold enough "gigantic power" to usurp the citizens' control over
their own government.

There are various ways of defining the so-called deep or administrative state. The hotly debated term usually refers to a "state within a

state" and has traditionally focused mostly on supposedly unaccountable and nontransparent intelligence agencies.

Now, however, references to a deep state encompass the entire permanent Beltway military echelon, as well as the intelligence and investigative agencies. It also often includes the top officials of the civil service bureaucracies and administrative agencies. In the case of the United States, it can also denote their multifarious and often incestuous—not to mention lucrative—bureaucratic relationships with the Washington–New York media, lobbyists, Wall Street, and elite universities.[1]

In the past, liberal critics especially warned of the deep state. They often cited the ominous power and overreach of the so-called military-industrial complex. In contrast, conservatives more often feared the power of regulatory agencies. They fought bureaucracies that tried to curtail the freedoms of private citizens and elected officials alike. They railed against the waste of public funds through inefficiencies and administrative bloat.

Both sides, however, shared suspicions of these unelected and often exempt careerists. Both suspected the vast government archipelago could become illegitimate and unwarranted without oversight—and might either hound individual citizens because of their political views, their singular success, and their fame or, in contrast, simply neglect their less powerful constituents without fear of consequences.

In past times, conservatives also criticized the deep state mostly in financial terms, talking of "cutting fat" and "trimming waste," or ridiculed useless "bureaucrats" and "functionaries" of a government that had grown enormously, both relatively and absolutely, after the New Deal of the 1930s. When Ronald Reagan's administration talked of "starving the beast," it meant cutting taxes to decrease incoming federal revenues. Reagan then assumed, wrongly as it turned out, that the ensuing reduced national income would demand massive cuts in government regulators. His administration failed to realize that the bureaucracy only grew as the government simply borrowed money from future generations to replace any lost tax revenue, even as annual deficits soared and conservatives lost their credibility as budgetary hawks.[2]

In contrast, liberals praised the deep state in terms of "making government work for you"—as in, evening out on the back end the inequities on the front end. They meant updating, reforming, but always growing the second great expansion of government as a result of President Lyndon Johnson's Great Society.

Grow the administrative state certainly did. By 2019 some 450 federal agencies were staffed by 2.7 million bureaucrats. The *Federal Register* now numbers 175,496 pages of various codes, encompassing 235 volumes. Its size increased yearly—until 2017 and Donald J. Trump's last-ditch efforts at radical deregulation and some thinning of the bureaucracy. An unfathomable amount of power has been transferred from state and local governments. The US Congress has ceded to federal agencies, manned by the unelected, the power to make regulations, administer them with the force of law, punish perceived offenders, and muster unlimited resources to quash citizens' appeals and objections.[3]

Contrary to popular belief, the term "deep state" never implied a secret cabal. Much less does it now convey any notion of official membership. Rather, it is a natural and loose alliance of those who see themselves as permanent custodians of US power, morality, and influence. The hierarchy is an anointed class, self-defined by its members' educations, résumés, incestuousness, and contacts. All too often they exude disdain and condescension for what they see as transitory, mostly clueless elected officials who come and go in Washington—and the ill-informed citizens who put them in office.

Of course, this worry over the powers of a deep state is no new development. Athenian democracy of the mid-fourth century BC was vastly more complex and bureaucratic than its founder Cleisthenes had originally envisioned in 508/7 BC. Even by the time of the latter fifth century, the Athenian bureaucracy was a constant butt of the comic dramatist Aristophanes's jokes for its graft, irrelevance, and self-importance. In the fourth century BC, some eleven hundred magistrates headed various boards and civil service organizations at Athens, whose citizen population numbered no more than thirty thousand adult males.[4]

To take other examples, the Great Palace of Justinian in Constantinople, the Vatican in Rome, the seventeenth-century Spanish El Escorial, the Versailles complex of Louis XIV, and the czarist and communist Kremlin all housed permanent bureaucracies. Their clerks alone knew how to run a state through their own intrigues and myriads of rules and regulations that always outlasted the particular monarch or autocrat in power. Note that the creation of a permanent caste of government officials that transcends the authority of its leaders is not confined to democracies. A deep state grows in monarchies and autocracies as well. Bureaucracy seems innate to human political nature. The key difference in democracies is that the government claims to be elected by and operate only at the will and pleasure of the people; it thus suffers the additional wage of hypocrisy when the administrative state becomes all powerful.

Woodrow Wilson and the progressives drew on the examples of the technocratic intellectuals of the French Revolution, such as Henri de Saint-Simon, in advocating that government could be entrusted to a professional class of unelected but "expert" functionaries, the precursors of modern "technocrats." Professionals supposedly could train and educate less capable, revolving elected and appointed officials. A meritocratic technocracy was supposedly certified by its members' knowledge of science, education and training certificates, and long state expertise. In contrast, elected officials gained legitimacy only from a mercurial and often uninformed mob of voters.

So the current American deep state is depressing in that we have seen it all before in a variety of contexts and different forms of government. We should have learned from history of its dangers to individual freedom and choice. Of all forms of government, democracies should be the least prone to negate the power of the people. But, on the other hand, democratic governments also singularly assume ambitious economic, social, and cultural challenges of bringing parity and equality to all their citizens—and occasionally attempt to nation-build democracies abroad as well. These were the very fears of the Founders, such as Alexander Hamilton and James Madison, who, in drafting the Constitution, sought to avoid Athenian-style democracy and imperialism through federalism and the checks of a constitutional republic.

Or as Robert Nisbet long ago observed of the ironic symbiosis between democracy and bureaucracy, "Through democracy, bureaucracy has constantly expanded, the result of the rising number of social and economic functions taken on by the democratic state. But when bureaucracy reaches a certain degree of mass and power, it becomes almost automatically resistant to any will, including the elected will of the people, that is not of its own making."[5]

Democracies are also masters of institutionalizing fads, popular beliefs, and new ideas. Sometimes they can galvanize the public brilliantly to avoid catastrophes, as in the mobilization during World War II against sudden existential enemies after December 7, 1941, or during the post-Sputnik space program of the 1960s, or during the same decade when the government and larger culture mobilized to address the threat of smoking, or in spring 2020 during the coronavirus pandemic when the United States recalibrated entire industries to meet medical supply demands and successfully created a commercial landscape to hasten a viable COVID-19 vaccination in less than a year.

Sometimes, the speed at which 51 percent consensus is reached and minority views are discredited is also frightening. Transgenderism, climate change, females in frontline combat units, and gay marriage, between 2008 and 2020, were transformed from topics of legitimate discussion and debate into rigid, politically correct orthodoxies—often more by regulators than legislators. When the deep state embraces new normals, its powers to target dissidents and mavericks and redefine them as dangers to the ideas of equality, fairness, and decency can become downright scary.[6]

In some sense, the best definition of the administrative state is just this absorption of the constitutionally separate powers of the executive, legislative, and judicial branches into one omnipotent entity—into the hands of people never elected to their positions of power. The regulator, after all, has no constituency that periodically audits his conduct at the polls. He can create a rule and then become the judge of whether the targeted citizen has broken it. Finally, as an executive, he has the power to enforce upon the offender his own prior legislative and judiciary rulings. In response, the citizen has no direct control over the anonymous bureaucrat. Of course, in theory, the power to elect new representatives and executives who can curtail or expand the deep state ultimately resides with the people. In reality, however, so often elected officials of both parties become overwhelmed by the permanent army of clerks, experts, and civil servants who must brief them, sometimes selectively, on the levers, gears, and wheels of their own vast and sometimes secretive government. Metaphors abound for the relationship, be it the parasite that eventually eats away its host, the Frankensteinian monster that cannot be controlled by its human creator, or the science fiction computer that goes rogue and devours its inventor.

Historically, most champions of constitutional government cautioned against creation of such central boards and bureaucracies and governmental agencies. They worried about the consolidation of the powers to make, enforce, and adjudicate laws. They saw the growth and inflexibility of the state as one of the prime enemies of democratic citizenship. So Alexis de Tocqueville warned, "I think that extreme centralization of government ultimately enervates society, and thus after a length of time weakens the government itself."[7]

The deterrent idea of a separation of powers that led to the foundations of the US Constitution began in ancient Greece, especially in Crete, Sparta, and other city-states. It was institutionalized in Republican Rome and refined and expanded during the British and French Enlightenments. The need to separate power among legislators, executives, and judges rested on a pessimistic view of human nature: officials would always seek to consolidate power and would do so under pretense of service to the public good or noble causes.

Thus, the only remedy to protect the citizen was to ensure that there would be tripartite and competing government interests—all overseen as well by the people, who in turn could elect their own officials. Each concern would be equipped with checks and balances upon the other. The ensuing tension would lead to a forced sharing of power and thereby prevent the inevitable emergence of a monarch, autocrat, or tyrant or rule by the mob—and also supposedly rule by unelected officials inside the government. For the Founders, these precautions would preclude an unelected, all-powerful caste, even though since the age of Aristotle political theorists had warned that once democratic man achieves political equality, he naturally soon expects additional equality in all realms of life—economic, social, and cultural—a dream that by definition demands legions of government regulators and interventionists.[8]

In addition, the deep state functionary is antithetical to the elected citizen official. Bureaucracies comprise workers with set hours. The pay of the bureaucrat is mostly guaranteed. Indeed, it is often higher than in the private sector. The regulator's success or failure is not predicated on the weather, the business cycle, finance, labor, or all the extraneous criteria that can destroy or elevate the self-employed amid a mercurial business cycle. Or it is worse still, given that the regulator's salary is paid by those he regulates—a source of often envy and mistrust?

The crisis is not just the canard that bureaucrats are frustrated utopians or failed entrepreneurs who resent the greater success of the businesspeople they so often regulate, fine, or indict. The paradox is subtler. When one's career is often predicated on various contractual tenures, civil service protections, and seniority, then a billet seems safe, if not guaranteed. An entitled worldview follows that events can and should be commensurately predictable, logical, controllable, and ultimately perfectible. Getting along rather than getting it right becomes institutionalized. The bureaucrat assumes that his own job guarantees and protected competence reflect his critical importance to the nation, in a way not necessarily true of those who grow, truck, or deliver our food and have no such sinecures.

The Internal Revenue Service (IRS) offers a fairly recent example of a Frankensteinian bureaucracy at war with the citizen. From 2010 to 2013, the IRS created a BOLO (be on the lookout) list. Its aim was to check the political affiliations of nonprofits applying for tax-exempt status. Purportedly nonpartisan IRS auditors began focusing on organizations with nomenclature that included supposedly telltale terms like "patriots," "Tea Party," or "Constitution." Lois Lerner, head of the IRS tax-exemption division (who would later be held in contempt of Congress and seek early retirement), inordinately delayed or refused these groups' requests for tax-exempt status.

No IRS official was ever charged with a crime. Yet the agency later offered profuse apologies for wrongdoing. Nonprofits had their applications delayed or deferred—in some cases to the advantage of the Barack Obama reelection campaign in 2012, which benefited from the noncertification of Tea Party–affiliated nonprofits. The boon of using state power to punish enemies outweighed any risk of disclosure and subsequent embarrassment. A certain sense of deterrence was also signaled: nonprofits were warned that it was foolhardy to complain about IRS overreach. The retirement of Lois Lerner, without loss of benefits, reminded the public not that the citizen controlled his bureaucracy but that a major scandal that may have affected a presidential election resulted in only a handful of abbreviated careers and prompted no loss of support for the administration that had unleashed Lerner.

Later studies authored jointly by Andreas Madestam (Stockholm University), Stanley Veuger (American Enterprise Institute), and Daniel Shoag and David Yanagizawa-Drott (Harvard Kennedy School) argued that the Obama administration had essentially weaponized the IRS. It had used its vast powers of bureaucratic oversight for patently partisan purposes and, successfully, to divert votes from Mitt Romney's 2012 campaign.[9]

Sometimes the clout of the administrative state can become tragi-comic. It can creep into the most unimaginable recesses far from Washington but exhibit the same sense of entitlement as those IRS officials who felt they could freely violate their own tax codes in confidence because either the public would never discover their violations or the administration in power would deem their efforts politically useful and thus, if they were caught, more as misdemeanors than felonies. An esoteric but instructive example of the reach of the deep state is the relatively tiny raisin industry of less than five thousand individual growers, seemingly the most unlikely target of a strangulating federal octopus.

In the 1980s and 1990s, I farmed Thompson seedless grapes that were dried into raisins, the fifth generation of my family to have done so on a small 120-acre farm where I still live. When prices crashed during the national recession of 1983, many raisin farmers contemplated not delivering their near worthless crops to packers to be sold. The contracted prices that growers were to receive remained far below the costs of production. Some of us instead planned on stemming and washing our own raisins and, in desperation, selling them directly to farmers' markets and local bakers and small stores—as if our typical-size small farm could ever sell its annual crop of four hundred thousand pounds locally.[10]

Yet the government quickly warned us that to do so was illegal—indeed, it was a federal felony. Bankrupt raisin farmers rediscovered that although they owned their ground and the vines on it, produced the grapes, dried them into raisins, stored them on their property, and lost money in the process, they still did *not own* their crop—or at least not completely.

The federal government in effect owns the nation's annual raisin crop before it is even harvested. Under the auspices of the fossilized, Depression-era Raisin Administrative Committee—created formally and overseen by the US Department of Agriculture in 1947, authorized and operating under the Agricultural Marketing Agreement Act of 1937—the government each year decides what percentage of farmers' raisin crops can be sold within the United States. The US government then confiscates the rest of the year's tonnage once it is delivered to packers. Sometimes the set-asides comprise up to 50 to 75 percent of the year's crop. It is still a crime to keep one's own harvested raisins on the farm without apprising the federal government. And further, it is a criminal act not to deliver to a federally authorized raisin packer any percentage of one's crop designated as a reserve tonnage portion.[11]

Delivered raisins determined to be reserve tonnage are set aside at packers' lots. They are kept off the domestic market and then eventually sold for below-production costs or given away, mostly abroad, as an annual "reserve pool" of raisins. That way the government controls the size of the domestic market and thus the pricing—all paternalistically in the supposed interest of the raisin growers themselves. So under such a marketing order, only raisins delivered to certified packers can be sold domestically once the government determines the percentage of such allowable "free tonnage" saleable within the United States.

Some years in the past, some of the reserve raisin tonnage—occasionally the majority of the crop—was, on the decision of bureaucrats, given away to domestic school lunch programs. It was also sold by administrative edict as animal feed or discounted at below-market prices overseas to create supposed new markets. The net result was often that farmers were forced to hand over much of their crops to the federal government without compensation to cover their costs of production. Again, those who refused or attempted to sell their own raisins without federal set-asides were fined or prosecuted. Again, elected congressional officials *could* serve as the people's auditors to investigate, audit, and punish overreaching bureaucrats. In fact, a mere 535 elected senators and representatives can hardly become acquainted with, much less even read, some 175,496 pages of the *Federal Register* or monitor 2.7 million employees—without the enlistment of more bureaucrats to monitor bureaucrats.[12]

Each year, the federal regulatory state creates far more similar "rules" that have the force of law than laws actually passed by Congress and signed by the president. In 2016, for example, federal departments, agencies, and commissions in toto issued 3,853 new rules and regulations. Yet that year Congress passed, and the president signed into law, only 214 bills. In other words, for every new law, there were eighteen new regulations and rules created by the unelected. Even if our 535 elected federal representatives knew the details of the 214 bills they passed, there is no way they could master the 3,853 new bureaucratic edicts that they did not pass.[13]

One example was the creation by the Environmental Protection Agency (EPA) of a new regulation in May 2015 known as the Clean Water Rule. The unelected EPA decided that under its new statute, it could now extend the law protecting "navigable waters" (streams and wetlands) from pollution and defilement to cover even standing water on private property. The law even extended to local irrigation district canals and ditches that run across private farm property but are neither navigable streams nor wetlands.[14]

Sometimes EPA regulators singled out farmers with low ground that collected temporary storm runoff or with irrigation ditch laterals, arguing that such temporary stagnant pools or tiny weed-filled ditches were subject to water analyses and possible punitive action. In my own environs, it became surreal that, after a dry ditch or low spot in an orchard filled with muddy water after a series of storms, farmers were apprehensive that either state or federal environmental officials might show up to test the water in order to determine whether the farmer was culpable of polluting an "inland waterway."

The point is that the bureaucracy had decided to reinterpret the law either to enhance its power over citizens or to advance an agenda it deemed to be in the state's long-term interest. And it often did so in violation of or indifference to the original intent of the Congress that passed the legislation. The EPA acted as a combined legislative, judicial, and executive entity that by fiat infringed on the citizen's private property. The aggrieved, of course, could always go to federal court to sue the federal government for overreach, but with limited means in comparison to the bureaucracy's legal resources.

The Clean Water Rule was just one of many efforts by federal government employees to harass small business owners, on the false premise that myriads of new regulations were cost-effective to society—or reflected proper and vital agendas that only experts such as themselves, certainly not an otherwise ignorant public, could appreciate. But, as public policy critic Oren Cass, for example, has pointed out, the drive for massive regulations is the work of elites who a priori assume that they have the money and influence to ensure the economic consequences of their new rules fall mostly on the working classes rather than on themselves: "Social justice activists argue that low-income and minority communities suffer disproportionally from pollution, therefore aggressive regulation advances a redistributive agenda. But the cost of constraining industrial activity lands far more disproportionally on blue-collar workers than does any benefit. They are the ones asked to 'pay' the most for environmental gains that high-income households value at least as highly."[15]

These fears of the unelected aggregating legislative, judicial, and executive power grew more pointed in the administration of Donald J. Trump. Because the bipartisan establishment and the professional classes of Washington disliked Trump so widely, especially in comparison to his far more accommodating predecessor Barack Obama, he uniquely became a test case of administrative overreach. The administrative state often saw the purportedly noble end of aborting his unpopular administration as justifying the often extraordinary and unconstitutional means of achieving it.

Trump campaigned not so much, as other conservatives had, on the financial waste, fraud, and abuse of the growing federal regulatory and administrative bureaucracy. Rather, he harangued on its perceived sinister ability to curtail the freedoms and opportunities of everyday citizens and to take out bothersome individuals such as himself. It was almost as if he were daring the administrative state to reveal its true nature by turning on him.

So "deep state" became by late 2016 a more common pejorative for the old "bureaucracy." The neologism implies that the functionaries of federal agencies comprised an organic entity "deeply" burrowed into the sinews of tax-payer-subsidized government. They thrived irrespective of elected overseers and often freelanced preemptively to emasculate perceived elected critics.[16]

Yet, in pushback, many in the federal government also recalibrated their own language and defense of the administrative state. The bureaucracy now praised rather than shied away from acknowledging a professional, permanent guild of what it called experts. This was especially true of the diplomatic corps, the current and retired military, the intelligence agencies, and the executive branch at large. Most dropped prior pretenses that they were supposedly apolitical and selfless technocrats with knowledge and skills lacking among elected officials and the mass of voters.

Now their redefined role "as adults in the room"—a much-used establishment phrase for those obstructing the president—was to act as custodians of normal protocols against dangerous "populists" and interloping "nationalists." Such advocacy was especially true of the intelligence and military communities that increasingly took on the look of a political party, eager to joust with elected officials who complained about either their incompetence or their partisanship or both.[17]

The bureaucratic threat, then, to classical citizenship is an ascendance of a virtual, unelected aristocracy or rigged oligarchy that exercises power in a manner that does not reflect consensual government. As part of their guardianship, the deep-state auditors were always on the lookout for trespassers like Donald Trump. His supposed uncouth and unethical presidency, they argued, might harm invaluable institutions such as the Federal Bureau of Investigation (FBI) or the Central Intelligence Agency (CIA) for posterity. Clearly, then, deep-state career officials supposedly were more than warranted to find ways, in partnership with the media, to mitigate the damage of any perceived populist mountebank like Trump.

Without a disinterested and investigated media, neither citizens nor their elected officials have any means of monitoring the huge federal octopus. For example, in 2020, four years after the FBI's extraordinary surveillance of Trump campaign officials, incriminating official internal bureau communications were finally released. Documents revealed that individual agents had worried about their own illegal behavior—to the degree that they fretted that even their government tenure might not save them from legal consequences. Thus many had purchased individual professional liability insurance policies to protect them from future civil suits lodged by those they had stealthily targeted and eventually ruined.[18]

Like those of the IRS, career Pentagon, State Department, or regulatory officials can draw on a wealth of bureaucratic contacts and lifelong knowledge of the permanent government to bend the will of a newly elected president. Days after the inauguration of Donald Trump, on January 31, 2017, the *Washington Post* reported, "180 federal employees have signed up for a workshop next weekend, where experts will offer advice on workers' rights and how they can express civil disobedience." The report also noted that federal employees were in "regular consultation with recently departed Obama-era political appointees" to affect the operation of their agencies to reflect political agendas. Among their strategies to undermine the incoming administration were instructions about slowing their work, at least if they felt they had differences with their new supervisors' instructions.[19]

A good admission of the arrogance of the deep state and its assurance that it knew government far better and could manipulate it far more effectively than the transitory elected administration came from controversial former FBI director James Comey. In a televised interview, he explained why and how as director he was able to insert his agents into the newly inaugurated Trump White House to interrogate National Security Advisor Michael Flynn. Comey did so without asking the permission of the president or his cabinet and without tipping Flynn off that the meeting might be adversarial and that thus having legal counsel present might be in Flynn's interest:

> I sent them. . . . Something we've, I, probably wouldn't have done or maybe gotten away with in a more organized investigation, a more organized administration. In the George W. Bush administration . . . or the Obama administration. . . . In both of those administrations there was process. . . . So if the FBI wanted to send agents into the White House itself to interview a senior official, you would work through the White House counsel and there would be discussions and approvals and it would be there. I thought, "It's early enough, let's just send a couple of guys over."[20]

The locus classicus of bureaucratic freelancing was the FBI and Department of Justice (DOJ) abuse of the Foreign Intelligence Surveillance Act (FISA) court process during the 2016 campaign and the first year of the Trump presidency. The inspector general of the Justice Department, Michael Horowitz, found that the FBI had systematically violated its own rules of conduct in deceiving or misleading FISA court judges in order to obtain surveillance of a minor Trump campaign official, Carter Page, on erroneous accusations of colluding with Russian interests. The voluminous Horowitz report confirmed almost all the key points of House Intelligence Committee chairman Devin Nunes's official report of his committee's findings about the FBI role in obtaining FISA surveillance. Most of the claims in his counterpart Representative Adam Schiff's contrasting minority report were discredited or exposed as untruths.[21]

Controversy followed the report concerning the reason why an apparently rogue FBI had sought to destroy citizen Page by surveilling and leaking false information about his purported profiteering and intrigue with high Russian officials. Good arguments were made that FBI and CIA operatives systematically targeted Trump's campaign staff on accusations of collusion that were never substantiated. Such administrative state paranoia illustrated institutional fears that the new president Trump was highly critical of and determined to prune what he called the "swamp."

By summer 2020, Christopher Steele, author of the dossier that supposedly had corroborated the Russian collusion hoax, had admitted that his research was unverifiable and his "research" notes destroyed. That fact had earlier been noted but ignored by the FBI in long-suppressed internal memos.

In addition, newly released federal documents showed that in fact Steele himself had relied on an unreliable Russian fantasist, Igor Danchenko. The latter had a criminal record and had been accused in the past of working for the Russian government. Yet Danchenko was employed at the Brookings Institution as a "researcher," and his various roles were likely known for some time to the FBI.

In this labyrinth of deceit, the US government was using the concoctions of a likely Russian asset and British ex-spy to compile dirt on Carter Page, a US citizen, himself once valued by the CIA as a helpful source. In sum, bureaucrats were colluding with those claiming to be in contact with Russian sources to concoct a crime of "Russian collusion" against one of their own informants, who was voluntarily offering them any expertise he possessed about Russia.[22]

Earlier in April 2020, amid the panic of the coronavirus epidemic, Inspector General Horowitz issued a second and subsequent report about FBI conduct in requesting FISA warrants that transcended the Trump campaign investigations. He additionally found a pattern of systematic abuse and disingenuousness on the part of the FBI lawyers, including thirty-nine major defects in forty-two applications. Translated, that means the FBI was habitually, improperly, or illegally monitoring American citizens by systematically deceiving a federal judge to obtain permission for such surveillance.[23]

In May 2020, still more federal documents were declassified. They included those from top FBI officials that showed how they had staged a January 24, 2017, interview with newly appointed National Security Advisor Michael Flynn. The FBI's clear intention was to snare Flynn in a perjury trap, or to charge him under the ossified Logan Act, or simply to so harass him that he might resign.

Before the agents—sent by Director Comey, who bragged of his audacity—went into the White House to interview Flynn, FBI supervisor Bill Priestap took handwritten notes of his briefing with them: "What's our goal? Truth/Admission or to get him to lie, so we can prosecute him or get him fired? If we get him to admit to breaking the Logan Act, give facts to DOJ & have them decide. Or, if he initially lies, then we present him [redacted] & he admits it, document for DOJ, & let them decide how to address it."

Eventually Flynn resigned, after promising Vice President Michael Pence that he had not discussed sanctions with the Russian ambassador during the presidential transition. That assertion, the FBI and other government agencies knew, did not square with their intercepted communications. A frightened Flynn essentially misled the vice president about a conversation of the sort that was not wrong and certainly common during presidential transitions. Flynn soon was nearly bankrupted by legal fees. The FBI and DOJ pressured him with threats to indict his son on questionable grounds. And he was charged with lying to FBI agents sent by special counsel Robert Mueller's investigation team—only to withdraw his guilty pleas upon the release of exonerating documents suggesting a government ambush. Flynn finally was freed from prosecution when DOJ officials dropped all charges—only to have a Washington judge refuse to end the case and instead call in a retired partisan justice to determine whether Flynn should be jailed anyway. A presidential pardon finally ended this entire sordid abuse of power.[24]

Nearly a half century ago, sociologist Robert Nisbet, writing in the wake of the Watergate scandal and the postwar growth of intelligence agencies, lamented,

> As everyone knows, it has been, since World War II under FDR, a constantly widening cloak or umbrella for government actions of every conceivable degree of power, stealth, and cunning by an ever-expanding corps of government officials. As we now know in detail, the utilization of the FBI and other paramilitary agencies by the President and other high executive department officers for the purposes of eavesdropping, electronic bugging, and similarly intimate penetrations of individual privacy goes straight back to FDR, and the practice has only intensified and widened ever since. Naturally, all such royalist invasions have been justified, right down to Watergate under the name of national security.[25]

What is now different from—and scarier than—past abuses is the radical change in attitude of the media and progressive community to such government abuse and overreach. If both were once careful to monitor FBI and CIA abuses, they now rationalize them. Both institutions, as is perhaps reminiscent of the New Deal era, see government power as a positive, a means of bypassing obstructive opposition to progressive agendas.

If some citizens, such as Carter Page, must be surveilled, even if illegally and unethically, or if a rambunctious and wayward general like Michael Flynn should be kept out of government and be reverse-targeted by the government surveillance of those with whom he spoke, then the liberal media assumes that such troublemakers should not have raised the suspicions of the state in the first place. If, in the Watergate age, the media inherently distrusted the permanent Washington bureaucracy, during the Trump administration journalists inherently distrusted those who distrusted the permanent Washington bureaucracy. All of these establishment "professionals" could condemn the excesses of Donald Trump; almost none would fault the excesses of professionals, in circular fashion, supposedly justified by the excesses of Donald Trump.

Given that progressivism self-identifies as a protector of civil liberties against government infringement on the rights of the individual, such modern overreach of the sort from 2015 to 2017 became a question of who will police the police. No public official, pundit, or media star who trafficked in the Steele dossier came forward to apologize to the public. Not one. None admitted that in prior court or congressional testimony, under oath, they had possessed no evidence to substantiate their often-televised wild charges.

For the bipartisan establishment, high rank in the deep state now exudes professionalism. It reflects trust in government. Selfless public servants put their exceptional talents in service to the public. And they sometimes note that they might have earned far more lucrative compensation in the private sector had they been less public spirited and more profit minded. Indeed, the sobriquet "deep state" became a badge of honor. And in most cases all this is true.

In contrast, the "shallow state" soon became a pejorative term for ignorant outsiders like those of the Trump administration who struggled to find even mediocre replacement talent, once they had ostracized the seasoned professional classes of Western government. Trump, for example, ran against both the Democratic Party and the Republican Party's veteran politicians, such as the Bush family, Mitt Romney, and many of the marquee veterans dating back to the George H. W. Bush and George W. Bush administrations.[26]

Another good example of how the administrative state, along with the media, judges its own came during special counsel Robert Mueller's 2017–2019 investigations of alleged Russian collusion and obstruction. Mueller put together what the media immediately dubbed a "powerhouse" lineup of career legal and investigatory bureaucrats. The team was peremptorily declared the veritable winner that would shortly dismantle Donald Trump's motley collection of inept and aged has-been lawyers.

At the outset, credentials—apparently defined as prior revolving-door government posts—seemed to be all that mattered. A *Vox* headline on August 2, 2017, summed up the progressive exuberance of the time: "Meet the all-star legal team who may take down Trump." The subtitle then clarified, "Special counsel Robert Mueller's legal team is full of pros. Trump's team makes typos." The media almost immediately recharacterized what had been authorized as an inquiry as a "takedown" by "pros" of the half-educated who could not spell—a referendum, as it were, on the sophisticated deep state versus those supposedly clueless about it.

As members of the Washington media perused the résumés of the New York and Washington government revolving-door veteran prosecutors and veterans of all sorts of federal bureaucracies and the prestigious Washington legal firm of WilmerHale, they soon became giddy. Indeed, Washington journalists immediately began writing of a "dream team" of "all-stars," a veritable "hunter-killer team." *Wired* immediately boasted of Mueller's team, "From the list of hires, it's clear, in fact, that Mueller is recruiting perhaps the most high-powered and experienced team of investigators ever assembled by the Justice Department."

If "high-powered" was the signature adjective of the Left, then the add-on superlative "ever assembled" was supposed to sound downright scary. Again, prior government service at the top levels of the FBI and DOJ and degrees from supposedly top-notch law schools—not necessarily long records of successful prosecutions in a variety of spheres—were taken for granted as proof of excellence.[27]

In contrast, Trump would predictably have little access to the bureaucratic elite and instead only to a limited pool of supposedly C-team legal talent due to a variety of reasons, from his status as an outsider and disrupter, to his known reputation for being mercurial and difficult with his own attorneys, to fear of career jeopardy that might accrue to any lawyer who defended him. No wonder he was soon supposedly bereft of Beltway legal resources entirely. Or as an NPR editorialist in June 2017 condescendingly tried to explain Trump's hapless plight, "If you asked a Washington insider to come up with a legal dream team for a situation like this, it's highly unlikely this is who they would come up with. But President Trump came into office as an outsider and continues to operate that way, and in a way his legal team is a reflection of that as well." Note the lack of any appreciation of irony in the use of "outsider" and "insider," as if they conveyed any notion of innate competence aside from tenure in Washington, DC.

Trump was certainly a difficult client for any attorney. And he was to be joined by sixty-nine-year-old Ty Cobb, an oddly named, rotund, eccentric-looking barrister. With his handlebar mustache, Cobb was typecast and caricatured in contrast to the suave, cool, and much younger Mueller head lawyer, the feared prosecutor Andrew Weiss- mann. Cobb's partner was initially John Dowd, a seventy-eight-year-old lawyer with degrees from Southern Benedictine College and Emory. Dowd seemed to the media another slow-talking, has-been lawyer who looked and acted his age. Hip and woke he was not.

Sixty-three-year-old TV and radio host Jay Sekulow, another Trump counselor, was a frequent Christian Broadcast Network and Fox News Channel commentator—and therefore an object of even more elite derision. The media often emphasized that Sekulow was a Christian convert and Messianic Jew. His degrees from Mercer and Regent uni- versities did not, for the most part, impress legal commentators. Nor did his job as past chief counsel for the conservative American Center for Law and Justice.[28]

Trump further confirmed the stereotype of a rube in autumn 2018 when he brought in the husband-and-wife team of Jane and Mar- tin Raskin as legal replacements and additions. The *Washington Post* headline could scarcely disguise its disdain—and glee: "Trump needed new lawyers for Russia probe. He found them at a tiny Florida firm."

One might have rejoined that geographical, chorological, and educational experience had advantages perhaps lacked by Beltway firms that recruited talent with predictable career and educational résumés.

The average age of Trump's original four-man, top-echelon legal guard of Cobb, Dowd, Sekulow, and Rudy Giuliani was seventy-one. None had a Yale, Harvard, Columbia, Chicago, or Stanford law degree. *Vox* remarked of another Trump attorney, Michael Bowe, and of Sekulow, "The last two are known more for their time on TV than their time in the courtroom, and don't have anywhere near the background Mueller's team boasts to take on this challenge." But, in fact, in terms of classical definitions of citizenship, the ancient reverence for experience and age, and modern ideas of diversity, perhaps the Trump team did indeed have the proper background.[29]

Soon deep-state legal and ethical blunders, not those of the outsiders, characterized the entire twenty-two-month, nearly $40 million Mueller investigation. Two of Mueller's all-stars, Lisa Page and Peter Strzok, were dismissed. The two had engaged in an unprofessional, stealth adulterous relationship while assembling an embarrassing phone text trove of expressed hate for Trump and his supporters, the very targets of their supposedly unbiased investigation.

Another all-star legal eagle, Kevin Clinesmith, was later found to have altered a document presented in a FISA warrant application. He faced felony indictment to which he eventually pled guilty. In an act of apparent illegality, on the eve of an inspector general's investigation into government wrongdoing, members of the Mueller team wiped clean the data from twenty-four of their own government-issued phones. They apparently feared, after their own failure to find grounds for a Trump indictment, that their communications would become part of the public record—and thus an incriminating narrative of their own partisanship, incompetence, and unlawful behavior. And the wrongdoing was multifold, given the mysterious loss of phone and text records, the suppressed circumstances surrounding the firing of Lisa Page and Peter

Strzok, and Mueller's own baffling testimony *under oath* to Congress. The special counsel bizarrely claimed ignorance about the key players and facts in his own investigation, from the Fusion GPS oppositional research team to the Steele dossier itself.

Worse, Mueller early on had grasped that he had little evidence to fulfill his primary mandate of investigating supposed Russian collusion with members of the Trump campaign to warp the 2016 election and instead turned to the DOJ-authorized blank check to investigate "any matters that arose or may arise directly from the investigation." Nonetheless, instead of apprising his superiors in the Department of Justice of his inability to find collusion, he sought to prolong and divert his mission into a hunting expedition that in the end was reduced to hopes of laying perjury traps and concocted obstruction charges for the president. As Trump lawyer John Dowd later put it, "That is when I knew he [Mueller] had lied to me in our original meeting (June 16, 2017) and every meeting thereafter. Robert Mueller—'D.C.'s great man'—completely and deliberately misled us in order to set up a perjury/false statement trap for POTUS. It was a monstrous lie and scheme to defraud."[30]

Some of the Mueller all-star team had proven indiscreetly partisan in broadcasting their anti-Trump venom before coming aboard. Weissmann, for example, had quite publicly announced that he attended a Hillary Clinton "victory" party on election night and later sent an email congratulating acting Trump attorney general and former Obama appointee Sally Yates for her stonewalling of a Trump executive order.[31]

In the end, the Mueller investigation, the FBI's various leaked investigations into the Trump campaign, transition, and administration, the so-called Steele dossier, and the "Russian collusion" narrative were *all* proved to be fantasy based though politically useful. Former federal prosecutor Andrew McCarthy summed up the "Ball of Collusion" charade as "counterintelligence as a pretext for a criminal investigation in search of a crime; a criminal investigation as a pretext for impeachment without an impeachable offense; an impeachment inquiry as a pretext for rendering the Donald Trump un-reelectable; and all of it designed as a straightjacket around his presidency."[32]

In reductionist terms, unelected bureaucrats had tried their best to overturn an election and deprive citizens of their right to elect whomever they wished as their president. Yet another example of the unelected resistance to an elected president was the case of "Anonymous," an unnamed "senior administration official" who, in a September 5, 2018, *New York Times* op-ed, unwittingly described a cabal in government. The writer thought of trying to declare Trump non compos mentis and having him removed from the presidency through the Twenty-Fifth Amendment, which entailed a clumsy process of the vice president and the cabinet instigating removal processes by a majority vote to refer their decision to the Congress. But then Anonymous thought better of it. So in his yarn, his colleagues resigned themselves to keep the government alive by thwarting the president until the Trump cancer was gone "one way or another": "Given the instability many witnessed, there were early whispers within the cabinet of invoking the 25th Amendment, which would start a complex process for removing the president. But no one wanted to precipitate a constitutional crisis. So we will do what we can to steer the administration in the right direction until— one way or another—it's over."[33]

Nowhere did Anonymous note that the president was duly elected by the people, in a way he himself was not. Also different in the age of Trump was an unabashed audacity in such resistance to the elected president, who has legal authority over executive agency employees. It was as if the vote of the citizenry in 2016 could and should be nullified by a group of bureaucrats with no such constituency. Nonetheless, Anonymous believed that he and others would thwart presidential orders in hopes of forcing the issue of presidential removal.

In late October 2020, just days before the election, Anonymous outed himself. Far from being an idealistic "senior administration official" (in the words of the *New York Times*), the author, Miles Taylor, was a relatively minor staffer in the Department of Homeland Security. Rather than a staunch conservative who felt betrayed by his president, Taylor, who had left government to work for Google, by 2020 had become a political activist in the NeverTrump campaign effort. Had Taylor simply resigned to shop his anti-Trump manifesto under his own name, then no major newspaper would have published it—given his low-level status, his lack of any prior government, literary, or academic achievement, and his obvious partisanship.

Yet the idea of a high-ranking mole, purportedly in the top echelons of the Trump administration, boasting that there were legions like him resisting an elected president provided a mutually beneficial hoax for the *Times*. The gambit ensured a lucrative platform for Anonymous-Taylor to land a book deal as a follow-up to his *New York Times* piece. In the end, Taylor and the *New York Times* merely accomplished further tarnishing of their reputations.

Worse, Taylor further deceived the nation by not coming forward earlier when the media had falsely identified Trump administration loyalist Victoria Coates as Anonymous. Indeed, Taylor not only denied he was Anonymous but fanned suspicions that it might be Coates by declaring, "No I'm not. . . . I've got my own thoughts on who that might be." Taylor finally came clean only when the Anonymous brand was no longer viable in leveraging either notoriety, profits, or anti-Trump momentum but apparently retained some marginal value as an "October surprise" in the final days before the election.[34]

Far more powerful bureaucrats than Miles Taylor, during their tenures and in their retirements, felt that the unelected should exercise authority over officials elected by the citizens. In autumn 2019, former acting CIA chief John McLaughlin proclaimed in a public forum, "Thank God for the deep state!"

McLaughlin was seconded by former CIA director John Brennan. The latter had previously admitted to lying on two occasions to

Congress while under oath—without legal consequences. Brennan praised the "deep-state people" for their marshaling of bureaucratic forces in opposition to Trump. He bragged that his former colleagues were analogous to soldiers in the trenches as they fought a comparable war against an elected president. But Brennan left unsaid that both the FBI and CIA had hired contractors to serve as informants to snoop about and monitor an ongoing presidential campaign, in pursuit of disrupting and indeed destroying a presidential candidacy.[35]

Less than a month into the Trump presidency, in mid-February 2017, former establishment conservative insider and later fervent NeverTrumper Bill Kristol tweeted out that he apparently preferred a coup by the administrative state to remove Trump if the constitutional means were not viable: "Obviously strongly prefer normal democratic and constitutional politics. But if it comes to it, prefer the deep state to the Trump state." Translated, "if it comes to it" meant that Kristol preferred the unlawful action of the unelected to the constitutional system that monitored any administration. "Deep state" was no longer a pejorative. It had become the brag of a Washington caste that felt itself more entitled to power and legitimacy than those elected through "democratic and constitutional politics."

Bob Woodward every year or so writes an insider's muckraking account of Washington politics. He had alleged that retired General James Mattis, serving in the Trump administration as secretary of defense, was so exasperated over policy disagreements with the president that he discussed with other high officials an intervention against an "unfit" and "dangerous" commander in chief. Or, as Mattis reportedly remarked to Dan Coates, the director of national intelligence, "There may come a time when we have to take collective action." If Woodward has accurately reported this quotation, one wonders why Mattis felt that he had the power or wisdom to unilaterally decide to even think about nullifying a US election and apparently to take steps to remove or emasculate an elected president.[36]

Apparently a "coup" became increasingly a part of the general discourse of bipartisan resistance to Trump among those unapologetic about removing a president before a scheduled election. The once unthinkable idea of a coup renewed confidence in the permanent state's efforts to oust Trump—or in fact anyone in the future deemed dangerous like him. The point again is not whether one voted for or loathed Trump but whether an unelected group of federal officials has a right to destroy a presidency on grounds of some "higher" cause and thus overturn an American election.

Retired generals, admirals, and intelligence heads now routinely appear as highly paid consultants on network and cable news shows. Some, almost immediately upon retirement, often land lucrative billets on corporate defense contractor boards. Apparently, defense suppliers consider their past knowledge and enduring influence with former subordinates in arms procurement and Pentagon bidding invaluable and pay them accordingly.

Many in retirement maintain top-secret security clearances, an entitlement rarely questioned. They are befriended by politicians and media celebrities alike. Often the most successful of them, especially State Department and national security officials, are enshrined as bipartisan "wise men" to be called upon in extremis by flummoxed American presidents, such as during the perceived stalemates of the Vietnam and Iraq wars.[37]

Yet traditionally CIA and FBI directors, the heads of the National Security Agency (NSA) and national intelligence, our highest-ranking military officers, and those who float among the State Department, military, intelligence agencies, and White House, both current and retired, were at least nominally apolitical. Their loyalties were first to the US Constitution. Their apolitical rationale was logical and twofold. First, by definition, in their three- or four-decade careers, high-ranking military and intelligence officers were asked to serve both Republican and Democratic administrations without partisanship. Second, they wielded such enormous power to marshal troops, to surveille, and to disseminate and massage intelligence reports that shape US foreign and even domestic policies that even the hint of political agendas might make them suspect—if not dangerous—in the public eye and thereby discredit the reputation of our most key services.

To be blunt, top-ranking officers, active and retired, in the military, CIA, FBI, NSA, and Defense Intelligence Agency have enormous ability to do either great good or great evil. And they can do so with the veneer of bipartisanship or disinterested government service, without a great deal of immediate oversight or repercussions when they err.

Periodically, the elected government pushes back. Sometimes furor arises over the incompetence of the military-intelligence complex. For example, it had little inkling of the Yom Kippur War, the Iranian Revolution of 1979, the Pakistani detonation of a nuclear bomb, the sudden collapse of the Soviet Union, the planned attacks on 9/11, the status of Saddam Hussein's weapons of mass destruction arsenal, the threat of the postwar insurrection in Iraq, the turmoil in Libya, or the rise of the ISIS caliphate.

On other occasions, outrage follows disclosures that the FBI, CIA, NSA, and military intelligence have become too intrusive and adept at spying. Or rather such agencies have become politicized and used their enormous powers of surveillance either in service of a particular ideology or political party or to preserve their own authority and influence—and often wielded them directly against elected critics and the American public. If in the past the Left deemed these federal organizations dangerous due to the conservatives and hyper-nationalists in their ranks, in the present they have earned equal suspicion from the Right that they are overly progressive, with a culture deeply skeptical of American influence and power abroad but eager to use it to advance agendas at home.[38]

The most famous—and to some infamous—check on the military-intelligence complex was the 1975 hearings of Senator Frank Church

(D-ID) on alleged abuses of the CIA, FBI, NSA, and IRS. The investigations nominally focused on supposed abuses during the recent Richard Nixon administration (1969–1974). But soon they encompassed wrongdoing dating back to the early 1950s. The Church Senate Committee—formally known as the United States Senate Select Committee to Study Governmental Operations with Respect to Intelligence Activities—issued a damning report in 1976. It charged the CIA with a series of targeted killings and assassination attempts on foreign leaders. It accused the US Army of spying on civilians and the NSA of intercepting the mail of private citizens and compiling "watch lists" of US citizens to be surveilled. The committee blasted the FBI for hounding American critics through illegal wiretaps and the use of informants.

The committee's findings were themselves predicated on the turbulent landscape of the 1960s and 1970s. They were seen as a liberal triumph over frightening government abuse, itself allegedly fueled by false patriotism and dark conservative worldviews redolent of the Cold War. Church had formed his committee in reaction to the Watergate scandal and resignation of President Nixon, with overwhelming bipartisan congressional support, in 1975. It was soon deemed authoritative after some fifty thousand pages of abuses were declassified and released to the public a year later. However, in the aftermath of the 2001 terrorist attacks on New York and Washington, DC, conservatives sometimes damned the late Senator Church ex post facto for constructing so many firewalls obstructing the intelligence agencies' mutual cooperation that the 9/11 plotters easily escaped detection as they sought to destroy the World Trade Center, the Pentagon, and the US Capitol. Such walls may have prevented the so-called twentieth hijacker's computer from being examined before 9/11.

Yet, after the news reports of the George W. Bush administration's "enhanced interrogation" of detained terrorists at US facilities at Guantánamo Bay, Cuba, and the Obama administration's misuse of the FBI, CIA, DOJ, and FISA courts to surveille the campaign and transition of President Trump, many Americans were once again convinced that the unelected military-intelligence complex had far too little oversight and far too much power.[39]

Recently many in the military and intelligence agencies, both active and retired, have acted in ways that can only be described as surreal. Some have committed crimes—leaked classified documents to the media, altered documents, destroyed evidence, lied under oath to congressional committees, illegally surveilled American citizens, unmasked redacted names and passed them on to the press, inserted informants into political campaigns, set perjury ambushes to entrap other federal officials, and in public attacked bitterly the commander in chief and other high-ranking administration officials.

All acted without the citizens' knowledge. Much less did they seek or earn approval for such behavior. These baleful actors in the current military-intelligence complex have two common denominators. First, they had either politicized the bureaucracies they directed or in retirement used their influence to weaponize them. Second, by 2021 these current and retired officials had worked in concert with the media to amplify their activism and rarely faced legal consequences for conduct that was often illegal.

Former FBI director James Comey unintentionally emblemizes one theme in ironic fashion in his memoir *A Higher Loyalty*. Comey inadvertently publicized the deep state's sanctimonious notion that violating laws and protocols in service of its own purported higher ethical agendas—in this case, opposition to the controversial president Donald J. Trump—was more than justified. Comey, for example, after he was fired, leaked classified memos of confidential conversations with the president in a successful gambit to force the appointment of a special counsel. Eventually his former FBI associate and close friend Robert Mueller would be tasked with investigating Trump's supposed "Russian collusion."[40]

Comey failed to mention in his numerous interviews and memoir that under congressional questioning he had claimed on some

245 occasions, usually in the context of compromising and self-incriminating information, that he simply could not remember or had no idea how to answer. From 2015 to 2020 Comey issued a series of questionable denials of his culpability in leaking confidential or classified documents, misleading FISA courts, ordering FBI agents to conduct suspect investigations, hiring the disreputable and eventually discredited Christopher Steele, and personally deceiving the president of the United States about the latter's being the target of an ongoing FBI investigation. Comey seemed to have little clue that a constitutional republic cannot function when its highest law enforcement officers simply will not or cannot answer simple questions under oath about their own purportedly illegal conduct.[41]

As unelected bureaucrats, those in the military-intelligence complex often show little appreciation of elected officials—much less realization that they themselves are appointed fixtures of the state. The deep state gains legitimacy only through appointment, while elected officials do so only through the voters. In popular American mythology, far-fetched stories of military coups, rogue officers, and revolts are common and often subjects of Hollywood movies like *Seven Days in May*, *Dr. Strangelove*, *The Rock*, and *Taps*—perhaps because heretofore such attempts have been rare or nearly nonexistent in the history of the American republic and are not periodic dangers. It is an American conceit that "tin-horn dictators" in Latin America who take power through coups and "strongmen" in the Arab world who assassinate their way to power or rig elections reflect extraconstitutional agendas impossible in the United States.

The now familiar Hollywood conspiracy genre channeled the tensions arising in the Joseph McCarthy era over the Cold War between former wartime allies the United States and the Soviet Union as well as Mao Tse-tung's unexpected communist takeover of China. Beginning in late 1945, a few conservative American military icons such Generals George S. Patton, Douglas MacArthur, and Curtis LeMay had questioned US wartime alliances with the Soviet Union and its communist appendages. These themes fed stereotypes of a cabal of fervent right-wing revanchists willing to disobey the orders of both military and civilian overseers in order to seize power and supposedly restore a lost constitutional America. All then were portrayed as potential threats to the American citizen and indeed the very idea of citizenship itself.

In reality, the dangers of an overreaching military and intelligence community rarely stemmed exclusively or even predominately from the Right—despite the constant warnings to the public of the dangers of rogue right-wing generals. The landscape of the Washington-centric military and especially intelligence agencies was predominately centrist or liberal. A progressive media that was always ready to fixate on a supposed furtive bemedaled right-wing insurrectionist or a Reaganite spook, such as CIA director William Casey, was ill-equipped to consider the deformation of military or intelligence institutions by the Left.

Journalists and academics assume that the CIA and military in particular have now evolved to become journalistic allies, not media adversaries. Both are occasionally seen as a far more rapid and sure mechanism to enact social change than lobbying for such agendas in the Congress, and they are often praised for their attention to rapid implementation of liberal reforms. Both represent a supposedly professional "deep-state" class that can resist supposedly know-nothing populism.[42]

Almost immediately after the 2016 election, a loose opposition group of current and former government officials and Washington functionaries, self-described as The #Resistance, sought to unify critics of the elected president. Defeated candidate Hillary Clinton, who did not entirely accept the verdict of the election, given the electorally irrelevant fact that she had won the popular vote by a wide margin, symbolically joined it. She announced in May 2017, "I'm now back to being an activist citizen and part of the resistance." She further promised to create a "resistance" political action committee.

The melodrama about "The Resistance" soon proved no mere pipe dream. Inspector General Michael Horowitz discovered communications between a high-ranking partisan FBI lawyer, Kevin Clinesmith, and fellow FBI lawyer Sally Moyer, in which Clinesmith insisted that he had no intention of resigning after the Trump inauguration ("Viva [*sic*] le [*sic*] resistance"). Clinesmith, however, worried that his signature was on incriminating documents that might put him in legal jeopardy ("Plus, my god damned name is all over the legal documents investigating his staff"). In August 2020, Clinesmith, a former member of the Mueller "all-stars," pled guilty to a federal felony of deliberately concocting evidence in a FISA warrant application, including altering a federal document submitted as evidence to the court.

The resistance nomenclature was melodramatic but also revealing. The president's opponents did not call themselves the traditional "loyal opposition" or even see themselves as mere "opponents." Instead, they deliberately chose a term from World War II's occupied France. La Résistance fighters had formed "underground" alliances across French society, especially to organize military attacks on the Nazi occupation forces and their Vichy collaborators.

Again, lost in all the frenzy was the central truth that the inaugurated Donald Trump was elected president for four years in a US election, as outlined by the Constitution and as approved by the citizens of the nation, and would exit only as a result of impeachment and conviction, resignation, a successful executive and congressional effort to declare him seriously mentally or physically unfit under the Twenty-Fifth Amendment, or a failed reelection bid in a constitutionally mandated four years. Any attempt to alter that apparently unhappy legal reality and to remove an inaugurated, sitting president, either in a way not specified by the Constitution or by perverting the spirit and letter of the law, was not patriotic and itself could soon turn unconstitutional if not insurrectionary.

Yet, just ten days after Trump's inauguration, Washington insider lawyer Rosa Brooks—a well-known and respected former adviser in the Obama administration to State Department legal adviser Harold Koh and a former special counsel to the president at George Soros's Open Society Institute—in *Foreign Policy* magazine offered the nation formal specific advice about *removing* the sitting president.

Brooks, remember, unlike the inaugurated President Trump, had never been elected to anything. She was no longer serving in government. But she seemed to sum up bipartisan Washington fears about the incoming administration in an article ominously titled "Three Ways to Get Rid of President Trump Before 2020." In it, she validated the acceptability of doing almost anything to prevent the elected president from remaining long in office. In other words, Brooks had needed a little over a week after the inauguration to conclude that Trump had to be ousted from his elected office by means other than a lost election in 2020.[43]

One might wonder not why a former government official of the now out party felt that a president was unqualified for office but rather by what logic she believed unelected administrators had a right, even a duty, to remove an elected president whom they did not particularly like. In her essay, Brooks first offered to the troubled military and diplomatic communities the option of immediate impeachment—but as a sort of European parliamentary vote of no confidence. Brooks reassured her readers, "If impeachment seems like a fine solution to you, the good news is that Congress doesn't need evidence of actual treason or murder to move forward with an impeachment. Practically anything can be considered a 'high crime or misdemeanor.'" Note her emphasis on "anything," which is a complete misreading of the precise constitutional language of grounds for impeachment—"Treason, Bribery, or other high Crimes and Misdemeanors."[44]

For those readers who might cringe at the broadness of "practically anything can be considered" an impeachable crime, Brooks next pointed to the fallback position of invoking the Twenty-Fifth Amendment:

"In these dark days, some around the globe are finding solace in the 25th Amendment to the Constitution." Here she advanced the idea to her apparently international audience that Trump could be immediately declared mentally unfit and removed from office. Also troubling was her seeming focus on "some around the globe," as if the effort to remove prematurely an elected US president were properly an ecumenical effort of the like-minded cosmopolitans of the sort discussed in the final chapter.

Brooks was clairvoyant, given what actually followed. Not much later, congressional Democrats and the media advanced the argument that Trump's presidency indeed should be terminated due to his mental incapacity. As a result, Yale psychiatrist Dr. Bandy X. Lee organized a conference at Yale where she met with members of Congress and diagnosed Trump as dangerously unfit. Indeed, Lee deemed the president an existential threat to the planet comparable to some sort of global pandemic. "Our survival as a species," she insisted, "may be at stake." When during the primary campaign of 2020 Democratic front-runner Joe Biden seemed to exhibit confusion at times about names, dates, and places, Dr. Lee was asked whether she might offer another in absentia analysis but refused. Nonetheless, her idea of removing a president by claiming he was non compos mentis without a physical or mental examination persisted—and took on even stranger manifestations.[45]

In 2019, fired former deputy and acting director of the FBI Andrew McCabe admitted that he and then deputy attorney general Rod Rosenstein had earlier discussed the possibility of removing the president from office. They pondered efforts to convince "the Vice President and a majority of either the principal officers of the executive departments or of such other body as Congress may by law provide" to vote him unfit under the protocols of the Twenty-Fifth Amendment. McCabe later claimed that Rosenstein had gone so far as to offer to wear a wire, supposedly to record Trump's inflammatory private speech in one of his purportedly more unhinged moments. One wonders whether either McCabe or Rosenstein had ever listened to some of the private, recorded, and unguarded taped presidential conversations of John F. Kennedy or Lyndon Johnson.

If McCabe was accurate in his description of yet another Twenty-Fifth Amendment caper, then the attempt might have been the first time in modern American history when the acting FBI director and the second-ranking attorney in the DOJ, who was his boss, both unelected bureaucrats, discussed ways to depose a sitting president. "Coup" is a strong word, but it is hard to find a more apt noun to describe what the two insiders were contemplating.

In part because of such spreading opposition narratives that he was deranged and should be removed from office, the president later conceded in mid-January 2018 to take the Montreal Cognitive Assessment test. He apparently wished to demonstrate that he showed no mental or cognitive decline. His White House physician, Rear Admiral Ronny Jackson, announced that Trump had scored thirty out of thirty on the exam. Trump, Jackson reported, had "absolutely no cognitive or mental issues whatsoever." In some sense, the media-contrived effort to brand Trump crazy by enlisting supposedly professional psychiatrists and psychologists mirrored the early-1964 liberal efforts to reduce presidential candidate Barry Goldwater to little more than an unhinged nut.[46]

Few constitutional lawyers stepped forward to remind citizens that the Twenty-Fifth Amendment (ratified in 1965) came in direct response to the 1963 assassination of President John F. Kennedy. After Vice President Lyndon Johnson assumed the presidency, he—himself a heart attack survivor—had no vice president until the January 1965 inauguration of Hubert Humphrey. At the drafting of the amendment, congressional leaders had also reviewed past cases of presidential physical incapacity due to health concerns, especially the illness of Woodrow Wilson. In the subsequent half century since its passage, it has been invoked or considered only during physical health crises or surgeries of incumbent presidents. The Twenty-Fifth Amendment was *never* envisioned as a tool of the opposition party or internal resistance to question the mental stability of a president whom they opposed in order to hasten his removal from office before or in lieu of an election.[47]

Brooks finished her presidential-removal essay with an even more chilling alternative: "The fourth possibility is one that until recently I would have said was unthinkable in the United States of America: a military coup, or at least a refusal by military leaders to obey certain orders." And she concluded, "For the first time in my life, I can imagine plausible scenarios in which senior military officials might simply tell the president: 'No, sir. We're not doing that,' to thunderous applause from the *New York Times* editorial board." Note the logic of gaming a scenario that spawns an illegal act that one regrets is "unthinkable," at least "until recently." That is, *less than two weeks after a new president has been inaugurated.* If not an outright resort to violence, Brooks envisioned "at least a refusal by military leaders to obey certain orders." Given what followed Brooks's essay in the ensuing months, she again proved prescient and scary all at once.

Brooks suffered little criticism in at least outlining a hypothetical avenue for removing Trump by military force. Strangely, three years later, during the campaign of 2020, Brooks reappeared in the public arena to cofound the Transition Integrity Project. It was a sort of war-gaming exercise, among mostly Washington elites, to determine whether there would be a peaceful transfer of power after the election. And her group not surprisingly seemed to suggest that only the hoped-for Joe Biden landslide would avoid a disastrous crisis—possibly involving the use of force—especially if Trump again won the Electoral College but not the popular vote. By late summer 2020, a number of retired military officers were envisioning several scenarios in which the military might surround the White House and force Trump to vacate, ostensibly based on their own conspiracy theories that he would not accept the verdict of an election and stay on after noon on January 20, 2021.

That paranoia was ironic. For two years, from 2017 to 2018, Hillary Clinton, the "Resistance," and former high officials of the Obama administration had sought to abort the Trump administration on grounds that the verdict of 2016 was not valid due to "Russian collusion," the debunked hoax birthed by the fabricated Steele dossier. The published scenarios of would-be architects of "patriotic" removal of a president became so common that one journalist dubbed the growing genre "coup porn."[48]

Just as disturbing to the idea that citizens, justices, and elected officials alone oversee a presidential tenure was the case of unelected officials organizing to obstruct an incoming elected administration. In early March 2017, Evelyn Farkas, an outgoing Obama-appointed deputy assistant secretary of defense, in a strange confession on MSNBC, detailed how departing Obama administration officials scrambled to leak and undermine the six-week-old Trump administration: "I was urging my former colleagues and, frankly speaking, the people on the Hill. . . . 'Get as much information as you can. Get as much intelligence as you can before President Obama leaves the administration. . . . The Trump folks, if they found out how we knew what we knew about the Trump staff's dealing with Russians, [they] would try to compromise those sources and methods, meaning we would no longer have access to that intelligence. . . . That's why you have the leaking." Note, inter alia, that former federal official Farkas apparently had expressed a worry that the incoming administration might discover prior Obama-era efforts to use intelligence information to damage the new president—on the ruse that there had been Trump-Russian collusion, a charge that no Obama administration official has ever under oath testified was justified by evidence.

Indeed, less than two weeks before leaving office, outgoing president Obama made a radical and unprecedented decision to increase the ability of the National Security Agency to disseminate and share its own globally intercepted and often personal communications. It was now to distribute such classified information to at *least sixteen other government intelligence agencies*, and to do so without pausing for the standard firewalls designed to protect the privacy of American citizens.

Note that in May 2020 the House Intelligence Committee, under administration pressure, finally released testimony that Farkas had given under oath in June 2017. Despite her melodramatic tales on MSNBC, a now meek Farkas, when under oath, apparently claimed that she had lied on television about knowledge of Trump-Russian collusion that might have justified leaking documents to the media. In short, she confessed, "I didn't know anything." In other words, her efforts to hamper a presidential transition were based not on real national security concerns but apparently on political and media-generated animosity.[49]

Unfortunately, these serial efforts to undermine an elected president were not limited to anonymous appointees or lifelong bureaucrats, as we have seen earlier with loose talk among retired military officers about obstructing a presidency. That latter effort marks an unprecedented development that also deserves further attention. The Uniform Code of Military Justice (UCMJ), which became effective law in May 1951, prohibits *active* generals from disparaging their commander in chief—in the way perhaps General Douglas MacArthur had bitterly pilloried then president Harry Truman over the Korean War. Indeed, Article 88 of the UCMJ makes it a crime to voice "contemptuous words against the President, the Vice President, Congress, the Secretary of Defense, the Secretary of a military department, the Secretary of Homeland Security, or the Governor or legislature of any State."

No one quite knows, and debate continues over, whether such codified prohibitions on free expression apply to *retired* generals receiving military pensions. Yet, given the spate of recent "contemptuous words against the President" leveled from retired top-ranking officers, it seems that few have worried much about another explicit regulation, AR 27-10 of the code: "*Retired* members of a regular component of the Armed Forces who are entitled to pay are subject to the UCMJ. (See Art. 2(a)(4)) They may be tried by courts-martial for offenses committed while in a retired status" (emphasis added). In the real world, the issue of proper military conduct versus First Amendment rights for retired generals remains nebulous. But the statute at least is unambiguous in that *it is clearly improper for retired officers to attack a sitting president publicly.*[50]

In the past generals and admirals of both political parties have rebuked their commander in chief or his chief cabinet officers in disparaging ways, from the so-called Seven Days in April retired military group who in April 2006 went on the attack against then secretary of defense Donald Rumsfeld to retired General Michael Flynn's tough talk against President Obama. Yet, most recently, an entire array of well-known and decorated retired officers have ignored such prohibitions in a fashion never before seen. Indeed, they came forward to denounce President Trump in extraordinarily contemptuous terms—from likening him to the world's most notorious mass murderers to declaring that he was utterly unfit to serve as president and *should leave office* before a scheduled election.

Retired four-star general Barry McCaffrey, for much of the Trump administration, lodged repeated ad hominem charges against the elected president, going so far as to state, "He [President Trump] is a serious threat to U.S. national security." By any standard, such venom would be characterized as "contemptuous" under the UCMJ's Article 88. McCaffrey alleged that Trump's loyalties lay more with Russian dictator Vladimir Putin than with his own country—essentially a smear that his commander in chief was treasonous: "He is for some unknown reason under the sway of Mr. Putin." McCaffrey certainly had a right to criticize Trump's policies. But for a retired four-star general to suggest, without any evidence, that his commander in chief was a virtual traitor was incendiary.

In a matter of policy disagreement, McCaffrey later called the president "stupid" and "cruel" for recalibrating the presence of US tripwire troops between Kurdish and Turkish forces. When Trump cancelled the White House's and other federal agencies' subscriptions to the *New York Times* and the *Washington Post*, McCaffrey equated him with the fascist dictator Benito Mussolini ("This is Mussolini"). Note that these smears were not based on any evidence of wrongdoing but grew entirely out of differences of policy and style.

When a high-profile retired military officer announces that the current president is in service to a foreign country and the equivalent of a fascist, mass-murdering dictator who seized power and defied constitutional norms, then what message is conveyed to other serving military officers and to the citizens who elected him? What would be the patriotic duty of active officers sworn to uphold the Constitution if they felt that one of their most respected former commanders was accusing the president of veritable treason?

McCaffrey was not alone.

Retired general Stanley McChrystal—removed from command by the Obama administration for, inter alia, allegedly not reprimanding one of his officers for referring to then vice president Joe Biden as "Bite Me"—publicly called the president "immoral and dishonest." Former CIA director Michael Hayden—a four-star air force general once smeared by the Left for defending supposed "torture" at Guantánamo—compared Trump's policies to Nazism. Hayden tweeted a picture of the Birkenau death camp to illustrate his criticism of the administration's use of detention facilities at the border—a plan inaugurated by the Obama administration to deal with tens of thousands of illegal entrants and followed as well by the Biden administration. That invective was only the beginning.[51]

Retired general John Allen attacked the commander in chief in morally disparaging terms rather than merely criticizing the president's strategic or operational judgment in pulling back US troops from the Kurdish-Turkish battlefront in Syria: "There is blood on Trump's hands for abandoning our Kurdish allies." Later Allen essentially accused Trump of destroying America as we have known it for railing against governors and mayors who refused help from federal troops and, in Trump's view, would or could not restore order in their jurisdictions and punish those who serially engaged in violence, looting, and arson: "The slide of the United States into illiberalism may well have begun on June 1, 2020," Allen wrote in *Foreign Policy*. "Remember the date. It may well signal the beginning of the end of the American experiment." So what exactly should the serving military do when one of its esteemed retired generals declares that the elected president destroyed America on June 1, when he contemplated using federal troops to restore order in the capital?

In perhaps the eeriest of all commentaries, highly decorated retired admiral William H. McRaven all but declared his president a subversive traitor. Apparently in reference to fellow military officers also working in some sort of resistance to the president, McRaven remarked, "The America that they believed in was under attack, not from without, but from within." Indeed, in the same *New York Times* op-ed, Admiral McRaven seemed to call for Trump to be removed *before* the 2020 election: "It is time for a new person in the Oval Office—Republican, Democrat or independent—*the sooner, the better*. The fate of our Republic depends upon it" (emphasis added). Just one year away from a constitutionally mandated election, an esteemed retired admiral of the US Navy publicly wished for a "new person" in the Oval Office— "the sooner, the better," a phrase reminiscent of Anonymous's earlier "one way or another." Exactly what scenario was the admiral referring to? Impeachment? Invocation of the Twenty-Fifth Amendment? Or the last of Rosa Brooks's various scenarios: a forced removal by the military? Did he reflect upon the notion that removing Trump "the sooner, the better" would equate to cancelling out the verdict of citizen voters?[52]

Esteemed retired marine general James N. Mattis, former secretary of defense in the Trump administration and a deservedly iconic figure, during the national protests, rioting, and violence of summer 2020 suggested that Trump had fostered disunity in much the same way that Nazis did. In a statement published in *The Atlantic*, Mattis wrote,

> Instructions given by the military departments to our troops before the Normandy invasion reminded soldiers that "The Nazi slogan

for destroying us . . . was 'Divide and Conquer.' Our American answer is 'In Union there is Strength.'" We must summon that unity to surmount this crisis—confident that we are better than our politics.

Donald Trump is the first president in my lifetime who does not try to unite the American people—does not even pretend to try. Instead, he tries to divide us. We are witnessing the consequences of three years of this deliberate effort. We are witnessing the consequences of three years without mature leadership.

How exactly was an elected president emulating the divisive methods of the Nazis, which included executing dissidents, establishing death camps, and torturing suspected enemies? What was the purpose of the indictment from Mattis—who had likely been forced out as commander of Central Command by the Obama administration and had worked for Trump for over two years—in the 2020 election year? Did he think his invocation of the Nazi simile might better "unite the American people" or instead enrage nearly half of the country who supported the president? Was ecumenicalism really the aim of his election-year simile?[53]

Such orchestrated furor next prompted four *former* chairmen of the Joint Chiefs of Staff—retired navy admiral Mike Mullen, retired army general Martin Dempsey, retired air force general Richard Myers, and retired army general Colin Powell—to join the chorus, in particular over Trump's notice that he might, if necessary, as had numerous past presidents, use federal troops to restore calm in cities where violence remained unchecked.

Democratic presidential candidate Joe Biden correctly assessed the thrust of the retired generals' attacks and the influence they exercised—and sought to capitalize on it. After breezily asserting, "This president is going to try to steal this election," Biden then charged additionally that Trump might not depart peacefully in January 2021 after losing the election. In other words, according to Biden, Trump would either steal the election, claim he won, and then not leave after really losing it, or he would clearly lose it and then refuse to vacate the White House.

But Biden was not worried because such revered retired generals had "ripped the skin off of Trump" and thus apparently could be counted on as muscle if need be: "I was so damn proud. You have four chiefs of staff coming out and ripping the skin off of Trump, and you have so many rank-and-file military personnel saying, 'Whoah, we're not a military state. This is not who we are.'" Biden then offered a final warning: "I promise you, I'm absolutely convinced they will escort him from the White House with great dispatch."

The irony notwithstanding of asserting that the United States is "not a military state" at a time when retired generals were weaponizing their military reputations and influence to attack a sitting president politically and personally and in some cases imagining his early removal by force, Biden was entering dangerous ground. In his use of the pronoun "they," he apparently counted on as his enforcers two groups of the military: the "four chiefs of staff," or retired generals, who had ripped Trump's skin off and the currently serving "rank-and-file military personnel." And together "they" would escort the cheating Trump out "with great dispatch."

The logic was twisted. But Biden seemed to suggest that retired generals who came out to criticize the current elected president might have to be pressed into action by Biden to enforce the results of an election. Biden apparently believed that, if necessary, he would have the support of the military, active and retired, to depose the interloper. This was preposterous. But it was a preposterousness that the retired generals themselves had spawned, because their current incendiary talk seemed not so preposterous to Biden. Further irony arose in their paradoxical idea that retired generals and admirals should use their influence in politics but all the same not be subject to the Code of Military Justice that governs the public behavior of retired high officers.[54]

At about the same time as Biden's "ripping the skin off" bragga-docio, the current chairman of the Joint Chiefs of Staff, General Mark Milley, apologized to the country for appearing in a "photo-op" with his commander in chief. Milley had come under intense criticism from both dissident retired military and the progressive media for stand-ing next to Trump at a time when the president had ordered federal police to stand by in order to maintain calm near the White House: "I should not have been there. My presence in that moment and in that environment created a perception of the military involved in domestic politics. As a commissioned uniformed officer, it was a mistake that I have learned from, and I sincerely hope we all can learn from it."[55]

If Milley were sincerely worried about "the military involved in domestic politics," he might have reminded retired generals of perti-nent articles in the Uniform Code of Military Justice. Yet it was not as if the president, without precedent, had ordered a few federal officers into the streets to quell violent protesters. In fact, *over a dozen* past presidents have sent the military into cities to stop rioting and looting. President George H. W. Bush in 1992 had characterized the racially sensitive riots in Los Angeles, over the beating of Rodney King, as mob-like: "What we saw last night and the night before in Los Ange-les is not about civil rights. . . . It's not a message of protest. It's been the brutality of a mob, pure and simple." Accordingly, as commander in chief, Bush ordered forty-five hundred marine combat troops into the city to quell the violence. He added of the order, "Federal effort will not be driven by mob violence, but by respect for due process and law." At the time of the riots, Bush's chairman of the Joint Chiefs of Staff, who oversaw the dispatch of the federal marines into Los Ange-les, was General Colin Powell. Powell, with the other former joint chiefs chairs, had criticized Trump for even considering the use of fed-eral troops. Yet in 1992, he reportedly had eagerly remarked to Bush about his request for federal troops to quell a domestic disturbance, "All you've got to do is say it."[56]

Note again, the common thread in these complaints from retired officers was never demonstrable high crimes and misdemeanors or, indeed, any evidence that the elected president would not leave office if defeated in the 2020 election—much less any popular groundswell among angry citizens for the retired or active military to act to remove a supposed danger to the republic. Rather, retired officers expressed venom over *policy* disagreements with the president about the Middle East or Russia. Further, they felt that they could demonize the president largely on grounds that he was controversial, unpopular, and completely at odds with the establishment of both political parties. Or they were furious over the president's own retaliatory and sometimes crass pushbacks, usually against prior ad hominem attacks both from serving and retired military officers. Retired admirals and generals somehow had gotten it into their heads that as far as the president was concerned, removal in some manner was far preferable to the downside of violating hallowed protocols of military conduct.

Note that the test of institutional resiliency and constitutional stability comes during times not of popular but rather unpopular leaders. When polarizing figures are elected, then popular cries arise to thwart them by sidestepping constitutional safeguards. And this certainly is the most dangerous time for a republic. Harry Truman left the office the most disliked president up until that time in US history. His unpopularity had earlier energized General Douglas MacArthur and his media and administrative enablers to intrude into political decision-making—this was dangerous for the constitutional system, even if MacArthur at times had proposed some strategic options superior to those entertained by the president.

Nonetheless, at a time of war in Korea, MacArthur serially disparaged his commander in chief to the press over American policy in Korea. And he did so to the extent that he imperiled the president's political and moral ability to establish strategy and see his military carry it out. Again, the crisis hinged on unelected public servants' assuming the right to remove or destroy a president without going through constitutional processes—such as impeachment and conviction or removal through the complicated process of determining a president medically unfit, as later entailed in the Twenty-Fifth Amendment—and thus nullify citizens' votes in a presidential election.

These insurrectionary impulses were not confined to the retired military. Some retired high-ranking intelligence officers—many of them actively engaged in the last months of the Obama administration in ordering surveillance of the Trump campaign and transition—were no less shy in seeking to undermine the new commander in chief. Most prominent was CIA director John Brennan, who had a long history of misleading or outright lying under oath to Congress. By 2020 his unchecked excesses had become emblematic of the dangers of the intelligence complex to constitutional government and indeed the sovereignty of the citizen-voter. Brennan's career additionally was a reminder that our administrative elite is rarely seriously audited and ignores laws that citizens, in fear of real consequences, do not.

For example, Brennan in 2009 falsely claimed that intelligence agencies had not missed evidence suggesting that Umar Farouk Abdulmutallab, aka the "underwear bomber," might blow up a US airliner in a manner well known to US authorities. In 2010, he offered a surreal redefinition of jihad (i.e., "Nor do we describe our enemy as 'jihadists' or 'Islamists' because jihad is a holy struggle, a legitimate tenet of Islam, meaning to purify oneself or one's community"). In 2011, Brennan's official statements about the Osama bin Laden raid were contradictory and had to be withdrawn or modified.

Also in 2011, Brennan, then the country's chief counterterrorism adviser, had sworn to Congress under oath that scores of drone strikes abroad had *not* killed a single noncombatant—at precisely the time when both the president and the CIA had received numerous reports of civilian collateral deaths. In 2014, John Brennan, by then CIA director, again lied, and once more emphatically, under congressional oath. He claimed that the CIA had not illegally accessed the computers of US Senate staffers who were then exploring a CIA role in torturing detainees ("As far as the allegations of the CIA hacking into Senate computers, nothing could be further from the truth. . . . We wouldn't do that. I mean, that's just beyond the, you know, the scope of reason in terms of what we do"). After months of prevarication, but only upon release of the CIA inspector general's report, Brennan belatedly apologized to the senators he had once deceived.

Brennan, in May 2017, as an ex–CIA director, again almost certainly did not tell the truth to Congress when he testified under oath, in answer to Representative Trey Gowdy's questions, that neither did he know who had commissioned the so-called Steele dossier nor had the CIA relied on its contents for any action. Yet both retired NSA director Michael Rogers and former director of national intelligence James Clapper have conceded otherwise: that the Steele dossier—along with the knowledge that it was a Clinton-campaign-funded product—most certainly *did* help shape the Obama administration's intelligence community interagency assessments and actions, often under the urging of Brennan himself. Andrew McCabe, former acting director of the FBI, testified under oath to Congress that without the unverified Steele dossier, the FISA court may well have not approved FBI requests to surveille erstwhile Trump campaign advisor Carter Page.

Years later, released government documents showed that Brennan had been well aware that the 2016 Clinton campaign had used the so-called Steele dossier to smear her political opponent in order to deflect media scrutiny from her own email scandals. Brennan knew of the ruse through intercepted communications from Russian intelligence sources.

Apparently, the Russians were baffled over why Clinton was falsely blaming them for colluding with Donald Trump. Their confusion arose perhaps because the Steele team may have been concocting its farcical dossier in part on falsehoods peddled by a Russian operative. In addition, when Brennan became aware of the intercept, he briefed President Obama on the Clinton gambit. Rather than investigating the subversion of the Trump campaign, high officials of the Obama State

Department, FBI, and CIA continued their efforts either to deny much knowledge of the dossier or, at least, to claim ignorance about those seeking to seed it within government agencies and the media.[57]

Indeed, numerous reports suggested that despite his denials about knowledge of the dossier, Brennan served as a stealthy conduit to ensure its wide dissemination. In an unusual private meeting in August 2016 with Senator Harry Reid, one that circumvented normal bipartisan briefings of relevant congressional leaders, Brennan himself apprised the senator about the Steele dossier's unverified contents. He hoped that Reid would pressure the FBI to further its investigations. Reid later bragged that he did just that, in a call two days later to James Comey.[58]

The list of John Brennan's unprofessional and bizarre behavior only increased after he left office, despite his retaining for over two years his top-secret CIA security clearance. On March 17, 2018, Brennan, in objection to the firing of deputy FBI director Andrew McCabe (who the nonpartisan inspector general would shortly find had lied on four occasions to federal investigators), tweeted about the current president of the United States, "When the full extent of your venality, moral turpitude, and political corruption becomes known, you will take your rightful place as a disgraced demagogue in the dustbin of history. . . . America will triumph over you." In mid-April, ex–CIA director Brennan followed up with another attack on Trump: "Your kakistocracy [rule of the 'worst people'] is collapsing after its lamentable journey. As the greatest Nation history has known, we have the opportunity to emerge from this nightmare stronger & more committed to ensuring a better life for all Americans, including those you have so tragically deceived." It is hard to find any comparable such statement about a sitting president from any of the other twenty-four former CIA directors. Yet Brennan continued to attack the president at a time when he was reportedly under federal questioning for his prior role in the so-called Russia collusion hoax and improper use of CIA operatives in the investigation of US citizens.[59]

None of Brennan's behavior raised eyebrows among his colleagues of the administrative state: far from it. Samantha Power, former UN ambassador and a past ethics professor on the Harvard faculty, almost gleefully warned, "Not a good idea to piss off John Brennan." Power was unabashedly conceding that powerful but unelected officials, even after retirement from the federal bureaucracy, exercised a greater degree of coercion than even high-ranking elected officials—and yet there was nothing anyone could or should do about it. Brennan's lies and long career of dissimulation were mysteriously exempt from legal, congressional, and public oversight. Few elected officials expressed such warnings about the intelligence services' reputed ability to stymie an elected president or worse—in a manner of admonition but also grudging respect for the omnipotence of these bureaucrats.

In a related and larger context, Senate Minority Leader Chuck Schumer warned Trump, shortly before his inauguration, about criticizing CIA officials in general and what the intelligence community could do to the president-elect, who had supposedly unwisely attacked such a permanent caste: "Let me tell you: You take on the intelligence community—they have six ways from Sunday at getting back at you." An elected US senator warned a newly elected president that he better fear the CIA and, by inference, its most prominent Trump critic—a *retired* CIA director. The latter purportedly had avenues of retaliation unimagined by the commander in chief. The strange case of the serial dissembler CIA director, the danger even his allies conceded he posed to elected officials, and the immunity under which he seemed to operate were all proof of just how dangerous the twenty-first-century deep state had become. It seemed utterly unaccountable to the very citizens who had indirectly created and were directly funding and supposedly auditing it.

Progressive former Cleveland mayor, erstwhile presidential candidate, and retired congressman Representative Dennis Kucinich (D-OH), at about the same time, warned of just these dangers to a constitutional republic:

The intention is to take down our President. This is very dangerous to America. It's a threat to our Republic. It constitutes a clear and present danger to our way of life. So, we have to be asking, "What is the motive of these people?" . . . This is a problem in our country. We've got to protect our nation here. People have to be aware of what's going on, we need to protect America. This isn't about Democrat or Republican. This is about getting what's going on in the moment and understanding that our country itself is under attack from within.[60]

Samantha Power herself was later found to have requested transcripts of FISA-court-ordered surveillance of Trump associates in the 2016 campaign. Indeed, she had gone further and made over three hundred such requests, most right before the 2016 election. She also asked to have the redacted names of American citizens in these files "unmasked," many of which were mysteriously subsequently leaked to the press—the latter act a felony.

Aside from the enigma of why a UN ambassador needed to know the whereabouts and the names of Republican officials in the midst of a campaign—*and after the election*—Power simply denied under oath to a House Intelligence Committee, without explanation, that she had herself actually submitted the requests made under her name. Who had made them? And why, if she had allowed others to make them, was it never disclosed?

I have mostly focused on John Brennan, the CIA director under President Obama, only because he was iconic of the deep-state intelligence service careerists who had mobilized against an elected president—especially, in Brennan's case, in the apparent expectation that he would never face accountability for his serial lying from the Congress or federal investigators. Unfortunately, Brennan was not an isolated example. Fired and would-be martyred FBI deputy director Andrew McCabe openly admitted to misstatements ("I was confused and distracted"). He had falsely assured investigators ("Some of my answers were not fully accurate") that he had not been a source for background leaks about purported Trump-Russian collusion, all of them harmful to Trump.

The inspector general released a report condemning McCabe for his serial false statements. McCabe had leaked FBI business ostensibly to deflect from charges that he was biased and had ignored conflict-of-interest charges arising from his own investigation of Hillary Clinton's purported destruction of several thousand emails under federal subpoena—after his wife, a Democratic candidate for the Virginia legislature, had received hundreds of thousands of dollars in campaign donations from Clinton-affiliated political action committees.

Former director of national intelligence James Clapper had also lied under oath to the Senate Intelligence Committee. On March 12, 2013, he had assured its members that the National Security Agency did not collect data on American citizens. Months later, Clapper was called out for his assertion. He then suddenly claimed that he had given "the least untruthful" answer. In late 2017 Clapper made an astounding charge, offering no proof: "I think this past weekend is illustrative of what a great case officer Vladimir Putin is. He knows how to handle an asset, and that's what he's doing with the president." We know that Clapper himself knew that he had been lying when he said that the president was a veritable Russian asset, because just months *prior* to that assertion, the House Intelligence Committee had subpoenaed him to testify on May 8, 2017. While under oath, he was asked directly whether he had any evidence that Donald Trump was colluding with the Russian government. Clapper testified that he did *not*—an admission that strangely was not released to the public until May 2020.

Clapper likely lied again when he also testified under oath to the House Intelligence Committee that he had *not* leaked the contents of the Steele dossier to the media. Later he apparently confessed that he had done just that to CNN's Jake Tapper. According to a House Intelligence Committee report, "Clapper subsequently acknowledged discussing the 'dossier with CNN journalist Jake Tapper,' and admitted that he might have spoken with other journalists about the same topic."

Clapper later became a paid CNN analyst, often criticizing those who had alleged that he had been serially untruthful.[61]

It is a threat to a free, constitutional republic when a retired general and director of national intelligence, in and then out of office, while retaining a federal security clearance, so frequently lies to the public. In the cases of Brennan, Clapper, Comey, and McCabe, for the first three years of the Trump administration, they were never held to account for their distortions. And they often ended up as paid media consultants to analyze various scandals in which they themselves were often key players. A cynic would conclude that once a professional bureaucrat or revolving-door appointee reaches a senior level in the government, he is immune from the sorts of perjury charges or ostracism that most all Americans would face.

What does all this have to do with the notion of citizenship? And why should we care that high-ranking career military officers and intelligence heads actively sought to remove or injure a constitutionally elected US administration?

The danger is that half the country will conclude that too many retired generals and admirals are going the way of past CIA and FBI directors. No longer just esteemed professionals, op-ed writers, and astute analysts, they have now become, in the public mind, political activists. They feel entitled to use their past authority and present contacts to challenge the very legitimacy of an elected president and the foundations of the US Constitution. That development is ruinous both to the reputation of a hallowed military and intelligence community and to the idea of a constitutional republic of citizens.

All of these abuses of the unelected might have been exposed and checked had the media played its assumed role as a watchdog of government and disinterested purveyor of the news. After all, reporters are not op-ed writers and opinion columnists. They supposedly report the news and leave editorialization out of their empirical investigations.

Yet recently many have lost their shyness in announcing that the era of past presumptions of neutrality is now over, even if in the past the media was, in fact, not always so disinterested. Journalists Jim Rutenberg of the *New York Times* and Christiane Amanpour of CNN both said that they could—*and should*—no longer be neutral reporters, given their low opinion of the president and the dangers he posed to America. Rutenberg indeed urged fellow journalists "to throw out the textbook American journalism has been using for the better part of the past half-century" and instead become "oppositional."

In Orwellian fashion, Amanpour claimed that declaring her bias was best described as being "truthful." She too defiantly announced, "Much of the media was tying itself in knots trying to differentiate between balance, between objectivity, neutrality, and crucially, the truth. We cannot continue the old paradigm." And Amanpour certainly did not. Later she simply refused to consider any of the concrete mounting evidence that Hunter Biden, son of then presidential candidate Joe Biden, had engaged in unethical if not illegal ventures with foreign-government-related concerns in order to peddle his influence on behalf of the Biden family. The subtext was that "journalists" like Amanpour could turn off and on the "old paradigm" of journalistic jurisprudence, depending on their own particular take on the object of their coverage.

Univision anchor Jorge Ramos more honestly declared of the "old paradigm" that it was the duty of the media to take sides, given the moral issues at stake: "Saying that reporters should abandon neutrality on certain issues and choose sides may seem at odds with everything that's taught in journalism school. But there are times when the only way we journalists can fulfill our primary social responsibility—challenging those in power—is by leaving neutrality aside."[62]

Amanpour, Ramos, and Rutenberg apparently did not contemplate that half the country held legitimate but antithetical views to their own. Other journalists could easily make the same argument if someone opposed to their own politics were president.

Unable to trust their time-honored sources of daily information, citizens could and did turn to talk radio, podcasts, the internet, blogs and websites, and social media for different versions of the news. In any case, what was stated rhetorically was soon born out in the concrete, as the following random examples illustrate.

In summer 2020, over a ten-day period, CNN reported that there was a "hate crime" at a NASCAR garage, after African American driver Bubba Wallace reported seeing a hanging noose. CNN tied the crime to the climate of hate purportedly fostered by Donald Trump. The noose upon FBI investigation was found to be a cord used as a garage door opener.

CNN additionally claimed that Trump did nothing when apprised by intelligence sources that Russians were paying Taliban terrorists to kill Americans in Afghanistan. Yet CNN never substantiated the truth of that rumor or reported that Donald Trump had never been briefed on such intelligence. Much later it was disclosed that the story was a fabrication.

CNN alleged that Donald Trump's July 3, 2020, address at Mount Rushmore was a veritable homage to Confederate Civil War racists. In fact, Trump did not mention a single Confederate in his long list of both white and black American icons.[63]

Sometime during the Obama administration years, the news division at CNN—a once-renowned and pathbreaking global media service—simply ceased being a news outlet. It soon would become an extension of the so-called Resistance and a defender of the administrative state—in a way well beyond both the center-left news networks and the strictly news division at center-right Fox News. Its new mission was stunning in the wide variety of its expression. Reporters Manu Raju and Jeremy Herb in December 2017, for example, falsely asserted that Donald Trump Jr. had advanced access to the hacked WikiLeaks documents belonging to the Democratic National Committee in general and to the emails of Hillary Clinton's campaign advisor John Podesta in particular. But Trump Jr. did not. Such a false charge may have spawned all sorts of subsidiary rumors that the younger Trump was on the verge of becoming indicted by special counsel Robert Mueller.[64]

Why did CNN's own "unnamed source"—namely, lawyer Lanny Davis—later deny he had ever given CNN information that Donald Trump had advance warning of a meeting between Russian interests and Donald Trump Jr. concerning purported "collusion" during the 2016 campaign? Why did the authors of the false story, Jim Sciutto, Carl Bernstein, and Marshall Cohen, not retract the allegation in full? Could they not at least have explained why their not-so-anonymous source, Lanny Davis, was claiming that he never told the three that his client Michael Cohen had professed foreknowledge of the meeting on the part of Trump?[65]

Why were Thomas Frank, Eric Lichtblau, and Lex Harris all forced to resign from CNN? Was it their collective, but false, report that Anthony Scaramucci, who had served briefly as Trump's press secretary, was connected to a $10 billion Russian investment fund and thereby, their insinuation went, part of the "collusion" conspiracy?

CNN's Gloria Borger, Eric Lichtblau, Jake Tapper, and Brian Rokus, remember, also had erroneously reported that former FBI director James Comey would, in congressional testimony, soon contradict President Trump's prior assertion that Comey had told him that he was *not* under investigation. That reporting proved false—and yet it too had helped to whip up anti-Trump hysteria on the eve of the Comey appearance. The problem was not just that news is untrustworthy but that it had become untrustworthy in a particularly predictable, biased fashion intended to warp coverage to advance a political outcome.[66]

Trump was controversial and often rude and enjoyed replying in kind to any media attack. So a certain media furor over Trump often erupted in repeated, obscene, and unprofessional anti-Trump outbursts by CNN journalists, contributors, and anchors—whether it was Anderson Cooper trashing a pro-Trump panelist by profanely retorting, "If he took a dump on his desk, you would defend it," or CNN religious scholar Reza Aslan referring to Trump as "this piece of sh-t," or perhaps the late CNN host Anthony Bourdain joking in an interview about poisoning Trump, or CNN New Year's Eve host Kathy Griffin's infamous photo in which she is holding a bloody effigy of Trump's severed head.[67]

Once journalists lose their reputations for disinterested reporting, they forfeit respect. Government entities then sense that, rather than serving as deterrents who keep officials honest, reporters can be enlisted as allies or indeed played. For example, critical to the selling of the Affordable Care Act to voters were the later cynical admissions of health expert Jonathan Gruber, who ex post facto bragged that he simply used a compliant media to dupe the public:

> This bill was written in a tortured way to make sure [the Congressional Budget Office (CBO)] did not score the [individual] mandate as taxes. If CBO scored the mandate as taxes the bill dies. In terms of risk-rated subsidies, if you had a law which said healthy people are going to pay in—it made explicit that healthy people pay in, sick people get money—it would not have passed. . . . Lack of transparency is a huge political advantage. And, basically, call it the stupidity of the American voter or whatever, but, basically, that was really, really critical for the thing to pass.[68]

Even more cynical was Ben Rhodes, former deputy national security advisor under Barack Obama. He bragged that he had counted on the inexperience, bias, and general stupidity of the news media to feed them narratives about an envisioned Iran Deal, which otherwise did not poll so well with the American people: "We created an echo chamber. They were saying things that validated what we had given them to say. . . . The average reporter we talk to is 27 years old, and their only reporting experience consists of being around political campaigns. . . . They literally know nothing."[69]

Meanwhile MSNBC anchor Brian Williams castigated the idea of a so-called fake news epidemic. Yet Williams failed to remind us that he was removed as NBC's evening news anchor for serving up all sorts of false details about his supposedly brave trips abroad in search of edgy news stories. Even worse, after the fatal shooting of Michael Brown in Ferguson, Missouri, the cohosts of the show *CNN Newsroom* collectively put up their hands in "don't shoot" solidarity with the progressive narrative of unjustified police killing, which a lengthy federal investigation conducted by the Obama administration later proved completely false.

Earlier, decades-long journalistic one-sidedness was apparently viable when there were no other news alternatives. Mainstream-media monopolies once were also highly profitable, and long ago news people, whatever their biases, were at least well-mannered and sought to appear neutral. In contrast, there is no such pretense today that television news is disinterested or hides some of its displeasure with conservative presidents. After just one hundred days in office, before President Trump could even enact his own agendas, the liberal Shorenstein Center on Media, Politics and Public Policy at Harvard University reported that 91 percent of CNN's initial coverage of the Trump administration was already negative. *Just one in every thirteen CNN stories proved positive.*

We are now apparently in uncharted territory. This radically asymmetrical pattern had *never* been seen before in the history of comparable media analytics. As the Shorenstein Center put it, "Trump's coverage during his first 100 days *set a new standard for negativity*" (emphasis added). No one in the media sought to explain the imbalance beyond asserting either that Trump deserved the asymmetrical coverage or that it was not biased but simply reflected his comprehensive failures. That inability to explain the slant left the impression that CNN, for example, had more or less joined the progressive opposition, in the fashion earlier outlined by Jim Rutenberg, Christiane Amanpour, and Jorge Ramos.[70]

It is easy to critique Donald Trump's often crass attacks on a press that was so one-sided in the coverage of his administration. But politicians' and even elected officials' crudity and invective are easily identified and contextualized in terms of transparent partisanship and politics. Far more pernicious than adversarial bias can be obsequious partiality or a willingness to be deceived for a purported higher good. The former is grating, the latter insidious and ultimately far more dangerous to a free citizenry, especially in the age of electronic and instantaneous communications.

Worse still is the level of contempt that officials harbored for the citizen (e.g., "stupidity of the American voter") and the surety by which they could manipulate the media (e.g., "they literally know nothing") to fool the public.

The duty of a journalist to the citizen *is* to stay neutral and disinterested and to report the truth, at least as it can be determined by testimonies, evidence, motive, and common sense—without concern for whether such reporting injures or aids a particular politician or agenda. Otherwise, the citizen has few sources of reliable news by which to form an independent opinion on any issue—and thus to participate in democracy in an effective manner.

So when journalistic bias is institutionalized and serves the state with the speed and electronic massaging of the internet, the citizen becomes orphaned from the world about him. Unelected bureaucrats, those who control electronic communications, the media, and the military-intelligence complex of the federal government all exercise enormous powers over American citizens without being elected to any office and while facing few consequences for their unethical or illegal behavior.

In the next chapter we shall see that there are also more formal and overt efforts to stifle the freedoms of American citizens, at least as envisaged by the founders. An army of political activists, judges, advocates, and politicians currently see the US Constitution and the centuries-old traditions that surround it as hopelessly outdated. They judge our founding documents and national traditions ill-equipped to meet their visions of the twenty-first century—and thus in need of radical changes. When ideologues cannot persuade Americans to support their agenda under the existing political rules and traditions of the nation, they seek to alter them for their own advantage—often by redefining citizenship as something never envisioned by the Founders.

Chapter Five

EVOLUTIONARIES

The Constitution was not made to fit us like a straitjacket.
—WOODROW WILSON, *"Speech on Americanism,"*
Cooper Union (New York, NY), November 20, 1904

E very consensual society that survives for a few decades eventually questions its original constitution and founding documents. Some evolve and dramatically change their protocols, usually to become more inclusive and redistributionist. The Athenian democracy founded in 508/7 BC by Cleisthenes and his supporters, subject to a number of ensuing radical coups and revolutions, was quite different from the far more bureaucratic democratic system of 180 years later described by Aristotle in his *Constitution of Athens*, written between 328 and 322 BC.

The US Constitution—the foundation of the oldest constitutional republic still in existence today—was primarily designed to protect personal freedom, property, and individual liberty from both oppressive government elites and periodic mob frenzies. The American Revolution, unlike the later French Revolution, was intended neither to ensure mandated equality of result (what we now call "equity") nor to extend state control over the private lives and thoughts of citizens, much less to create a communitarian ideal of citizenry. Few, if any, of the Founders embraced what the later French Revolutionaries would champion as *égalité* and *fraternité*.[1]

This American foundational idea of citizen control of government on major matters of life and death, however, is waning. And given that the Constitution is difficult to amend, reformists are constantly seeking evolutionary avenues to render it inert or to change it by unconstitutional means. These "evolutionaries," who wish to move beyond the Framers' ideas, assume that the public has lost confidence in its ability to control its own republic or now prefers a radical, equality-of-result democracy to its own prior 234 years of constitutional history.

Indeed, rarely in American history have so many powerful and influential Americans become so unhappy with the US Constitution and its emphases on liberty and individual freedom rather than on government-mandated equality. Most critics see the need for a far more powerful presidency to ensure that an obstructionist Congress does not stymie progressive issues such as immigration expansion, climate change, and income redistribution.

Political scientist Terry Moe, for example, argues that the Founders "designed a government for a tiny agrarian nation—and they assumed that, as society changed, future generations would change the Constitution to meet new and evolving needs. But future generations didn't do that. Instead, they put it on a pedestal to be worshipped." Democracy scholar Larry Diamond has argued that to ensure fairness in American presidential and national elections, we need both to abolish the Electoral College and to adopt ranked-choice voting (RCV), that is, allowing citizens to rank their preferences for multiple candidates, as a way to green-light further changes in how we conduct elections. Of the latter, he argues, "Once RCV is adopted, with its greater incentives to moderation and diversity in our electoral process, other democratic reforms may become more achievable." Such constitutional critics assume that as the nation constantly becomes more just, fair, and humane—reflecting the natural moral progression of human nature—it also needs to rewrite its charters to improve on the blinkered documents of the late eighteenth century.[2]

Of course, throughout American history there have been lots of both necessary and questionable legal and formal attempts to redefine citizenship as set out in the Constitution—well beyond the formal efforts of adding twenty-seven amendments, the last in 1992. Federal and state courts, the administrative state, and presidents wielding sweeping executive orders have all become would-be modernizers. All felt the eighteenth-century Constitution's singular devotion to liberty hindered the natural progression to an equality of result. And all presidents, on the Left and Right, increasingly feel that executive orders should augment or even replace congressional legislation, especially when a president does not enjoy party majorities in the Congress.

Yet never have such efforts of the evolutionaries been so focused and holistic as they are today. Original constitutional avenues for amendments are now often seen as too cumbersome to effect change, given the need for three-quarters of the states to ratify what two-thirds of the Congress has previously enacted. Instead, the subtext for radical reformers remains, why let old white men of a bygone age continue, from their graves, to impose their ossified values on a far more enlightened, ethnically and racially diverse, and knowledgeable twenty-first-century nation? Why not allow a simple majority of Americans or a panel of distinguished jurists to fix what is obviously irrelevant or wrong in the Constitution? After all, the naive and blinkered Founders assumed that human nature is fixed and constant rather than fluid, which—with enough mandated correct education, funding, and technology—would be malleable and subject to radical improvement in its expression.

So the latest discussions about "updating" American institutions are not matters of adding a twenty-eighth, twenty-ninth, or thirtieth constitutional amendment. Instead, they are far more structural and cover everything from admitting new states to redefining the way we elect presidents. And the efforts represent an assault on the origins, spirit, and current status of our constitutional republic. Progressives no doubt would redefine a citizen, first, as a sort of judge, legislator, and executive through more direct elections and plebiscites and, only second, as a constitutional republican if he does not get his way and needs to fall back on constitutional redress through the courts.

The overarching theory of social scientists and historians is the shift from an "equality-of-opportunity" to an "equality-of-outcome" society. This transformation during the New Deal was the requisite for the entire 1960s continuance under the Great Society programs and their redefinition of civil rights to encompass government-ensured economic parity through higher taxes, income redistribution, massive new government spending, and forced proportional representation by race and gender in hiring and admission. Up until then, Americans traditionally had been open to new and stronger laws protecting equality of opportunity but were wary of the destructiveness of envy, the ancient fuel of an equality-of-result society that saw government punish its more successful citizens. As Alexis de Tocqueville warned of upward mobility and the resentment it incurs in a democracy, "In a democracy private citizens see a man of their own rank in life who becomes possessed of riches and power in a few years; this spectacle excites their surprise and envy, and they are led to inquire how the person who was yesterday their equal is today their ruler. To attribute his rise to his talents or his virtues is unpleasant; for it is tacitly to acknowledge that they are themselves less virtuous and less talented than he was."[3]

As we will see, the mostly elite and formal efforts to change the Constitution—whether by systematically nullifying federal laws, using the courts and the bureaucracy to circumvent the will of Congress, or ignoring or replacing parts of the Constitution itself—share the same ideological geneses that have led to the ad hoc diminution of the middle class, the conflation of citizenship with residency, and the multicultural tribalism discussed previously. The common theme once more is an effort to erode traditions and laws in order to mandate equity and to empower an alliance of the elite and the poor at the expense of the power and influence of the middle class.

Increasingly the Constitution is seen as an obstacle to popular policies and thus ripe for circumvention. Take war and peace. Governments, left and right, have begun wars in Afghanistan, Iraq, and Libya on the principle that such conflicts—at least since the Korean War (1950–1953)—were not existential struggles and thus were not quite real wars. Instead, they were loosely defined paradoxically as both admittedly optional and also quite necessary "police actions." Therefore, the deployments supposedly did not require a formal congressional declaration of war, as specified in Article I, Section 8 of the Constitution, which has occurred on five occasions in US history.

Instead, the fighting only needed a budgetary authorization by Congress, enabled by various congressionally enacted requirements to fund and authorize the continued use of force abroad. Major "police actions" are far more common than declarations of war and have occurred on some ten to fifteen prior occasions in US history. Of course, one could imagine that a "police action" of a few weeks' duration was not synonymous with "war," but this is not so easy with "interventions" that last twenty years, such as the ongoing, as of this writing, two-decade Afghanistan conflict (2001–2021).[4]

In truth, not just the size of the force or the cost involved or even the seriousness of the perceived threat to the safety of the homeland distinguishes a war from a police action. "Police actions" mostly include any conflict after World War II in the age of nuclear weapons. Given the peril of nuclear escalation, the fact that the United States did not choose to use its full arsenal to fight an enemy and quickly end the war apparently meant that the war was an "action" or "conflict" and therefore did not require a formal congressional declaration of war. More cynically, the United States has never lost a declared war, given that a formal declaration seems to prompt a national mobilization for victory. But it has arguably lost "police actions," like the troubled Vietnam intervention and withdrawal and the 1983–1984 misadventure in Lebanon, neither of which were always supported by the citizenry.

Well beyond the redefinition of war making, recent administrations have also more often tried to circumvent the constitutional right of the Senate to ratify treaties, most recently in the case of the so-called Iran Deal (Joint Comprehensive Plan of Action) and the Paris Climate Accord. In fact, in 2015, the Obama administration proposed shared national climate-change commitments with the Chinese government that were to be sent on to the United Nations as a veritable treaty without need for Senate ratification.

The administration was not shy about abrogating the Constitution on grounds that the Senate would be essentially unqualified to consult with the president about or eventually ratify the treaty or would illogically oppose the entire agreement. Or as White House press secretary Josh Earnest said of the likely unconstitutional decision to exclude the US Senate without any sense of embarrassment or irony, "Well, again, I think it's hard to take seriously from some members of Congress who deny the fact that climate change exists, that they should have some opportunity to render judgment about a climate change agreement." Translated, that meant if more than a third of the Senate might disagree with President Obama and refuse to help craft or to send his treaties onward for ratification, then the president should illegally bypass the Congress itself on the grounds its members lacked the education or intelligence to make informed favorable decisions. And that was exactly the case with both the Iran Deal and the climate accord. Note the trend: we increasingly make war without constitutionally required declarations, while crafting peaceful accords without constitutionally mandated treaties.[5]

The Framers, federalists particularly, worked in conscious antithesis to radical democracies of the past, ancient Greek democracies in particular, which simply voted to enact most policies without constitutional guardrails, judicial review, or tripartite checks and balances. And perhaps the Founders worried also about growing social turmoil in Europe that would erupt most dramatically in the French Revolution little more than a year after the ratification of the US Constitution. Consequently, at least some of the current overt dissatisfaction with the Constitution is old. It represents the eternal war of individual liberty and limited government versus an all-powerful, all-knowing state ensuring government-engineered equity—what is sometimes informally referenced as the antitheses between the American (1775–1783) and French (1789–1799) revolutions.

There continue to be formal, though so far still ineffective, efforts to end or alter the Electoral College—the presidential election system that allows the states, not a direct popular vote, to determine the voting citizens' choices for president and vice president. Rarely in our history has the presidential candidate with the greatest popular vote *not* gained the presidency. But when these anomalies have occurred, renewed debate centers on whether America is, or even should be, a constitutional republic rather than a direct democracy. A "selected not elected" George W. Bush, for example, won the 2000 election without a popular vote majority—and only after a split Supreme Court decision adjudicated the disputed popular vote in Florida.

The unlikely happened again less than two decades later in Donald Trump's 2016 win over Hillary Clinton, also without a majority of the popular vote. The two rare occurrences—of five such events in American history—and disdain for a supposedly outmoded eighteenth-century relic outraged progressives. After Trump's election, they began more systematically to investigate ways of repealing the Electoral College.

The Founders initially worried about such alterations of their Constitution. They made it difficult to amend without considerable debate and delay. As a result, it remains almost impossible in the current polarized political climate of the last thirty or so years properly and legally to repeal the Electoral College through a constitutional amendment. Such passage would require, first, a two-thirds vote of both houses of Congress and an additional ratification of the amendment by three-fourths of the states through votes of their own legislatures. How then are progressive critics to dispose of the now reviled Electoral College?

Opponents apparently believe where there is a will, there will be a way to circumvent the Constitution. In autumn 2019, *fourteen* of the Democratic candidates for president came out officially in favor of eliminating the Electoral College. Front-runner Elizabeth Warren summed up the prevailing consensus and confidence: "My view is that every vote matters. And that means get rid of the Electoral College!" She later elaborated, "I plan to be the last American president to be elected by the Electoral College. I want my second term to be elected by direct vote." But how exactly did Warren "plan" to alter the Constitution, given that at the time the Democrats enjoyed neither a two-thirds majority in the Congress nor control of three-fourths of the state legislatures?[6]

Nonetheless, other vocal candidates such as Bernie Sanders, Beto O'Rourke, Pete Buttigieg, and Kamala Harris joined Warren. The issue soon became a barometer of progressive fides. A Democratic presidency, elected in 2020, if it controlled the Congress, would pledge to concoct some sort of formal measure to do away with the College. Progressive proponents oddly complained that their own heavily populated states, such as California, Illinois, and New York, were so asymmetrically Democratic and so predictably progressive that presidential candidates did not campaign there. And they seemed to argue that their voters as a result might become uniformed about, and irrelevant in, national elections—an argument, ironically, that some conservative Texans had also voiced about their own predictable red-state affiliations, which limited presidential campaigning in their state as well.

Since a constitutional amendment is considered too lengthy, cumbersome, and unlikely a method to repeal the Electoral College, Warren and other presidential candidates in 2020 assumed that simply bypassing the Constitution would be much quicker. State legislatures could pass laws mandating that their own state electors follow the national popular vote, making individual state vote totals irrelevant. Note, however, that under our federal system, there is officially no such thing as a "national popular vote" in presidential elections, only individual state totals that determine the selection of electors.

The plan to render the College inert may be unconstitutional, especially given that the US Supreme Court in 2020, without dissenting votes, upheld state legislation that removed or punished "faithless" Electoral College delegates who refused to vote for the presidential candidates whom they had previously pledged to support. As in the case of sanctuary cities, ending the Electoral College without passing a formal constitutional amendment is yet another way for states to nullify federal law. Nonetheless, the movement is gaining popularity after the 2016 and 2020 elections.[7]

A somewhat similar but easier to implement and more nuanced effort is called the National Popular Vote Interstate Compact. This equally unconstitutional idea would require only *some* states to pledge all of their electoral votes, regardless of the particular vote tally in their jurisdictions, to the top national vote getter. Yet the compact seemingly violates Article I, Section 10 of the Constitution (i.e., "No state shall, without the Consent of Congress . . . enter into any Agreement or Compact with another State") in its implied effort to join states together in circumventing the Electoral College.

The aim of the compact is not to dismantle outright but rather to render irrelevant the Electoral College. It would require only enough states to sign on that in toto have the sufficient 270 majority of electors (of 538 total) to choose the winning presidential ticket. That is, participating states would pledge their assigned electors to any presidential candidate who won the greater nationwide vote. Currently some fourteen states—with two hundred electoral votes, just seventy shy of the needed majority—have passed the compact. More are planning to take up the issue on the theory that the Constitution can be altered without a constitutional amendment.[8]

But the logic is again perverse. It reflects the particular partisan political landscape of the early twenty-first century, given that most of the states in the compact are blue and most outside it are red. In sum, we would have two American voting systems working simultaneously yet antithetically to each other: mostly blue states ignoring the Electoral College and red states following constitutional mandates.

Yet what if state voters rebelled after seeing their majority votes nullified in the Electoral College? What if changes in political affiliations caused some states to renege on their promises once they saw unwelcome vote tallies? In a hit-and-miss nullification of the Electoral College, on a state-by-state basis, without a constitutional amendment, individual states could enter and leave the compact with majority votes of their legislatures and governors' assent. In other words, after 234 years of a uniform federal system of voting, some states would follow the Constitution and pledge their electors to the candidate who won the popular vote in their jurisdiction—and some would not.

A more hare-brained scheme for destroying both the Electoral College and the US Senate was recently proposed in a *Harvard Law Review* article:

> If we truly hold to be self-evident that all are created equal, then it is time to amend the Constitution to ensure that all votes are treated equally. Just as it was unfair to exclude women and minorities from the franchise, so too is it unfair to weigh votes differently. The 600,000 residents of Wyoming and the 40,000,000 residents of California should not be represented by the same number of senators. Nor should some citizens get to vote for President, while others do not.

And the solution such scholars propose?

> To create a system where every vote counts equally, the Constitution must be amended. To do this, Congress should pass legislation reducing the size of Washington, D.C., to an area encompassing only a few core federal buildings and then admit the rest of the District's 127 neighborhoods as states. These states—which could be added with a simple congressional majority—would add enough

votes in Congress to ratify four amendments: (1) a transfer of the Senate's power to a body that represents citizens equally; (2) an expansion of the House so that all citizens are represented in equal-sized districts; (3) a replacement of the Electoral College with a popular vote; and (4) a modification of the Constitution's amendment process that would ensure future amendments are ratified by states representing most Americans.[9]

In other words, create new states to obtain the votes to change the 234-year-old rules about amending the Constitution. Then abolish the existing Senate and the Electoral College and change the House membership. The aim is a predetermined, ends-justify-the-means goal of radical equality of result. The problem with even these abstract, often unhinged proposals is that they expand the parameters and lower the bar of the absurd. They make once radical ideas like ending the Electoral College seem like a moderate compromise in comparison.

But *why* are some Americans complaining at all about the Electoral College—and why now? On the one hand, progressives—there are no comparable conservative efforts to alter the Constitution—currently have done quite well in the Electoral College. Since 1988 Democrats have guaranteed the prizes of two of the three richest electoral-vote states, California (fifty-five) and New York (twenty-nine). They are therefore freed to spend more resources in so-called purple swing states.

That latitude is why after the two successful Obama elections and Electoral College blowouts of 2008 and 2012, Democrats were relatively silent on the issue. They supported the Electoral College, especially its supposedly invulnerable "blue wall" in the industrial Midwest and on the two coasts, which had been more or less invulnerable from 1992 to 2012. Indeed, until many states of the blue wall—most prominently Democratic Michigan, Ohio, Pennsylvania, and Wisconsin—began to erode in 2016, it had been considered an unassailable bulwark of Democratic electoral strategy. When most of the blue wall was resurrected in 2020, some talk of immediately ending the Electoral College vanished.

Partisanship, of course, is never one way. After their 2012 election disappointment, some Republicans objected that it would be nearly impossible for Republicans in the future to win the presidency, given that elector-rich states like California, Illinois, and New York all but ensured Democratic presidential candidates 104 electoral votes before a presidential campaign even started. A few Republicans and conservative spokespeople supported the "compact" to render the College meaningless.[10]

But, as the Framers knew, states change sympathies, ideologies, and allegiances. Elections in just four years can redefine a state as either a bellwether or irrelevant; states can swap from blue to red or red to blue. In the fifty-three years between 1966 and 2018, the now bluest of the blue states, California, elected four Republican governors (for thirty-one years of Republican administrations versus twenty-one of Democratic). The so-called eleven states of the Old South were Democratic for roughly one hundred years. Yet, after 1968, they began metamorphosing into their current solid-red status. Democrats currently believe they can soon flip red Georgia, Florida, and Texas into permanently blue states. And they may, given fundamental demographic changes. In any case, data suggest that historically the Electoral College has benefitted no particular party inordinately.[11]

Circumventing the Electoral College to achieve hypothetical and transient political advantages would also help to transform a unique constitutional and federal republic into a direct democracy. The ultimate aim once more is the end of the idea of republican citizenship itself, of some elements of constitutional government not being decided simply by an up or down vote.

We might remember the original purposes of the Electoral College as envisioned by the far-seeing Framers. Their chief task was to unite quite different states into one federal union. That is, they aimed to protect states by fusing their independent resources into a single defensible nation—but not to the extent of obliterating their local sovereignty and distinctive state and regional cultures.

Central was the federal idea of diffusion of power and authority. The Electoral College was one resource in that holistic effort to ensure that distinct states qua states had a voice in selecting a chief executive. Thus the college provided a check on the national candidates who otherwise might have focused entirely on popular ideologies directed at 51 percent of the mostly urban voting public at large. The Founders did not wish to render smaller states irrelevant in national elections by favoring more urban states with larger populations. The idea of a state as a check on federal power was stronger even than the commitment to the popular election of federal officials. It is no accident that today we speak of unique Vermonters or Virginians rather than just anonymous Americans who happen to live in those two states.

Some Founders, as students of eighteenth-century European politics and classical political theory and history, distrusted the mercurial nature of large urban populations. Others also feared the greater risk of fraud and corruption in a single-vote national election. They feared the possibility of, for instance, the sometimes irregular tabulation in Mayor Richard J. Dailey's Chicago of the 1950s and 1960s, or contemporary vote harvesting—the registering of voters and collecting and delivering of ballots by third parties—in many states, or the controversies that surrounded the 2020 election.

Yet, in theory, such warping of the voting would only affect one or a few states' electors and thus lessen the chance that conspiratorial fraud might encompass numerous states simultaneously. The Constitution's architects also thought that the Electoral College would discourage crowded fields of all sorts of fringe and mostly regional presidential candidates in which the eventual president might have won only a small plurality of the popular vote.

The current American two-party system, for better or worse, largely evolved naturally from the idea that candidates must win a *majority* (currently 270) of the combined individual states' electors rather than a possible small *plurality* of the national popular vote. The Founders, then, had no need to specify that presidential candidates would first run in their party's primary election, followed by a general election between the two top vote recipients of the two major parties that alone had a shot at obtaining 270 electoral votes. Instead, they assumed that under the likely workings of an Electoral College, the popular vote would never be atomized by lots of candidates and political parties.

No president, for example, has ever been elected simply by a small fraction of the popular vote. Even in the anomalous 1912 election, in which former Republican president Theodore Roosevelt, running as a third-party candidate (27 percent of popular vote), and incumbent William Howard Taft (23 percent) split the Republican total, the Democratic beneficiary Woodrow Wilson still garnered nearly 42 percent of the popular vote. Nonetheless, that nonmajority margin won him an overwhelming 435 of 531 electoral votes. Wilson's victory reminds us that the Electoral College can add legitimacy to presidents-elect who did not achieve a 51 percent popular-vote majority.

A similar result occurred earlier in the pivotal election of 1860. In a four-way race, Abraham Lincoln won less than 40 percent of the popular vote, but he gained legitimacy for his victory by capturing 180 electoral votes—some 28 more than needed for victory, nearly 60 percent of all Electoral College votes cast, and over twice the total of his closest competitor, former vice president John C. Breckinridge.

In the Jeffersonian sense, large cities were not felt to inculcate the self-reliance, resilience, and independence of the rural small towns and farms, and the country needed such balance. It still does today. The Electoral College, in modern times, continues to force politicians to campaign in those areas—like Cody, Wyoming; Carson City, Nevada; or Lincoln, Nebraska—where voters' concerns might prove a check on growing urban majorities. Thus it preserves and reminds the country at large of timeless values essential to republican government—which, after all, originated in rural ancient Greece and Italy.

Without the Electoral College, millions of rural citizens would be reduced to second-class status, given that candidates could focus on millions of voters in a large American city in a few hours, while it might take a week to reach commensurately sized but dispersed audiences spread across several states. In our global era, California and New York may be more economically reliant upon and even culturally sympathetic to, respectively, China, Japan, and South Korea or London and Paris than Ohio, Oklahoma, and Utah—as the blue coastal corridors of the United States look outward rather than within. Yet every four years the Electoral College reminds the country that the coastal economic clout of Silicon Valley and Wall Street, the cultural influence of the Ivy League and California's marquee universities, and the political leverage of Washington, DC, do not necessarily define America or always determine its political present and future.

Certainly, the Electoral College has not proved as antidemocratic as the European parliamentary system, in which prime ministers and presidents, as national leaders of their particular parties in power, can be changed without any national popular referendum. Unlike in Europe, American executive power is not contingent upon a labyrinth of alliances with and concessions to small and sometimes extremist political factions and parties.[12]

In sum, American presidential candidates usually do visit both rural and urban America. Those who would be president of the United States do campaign in Delaware, Kansas, New Hampshire, New Mexico, West Virginia, and Vermont, whose aggregate population is smaller than that of Los Angeles County alone.

Elections, until recently, have rarely been questioned. Periodic criticism of the Electoral College arises mostly after the rare occasion of a defeated party in an election having won the popular vote and thus claiming that the system is rigged against it by its opposition—even though both parties geared their campaigns to capture key swing states rather than just running up national vote pluralities.

In the present atmosphere, the Electoral College system remains a way of harmonizing an increasingly divided America, cloven into a globalized, coastal culture and a vast, more traditional interior. In a radically democratic age, it offers a continuing reminder that Americans are citizens of a constitutional republic, not of a radical democracy. They expect to be protected, by the Bill of Rights, the checks and balances of the executive, legislative, and judicial branches of the US government, and their own elected representatives, both from what 51 percent of the people wish to do on any given day and from the permanent caste of unelected bureaucrats.

There are lots of additional efforts either to change the Constitution formally or to find ways to nullify its articles and amendments, such as avoiding treaties and declarations of war. As in the case of ending the Electoral College, the effort at radical democratization ultimately would reduce the power of individual states and render them electorally all but lifeless.

Another long-standing progressive complaint focuses on the reality that one hundred US senators have never been elected by proportional demography, as is the House of Representatives. Originally, the Constitution tasked state legislatures with choosing senators. Such selection was an effort of the Framers to emulate ancient senatorial practices, such as those in Rome, in both name and spirit—a model of checks and balances deemed far superior to the ancient Greek brand of radical democracy and some later versions advocated by members of the French Enlightenment. Roman *senatores* ("the older ones"), for example, were appointed (for life) originally by the two consuls—themselves popularly elected in the Comitia Centuriata, an assembly of the people—and then later by elected *censores*. Thus, by design, the Senate itself originally provided a popular check on the zeal of Roman popular tribal assemblies.

After 125 years of American senatorial selection by legislatures, the progressive movement in 1913 finally "reformed" the Constitution with the Seventeenth Amendment, which mandated that each state choose its two senators by direct popular vote. Many conservatives continue to doubt the wisdom of amending the Constitution to allow direct election of senators. They suggest that the formerly appointed representatives of the Senate reflected the interests and will of popularly elected state legislators—and thus senators empowered the states, strengthened the federalist system, and better balanced the directly elected members of the House of Representatives.

But in the logic of always more progressive trajectories, direct election was soon seen as only the first step in a longer march to ensure professed radical equality. In recent years, momentum has increased again to redefine the Senate. It is no longer seen, as originally envisioned, as a smaller, mostly older, and more powerful body designed to "deliberate" or to slow down the popular energy of the House of Representatives and to harness some of the foreign policy exuberances of the presidency.

Instead the Senate is now to be rebooted as an accelerant of popular consensus. The driving force to end the Senate as we have known it over the last one hundred years is current political protest that it is far too conservative in comparison with the House. It purportedly enjoys too much power as a deliberative body in blocking a progressive president and liberal judicial appointments. In addition, complaints arise that smaller states are likely to be "whiter" than the new demographic normal of the most densely populated and urban states. Thus the Senate has allegedly become a tool of a tyrannical racial majority.[13]

Certainly, there is no black or Latino caucus in the Senate commensurate with such groupings in the House. Yet, given the logic of the Constitution, there was nothing inherently antidemocratic about the fact that for some twenty-three years California Democratic senators Barbara Boxer and Diane Feinstein were hardly representative of the state's rich gender, ethnic, economic, regional, and political diversity— inasmuch as both were liberal, senior, multimillionaire females living within a few miles of each other in exclusive neighborhoods of the San Francisco Bay Area, a profile further enhanced by Democratic Speaker of the House Nancy Pelosi, another Northern California female.[14]

By intent, there were at the founding constitutional antitheses between representatives and senators. In tandem, they were designed both to reflect and to modulate popular groundswells. Senators are elected for six years, not two, as representatives are—a way of shielding senators from expressions of occasional, transitory popular frenzy. House candidates who identify primarily by race or ethnicity may find constant congressional redistricting conducive to their constant reelection. But statewide elections for senators are a different matter. By definition, they encourage more moderate candidates who must win a wider group of voters beyond their own race, class, gender, and local tribal affinities prominent in increasingly gerrymandered congressional districts. Barack Obama, for example, in 2000 was trounced (61 to 30 percent) in his effort to unseat radical incumbent congressman Bobby Rush, a former Black Panther, in the Democratic primary election in Illinois's First Congressional District—a mostly Chicago and predominately African American district. Yet the more radical Rush would have had no chance of being elected a US Senator from Illinois—in the fashion of Obama's successful statewide effort four years later.

Senators also must be thirty years old, not twenty-five—on the idea that adults are soberer and more experienced (if less idealistic and impulsive) at thirty. Senators must have been citizens for nine, not seven years. They must live in the districts (i.e., the states) they represent, whereas congressional representatives need only live in their states and thus can reside outside their districts if they wish. In general, senators usually are on average from three to four years older than representatives.

Rather than the entire one-hundred-member Senate, just one of its three cohorts turns over every two years. That is, only one-third of all senators is elected during each national election every twenty-four months. The point is that at the creation of America, the Founders designed the Senate, in Roman style, to complement or, in paradoxically antithetical fashion, balance the more popular House with its current 435 representatives.

The nature of senatorial elections every two years usually hampers a party's possible presidential landslide every four years. Senate elections can also balance radical shifts in House representation that otherwise would completely refigure the legislative branch and easily green-light particular popular but occasionally transitory and poorly thought-out agendas or demagogic politicians of the age. Gridlock is not a modern notion. It is engineered into the original nature of the legislative branch to ensure that Americans, in the words of the emperor Augustus, "make haste slowly."

Moreover, we should remember that in the last half century, when Republicans were more frequently holding the presidency (1953–1961, 1969–1977, 1981–1993, 2001–2009), the Democrats more often controlled at least one house of the Congress. The reverse was true during the sixteen years of the Clinton and Obama presidencies, when Democratic administrations rarely controlled both houses of Congress for long.[15]

Many of the current complaints against senatorial selection center on purported inequality. As we have seen, critics point to some low-population states enjoying inordinate senatorial representation. Wyoming, for example, currently elects one senator per roughly 288,000 people. In contrast, in California, the nation's largest state where I reside, each senator theoretically represents roughly twenty million voters. In other words, in the logic of popular representation, a California senator serves a constituency nearly seventy times greater than that of his Wyoming counterpart and thus, in theory, should enjoy more senatorial clout. Or put more negatively, a mostly urban or suburban California voter has only one-seventieth the senatorial representation of his traditionally more rural Wyoming counterpart.

The Founders, as in the case of the Electoral College, were well aware of such asymmetries. But by intent, they saw the House of Representatives as a sufficient grassroots corrective and the two legislatures together as the ideal balance between collective state and popular interests. Of course, in a free, postmodern republic with fluid borders, millions of Americans change their state residencies yearly and with them the demographic ratios of senatorial representation. The Founders also envisioned that reality.

Likewise, they were aware of the role of population growth and understood that a House member represents an increasingly larger constituency. In 2020, each is elected from about 750,000 voting constituents. While the House has enlarged since the founding, its current membership of 435 representatives has been static since 1912, when it was readjusted based on the 1910 census; that number was set in stone by the Permanent Apportionment Act of 1929.

Put in democratic terms, if the House itself does not enlarge its membership, then each representative steadily represents more voters. In theory, if population continues to grow, voters' power is diluted by less proportional representation. Given that small-population states are allotted at least one member in the House and that some are smaller than 750,000 people (e.g., Alaska, Vermont, and Wyoming), there exists not just a steady loss of popular representation but "unequal" representation as well. In reaction to both population growth and the radicalization of the contemporary Democratic Party, there are also increased calls to expand the House of Representatives. After all, it is argued, the actual *size* of the House, like that of the Supreme Court, was never set in the Constitution. The proper makeup of the House and the intent of the Founders are a constant source of debate among constitutional scholars.[16]

What are the progressive remedies? Suggestions based on different algorithms and progressive agendas range from increasing the House to 930 or even some 2,800 members or more—on the theory that the House's mission is to equalize representation by population and not to reflect geographical diversity. Even more radical popular remedies, voiced in the media and universities and by progressive activists and politicians, would undo the traditional Senate and House. These ideas range widely from breaking up states into smaller ones, to admitting Puerto Rico and the District of Columbia as new states, to refiguring the Senate by increasing the allotment and number of senators to reflect proportional representation, to allowing allotment of fifty senators by national popular votes and fifty by state votes, to abolishing the Senate and elevating the House to a huge unicameral legislative body.

Others seek more practical and quicker remedies to thwart perceived conservative bias built into the constitutional system. In 2020, ex-president Barack Obama, while delivering the eulogy at the funeral of Representative John Lewis (D-GA), blasted the incumbent Republican administration and called for statehood for liberal Puerto Rico and Washington, DC. Obama was certainly correct that adding two states might be the quickest way both to enlarge the Senate by four members and, more germanely, in the short term to ensure a Democratic majority possibly for decades.[17]

As in the case of ending the Electoral College, progressives accept that the Founders largely flummoxed their current agendas by making it difficult to amend the Constitution. So other, extraconstitutional remedies for change must be found, often with allusion to foreign democracies seen as more popular and democratic. Whether they are more stable and functional, with a commensurate stable history, is seldom discussed.

More imaginatively, some progressives turn to the courts. They have sought to apply the Warren Court's 1964 "one man, one vote" ruling to the Senate. The latter decision—itself based on earlier preliminary and inspiring later court cases (e.g., especially *Gray v. Sanders* [1963], *Wesberry v. Sanders* [1964], *Reynolds v. Sims* [1964], and *Avery v. Midland County* [1968]) and used to argue for further expansion—ruled, inter alia, that states also must reapportion their allotted congressional districts on the basis of the latest census, ensuring all contain roughly the same population. Further and more radically, in a series of decisions the Warren Court also held that *both* houses of state legislatures must embrace similarly sized demographic state assembly and senate districts.

There are more current evolutionary arguments to change the Constitution. If the Supreme Court has already affirmed that the US House of Representatives and *both* houses of state legislatures must have districts of equal population size, then why, the argument goes, does the state-based US Senate stay exempt? Why is it not logically subject to the same popular ruling, if not de facto at least in spirit?

In other words, the courts, guided by the more abstract overriding doctrine of equality of result and the concrete issue of "one man, one vote," should be freed to overrule one of the fundamental tenets of the Constitution throughout its 234 years of existence. A cynic, of course, might reply that if a wave of radical conservatism should sweep the country in the next decade, then current reformers might praise the existing Senate as a necessary check against deplorables, irredeemables, clingers, and "Make America Great Again" know-nothings, whose national populism they found frightening and in need of slowing by soberer constitutional and judicious establishmentarians.

Finally, the Left has increasingly targeted the Senate filibuster, a maneuver not found in the Constitution but a well-known senatorial legacy with a pedigree of well over 180 years. The mechanism to stop a law's passage in the absence of a majority of senators to do so channeled the ancient Roman idea—made most famous by the loquacious Cato the Younger—of stonewalling any proposed legislation by deliberating it to death and thus precluding an actual vote. The filibuster's ostensible aim was to prevent one party's control of all three levers of governing—the presidency, the House of Representatives, and the Senate—from steamrolling through polarizing, extremist, or hyperpartisan legislation. Three-fifths of voting senators, or usually sixty votes—reduced in 1975 from a previous two-thirds requirement (66.7 percent)—are required to invoke "cloture" in order to stop a filibuster. Such a supermajority is somewhat rare in American history.

At Representative John Lewis's funeral in 2020, former president Obama also damned the filibuster as a racist relic of the Jim Crow era ("And if all this takes eliminating the filibuster, another Jim Crow relic, in order to secure the God-given rights of every American, then that's what we should do") and called for its repeal. Obama perhaps believed (correctly) at the time that in November 2020 Donald Trump would lose the presidency, lose the Senate, and not regain the House. And yet he may have (also correctly) feared that the Republicans still might salvage forty-one to fifty Senate seats and thus impede a radical proposed progressive agenda.

Oddly, as a senator in the minority party, Obama himself in 2005 had blasted any notion of eliminating the filibuster. In 2006 he even sought to filibuster the confirmation of Supreme Court nominee Judge Samuel Alito. Later in 2009–2010, as a president with a Democratic Congress and a filibuster-proof Senate supermajority, a content Obama never spoke out against the filibuster. And again, during all of 2017–2018, when the Republicans held the presidency and both houses of Congress, Obama and most Democrats grew quiet, as the filibuster was their only lever left to stymie the Trump agenda.[18]

More ironically still, Senate Majority Leader Harry Reid (D-NV) in 2013 had sprung the "nuclear option" and used his Democratic Senate majority to end the filibuster as it applied to judicial nominations. Reid planned to fast-track confirmation of Obama administration judicial nominees. Yet he never imagined that his party would lose the Senate the very next year. So he had inadvertently ensured that just four years later, the Trump administration would use its small Republican majority in the Senate to confirm nearly three hundred federal judges without worry of Democratic obstructionism.

The filibuster has been used both wisely and foolishly by both parties. Yet its current unpopularity reflects three recurrent themes of the present age. One, ending the Senate filibuster "democratizes" government by transforming policy debates into a 51 percent up or down vote. Two, it erases constitutional and nineteenth-century traditions designed to balance and check power and the asymmetrical momentum of one particular party or ideological movement. Three, it reflects a new short-term willingness to change the rules when they suddenly seem to have become politically obstructive to progressive agendas.[19]

Citizens must not only worry about the erosion of their current state and national votes. The courts, too, are now envisioned as political

operatives whose membership in turn must be more equally propor-
tioned. They are asked—and often agree—to assume legislative roles in
making rather than just adjudicating laws.

Article III of the US Constitution delineates the nature of federal
courts. Given that the president would appoint judges, political motives
in such selections could be assumed. Partisanship could be checked
somewhat by the need for Senate confirmation of judicial appointments. Yet the Constitution never mandated the *size* of the Supreme
Court other than to require one chief justice; thus by default it allowed
Congress to determine the actual number of associate justices on the
highest court.

Since 1869, the Supreme Court has had a static nine justices. That
century-and-a-half continuity had been somewhat at odds with the
chaotic practice of the prior eighty-two years. The original Judiciary
Act of 1789 placed six justices on the Supreme Court. But the number
waxed to nine and ten justices, then waned by 1863 back to six. The
changes almost always reflected contemporary efforts to warp court rulings to reflect the ideological agendas of the dominant political party.[20]

The most infamous effort at politicizing the court, of course, was
President Franklin Roosevelt's "court-packing" scheme of 1937 (formally known as the Judicial Procedures Reform Bill of 1937). Roosevelt's
efforts were designed to end Supreme Court opposition to the New
Deal, especially to his keystone National Recovery Administration.

Coming off a 1936 landslide reelection victory, an emboldened Roosevelt tried to alter the number and age of Supreme Court justices. His
"reform" would allow a president to nominate up to six new judges
(i.e., in theory to reach a maximum Supreme Court of fifteen justices),
one for each sitting justice who had served at least ten years and had
refused to retire within six months after turning seventy. There were
similar packing provisions for the perceived unsympathetic lower federal courts.

But the scheme was so blatantly partisan and the sixty-eight-year
tradition of a nine-justice court was even then so strong that even

Roosevelt's new and huge congressional majorities balked. Finally, the Democratic-led Senate (seventy of ninety-six senators) defeated the plan 70–22. Yet Roosevelt nonetheless may not have failed entirely. The existing nine-justice court subsequently tended to rule more favorably on the administration's New Deal legislation—apparently for fear of renewed efforts to remove or neuter perceived uncooperative and aged justices.

Court packing since that infamous failure has suffered an odious and infamous pedigree and reputation—at least until recently. Perhaps because increasing the number of Supreme Court justices requires no constitutional amendment and yet is seen as so patently political, the bipartisan establishment for the last nine decades has seen the gambit as explosive. Yet a number of 2020 Democrat presidential candidates advocated various new versions of Roosevelt's court-packing scheme—even resurrecting Roosevelt's earlier, discredited idea of a fifteen-justice court. Like Roosevelt, Democrats have grown furious over the recent revised ideological makeup of the court, especially President Trump's three conservative appointments, Neil Gorsuch, Brett Kavanaugh, and Amy Coney Barrett, who apparently ensured in some instances a 5–4 or occasional 6–3 conservative consensus on the Supreme Court.

During the election year 2020, the Senate often fought over the nature and viability of the so-called Biden rule. The purported Senate precedent maintained that no president in an election year should expect any Senate, controlled by the *opposite* party, to hold a vote on a presidential Supreme Court nomination until *after* the inauguration of the elected president the following year. Both Republicans and Democrats fought over whether there was ever such a rule. They battled over whether there should have been such a rule and, if so, whether either party was hypocritical in its application. The subtext of the argument on both sides was that the Supreme Court for the past sixty years had become activist, and justices were counted on to serve as a legislative accelerant for progressivism—a trend vehemently opposed by conservatives.

Rarely asked, however, was whether the political affiliation of a Supreme Court nominee really mattered all that much. Republican-appointed justices (e.g., Harry Blackmun, William Brennan, Lewis Powell, David Souter, John Paul Stevens, Potter Stewart, and Earl Warren), of course, had established a modern tradition of tacking to the left more frequently than their Democrat-appointed counterparts embraced conservative opinions.

In that context of ideological "maturation," Roosevelt's successful warning shot across the conservative Supreme Court bow may have encouraged contemporary court-packing advocates. FDR's implicit message was that if stubborn justices insisted on entertaining moderate strict-constructionist and originalist views, then someday they would face either reprisal removals or at least dilution of the court with additional, more liberal colleagues. Indeed, the current "conservative" court is beginning to experience just such flexibility. Chief Justice John Roberts especially, but also occasionally Associate Justices Neil Gorsuch and Brett Kavanaugh—unlike strict-constructionist associate justices Samuel Alito and Clarence Thomas—have strayed from conservative orthodoxy.[21]

No matter: Democrat presidential candidate Pete Buttigieg on the 2020 campaign trail hinted that as president he would seek to raise the number of Supreme Court justices to fifteen—supposedly half appointed by Democrats and half by Republicans. Other candidates at that time—Kamala Harris, Beto O'Rourke, and Elizabeth Warren—also promised, if elected, to consider packing or reformatting the court. Former attorney general Eric Holder likewise supports increasing the number of justices to ensure greater progressive representation and to balance Trump's three conservative picks.[22]

Various Democratic activist groups—including the unabashedly named Pack the Court ("The court has become a mechanism for the revanchist right to avoid electoral consequences for their unpalatable agenda.")—have not been subtle about their agendas. Pack the Court has advocated that any future Democratic-majority Congress simply select additional judges to correct what is now perceived as a 6–3 Republican majority that could exist for years and might undo much of the activist progressive judicial agenda of the last sixty years following the appointment of liberal Republican Earl Warren as chief justice.

All these ideas are not to be discounted. They are not just the musings of irrelevant academics or marginal political candidates. During the 2020 presidential campaign, a key controversy surrounded Democratic candidate Joe Biden's refusal to rule out a Democratic plan to pack the court in 2021 and beyond.[23]

So change, both political and institutional, in America has often followed a predictable trajectory: erstwhile abstract and apparently radical theories of the faculty lounge soon gain credence among and are fueled by foundations and activist groups, then culminate as official agendas of political candidates. The quite short campus-to-court-sanction lifespan of sanctuary cities, legal recognition of multiple genders, and the decriminalization of vagrancy often bypassed legislative consensus and at times overruled popular referenda.[24]

For much of the history of the United States, Americans above all cherished the Constitution's First Amendment ("Congress shall make no law respecting an establishment of religion, or prohibiting the free exercise thereof; or abridging the freedom of speech, or of the press; or the right of the people peaceably to assemble, and to petition the Government for a redress of grievances") and its Second ("A well-regulated Militia, being necessary to the security of a free State, the right of the people to keep and bear Arms, shall not be infringed").

Americans in general, and progressives in particular, had always held the First Amendment as sacrosanct. They championed it as their bulwark to protect edgy cultural expression, to curtail public school prayer, to ensure the safety of demonstrators and encourage mass protests, to stop censorship of unpopular expression, and even to mainstream pornography. In all these various ways, the Left felt the First Amendment was essential to expanding civil rights and freedom of thought, speech, expression, and association. They argued that an entrenched and potentially authoritarian, reactionary, and tradition-bound establishment endangered it. Traditionalists were felt to be unduly fearful of controversial art and avant-garde literature and expression, and a perennial impediment to needed cultural enlightenment.

The Left had even occasionally championed the right to bear arms, given its occasional fear of a powerful military-industrial-intelligence complex, as well as the history of well-armed majorities coercing vulnerable minorities. But not now. Our first two amendments are currently the most targeted of the Bill of Rights for radical changes to reflect contemporary political and ideological agendas. They are seen as obstacles to efforts that would further equality, diversity, inclusion, and, most importantly, the power of the federal government to enact such agendas.

In the case of the First Amendment, current progressives are waging a constant war with the courts and the public, mostly over the freedom-of-speech clause. The battle is mostly fought on university campuses and within local, state, and federal government bureaucracies. The debate generally reflects both ancient and modern ideological fault lines.

The debate also includes lots of transformative terms. One is "hate speech." A popular argument in universities and government agencies holds that particular political speech, texts, books, art, and music can become so incendiary, so hurtful that such expressions—appealing to prior court-approved narrow restrictions on free speech—should be banned as they often now are in the European Union. The assumption is that today's students, for example, are "snowflakes," too vulnerable to hear contrary arguments that they find "hateful," or "demeaning," or "marginalizing," or "hurtful." Censors, when issuing campus speech codes, often refer to Oliver Wendell Holmes Jr.'s 1919 admonition about the First Amendment's not protecting people falsely "shouting 'Fire!' in a crowded theater."[25]

Unfortunately, on campuses today, the definition of "hate" is fluid and flexible. It is often used to brand politically unorthodox or unwelcome expression as so hateful and inflammatory that it must be restricted to protect the vulnerable. In some sense, today's "hate speech" is now analogous to the "un-American speech" of the 1950s, whereby those supposedly espousing pro-communist themes were considered to have forfeited their First Amendment rights.

These current curbs can include efforts to silence faculty in the classroom, to punish students in their private conversations and social media postings, to prevent certain types of electronic communications, and to ban controversial speakers from campus. The restrictions are fought constantly in the courts. These suits are often resolved in antithetical ways, depending on the distinction between public and private universities, whether campuses do or do not receive federal funding, the particular ideological landscape of the ongoing debate, and, of course, the ideological makeup of the federal and state courts in which these cases are heard.[26]

Some of the most flagrant examples of speech indoctrination occur in mandatory diversity workshops on American campuses. In addition, government agencies and universities require the use of particular personal pronouns or expressions felt essential to promoting their notions of inclusivity and diversity. Certainly, as a senior fellow at the Hoover Institution at Stanford University, I have learned that I cannot talk or write freely and dispassionately about certain topics—illegal immigration, global warming, identity politics, abortion, affirmative action, Donald Trump, or policies concerning COVID-19 quarantine—without campus or student and faculty efforts to restrict my free expression or threaten me with career reprisals. In general, over the last three years, anywhere from 62 to 71 percent of Americans have expressed new fears of personal and career repercussions for speaking candidly.[27]

A new phrase, "freedom of speech, not of reach," is used mostly by the media, publishing, and especially Big Tech to suggest that while the government protects free speech in the public sphere, courts have clearly decided that private companies have the right—and sometimes the responsibility—to apply codes of conduct and censorship in their own domains. They have done so partly on the assumption that those denied or cancelled have freedom of choice and can go elsewhere. For example, if airline attendants do not like the speech codes at United Airlines, they can leave for other jobs in or out of the industry.

But do employees and customers always have such alternatives? When Twitter, Facebook, and other social media outlets in ideological and often haphazard fashion censor particular expression and suspend or ban citizens from their platforms, they increasingly begin to revisit constitutional questions of the 1960s. Back then some restaurants and motels claimed that their First Amendment freedoms included the right to serve anyone they wished—or did not wish. Often they assumed that those denied services because of their race, gender, or sexual orientation had lots of alternatives to eat elsewhere, when, in fact, on occasion they did not. So, if Twitter, for example, bans, or bars the expression of, one customer—such as the president of the United States with over seventy million followers—it need not show that it does not allow other social media users to express thoughts far more obscene, libelous, insurrectionary, or fallacious—such as the organizers of Antifa, for example, who used Twitter to coordinate their often violent street protests between 2016 and 2019. After all, a cancelled Trump can then simply use another social media provider.

But what if there are *no* other Twitter, Facebook, or Google competitors with comparable reach in an industry where the leading companies enjoy near-cartel status and are virtual monopolies, increasingly involving the chief ways in which Americans communicate with one another? In monopolistic fashion, Big Tech has the ability to choke off and shut down upstart rivals. Consider the case of Twitter's small, new rival Parler. It exercised no comparable restrictions on the free expression of its users. Yet its internet and smart phone access were virtually shut down by the collusive efforts of Amazon, Apple, and Google—at the very moment millions of former Twitter followers of the now cancelled Trump were moving over to the new company.[28]

One of the most bizarre paradoxes of contemporary liberal support for restrictions of free speech has been the return of versions of 1950s-era "loyalty oaths" that in many states once required each faculty member, as a condition of employment, to swear "that I am not a member of, nor do I support, any party or organization that believes in, advocates, or teaches the overthrow of the United States Government, by force or by any illegal or unconstitutional means, [and] that I am not a member of the Communist Party." Today, many universities require applicants for employment to send in a "diversity statement." It is certainly a far more sophisticated pledge than the old loyalty oaths. But perhaps it is even more dangerous—given the sanctimonious denials that it discriminates against free thought and expression. That is, potential hires must outline past contributions to diversity and the methods by which they would exhibit in their courses "the skills and experience to advance institutional diversity and equity goals." That is bureaucratese for ensuring that future faculty members will share, in their teaching, assignments, and advising, the same ideological approaches to controversial issues, such as affirmative action, disparate impact, and proportional representation in higher education. Such intrusion interferes with the professor's academic freedom to control the content of his curriculum and expression.

Universities reportedly use detailed "scoring systems" to rate applicants' ideological purity and suitability that go well beyond their expertise and experience in educational preparation, scholarship, teaching, and publication. Indeed, on many universities' standard forms any diversity statement that "defines diversity only in terms of different areas of study or different nationalities, but doesn't discuss gender or ethnicity/race" was seen as disqualifying, as were any that discounted "the importance of diversity."

Once-liberal monitoring groups such as the American Association of University Professors and the American Civil Liberties Union (ACLU)—which, as wealthy and huge bureaucratic organizations, often still boast of their prior grassroots opposition to "loyalty oaths" designed to prevent former or current Communist Party members from teaching—now are either silent on the issue of mandatory "diversity statements" or support them.[29]

In particular, perhaps most emblematic of the radical erosions in free expression is the current metamorphosis of the American Civil Liberties Union from a professed protector to a critic of the First Amendment. In past times, both Left and Right often denounced the ACLU for protecting the demonstrations and free speech of unhinged reactionary and radical groups, from Nazis to Stalinists to Klansmen, who were roundly hated by most Americans. The one predictable constant was that the ACLU would sometimes go to radically unpopular lengths to remind the nation that reprehensible people still had the right to say disgraceful things—this was the unfortunate but necessary price to ensure free expression for everyone else.

The ACLU's supposed position was the common one that the First Amendment was not intended to protect consensus, or inoffensive expression, or politically popular speech. Rather, the Founders enshrined it to stop Americans from banning what most usually despised or just opposed and certainly what they did not wish to hear or otherwise deemed politically unwelcome. Yet, after the 2016 Trump election, the ACLU announced it was joining progressive efforts in what former Democratic senator Joe Lieberman called "issue-based electioneering." That was a pleasant way of saying that the ACLU's protection of the First Amendment would now hinge on the particular ideology of those requesting the organization's help.[30]

The ACLU has since announced the creation of programs of "resistance training" to prep volunteers to sue the former Trump administration on partisan issues. It has also proclaimed that anyone legally bearing a licensed firearm at a demonstration will not be eligible for ACLU defense—on the theory that citizens' civil rights are not necessarily defined by the Bill of Rights. In sum, the ACLU no longer believes in its past defense of the First Amendment (or Second

Amendment), which it now sees as an obstacle to banning purported "hate speech." Or as the left-wing *Nation* magazine put it, "In a fundamental transformation, the ACLU is now incorporating volunteer organizers to work in tandem with its staff attorneys. The hope, said executive director Anthony Romero, is to seed a kind of citizen-led civil-rights defense force, and to transform the ACLU into an organization with clout at the ballot box." The First Amendment, once a shield for liberty, is now often viewed as an obstacle to equity.[31]

There are also renewed efforts to ban the sale of particular weapons, restrict those eligible to buy them, and even seize legally purchased weapons. Failed 2019 presidential candidate Beto O'Rourke—for a time mentioned as a possible "gun czar" in the next Democratic administration—promised to confiscate some types of guns ("Hell yes, we're gonna take your AR-15, your AK47!"). Fellow candidates Kamala Harris and Cory Booker echoed his support for government-mandated buybacks. "Buyback" programs for decades in larger cities have offered cash for voluntary *surrender* of firearms. But for the most part they have had not much, if any, effect in reducing gun violence—given the huge number of unlicensed and illegally obtained guns that circulate easily in municipalities and increasingly fewer arrests for felons illegally in possession of firearms, many of them models that are illegal themselves.[32]

Note the Orwellian terminology of an envisioned coerced "buyback." The federal government had neither owned individuals' guns nor sold them to individuals. So Washington can hardly buy "back" something that it never possessed. How any proposed mandatory "buyback" of semiautomatic rifles would work is never quite specified. Given that there may be fifteen to twenty million semiautomatic rifles capable of holding large clips (inaccurately called "assault weapons") in private hands, would law enforcement visit private homes and use force to confiscate them?

In March 2020, the city of Los Angeles and the LA County Sheriff's Department closed all gun stores inside city limits, in unincorporated areas, and in forty-two cities. The rationale was that they were unessential businesses, like liquor stores, and might facilitate panic gun purchasing—especially by first-time buyers unacquainted with gun safety and usage—following the release of some seventeen hundred inmates from area jails due to COVID-19 fears. Soon, facing lawsuits and popular demonstrations, authorities relented and allowed stores to reopen, given that they never had offered a coherent reason for singling out arms sellers for closure. In late May 2020, major city police forces in Minneapolis, Portland, Seattle, and Los Angeles stood down in the face of thousands of looters and arsonists who roamed streets and ransacked small businesses in the wake of the protests over the death of George Floyd while in police custody in Minneapolis. A few owners who had access to legal semiautomatic rifles used them successfully to save their stores, while the establishments of others less fortunate in the vicinity burned or were destroyed.[33]

Three relatively recent developments have spurred these renewed progressive efforts to curb citizens' rights to bear arms. One, the spate of mass shootings, often on school campuses, infrequently through the use of semiautomatic rifles with large-capacity clips, has fueled public furor over the state's inability to stop such rampages. In a cacophony of calls to hire school guards, or to arm teachers, or to expand mental health screening, the solution of just banning or curtailing the sale of particular weapons is seen as the easiest and most effective—even though the great majority of the nation's homicides are committed with handguns, not with rifles of any type.

A second impetus to amend or repeal the Second Amendment comes from virtually annual mass killings of mainly minority youth in many of our inner cities, especially in St. Louis, Baltimore, Detroit, and Chicago—as witnessed during 2020–2021 when homicide rates soared. Over seven thousand African American males are murdered each year on average in the United States, the vast majority by handguns and at the hands of other blacks. Although most large American municipalities already have the strictest gun controls among the nation's local and state jurisdictions, such statutes either have not stemmed handgun violence or, in fact, may have facilitated shootings by making it difficult for law-abiding citizens to purchase and use firearms in a deterrent fashion.

In any case, if strictly enforced, these gun-control laws would lead to increased incarceration of minority youth—at a time when many of the latter are being released early from prisons before the completion of their sentences. Nonetheless, "banning guns" becomes a rallying point for reformers, especially given the shift in the blame for homicide from the shooter to his tool. Cracking down on illicit guns or beefing up penalties for their use is a far more difficult task than restricting the access of law-abiding citizens to firearms. Banning so-called assault weapons like the AR-15 for a decade (1994–2004) did not statistically result in fewer gun deaths.[34]

Third, with the election of Donald Trump came progressive calls especially to monitor supposed alt-right racist groups, whose members were legally well armed and, on some occasions, had visited public spaces armed to publicize their Second Amendment rights. Some had bragged of their vigilante willingness to protect themselves from both criminals and the federal government or had battled in the streets with leftist counterparts. From 2018 to 2020, loose talk of a virtual "civil war" was in the air. Antifa—a generic term describing a loose organization of local and state hard-left "antifascist" militant groups—marches, for example, were beginning to draw smaller crowds of right-wing counter-demonstrators, who were often armed and seemingly more familiar with guns than were the occasional left-wing protesters who bandied them about.

In all these instances, progressives have argued for the need to enhance prior court-approved restrictions on the easy sale and use of particular weapons, given new existential challenges. America is an increasingly urban and suburban society. There are ever-fewer rural residents, who are most likely to grow up and use weapons for hunting and personal defense. Consequently, some of these restrictionist efforts enjoyed majority public support—at least until the national defund-the-police efforts in summer and autumn 2020 in reaction to the death of George Floyd.

Urbanization, along with the end of national conscription, accelerated the general trend in which millions of Americans had not only never bought or used a firearm but likely had never seen one. Yet gun sales reached record heights during the 2020 COVID-19 quarantines and in reaction to rioting, looting, and arson in the streets of major cities. Apparently some five million first-time buyers, without prior firearms experience, abruptly concluded that they no longer could rely on local police for their personal safety in times of national protests and violence.

Yet past strict restrictions of the Second Amendment have rarely curtailed mass shootings. Proposed further curbs likely would not either. So-called red-flag laws—allowing the state to curtail the Second Amendment rights of those perceived as unstable or posing threats, in some cases based on the claims of a family member—would likely not have stopped many mass shooters. Unfortunately, most mass murderers kept quiet and to themselves and rarely gave prior evidence of either a propensity for gun violence or mental instability. Most mass shooters also passed universal background checks and bought their guns months or even years before the commission of their crimes, thus making increasing waiting periods for gun purchases often seem noble but ultimately too often irrelevant. Other proposals, from limiting gun purchases to one per buyer per month or raising the eligible age to twenty-one or even thirty likely would also not have precluded most mass shooters.[35]

In general, data reveals that in 2017 about forty thousand Americans were killed under various circumstances by firearms. A minority (37 percent) of those deaths were homicides. In 2017, the latest year for gun *murder* statistics, the rate of gun deaths of all sorts (including suicide) per 100,000 people was 4.6—a much lower figure than the per capita rate of 7.7 in 1974, some forty-five years ago.

Banning or confiscating so-called assault weapons does not change the reality that most shooting homicides are committed with handguns. Rifles, including so-called assault weapons, account for only 4 percent of annual gun murders. Instead of contextualizing the Second Amendment per se, it might be wiser to ensure stiffer enforcement of existing laws, such as those applicable to the possession of stolen guns and the use of a gun by a convicted felon or guns used in the commission of a felony.

Finally, we should remember that the Founders in some sense saw the Second Amendment as the most important of the Bill of Rights. It alone ensured that the people themselves could enforce the other nine amendments in extremis. Indeed, in the arguments over the Constitution, the federalists assumed that the right to bear arms precluded the need for a Bill of Rights, given that a federal government could not deny civil rights, even if it wished, to any populace adequately armed.[36]

There are other formal efforts to undermine the Constitution besides watering down the First and Second Amendments. Among them are the deliberate nonenforcement of existing federal laws and increasingly state laws as well. Certainly, citizens of a republic expect *all* their federal laws to be equally enforced throughout their nation across state lines. The sometimes radically diverse regional, religious, racial, ethnic, and gender composition of the citizenry does not nullify that duty. So each instance in which a city, county, or state decides to ignore or override a federal statute weakens the fabric of the entire republic and favors some citizens at the expense of others.

Formal nullification of particular federal law has a long, usually checkered history. Sometimes nullifying states have deemed the federal law in question unconstitutional, regardless of federal court rulings. Or, more flagrantly, they have simply determined it to be unpopular with, or at least not supported by, a majority of state residents. Therefore, they have chosen to nullify particular federal laws by overriding them with state legislation, ordering law enforcement agencies not to comply, or simply ignoring them altogether.

At times, states have anchored their defense in the "compact theory." This strategy dates back to the original arguments of the Framers regarding state versus federal jurisdictions. The proposition ultimately argues that state legislatures should have the power to override the US Congress or at least the rulings of federal judges. The US Supreme Court has repeatedly rejected such states' rights doctrines, emphasizing that Article III of the Constitution gives the Court final authority to interpret all laws. States also cannot make arrangements with each other that sidestep the federal government, as outlined by the so-called supremacy clause in Article VI, Paragraph 2 of the US Constitution.

Of the dozens of state nullification efforts in American history, at least four stand out as serious challenges to the idea of a federally unified and cohesively law-abiding United States. In 1832, deep antipathy within the cotton-exporting South to the North-inspired federal tariffs of 1828 and 1832 prompted an emboldened South Carolina to announce that it simply would not enforce federal tariffs within its own state jurisdiction. One subtext of the South Carolina decision to annul federal law was, of course, the battle over slavery: successful defiance by South Carolina of tariff laws might embolden the entire South to ignore increasing federal efforts, also initially anchored most commonly in New England, to prohibit slavery nationwide or at least in new territories and states. President Andrew Jackson threatened to send federal troops into South Carolina to enforce the tariffs and thereby ensured that South Carolina would back down—and no other southern states would join its nullification efforts.[37]

The issue arose again in the 1850s in a series of court decisions concerning state fugitive-slave laws. In the most infamous, 1857's *Dred Scott v. Sandford*, the Supreme Court found that fugitive African American slaves did not legally possess US citizenship rights. Thus, even when they resided as free men in the North, federal law—as interpreted by the Court—still defined them as mere chattel property belonging to their former masters in the South; thus they had to be returned.

In contrast, until the outbreak of the Civil War in April 1861, some northern states attempted to nullify federal court rulings deemed pro-slavery, more often by ad hoc private efforts to rescue runaway slaves and shepherd them northward. The idea of nullifying federal law no longer had a consistently ideological basis. It was either opposed or supported on the merits of the convenient politics of the times. On occasion, southern nullificationists insisted that northerners be punished for disobeying rulings of the Supreme Court with the force of federal law.

Far more commonly, most of the eleven states of the future Confederacy assumed that they had the right to ignore increasing federal efforts to curtail slavery—eventually to the point of illegally appropriating federal property within their own state jurisdictions, which inevitably led to secession and civil conflict. The result was the bloodiest war in American history. After the loss of nearly seven hundred thousand Americans, the nullification issue was rendered largely moot, given its proven propensity to lead to civil strife, based on both ideology and geography, and its odious association most often with Confederate efforts to protect slavery.[38]

The third famous epidemic of nullification came to a head, again in the South, during the 1950s and 1960s over the issue of federally mandated racial integration and the reestablishment of legal protections for African Americans living in the South. Since the end of Reconstruction, a number of state laws that were often in conflict with federal laws and court rulings had deprived blacks of their civil rights. Ultimately, Presidents Dwight D. Eisenhower and John F. Kennedy both sent federal troops into the South to uphold federal law and sometimes federalized state police to ensure enforcement of US government court rulings.[39]

In all these examples, nullification turned out poorly for the wayward states involved, whether in matters of tariffs, slavery, or Jim Crow. In the case of the Civil War, nullifications proved disastrous for the nation at large. No wonder, then, that until recently progressives considered nullification insurrectionary, an archaic states' rights throwback to the antebellum South, as well as crackpot, racist, and a relic of Jim Crow.

Not now. In the last decade, new forms of nullification have emerged. As with the new "diversity statements," it is oddly a progressive trend and contrary to past liberal denunciations of "states' rights" efforts. Sanctuary cities—a euphemism paralleling American cities with medieval churches, which offered asylum to those unjustly arrested and sought out by monarchs—seek to render elements of federal immigration law null and void.

"Sanctuary" exempts from deportation not just those who entered and continue to reside in the United States illegally. It also applies to foreign nationals without legal status who are arrested for criminal violations and detained by local authorities pending trial but not turned over to Immigration and Custom Enforcement (ICE) officials for possible deportation. Instead, suspects are often bailed and released from temporary custody, and information about their status is deliberately withheld from federal immigration officials.[40]

There are currently in the United States an estimated 550 or so sanctuary jurisdictions—entire states, counties, cities, and municipalities. Sanctuary officials feel that federal enforcement of the southern border is either unnecessary or immoral. Thus, they have decided that entering and residing in the United States at will and without permission should be no real, punishable crime. They also assume that they lack legislative majorities in the Congress to amend or overturn the federal immigration laws that they so often ignore. While the majority of illegal aliens are no doubt law-abiding and have avoided public dependency, the pool of unlawful immigrants, at somewhere between eleven million and twenty million, is so large that even small percentages of lawbreakers can translate into hundreds of thousands of criminal aliens.[41]

The liberal Migration Policy Institute found that there are over eight hundred thousand illegal aliens with criminal records, nearly seven hundred thousand of them for felonies. These numbers, of course, reflect only those who have been arrested and faced trial, not the unknown number who have committed crimes without being apprehended or charged. In some sanctuary cities, lawlessness among undocumented immigrants has reached epidemic proportions.

Heather MacDonald of the Manhattan Institute had long ago argued that in 2004 two-thirds of all outstanding felony warrants in the city of Los Angeles, as well as 95 percent of outstanding murder warrants, involved illegal aliens. Sanctuary cities are on record as having released into the general population over ten thousand known criminal aliens whom ICE agents were attempting to deport. In addition, hundreds of thousands of criminals are currently protected from deportation as they await trial and sentencing. Among the most infamous cases is that of Juan Francisco Lopez-Sanchez in 2015. He was a *seven-time convicted felon and five-time deported illegal alien* who was not turned over to ICE by the San Francisco Sheriff's Department, which had him in custody on a drug charge. He was instead released and just weeks later shot and killed San Franciscan Kate Steinle—only to be later acquitted by a San Francisco jury of both murder and manslaughter charges, while his felony weapon-possession conviction was later overturned on appeal.[42]

The sanctuary city principle is akin to roulette. The odds suggest that most illegal aliens detained by local officials are not career felons and thus, in the eyes of those officials and activists, supposedly need not be turned over to ICE for deportation. Concerning the chance that some of the ten thousand released criminals will go on to commit further crimes in the manner of seven-time-convicted felon and five-time-deported illegal alien Lopez-Sanchez, officials assume that the public outcry will be episodic and quickly die down—or will at least not pose political problems as great as would deporting them.

The problem with legal nullification is always the enduring principle, never just the immediate landscape, of its implementation. For example, many in the rural West oppose the Endangered Species Act. Might Wyoming declare that federally protected rodents and insects are not protected inside its huge expanse when such pests obstruct construction of dams or highways?

Many conservatives oppose federal restrictions on gun sales. Could Boise, Idaho, declare handgun purchases within its city limits immune to federal firearms statutes? In fact, in 2020 local officials announced that Utah County, Utah, was a "Second Amendment sanctuary." They then proclaimed that state and federal laws deemed in conflict with the Second Amendment simply would not apply.

Perhaps Little Rock, Arkansas, could ignore a Supreme Court ruling and declare gay marriage illegal within its jurisdiction. What legally consistent rationale would supporters of the sanctuary state of California have for objecting to such nullifications—that neither the state nor city had the right arbitrarily to ignore a federal law or to obstruct the law enforcement duties of federal officials?

As a remedy to such reactionary nullifications of liberal federal laws, would San Francisco or Los Angeles advocate cutting off federal funds, sending in federal agents, or nationalizing the local or state police? All of these were proven remedies imposed on recalcitrant southern states that refused to abide by federal integration and civil rights laws in the 1960s.[43]

Such hypocrisies were evident when many local and county jurisdictions were considering nullifying the 2015 Supreme Court ruling making gay marriage legal throughout the United States. In shock that any local or regional entity would dare defy the Court's ruling, liberals correctly emphasized, "This concept [nullification] has a long but not especially honorable pedigree in U.S. history"—apparently oblivious that such a dangerous doctrine underpinned the entire sanctuary city movement.[44]

Again, these scenarios of conservatives nullifying federal laws in tit-for-tat fashion, empowered by the liberal success of the sanctuary city nullification movement, are not the stuff of make-believe. Recalcitrant Nevada rancher Cliven Bundy in 2014 invoked the doctrine of federal nullification in accordance with the supposed protocols of the "sovereign citizen movement." He certainly enjoyed some rural public support in the West as a die-hard rebel for his refusal to pay his federal grazing fees on lands that his family had ranched for decades. Yet the federal government eventually arrested him and charged him with a variety of felony counts—until a federal court judge forced the government to drop all charges on grounds of prosecutorial misconduct.[45]

In reaction to the election of Democratic legislative majorities in Virginia that promised tighter gun-control legislation than current federal restrictions, more than one hundred conservative Virginia cities and counties announced that they were to become sanctuary jurisdictions not subject to *state* gun laws. In a sanctuary city twist, they appealed to a higher *federal* law grounded in the Second Amendment.[46]

That trend of local jurisdictions defying state authority on the theory of adhering to overriding federal law is spreading. In California, a number of county and city jurisdictions are nullifying sanctuary state laws. They are citing their fealty to a higher federal law over their own state's apostasy. Will the federal government then intervene to offer kindred counties protection from a wayward state? Some fourteen California cities and counties have announced that state sanctuary laws simply do not apply within their jurisdictions.[47]

When states nullify federal law of any sort, utter chaos follows. A Byzantine series of suits and countersuits arises among local, state, and federal agencies. The only paradox is the convolution of politics: former conservative states' rights advocates often champion the omnipotence of federal jurisdiction while erstwhile liberal federalists now support formerly conservative nullification of federal law.

Perhaps the most recent and dramatic instance of the nullification of state and local laws—"de facto nullification" as a result of politicized decisions by mayors and governors—came during the mass rioting following the police killing of George Floyd in May 2020. For the first few days of violent protests, arson, looting, and destruction, mayors in Minneapolis, Portland, and Seattle, as well as dozens of other cities, did not provide police protection for vulnerable small businesses or for state and federal buildings from police precincts to federal courthouses. Nor could authorities protect the right of citizens in their jurisdictions to have their persons and property protected from violent looters and protesters. Nor did governors consider calling in National Guard soldiers or asking Washington to send military help, until they feared the violence would turn their downtowns into no-go zones. In part, their decisions reflected unpreparedness and lack of sufficient resources to deal with mass rioting and arson.

Initially nullification also stemmed from officials' sympathy with the national protests against instances of police brutality and hopes that such government laxity would be interpreted as magnanimity, to be reciprocated by protesters' rejecting illegality, rather than as a lack of deterrence and sanctioning of further violence. When violent demonstrators simply declared a section of downtown Seattle as their own sovereign territory, Mayor Jennifer Durkan declared that such lawlessness might well mark a "summer of love" and that the atmosphere was analogous to a "block party." Those euphemisms served to justify the reality that she did not order the arrest of violent protesters for weeks. But most of all, the 2020 instances of nonenforcement of laws—and opposition to the arrival of federal marshals to protect federal property within states as well as the safety of citizens—were political acts deemed useful for an array of political agendas in a landscape of mostly liberal mayors and governors at odds with a conservative Trump administration.[48]

The concept of giving violent protesters free rein by deliberately not enforcing existing criminal statutes was likely first institutionalized by liberal Baltimore mayor Stephanie Rawlings-Blake, under the doctrine of allowing "space," during the April 2015 riots in her city: "I made it very clear that I work with the police and instructed them to do everything that they could to make sure that the protesters were able to exercise their right to free speech. It's a very delicate balancing act. Because while we try to make sure that they were protected from the cars and other things that were going on, *we also gave those who wished to destroy space to do that as well*" (emphasis added).

Five years later, Minnesota governor Tim Walz likewise did not call in the state National Guard to quell unchecked violence in the state's capital. He too adopted a doctrine of giving "space" to protesters in hopes that nullification of laws might lead to peaceful demonstrations. Minneapolis mayor Jacob Frey explained why he had even allowed arsonists to burn down an entire municipal police precinct with immunity from criminal indictment: "We could not risk serious injury to anyone, and we will continue to patrol the third precinct, entirely. We will continue to do our jobs in that area. Brick and mortar is not as important as life. Happy to answer any questions on this topic. . . . The resources that we will offer to the people of the third precinct will continue. Period. The building is just bricks and mortar. It's a building."[49]

Frey seemed clueless in a number of ways when he did not contest the burning of a police station. Apparently, he did not fathom that such indulgence only fueled more violence, as followed in the ensuing days. Buildings and real property are not merely "bricks and mortar." They are public properties and, as such, symbols of civilization, none more so than police stations. Moreover, they are paid for and owned by citizens, not the private domain of the mayor. He is elected as an executive to enforce and execute existing laws, not to selectively ignore them.

What prompted the doctrine of nullifying law enforcement in times of riot and arson? Again, ideology mostly. All the mayors of the cities that experienced the most widescale violence—Los Angeles, Minneapolis, New York, Philadelphia, Portland, and Seattle—were progressive Democrats, as were many of the police chiefs, governors, local prosecutors, and state attorneys general. The consensus was that, given society's culpability for allowing a racist police officer in Minneapolis allegedly to kill an African American in custody, protecting its infrastructure was simply not a high priority, in comparison with virtue-signaling solidarity with the protesters—at least initially before entire swaths of such cities became war zones.

Who in the end paid for the nonenforcement of laws prohibiting violent protests and street violence? For the "tolerance" granted looters to give them space for their theft? For government officials romancing of Antifa terrorists? Mostly African American and other inner-city citizens, many of whose stores and businesses were closest to the downtown violence and thus left vulnerable to the looting and burning. As it turned out, the wages of not enforcing the law fell most heavily upon the citizens with the least ability to object to the nullifying of enforcement of the very statutes that civilization relies upon to protect the vulnerable. Indeed, in the midst of defund-the-police movements and reluctance among dispirited officers to enter dangerous crime-ridden areas, murders in 2020 soared in most American cities. In some cases, district attorneys failed to prosecute crimes; in others, law enforcement simply lost all sense of prior deterrence on the assumption that either criminals would not be arrested or, if arrested, would not be prosecuted.[50]

In sum, state and local nullification erodes the rights of the citizen. He loses federal protection by reason of living within a state that rejects full implementation of federal law. He forfeits the vaunted idea of equal protection under the law, given that jurisdictions or authorities pick and choose which elements of federal law they will obey, predicated on the race, class, gender, or ideological profile of the particular offender and his victim or the particular political agenda they seek to enhance. All efforts of the Trump administration to disallow sanctuary city nullification failed, due either to court challenges to executive orders or to congressional infighting among Republicans during their brief 2017–2018 majorities in the House and Senate.

Nullification additionally threatens to add, in Civil War fashion, a geographical element to national disunity. Southern and Western jurisdictions consider nullifying federal gun laws, while coastal enclaves vow not to enforce federal immigration law. For every left-wing attempt to disregard federal or state law, there will no doubt soon appear a right-wing effort to do the same. Then the federal law itself will have little authority. The citizen will be living in an Athenian-style ochlocracy, in which what 51 percent of the people in local or state polls wish on any given day becomes de facto law—until they change their minds on the next.

There are yet other efforts to render the Constitution and the intent of the Founders increasingly negotiable, to facilitate contemporary political agendas at the expense of the citizen—a prime example being the use and abuse of impeachment. On December 19, 2019, the House of Representatives impeached President Donald Trump in the midst of a national debate over a temporary halt in assistance to Ukraine— just as news began to leak of the spread of a strange new coronavirus from China. On February 5, 2020, the Senate acquitted Trump of two impeachment charges, almost as soon as the articles of impeachment were belatedly delivered to the upper house after a deliberate delay of nearly six weeks. Then, again, on January 13, 2021, during the waning days of the one-term Trump administration, the president was again impeached. His trial (February 9 to 13) occurred *after* he left office and may well have been unconstitutional, given that he was by then a private citizen. In any case, Trump was the first president to have been impeached, tried, and acquitted twice, the first to have faced a Senate impeachment trial after he left office, and the first to be tried without the participation of the chief justice of the Supreme Court, who refused to take part in the *post officium* proceedings.

Note that the impeachment of "the President, Vice President, and all civil Officers of the United States" has been rare in American history. Although the Constitution does not specify exactly who "civil Officers of the United States" are, so far the House has impeached only nineteen federal officials, with the majority acquitted by the Senate. The impeached include fifteen federal justices (with eight convictions in the Senate), one senator (acquitted), one cabinet officer (acquitted), and only three of forty-six presidents (all acquitted).[51]

Article II of the Constitution lists, if somewhat opaquely, the grounds for impeaching a president and other high officers: "The President, Vice President and all civil Officers of the United States, shall be removed from Office on Impeachment for, and Conviction of, Treason, Bribery, or other high Crimes and Misdemeanors." The details of the last category, "other high Crimes and Misdemeanors," were never spelled out, however, and that lacuna has led to a great deal of controversy over that phrase's precise meaning ever since. The dispute may explain why impeachment and subsequent conviction in the Senate has been extremely rare. And in the case of the presidency, it has been nonexistent, as the Founders perhaps had hoped.

In Article I, the Constitution sets out the procedures for an odd characteristic of American republican government: the House has the sole power of impeachment; the Senate alone tries those successfully impeached—a bicameral procedure borrowed from the British House of Commons and House of Lords. Conviction requires a two-thirds vote of the senators *present* during the trial, making it a much more difficult proposition than indicting a president in the House by a simple majority vote. A president who is convicted and removed is not exempt from subsequent legal indictment and trial. More practically, since all House members face reelection every two years, such elections can become referenda on either warranted or superfluous presidential impeachment hearings and votes.

The Founders thought a great deal about instituting checks on the power of each of the three branches of government, especially the presidency, beyond the election cycle. The two houses of Congress together can override presidential vetoes, and the Senate alone can reject presidential nominees and submitted treaties. Congress alone can declare war and fund the government. Giving the House the power to originate financial bills and bring articles of impeachment is further compensation for the Constitution's supposed "democracy deficit."

In *Federalist Papers* Nos. 65 and 66, Alexander Hamilton took up at length the problem of impeachment of the president—an act that in effect overruled a vote of the Electoral College and by extension the will of voters. Hamilton worried that inevitably the president's political opposition would wield impeachment as a political tool. He feared the outcome ultimately could be decided more "by the comparative strength of parties, than by the real demonstrations of innocence or guilt."

In other words, periodic impeachment could in theory become an endless replay of a prior election—or a way to warp a future one. Presidents, then, would likely not be impeached when their party controlled the House. But they certainly might be when their party did not—another prescient observation by a somewhat cynical Hamilton. Impeachment was largely envisioned as a congressional deterrent to presidential power that might turn criminal, but in fact, Hamilton worried, it could devolve into a political attack on an otherwise successful president whose popularity would likely ensure reelection. The vote of the citizen, then, could be nullified after or before an election.

Addressing worries such as these, the Framers listed the necessary criminal criteria for impeachment and required a two-thirds vote for conviction in the Senate. That fact suggests that while the House alone could impeach a president if he committed treason, bribery, or other high crimes and misdemeanors, it was under no obligation to do so.

Furthermore, crimes were specified, not simple poor judgment, supposed abuse of power, alleged incompetence, unpopularity, obnoxiousness, vague misbehavior, private sexual peccadillos, or even fights with or "obstruction" of the Congress. Given the relative ease of a majority impeachment vote and the extreme difficulty of a two-thirds Senate conviction vote, the Framers expected the former to be rare, the latter almost impossible. And until recently, they were mostly right.[52]

Indeed, Hamilton in *Federalist Papers* No. 65 and especially No. 66, and in other papers as well, defended the privileged role of the US Senate as the final arbiter of an impeachment trial in a larger context of replying to contemporary skepticism that the Senate already might enjoy too much power under the proposed Constitution. Hamilton's various arguments focus on the likely greater sobriety of the Senate.

In hysterical times, the upper house would not be likely to convict a president barring "evidences of guilt so extraordinary." In relation to the four successful impeachments of presidents in US history—those of Andrew Johnson, Bill Clinton, and Donald Trump twice—Hamilton again proved far-seeing. All the writs were initiated by opposition parties, with the foreknowledge that, while they had the simple majority of House votes to impeach, they would likely not have the votes of two-thirds of the Senate to convict. In essence, the Founders for all practical purposes envisioned impeachment either as a rare political rebuke of a sure-to-be-acquitted president or as a stain upon the House for initiating a wasteful and divisive gambit for political purposes—with no chance of removing a president from office.

Since the embarrassing impeachment and failed conviction of President Andrew Johnson in 1868, Americans had left that ultimate constitutional method of ending presidential power well enough alone. The Johnson impeachment had been so steeped in personal hatred, political rivalry, and bitter post–Civil War agendas that the failure by one vote in the Senate to remove Johnson more or less discredited the process for a century.

The 1974 Watergate scandal was framed in opposition to the way Andrew Johnson had been impeached, inasmuch as anyone still remembered the particulars of that long-ago nineteenth-century fiasco. That is, a special prosecutor, first Archibald Cox and then Leon Jaworski, was appointed to investigate the break-in and the so-called Watergate cover-up by President Richard Nixon. Democratic centrists such as Peter Rodino (D-NJ) in the House and Sam Ervin (D-NC) in the Senate gave the impeachment inquiries against Nixon a patina of bipartisanship. Both houses gave time for the targeted president's defenders and legal team to produce witnesses and conduct cross-examinations. By the time a now unpopular Nixon resigned in August 1974 to avoid an impending and likely overwhelming vote to impeach, he had lost majority public support and earned near-total bipartisan congressional opposition.

Bill Clinton, unlike Nixon but like Andrew Johnson, was both impeached and acquitted. Like Nixon, he had easily won a prior reelection (1996). But, unlike Nixon at the time of a likely impeachment proceeding in summer 1974, Clinton still reigned over a booming economy and enjoyed relatively strong popularity. Special counsel Ken Starr, like Leon Jaworski with regard to Nixon, found Clinton likely to have committed felonious acts. Indeed, the full House, on a mostly partisan vote, impeached him on grounds of obstruction of justice and perjury in efforts to cover up a sexual affair. Nonetheless, the impeachment vote saw a handful of both Democrats and Republicans cross party lines.

Prior to the December 1998 impeachment, the Republicans had lost some congressional seats the month before in the November election. Debate continues over whether the political chaos before an impending impeachment vote had earned an ominous warning from the country, in the form of that setback, *not* to impeach Clinton for lying about largely private matters at a time of economic vibrancy. The Republican-controlled Senate did not even get fifty-one votes on either count of perjury or obstruction. Sizable numbers of Republicans—five and ten, respectively—voted for acquittal on the two counts. Earlier, in 1998, before the midterm election, Republicans had predicted that they would not pay a price for impeachment—but they did just that, despite accurate warnings from Democrats.

The public at the time overwhelmingly opposed removing their elected president. Voters apparently accepted that, inter alia, Clinton had been less than truthful about an affair with a White House intern. And further they had elected Bill Clinton twice with full knowledge that he was a past serial adulterer and had likely lied when presented with prior incriminating evidence of sexual improprieties.[53]

After the three modern impeachments of Clinton and Trump, certain lessons had emerged—given that still no president in the history of the United States had ever been impeached, convicted, and removed from office. Most assumed no future president ever would be.

The House impeachments and subsequent trials in the Senate of President Trump tore the country apart. Trump supporters saw the first ordeal as yet another partisan effort to abort a presidency after the failure of Robert Mueller's special counsel investigation and the collapse of the "Russian collusion" hoax. Mueller in March 2019 had de facto cleared the president of *actionable* "collusion" with Russia and "obstruction" of justice in hampering any investigation into what proved the noncrime of collusion.

Even Trump's House of Representatives opponents, who had recently gained a Democratic majority in 2018 after eight years as the minority party, had no confidence that if they impeached the president, a Republican-controlled Senate would vote by the necessary two-thirds to find Trump guilty. But House Democrats wagered that the resulting embarrassment would weaken an impeached candidate Trump as he began his 2020 reelection bid. And perhaps it did, or worse, perhaps it distracted the country from the looming COVID-19 pandemic.

Unlike Clinton, Trump was never impeached on grounds of bribery, treason, or any other criminal or civil statute as outlined in the Constitution or within the existing corpus of federal or state laws. He was not even charged specifically for holding up aid to Ukraine for political advantage, the allegation that had prompted the original House investigation and hearings. Instead, he was impeached on murky grounds of "obstructing Congress" and "abuse of power," vagaries that are not crimes, were not intended as such by the Framers, and could be leveled at almost any president by his opponents.

Little need be said of the second Trump impeachment proceeding on a single article of "incitement of insurrection." In the furor over the aftermath of the January 6, 2021, riot of renegade Trump supporters inside the Capitol, it was even more a rushed partisan act than the first attempt. Again, there was no special counsel's report. There were few if any opportunities to produce all the key witnesses. No real time was allotted for cross-examination or to mount a defense. The FBI investigation of the riot had only just begun. Much of the media coverage of the event at the time of the impeachment and Senate trial was either incomplete, contradictory, or later revised. The trial was conducted without the chief justice. Instead, Senator Patrick Leahy, a senior Democrat from Vermont, served as witness, judge, and juror in the Democratic-driven effort to convict Trump, who was no longer in office.

Only after the impeachment and trial did the fact emerge that four of the five who tragically died in the melee were Trump supporters. The fifth fatality, officer Brian Sicknick, did not die violently at the hands of a Trump supporter as alleged frequently during both the impeachment and trial proceedings—and in lurid media accounts.

Trump may well have been reckless, in a time of national post-election tensions, in revving up a protest crowd of over one hundred thousand supporters and even giving them unrealistic hopes that Joe Biden would not be sworn in as president, as the November 3, 2020, vote count indicated. But Trump likely was not directly responsible, as alleged, for a breakaway group of about one thousand protesters who had already surrounded the Capitol. And the mob break-in was hardly an "armed" insurrection to overthrow the government; much less was it the result of a direct Trump prompt to use violence. Of the many intruders arrested in the aftermath of the riot, *not one was later charged with possessing or using a firearm.*[54]

Unfortunately, the effects on citizenship of these low-bar Trump impeachments are manifold. Impeachment now can be used against *any* first-term president, even one with a record of success. The opposition party—possibly the very House or Senate members who as candidates will seek to replace the president while first passing judgment on him—will likely invoke it solely as a political strategy to weaken the incumbent president's reelection chances. There will be no need for a special prosecutor's report of wrongdoing. There will be no need for hard, actionable violations of statutes. There will be no need for firsthand witnesses of *legal* wrongdoing. The entire rushed indictment will take days, not months, to stain the president with impeachment as he faces reelection. The impeaching party need not worry about the absence of either public or bipartisan congressional support and can sit on its indictment for weeks before handing it to the Senate for trial to cast a shadow of guilt over the president.

All that is now regrettably the legacy of the first Trump impeachment. As for the second, which followed much the same script, an additional precedent has been established: a president may be impeached and tried twice, both attempts proceeding with no hope of conviction. The process can be used against a one-term, lame-duck president in hopes that he might be convicted while out of office as a private citizen—and thus prevented, while still the de facto head of his party, from ever seeking a second term. A Supreme Court justice no longer need preside over the trial.

As a result of these two impeachments and trials, we have altered and diminished the authority of the US Constitution without any formal effort to amend it. More importantly, we sought not just to nullify the presidential election of 2016 but to preclude that of 2020, again without citizens' exercising their right to weigh in with their votes.

The next and final chapter discusses yet another sort of effort at transforming the idea of American citizenship—one well beyond the idea of ceding power and authority to the unelected or attempting to dissipate the powers of the US Constitution and erode the traditions of constitutional citizenship as envisioned by the Founders.

Increasingly, many Americans, mostly our wealthiest and best credentialed, do not believe in American singularity. Instead, they see themselves as universalists. They claim that while they are nominally residents of the United States, Americans are in truth spiritually and politically citizens of a wider, but also increasingly narrowing, world—and they use their networking, money, and public influence to advance these cosmopolitan agendas.

At best they see their American citizenship as no different from any other nation's. At worst they feel embarrassed that in an increasingly diverse, statist, and interconnected world, they are shackled by the baleful legacy of an eighteenth-century elite aristocracy with its ossified constitutional ideas of American citizenship that selfishly put too high a premium on individual liberty and freedom.

Chapter Six

GLOBALISTS

I am a citizen of the world (*kosmopolitês*).
—DIOGENES THE CYNIC *(fourth century BC)*

How can nations abroad in any way endanger the citizenship rights of Americans at home? In this chapter we are not so concerned with hostile military actions of the sort that characterized much of the twentieth century or the attacks on September 11, 2001, that killed some three thousand Americans and endangered the social and economic fabric of the country. Rather, this chapter examines how putting global concerns above national interests insidiously erodes the financial health, freedoms, and safety of Americans. In blunter terms, when American elites feel their first concerns are with the world community abroad rather than with the interests of their own countrymen, there are consequences for American citizens. In this case, the threat to citizenship comes not from foreign countries curtailing our liberties but from Americans themselves deliberately widening the idea of citizenship to include the peoples of the entire world, thereby rendering Americans mostly unexceptional. And never has this been truer than in the current era of globalization.

Globalism is not new. It is recurrent, cyclical, and at best a morally neutral phenomenon, at worst a destroyer of local customs, traditions—and citizenship. Efforts at world unification have always, at least in relative terms, come into and out of vogue over the past twenty-five hundred years of civilization. Yet globalism's recent manifestation carries greater chances of dangerous consequences for American citizenship in our era of instant electronic interconnectedness.

By the early third century, a globalized Roman world comprised seventy million citizens. "Rome" encompassed a vast area of two million square miles, extending from Hadrian's Wall to the Persian Gulf and from the Rhine to northern Africa. In AD 212, the money-hungry emperor Caracalla had issued an edict (the Constitutio Antoniniana) declaring all free residents living within the confines of the Roman Empire instantly legal (and thus now much-needed taxpaying) citizens of Rome: "I grant, therefore, to all foreigners throughout the Empire the Roman citizenship." Yet declaring someone a Roman citizen did not ensure he would come to speak Latin, adopt the original values of Italian republicanism, or shoulder the responsibilities of citizenship rather than just enjoying its rights.

Like frogs around the pond of Mare Nostrum, ancient elites conducted all official business of the westernizing world in Latin or, increasingly in the East, Greek. After the first century AD, emperors were rarely Italian born. A Roman citizen, at least in theory, could enjoy habeas corpus from Bithynia to the Atlantic. A veneer of standardized forums and agoras, colonnades, and basilicas marked thousands of small towns from Syrian Apamea to Segedunum on the Scottish border, three thousand miles distant. Multiracial and non-Italian, uniformly equipped and trained legions for a time secured the vast borders.

Providing aqueducts, security, and property rights to so many millions of disparate peoples proved quite an achievement in an age of difficult communications and travel. But the new facade of uniformity did not mean the culture beneath was necessarily still that of the earlier

Roman Republic of the Scipios or the idyllic Italian countryside of Virgil's *Eclogues* and *Georgics*.

By AD 500, this transitory but vast sameness was rapidly eroding. Vandals, Visigoths, Ostrogoths, Huns, Sasanians, and a host of other tribes and migrant and aggressive peoples had picked apart most of the empire in the West and the old borders in the East. Roman globalization was dead, the empire fragmented into mostly early-European and Byzantine regional hegemonies.

Not surprisingly, the Roman Empire in the East, administered from Constantinople, would survive for another one thousand years. In part, what became known as the Byzantine Empire was, amid general collapse, better able to establish defensible borders and to ensure greater uniformity in language, population, and values, better codification and fair application of Roman law, and a more clearly defined, uniform, and enforced idea of its citizenship. Today "Byzantine" may be a pejorative term denoting either inefficient bureaucracy or a garrison state. But in late antiquity, Byzantium's more unyielding, alternative idea of Romanity, not the Western fluidity of unchecked migrations across the Rhine, Danube, and Mediterranean, proved the more enduring.[1]

History's succession of subsequent would-be imperial globalists—the various Islamic Caliphates, the Mongols, the Ottomans, the British imperialists, and later Napoleon, Stalin, and Hitler—for a while collapsed national borders and spread uniform language, architecture, customs, and culture, usually by force of arms. But eventually—or sometimes quite quickly—their dreams imploded. The causes were usually self-inflicted and variously included overreach, financial insolvency, military defeat, corruption, bankrupt ideology, demographic calcification, rampant inflation, sheer inefficiency, and bloated bureaucracy—as well as, in the case of the British, imperial weariness.

These past failures should have made clear that globalization occurred mostly through coercion and usually prompted regional resistance from even its beneficiaries of greater wealth and security. In overcoming tribal chauvinism and identity politics, usually nations—with clearly defined borders, shared traditions and histories, and nationalist confidence—were more successful than globalist abstractions of universal caring and community. Consequently, it was never clear that the current European Union could forever abolish national borders and invent something permanent called Europeanism or a New European person. Or that the international containment and quarantine protocols of the World Health Organization (WHO) would make something like the coronavirus outbreak virtually impossible—or at least allow a united world to combat its global spread. Or that the world would shrink as tens of millions flew on identical American Boeing 737 MAX jets.

History does not end in one something. It is erratic, unpredictable, and heads in lots of directions rather than following a single fated trajectory. Tribalisms, nations, empires, and globalizations grow and collapse—not unlike natural long-term, cyclical changes in climate. Or, as the Greeks believed, societies are like the endless natural phases of birth, aging, and decline of humans themselves. Nationhood survives not because it is ideal but because it is the *least* pernicious system compared to the alternatives.

So globalization, while not new, is hardly history's norm. Its transnationalism is less natural and requires more violence, not less, to enforce its inconsistencies and paradoxes on too many different, restless peoples continually seeking, in irredentist fashion, to return to what is comfortable and familiar. But the chief flaw of globalism is the often-caricatured law of "limited good"—that only so much of a resource can be shared before it is diluted for all. For every extension, every exemption, every redefinition of citizenship, the original citizen of a republic loses his exceptional status to mostly distant, unknown, and unseen others. In a parochial sense, when American companies outsource their jobs overseas, the American worker usually becomes weaker, not stronger. When elites enjoy trillions of dollars in joint-venture investments in China, they are less, not more, likely to speak out against authoritarian Chinese anti-Americanism. When the international community seeks to establish climate change canons for the United States without a constitutionally mandated treaty, the US Congress becomes weaker, not stronger.

Or, to put it another way, in an age of instant global connectiveness and increasing homogeneity of ideas, there remain limits to Americanized elasticity: the more regional concerns, the more languages, the more transnational issues, the more lands, the more customs that America must oversee, the more its original core is attenuated. The more Silicon Valley looks westward across the ocean for its talent, the less it seems to look eastward to invest in its kindred Americans; the more it seeks to synchronize global norms of censorship and deplatforming, the more it will come into conflict with the Bill of Rights. The more the United States puts its money, its military, its people, and its resources at the disposal of others, the fewer such assets will be available to serve the interests of its own citizens. And the more Americans recalibrate their values with those of the wider world, the less resonance their own constitution will have.[2]

We should keep these incongruities in mind as we seek to harmonize the world in the late twentieth and early twenty-first centuries in our own image. In truth, globalization is the ongoing cultural westernization of the planet—at least in a *superficial* sense. In 2020 nearly eight billion diverse peoples dress, listen, talk, travel, and communicate in an increasingly homogenous manner that mostly follows the examples of those in the United States, Europe, many of the English-speaking former colonies of the British Empire, and the Asian democracies of Japan, South Korea, and Taiwan. Yet these societies' popular commonality remains a quite thin veneer of civilization, easily exposed as such in times of war, plague, and famine. Globalization's real transnational cultural and political harmony encompasses a group of a few million elite architects of pan-worldism. They are heavily invested in ending nationalism and making Americanism incidental rather than essential to Americans as they synchronize their values, laws, and traditions with those abroad.

Consider the annual, invitation-only assembly of some three thousand of the world's elite at the World Economic Forum, held for the last fifty years each January at Davos in the eastern Swiss Alps. Most of the Davos community's recent efforts have aimed, at least rhetorically, to systematize global finance and trade. Davos seminars loudly fixate on climate change. With like-minded certainty, attendees deplore global poverty, strategize how to stop epidemics, and worry about wealth inequality.

But so far, the so-called Davos Man—a term coined by political scientist Samuel P. Huntington—is a similarly wealthy, sophisticated, highly educated Western or westernized cosmopolitan. He is heavily invested in global capital profit making in an increasingly homogenized seven-billion-person market. And by needs, his mindset, ethics, and loyalties often transcend those of his own country. Davos Men—and Women—certainly seem to have a shared vision of how their own ideas, rather than those of the less gifted, should permeate the governments of the world.

As such, the crowds of Davos are often insensitive to the effects of their policies and methods of global wealth creation on the middle classes and poor of their own countries. Instead, they feel nationalist efforts to retain regional and local traditions often impede superior transnational government organized by elites such as themselves and reflect a lack of education or awareness among the working classes of the world beyond their borders. Globalists' chief constituencies are consumers who have the wherewithal to buy their products and services, or are not affected by their policies, or seek to enlist their money and influence.

The sight of hundreds of private, carbon-spewing private jets flying into Davos to discuss curtailing excessive carbon emissions offers insight into the mindset of the gold-plated globalist class. *Res ipsa loquitur*: the thing speaks for itself. Of such a global elite, Huntington once wrote,

They constitute a world within a world, linked to each other by myriad global networks but insulated from the more hidebound members of their own societies. . . . They are more likely to spend their time chatting with their peers around the world—via phone or e-mail—than talking with their neighbors in the projects around the corner. Contemporary intellectuals have reinforced these trends. They abandon their commitment to their nation and their fellow citizens and argue the moral superiority of identifying with humanity at large.[3]

There are lots of things to fault globalists for, such as their borderless sophistication and their contempt for supposedly ossified nationalism and local governments. So often they pay homage to the abstract humanity of the planet rather than to the flesh-and-blood humans of their countries. Yet the central problem with global elites remains a sort of retrograde tribalism. For all the grand talk of being citizens of the world, they really owe their limited allegiances only to like kind—westernized elites with proper credentials—or rather, to the systems and fonts of their wealth and success. They are like the royal families of Europe before World War I, incestuously related and essentially more akin to each other than to their constituents.

Globalists may claim to have transcended barriers of race and gender as well as nationality. But they certainly have not risen above a shared class, training, education, and culture, which bind the men and women of Davos together just as much as ethnic chauvinism or nationalist pride did in the past—and blind them to their own antidemocratic and narrow self-interests. Or as Walter Russell Mead put it of the Daviosi,

There is something inescapably ridiculous about a gathering this self-important; certainly Marie Antoinette and her friends dressing up as shepherdesses to celebrate the simple life have nothing on the more than 100 billionaires descending, often by private jet, on an exclusive Swiss ski resort for four days of ostentatious hand-wringing about the problems of the poor and the dangers of climate change. This year an earnest young aide at registration told me that, to reduce the event's carbon footprint, no paper maps of the town were being distributed; one could almost feel the waves of relief from the nearby Alpine glaciers at this sign of green progress.[4]

Globalization and its architects are not just hypocritical but often absurd. Michael Bloomberg, who spent $1 billion in failed efforts to win the 2020 Democratic nomination, censured his own American reporters at *Bloomberg News* when they criticized practices of the grandees of the Chinese Communist Party. This was a corrupt government for whose start-up companies Bloomberg himself, quite lucratively, was helping to raise billions in Western capital. Bloomberg, throughout his brief presidential campaign, was also quite critical of what he considered blinkered and hidebound Americans. Yet no deplorable or "clinger" had the power or desire to oppress hundreds of millions of their fellow citizens, in the fashion of the Chinese Communist Party, for whom Bloomberg himself had become a veritable banker.

During the coronavirus pandemic, when thousands of Americans had died from the so-called Wuhan virus and over thirty million had lost their jobs during the massive quarantine, Bill Gates, the multibillionaire cofounder of Microsoft, the largest landowner in America, and one of the first to invest heavily inside China, strangely warned America not to criticize China, which he later praised for its handling of the pandemic that it had both spawned and lied about. That admonition did not extend to efforts to calm partisan attacks on his own elected officials. Gates, indeed, seemed to dismiss efforts to hold China responsible as somehow unfair: "So that's a distraction, I think there's a lot of incorrect and unfair things said, but it's not even time for that discussion." The call for accountability from Beijing was certainly a distraction for Microsoft—but not for sheet-metal fabricators in Addison, Illinois, or Flint, Michigan, or bankrupt restaurant owners in Reno, Nevada.

Gates apparently did not see the origins of the crisis in nationalist terms of the self-interests of his own compatriot American citizens: an imperialist China, worried about its loss of stature over the mysterious genesis of the coronavirus, simply misinformed the WHO and the rest of the world about the realities of COVID-19. Beijing allowed thousands of its own citizens already exposed to the virus to fly on nonstop flights into America from Wuhan—at a time when it had barred such travel within China. Instead, Gates saw the problem in terms of the misunderstandings to be worked out among the global elite, whose shared directives were to stay on a common message to tutor the xenophobic and undereducated at home.

He seemed unconcerned that China was a Stalinist-like government: it had interned over one million of its own citizens, caused global havoc due to its incompetence, deceit, and contempt for non-Chinese, and deliberately allowed the virus to spread to others when it knew it could not be contained within China. For Gates and other globalists, there was no reason to pull back from China because it was a communist dictatorship. It mattered little that Beijing had crafted a neoimperialist Belt and Road Initiative, or destroyed Hong Kong's democracy and absorbed the indigenous culture of Tibet, or become the protector of a reckless nuclear North Korea. He was unaware or unconcerned that China had serially threatened its Asian neighbors, imprisoned its own people, systematized racism, and violated the basic rules of international trade and commerce.

Still, Gates's attitude toward China was not unusual. It simply reflected a widespread sense among corporate elites that either China's wealth or its ability to effect top-down change in near-instantaneous fashion earned it admiration or at least exemption from criticism. Or perhaps Gates simply saw his role as that of world citizen, for whom global ecumenicalism was a much more important value than affinity for his fellow citizens or pride in the exceptionalism of American culture.

Americans have grown to expect lectures on American shortcomings from their own globalists. In the reductionist sense, when Western corporate CEOs, international professionals, and philanthropists attack their own countries, the greater become their globalist fides. So Gates displayed another common characteristic of the globalist: eagerness to criticize the clumsy illiberality of his own society coupled with laudation of efficient illiberality abroad.

Gates shared with Americans the abstraction of citizenship; with the Chinese government he shared multiple billions of dollars in investments. We should remember that the drivers of US globalism are not necessarily elected officials, much less popular opinion. More often, those in media, corporations, finance, professional sports, entertainment, and academia freelance and profit in joint global projects and then ex post facto provide—whether naively, sincerely, or cynically—the collective moral justifications for their own self-interest. Yet what has been good for Google, Apple, Goldman Sachs, the Los Angeles Lakers, Disney, Stanford, and Harvard has not always been in the interests of the US government or the American people.[5]

At about the same time as Gates's caution about criticizing the laxity of China's initial response in the midst of the pandemic, American legal scholars Jack Goldsmith and Andrew Keane Woods—in the months before Donald Trump's banning from Twitter and Facebook—argued that in the debate over free expression and the state's right to censor and control, China, not America ("China was largely right and the United States was largely wrong"), had the right idea of censoring internet expression for the greater collective good:

> Significant monitoring and speech control are inevitable components of a mature and flourishing internet, and governments must play a large role in these practices to ensure that the internet is compatible with a society's norms and values. . . . The First and Fourth Amendments as currently interpreted, and the American aversion to excessive government–private-sector collaboration, have stood as barriers to greater government involvement. Americans'

understanding of these laws, and the cultural norms they spawned, will be tested as the social costs of a relatively open internet multiply.[6]

These postcitizen authors apparently believe the coercive mechanisms available to a communist and totalitarian dictatorship are superior to the freedoms guaranteed by the US Constitution. Correct and enlightened views of elite experts should not be challenged by just anyone on the internet. Yet, during critical early days of the COVID-19 pandemic, the American masses were *not* the first to swear that the virus was not transmissible among humans, that masks and quarantines were of little utility, and that xenophobia, not health concerns, drove travel bans. Instead the experts of the World Health Organization promulgated such disinformation—often on the prompt and under the influence of the nontransparent communist Chinese government.

Another shared trait of contemporary globalism is a thinly veiled desire to use an autocracy's coercive means to enact progressive ends as defined by global standards. In the case of China, globalists praise Beijing's supposed concern with global warming and its strong-arm ability to implement mass transit and vertical urban living. Its family planning and easy abortion, its seduction of Western academia and universities, and its feigned victimhood as the target of Western racism combine to hypnotize elites. The use of absolute non-Western power for absolute Western good is seen as a good thing indeed.

Economically, westernized capitalism of sorts—whether under the aegis of consensual, or controlled by autocratic, governments—is sweeping the globe. Its central achievement is lifting billions out of poverty in a way that subjects under postwar Soviet, Eastern European, Asian, and Chinese communism or Middle Eastern, African, and Latin American autocracy never imagined. Globalization spread so quickly because Western-spawned, mass-produced, and inexpensive technology—mobile phones, satellite television, the internet, email, social media—made instant communications easy, cheap, profitable, and fun.

Such transparency allowed most of the world in real time to enjoy at least the semblance of alternative Western consumerism and leisured lifestyles, along with instant access to Western medical information and scientific research.

Apparently, the non-West perceived such benefits of free market capitalism in most ways as superior to their own economic systems, business acumen, and commercial expertise, at least as evidenced by their efforts to buy or copy Western products and customs. In the beginning, under the new fusion of the non-West with Western commercialism, the Western world assumed that its elite coders, designers, and engineers would create the blueprints, while the world's poor in Asia and Latin America would cheaply assemble their devices and corporations would ship them back to the West for redistribution there and worldwide. And many of the outsourced products were to be bought inexpensively by the often struggling and sometimes out-of-work American middle and lower classes whose jobs had been shipped abroad in the first place. But eventually China's westernized engineering graduates and corporate teams began replacing their erstwhile mentors, as Beijing began to vertically integrate and absorb an increasing share of world manufacturing and assembly.

Inexpensive and mass jet travel likewise eroded borders. It translated entering and leaving a country into a mere bureaucratic process of airport security rather than waiting for visas, butting against border walls and fences, crossing rivers, or climbing mountains. Border security was no longer defined as the ancient way of protecting the common space of fellow Americans. Instead it was recalibrated as an ossified concept of territoriality, now adrift in a mobile and interconnected world. One could get up in the morning in Wuhan, China, and be in San Francisco by evening without audit, background check, or worry of contagion or threats to national security—and all for the cost of a week's pay.

All too often Western elites felt smug satisfaction in what westernization of the planet had accomplished, rather than expressing any worry over what globalization had wrought in their own homelands—lost jobs, investment, control over borders, and national cohesiveness. While at its origins mostly economic and technological, globalism also soon certainly spread the facade of westernized culture. Residents all over the world watched international movie stars in Western jeans and T-shirts. They heard rap music and country music. They were entranced by Western lifestyles of risqué exhibitionism, unapologetic promiscuity, and coarse expression. They were glued to televised sports.

Soon such Western casual culture became cool, not because of some Western conspiracy but due to the ease and informality of European and American language, fashion, music, and cinema. Popular culture from the European Union and the United States—the world's two largest economies—resonated laxity and the absence of hierarchies. Energized by Netflix, Amazon, YouTube, and Facebook, globalization soon eroded indigenous and local customs and traditions the world over.

The public relations themes of the World Cup or the Olympic Games were superficial celebrations of global diversity under agreed-upon shared auspices and values. The unspoken reality was that politically, racially, and religiously diverse athletes looked about the same, adopting similar lifestyles, uniform dress, and the English language during such competitions. So-called fast fashion allows designers to aggrandize basic designs, update and change them monthly, outsource the production of clothes to low-labor-cost countries, use westernized advertising to promote transitory fads and tastes, and then sell trendy, globally homogenized clothes for affordable prices.[7]

Many young urban women in Africa found emulating Beyoncé's swagger, tight jeans, and T-shirt blouse preferable to wearing the traditional *kanga*—and certainly cooler and in sync with what they saw and read on their mobile phones. When a Brazilian or Ghanaian or Indonesian said "F**k you!" or "OK," he did so because he heard those bits of English in movies, listened to them on the radio or the internet, or met thousands of tourists who talked like that—and concluded a smidgeon of English exuded a global hipness and commonality with famous, rich, and enviable celebrities. The English language is becoming

Americanized and in turn globalized into a common vernacular patois with its own particular grammar and syntax.[8]

Yet all that is a mere facade, a Potemkin village. Despite the prodigious efforts of Western intellectuals, the media, and politicians, globalization has not yet achieved, and probably never will, global political or moral consensus—much less harmony about constitutional government, human rights, the fair enforcement of international commercial agreements, or common moral or democratic values. True, there may in theory be more "democracies" than at any time since the 1990s (96 of 167 nations), at least in name and occasional practice. Indeed, about half the world's population now lives under nominal consensual government. But such reassurance does not translate into a world unified by the supposedly dominant Western ideas of progress, tolerance, human rights, and liberal democracy. Much less should we think that Western progressivism is history's fated global telos or even America's final stop.

Barack Obama often framed such bromides of historical determinism as "being on the right side of history," saying, "The arc of the moral universe is long but it bends toward justice." However, China will likely appropriate and enhance Western technology and market capitalism to kill, torture, or incarcerate far more people than it will save by following our notion of a predetermined arc of a moral universe. To take one small recent example, researchers from liberal Stanford University—recently found lax, like a number of other American universities, in reporting to the federal government $64 million in gifts from companies and individuals associated with the Chinese communist government—partnered with Chinese counterparts to develop facial recognition mechanisms to find suspect individuals amid large crowds. And so all the better for the communist Chinese government to use such Western technologies to surveille, monitor, and ultimately oppress its religious and ethnic minorities.[9]

Progressives are indeed globalists, but they would dissent from the notion of a prosaic "new world order" common thirty years earlier, which was more classically liberal. Instead, progressive globalism is not so much about convincing the world of the superiority of democracy and free market capitalism as hoping that those modalities more quickly lead to the predetermined results of promoting social justice, addressing climate change, and encouraging global homogeneity of abortion rights, identity politics, and eventual collective world governance.[10]

Thomas Friedman seems confident that a globalizing world deep down really wishes to embrace not just Western technology and mutant forms of its capitalism but also constitutional government, individual freedom, and Western progressive culture and lifestyles. But what if China, or Russia, or Iran, or for that matter much of Africa, Asia, and Latin America, do not especially wish to embrace globalization in such an entirety, defined as Westernism in general and Americanism in particular? Perhaps what Friedman sees as the world arcing toward a model progressive society, other illiberal nations view as dangerous laxity. Why then should Americans as global citizens spend their blood and treasure from Libya and Syria to Afghanistan to apply American progressive nostrums to the economic ills and religious and cultural dislocations wrought by globalization, as if we had the wisdom to know the needs of over seven billion people and the power to grant their wishes?

This hubris is especially disconcerting. Half the country did not fare well under globalized offshoring, outsourcing, and free but asymmetrical trade. And others, the more progressive and supposedly empathetic 30 percent of the population, did not much care about the fate of such deplorables. Much of the more traditional and religious world abroad may perhaps wish to opt out of what we now consider our norms—from gay marriage, to racial quotas and identity politics, to abortion on demand—as we might their own religious intolerance, tribal violence, state atheism, or absence of constitutional freedoms.[11]

So beware of Western-centric arrogance among our elites, who believe their own careerist successes or private materially blessed lives are objects of emulation the world over. Such haughtiness explains both their confidence that globalization is turning the world into their version of America or at least of the West and their own privileged ability to pose as critics of the very free market economic system that enriched them. It is almost as if caricaturing and deprecating America is proof of such overweening confidence, as if the United States is so preeminent and resilient that it hardly needs nourishing by old-fashioned nostrums like civic education, patriotism, and collective national pride. The irony, of course, is that today's immigrants are not risking their lives to reach America because they think it is striving for a solar/wind-powered managed economy or institutionalizes racial and ethnic reparatory college admissions and hiring or is systematically destroying the statues and monuments of its past; they are doing so because they sense its market capitalism and Constitution allow the lower and middle classes economic opportunities and freedoms rarely found elsewhere.

The nineteen Middle Eastern hijackers who on September 11, 2001, crashed four large jets, took down the World Trade Center towers, and hit the Pentagon dressed like Americans. They tried to talk like Americans. They were treated as ordinary Americans in their education, jobs, and entertainment, in a liberal live-and-let-live society that does not inquire about legal status. They watched everything from American sports to strip shows—and still deeply despised America's religion, popular culture, and politics, whether defined as atheism or Christianity, equality of the sexes, and a freely elected Congress supporting Israel. Perhaps their odium of the West arose because their appetites were so hooked on it. Indeed, their natural indulgence was exempted because as "martyrs" that sensual behavior would not be held against them in the hereafter.[12]

Indeed, this confusion of fundamental values with superficial tastes is one of the strangest but most important fetishes of globalization. In reality non-Westerners superficially emulate Westerners and sometimes have as much money as Westerners. They use the same technology as Westerners. They echo the same political sloganeering as Westerners. Yet they are hardly political Westerners at all. About half the planet prefers communism, theocracy, and monarchy in the Middle East, autocracy in Turkey, a vestigial caste system in India, and all sorts of non-Democratic -isms and -ologies in Latin America, Asia, and Africa. And yet so often we romanticize the antithesis of America abroad, while caricaturing or ridiculing America's traditional manifestations at home.

Sometimes the citizen becomes bewildered by globalized popular culture that tends to contextualize or excuse the truly awful and evil on the reductionist grounds that it is not American. The citizen wonders why even the veneer of foreignness attached to something not innately American is considered not just exotic but worthy of an exemption never commensurately extended to the citizen. After the so-called Boston Marathon bombing in 2013, *Rolling Stone* put on its cover a flattering, if not glamorous, picture of the cruel killer Dzhokhar Tsarnaev, a recently naturalized American citizen, whose parents had fled Kyrgyzstan and whose Islamist sympathies were part of a larger disgust for the very culture he so eagerly dove into. Or as *Rolling Stone* put it,

Jahar to his friends—as a beautiful, tousle-haired boy with a gentle demeanor, soulful brown eyes and the kind of shy, laid-back manner that "made him that dude you could always just vibe with," one friend says. He had been a captain of the Cambridge Rindge and Latin wrestling team for two years and a promising student. He was also "just a normal American kid," as his friends described him, who liked soccer, hip-hop, girls; obsessed over *The Walking Dead* and *Game of Thrones*; and smoked a copious amount of weed.

But once the FBI found the "beautiful, tousle-haired boy" wounded after committing murders of the innocent, *Rolling Stone* almost inadvertently referenced a rather different side of the "laid-back manner" of "Jahar":

He admitted he [Dzhokhar/Jahar] did not like killing innocent people. But "the U.S. government is killing our innocent civilians," he wrote, presumably referring to Muslims in Iraq and Afghanistan.

"I can't stand to see such evil go unpunished. . . . We Muslims are one body, you hurt one, you hurt us all," he continued, echoing a sentiment that is cited so frequently by Islamic militants that it has become almost cliché. Then he veered slightly from the standard script, writing a statement that left no doubt as to his loyalties: "Fuck America."[13]

The same strange combination of shallow contextualization of a foreign monster and misguided triumphalism in seeing the other superficially emulate the West led naive media to sensationalize Kim Yo-jong, the stone-hearted sister of North Korea's murderous leader Kim Jong-un, during the televised 2018 Olympic games. The *Washington Post* gushed in a headline about Jong, "The 'Ivanka Trump of North Korea' captivates people in the South." CNN nearly deified Jong, who wore trendy Western dress and seemed Americanized in her manipulation of the media, as if Western clothes automatically made a person Western inside. Or as the *Wall Street Journal* characterized CNN's coverage,

> "Kim Jong Un's sister is stealing the show at the Winter Olympics," said an actual headline on CNN Saturday. The story was an encomium to the heretofore undetected charms of North Korea's first sister, who is the North's lead emissary to the games: "With a smile, a handshake and a warm message in South Korea's presidential guest book, Kim Yo Jong has struck a chord with the public just one day into the PyeongChang Games. Seen by some as her brother's answer to American first daughter Ivanka Trump, Kim, 30, is not only a powerful member of Kim Jong Un's kitchen cabinet but also a foil to the perception of North Korea as antiquated and militaristic."[14]

At the time of this reporting, the once "antiquated and militaristic" Kim dynasty had threatened to send nuclear missiles to the American

West Coast and was a United Nations pariah for its systemic oppression and murdering of its own people.

Incidentally, the bourgeois fascination with the clothing, style, and chic of the edgy "other" is not always confined to romance with the dress of those abroad. During the rioting of 2020, the *Washington Post* ran a fawning photo spread of various Antifa and Black Lives Matter emulators who were dressed as "their unique selves," which the *Post* explained was "part of their power." The photo spread and hagiography focused on their idiosyncratic embrace of various items of demonstration and riot dress—body padding, leaf blowers to expel chemical agents, bull horns, helmets, and other assorted protective and offensive gear—a chic revolutionary brand of performance art that has gone global. Enhanced methods of committing politically correct violence were cool.[15]

If globalization tends to dilute and warp classical American citizenship, why have so few critics questioned its spread? In other words, how did America become so enmeshed in global affairs, so powerful as to craft a universal popular global culture, and yet so divided over whether a once insular republic, concerned foremost with the safety and prosperity of its own citizens, should seek to remake the world in its own image? After World War II, only the triumphant United States possessed the capital, military, freedom, and international goodwill and reputation to arrest the spread of global Stalinism, emanating from a triumphant Soviet Union that had reached the Brandenburg Gate in Berlin. There seemed no reason why the USSR could not spread its hegemony across western Europe to the English Channel. To save the fragile postwar, capitalist, and democratic West, America was soon willing to help rebuild and rearm war-torn former democracies—in the manner that it felt that it had saved Europe, and Western civilization itself, from the evils of national socialism by entering another foreign war that initially did not immediately or directly threaten its own borders. But the United States did not stop its postwar political and cultural interventions with merely restoring only consensual states that had some prewar history of parliamentary government. Its ambitions transcended ending global communism and encompassed spreading American-style capitalism and noncommunist rule almost anywhere and everywhere.

Over seven decades, the United States intervened in proxy wars against both Soviet and Chinese clients and radical rogue regimes. It often sought to create anticommunist governments, democratic if possible, autocratic if necessary. In this fashion, America's role was not unlike that of late-republican and imperial Rome, which habitually and sometimes brutally put down or bought off local tribal insurrectionists such as Boudicca, Jugurtha, Mithridates, or Vercingetorix for the greater security and expansion of the global Pax Romana. In the American context, young Americans of the lower and middle classes were often sent to fight abroad, at a time when increased outsourcing and offshoring were beginning to curtail their own traditional job prospects at home. Postwar youth remained unsure whether, in cost-to-benefit analyses, their sacrifices from South Korea to Vietnam to Afghanistan were making Americans more prosperous and secure. And they doubted that the beneficiaries of their interventions became friendlier and more thankful for the sacrifice of American blood and treasure.

Commercial sacrifices accompanied military costs in the growing global project. An unprecedentedly rich postwar United States also soon accepted institutionalized asymmetrical and unfavorable trade as the price of leading and saving the West—at first with former enemies such as Germany and Japan, later with most of Europe and Asia, which had been considered on the front lines of World War II. The last US trade surplus was some forty-five years ago in 1975—after a century of continued trade surpluses. Trade deficits, of course, and concomitant cheaper prices were not always disadvantageous for American consumers, at least in the short term. The use of the dollar as a universal currency and the Americanized nature of international financial institutions likewise helped the United States. But as the deficits soared, strategic ends raced ahead of operational means. And outsourcing and offshoring increased. The result was a hollowed-out US interior bereft of well-paying manufacturing and assembly jobs and two coasts with global rather than just American responsibilities.[16]

America became the chief patron for dozens of needy clients and opportunistic friends—with no time limit on such commercial asymmetry. An entire corridor of bureaucratic elites and revolving-door lobbyists, lawyers, and government officials promulgated a bipartisan consensus. America was to anchor and perpetuate an unchanging and static global mercantile and security order that arose after 1945. It was now to be overseen by new transnational organizations such as the World Bank, the International Monetary Fund, the World Trade Organization, and various subcommittees of the United Nations. All were international in theory. In fact, they depended largely on American money, American or American-trained technocrats, the American military, and a secure US-led and enforced international order.

Only US taxpayers could afford the staggering costs of making billions around the world richer and safer through annual budget deficits, the Pentagon budget, and American technology and business practices. The postwar Americanized global system, of course, achieved many of its goals. The former Axis powers became model democracies. Soviet imperialism was contained, and eventually the Soviet Union itself imploded. Europe avoided most suicidal civil wars; when it could not, the United States intervened in the former Yugoslavia to quell the violence. Eastern and western Europe were again reintegrated.

The narrative of American postwar global success is certainly positive—as long as it ignores the increasingly bleak landscapes of the American interior and of the large rust belt cities of the 1960s and 1970s. With plenty of hypocrisy and paradox, and often without rational cost-to-benefit analyses, American power has, over the last seventy-five years, either removed, emasculated, contained, isolated, compromised, or bought off a number of dictators and tyrants who threatened this westernized international postwar order—Fidel Castro, Saddam Hussein, Muammar Khadafi, the North Korean Kim dynasty,

Osama bin Laden, Slobodan Milošević, Manuel Noriega, and a host of others. Radical Islam was eventually contained and, so far, checked. The indigenous in the Amazon basin got access to eyeglasses. Amoxicillin made its way into Chad. Jay-Z could be heard in Montenegro. The impoverished from Oaxaca became eligible for affirmative action the moment they crossed the US border.

Other thuggish rulers, such as Idi Amin, the Syrian Assads, Robert Mugabe, and Pol Pot, were isolated and left to their own devices, often with disastrous results for their own peoples. In general, after costly and often unpopular interventions in Korea, Vietnam, the Middle East, and Latin America, Americans questioned the wisdom of removing dictators, even communist ones—only to be lectured on their heartlessness by would-be beneficiaries when they hesitated to act in the Balkans, Rwanda, and Somalia, where mass deaths ensued.

The average twenty-first-century American eventually came to see this globalized project as predicated on lots of flawed and unquestioned assumptions. The first was the notion that the great wealth and power of the postwar United States were not just limitless but owed in service to the Western agenda for the global population. Americans supposedly alone could afford to subsidize other nations through trade concessions, foreign aid, and military subsidies and by keeping the sea lanes and air travel safe. Any ensuing commercial or military wound to the American industrial heartland was always considered transitory or at least collateral damage well worth the cost of protecting the civilized order—at least as those westernized elites invested in globalism envisioned it. More cynically, the architects of US foreign and commercial policies rarely lived in the Midwest, the rural North, or the South, the recruiting grounds of the US military and the areas most hurt economically by the consequences of their elite theories and practice.

It was also assumed that the more American largess and concessions, the more likely disparate places from Shanghai to Lagos would eventually operate on the Americanized premises of Salt Lake City or Los Angeles—or at least not trouble the global order. The world itself would inevitably reach the end of history in terms of democracy and market capitalism, as it progressed on its trajectory to something like Palo Alto, the Upper West Side, or Georgetown, the assumed apogees of democracy, social welfare, and capitalism. Globalists sometimes felt that new westernized populations abroad possessed a vigor and energy lacking among the played-out population of the deindustrialized Midwest, as if an exhausted people had driven out industry instead of the corporations that had previously employed them having fled abroad for cheaper labor.

Or as Bill Kristol, former editor of the *Weekly Standard* and subsequently editor-at-large at the *Bulwark*, explained, illegal immigration should not be an issue. Instead, there was a need to replace an increasingly pathological American white working class that was not quite up to the standards of a globalized world: "Look, to be totally honest, if things are so bad as you say with the white working class, don't you want to get new Americans in? . . . You can make a case that America has been great because every—I think John Adams said this—basically if you are in free society, a capitalist society, after two or three generations of hard work, everyone becomes kind of decadent, lazy, spoiled—whatever."[17]

Despite controversy over immigrants' use of public assistance, there was no data to support Kristol's assertion of a lazy and decadent working class. Much less did Kristol elaborate on what he thought should be done with this supposedly played-out and used-up "spoiled" working class. In fact, dependence on government assistance, such as welfare and food stamps, is often far higher among immigrant households (63 percent) than among American citizens (35 percent).[18]

In this same Bill Kristol way of thinking, twenty-first-century open borders would draw into America—and later to Europe and the British Commonwealth of Nations—the most daring and adventurous of the world's poor, uneducated, and dispossessed. They would soon become model citizens, reinvigorate a stagnant population, reinforce the global resonance of the West, and improve the political dialectic within America—even if millions of immigrants did not come legally, in measured numbers, with high school diplomas and knowledge of English, and in diverse fashion, and even if host America had lost confidence in the melting pot.

By the twenty-first century a number of contradictions in the global order had also became self-evident. As noted, consumer quasi-capitalism did not always lead to democracy and consensual government. Just as often, it enhanced and enriched authoritarianism, at least for millions in Russia, China, and much of Africa and Latin America.

More worrisome, globalization in religious fashion demanded faith in its canons rather than proof of its logic and assumptions. That is, did globalization really reflect robust democratic culture? Within the West, democratic legislation and referenda that questioned globalization were demonized as the moody fickleness of the provincial and undereducated and often ignored—witness the French and Dutch referenda that rejected the European Union constitution and the English working class's much scorned vote to leave the EU, leading to years of elite haggling in efforts to derail Brexit. The prevailing global wisdom was that the proverbial people did not know what was good for them. Such a sentiment was illustrated by rising populist movements that voiced resentment of unelected "globalists," or sought to bring American troops home, or favored raising tariffs on known commercial cheaters. Ironically, democratic resistance at home to democratic nation building abroad was often slandered as undemocratic.

Opposition to globalism became defined as support for everything from racism to mass extermination. "Nativism versus globalism" framed the divide between those who favored the supposed tolerance of a mostly illiberal wider world versus the purported bigotry of democratic America. Nancy Rockwell, in surreal fashion, managed to warp the globalist controversy into one of noble globalists, who were tolerant and ecumenical, versus antiglobalists, who were racist, bigoted, homophobic, gun toting, xenophobic, and callous toward those with disabilities. In truth, she meant that anyone who voted for Donald

Trump was a nativist bigot and anyone who did not was an enlightened globalist:

> And here we are, in 2016. Our election rhetoric dances with all these ideas, examining their possible strengths, and labelling many of them virtuous. Are Moslems Americans? Should we quarantine them? Expel them? Put them through rigorous tests of fealty? Does God despise gays? Is it alright to kill them or not? What kind of money should we spend on special needs programs and people? Are black people more murderous, more sexually deviant, than whites? Do they all carry guns? Should we stop allowing immigrants? Who will save us? And what is going on here?[19]

America itself split in two on attitudes toward globalization. On the one hand, in reductionist terms, those cognitive elites who did well by running the global show—politicians, bureaucrats of the expanding federal administrative octopus, coastal journalists, the professionals of the high-tech, finance, insurance, and investment industries, and white-collar entertainers, lawyers, academics, and consultants—all assumed that aspiring populations in the former Third World could not replicate their First World skills. Indeed, they had now a market of billions of new consumers for their wares. They enjoyed the idea that who they were and what they did were objects of emulation worldwide, at least as adjudicated by profits, consumer tastes, celebrity, and popular culture. As Thomas Friedman, safe from the globalist Frankenstein in his *New York Times* billet, once cheered, "Thank goodness I'm a journalist and not an accountant or radiologist. There will be no outsourcing for me—even if some of my readers wish my column could be shipped to North Korea."[20]

On the other hand, those who did with their hands things that could be done more cheaply abroad—due to inexpensive labor and an absence of most government safety, environmental, and financial regulations—were replicated there and rendered redundant at home: factory workers, manufacturers, miners, mill workers, small farmers, and anyone else whose job was predicated at least in part on muscular labor and the use of natural resources.

The logic of globalism was that anything foreigners could *not* do as well as Americans was proof of the intelligence and savvy of US elites. Anything that foreigners *could* do as well as Americans was confirmation that some Americans had never evolved much beyond use of their arms and backs. All this is not to say that the poor and working classes were completely exempt from culpability for rising rates of illegitimacy, drug use, criminality, and suicide—only that preexisting social and cultural pathologies were best alleviated by economic opportunities and methods of self-help, not through government dependence in lieu of well-paying jobs. Once deindustrialization impoverishes communities, it often rekindles repressed or dormant social and cultural toxins that in turn become force multipliers of suicide, criminality, and drug use. Similar examples were the more frequent incidents of family, spousal, and drug abuse, suicides, rioting, looting, and arson, and mental health issues that rose during the national 2020–2021 COVID-19 quarantine, when millions stayed home, lost jobs and income, and relied more on government assistance.[21]

Globalism was not necessarily an organic process that just appeared out of nowhere. Some of westernization abroad and de-westernization at home—in the sense of eroding citizenship—was ad hoc. Yet masters of the universe articulated aims, principles, and methodologies of the global project. Few, if any, of their agendas were in the interest of the constitutional freedoms, autonomy, and traditions of the US citizen.

Certain canons of globalism are mostly at odds with traditional American ideas of constitutional citizenship. In the globalist creed, democratic socialism is preferable to free market capitalism under the aegis of constitutional republics. The wisdom of the elite managerial class is far superior to the common sense of the public. Those whose jobs are outsourced and shipped abroad are themselves mostly deemed wanting, given their naïveté in assuming that building a television set in Dayton or farming one hundred acres in Tulare is as valuable as designing an app in Menlo Park or managing a hedge fund in Manhattan. To paraphrase again the earlier referenced quote of former treasury secretary and Harvard president Larry Summers, if the new meritocracy fueled inequality, this was because people were being treated as they deserved.

Predictable consequences followed from the gospel of Americanized globalism. Language, as it always does in times of upheaval, changed to fit new political orthodoxies. "Free" trade now meant that Beijing could expropriate technology from American businesses in China without much worry about countermeasures. Under free trade, dumping products on the world market below the cost of production to garner increased market share—in violation of the protocols of the World Trade Organization, to which Beijing belongs—was tolerable for 1.4-billion-person China. But tariffs remained mortal sins for America and so were denounced as nineteenth-century "protectionism."

Likewise, vast trade deficits were redefined as nearly irrelevant. Still, for some strange reason almost all countries preferred trade surpluses to deficits. Most elites privately confessed that China and other countries had distorted the international trading system. Even the very architects who drafted the policy of offshoring and outsourcing to China by 2020 claimed they had come to rue it.[22]

Pessimists publicly asserted either that America could do little about Chinese ascendance and globalization or that any proposed remedy would be worse than the disease. By summer 2019, the financiers, economists, and policy wonks of the Western world feared "the end of the world" if Donald Trump insisted on leveling tariffs on the Chinese to force them to comply with trade rules and norms. How strange the Western mindset of silently conceding that the current deformation of world trade could not go on as it was under systematic Chinese commercial cheating, while publicly damning those who searched for ways to ensure that it did not go on.[23]

"Managing decline," not arresting it, much less denying it, gradually became a cottage industry of American globalists. They openly talked of following the British model of planned downsizing in the late 1940s and 1950s in deference to a then rising America. Most pessimists were determinists. Some felt American decline was inevitable rather than the choice of a particular generation—and that a far healthier global ecumenicalism might at last replace Americanism and Westernism. Some felt the fading of America was deserved and long overdue payback for its innate sins. Still others discounted facts suggesting that America still ranked at the top of most comparative studies in terms of traditional barometers of national vitality—food and energy output, relative business costs and climates, strategic independence, military power, cultural influence, constitutional stability, technological innovation, graduate university programs in science, engineering, and professions, and immigration.[24]

The globalist vocabulary is inherently anti-American, at least in the sense that critical standards that apply to the United States do not always do so elsewhere. "Nativism" in the globalist lexicon does not refer to the highly restrictive and ethnically chauvinistic immigration policies of Japan, China, and Mexico. Instead, it mostly applies to the United States, which annually takes in more immigrants than any other country and currently has the world's largest resident immigrant population.

In the global media community, "intolerance" does not denote so much China's mass incarceration of Muslim Uighurs in reeducation camps, or destruction of Tibetan culture, or strangulation of Hong Kong's democracy, or systemic racism shown African students and resident workers in China. Instead, America's purported sin is occasional consideration of recalibrating its open-borders policies and requiring legality before entering the country. Or more candidly, America, the most globalist of all nations, sometimes amplifies the complaints of those who cite immigration misdemeanors, in contrast to other countries that do not care much about critics of their own felonies.[25]

"Isolationism" has been a new charge leveled at Americans. By 2017, many Americans, and certainly the Trump administration, thought affluent allied nations like Germany—the world's fourth-largest economy—not just could but must, as once promised, spend more than 1.2 percent of their annual GDP on defense, about half to a third of what Americans routinely did. Refusing to intervene in nihilistic civil wars or declaring that North Atlantic Treaty Organization (NATO) nations needed to keep their promises on alliance contributions somehow evidenced an isolationist mind. Transferring some twelve thousand troops out of Germany to other less prosperous NATO countries such as Belgium, Italy, and perhaps soon Poland was considered foolish nationalist "chauvinism."

The subtext of the NATO outrage at the move was furor that members might have to honor their benchmark promises of defense expenditures or lose American bases, together with fear of a dominating Germany and a fracturing alliance with no idea how to handle a strategically unreliable Turkey or Vladimir Putin. Few in the United States, but apparently many in Europe, still remember that NATO's informal charter mission was, according to its first secretary-general, Lord Hastings Ismay, "to keep the Russians out, the Americans in, and *the Germans down.*"[26]

Rhetoric aside, the United States currently maintains over three hundred embassies, consulates, and diplomatic missions overseas (far more than any other of the world's 195 nations). It posts some 11,000 Foreign Service employees abroad. Over 37,000 employees work in US embassies and consulates outside the United States. Somehow stationing 225,000 US military personnel overseas, or paying the largest member share of the NATO budget (22 percent of actual dollars spent), or promising to protect dozens of democracies under the American nuclear umbrella, or keeping thousands of troops for seventy years in the Demilitarized Zone between the two Koreas nonetheless qualifies as isolationism and a retreat from global responsibilities. By 2018, the United States alone accounted for 69 percent of total defense spending by all NATO member states, funding a huge military machine pledged to keep the alliance's members safe.[27]

"Populism" is also a pejorative, usually referring to supposedly uninformed voters' majority opinions overriding an unelected elite's master planning and protocols. Given that populism is felt to be symptomatic of an uneducated, unenlightened, and superstitious mind, it should be impeded or at least diluted by administrative guardians, sober courts, and judicious politicians. The latter know best the historical perils of letting the mob speak, as it does in America mostly by electing state and federal representatives.

"Progressivism," in contrast, is more often considered by academicians and journalists as a popular movement of the educated and the more socially respectable. Increasingly it encompasses the wealthier and more credentialed. They feel that their education and compensation, not just their self-interests, explain their globalist allegiance. Or as recent commentator George Packer put it in the *New Yorker*, channeling the dichotomies of liberal historian Richard Hofstader's 1955 dissection of populists and progressives, "Populists looked with anger upward rather than with sympathy downward. They didn't come from the professional middle class, though some of their champions did, and they didn't put their faith in the training and education of experts." Suspicion of expert opinion was apparently something to be regretted. In contrast, progressive reformers

> came from the successful ranks of American society, they identified with the interests and aspirations of the educated and well-off, but their sense of civic responsibility was scandalized by the corruption of political machines and the evils of corporate capitalism. They were driven by moral conscience and pragmatic concern to crusade for a range of reforms, from the primary election to the income tax. Their impulse, individual and ethical in nature, was to cleanse and restore. Their model was the disinterested, public-spirited citizen who brought expert knowledge to solving social problems.[28]

Translated, a cynic might suggest that elites see progressive globalists such as themselves as a sort of Platonic guardian class. Their education, training, and like values should elevate them above base instincts, biases, and emotions. If their inferiors would only entrust their affairs to such enlightened and mostly unelected reformers, then the impediments to civilizational progress—the wild agendas of the uneducated, self-governing middle class, ossified borders, nationalism, patriotism, suicidal fossil fuel use, singularly American obsessions with gun ownership and resistance to abortion, and skepticism of credentialed expertise and higher education—could all be neutered and overcome. Such elitism was innate to progressive icons such as the eugenicist Margaret Sanger, the racialist Woodrow Wilson, and the elitist journalist Walter Lippmann.

Yet, world economic growth aside, globalization did not deliver as promised for its creators at home. Perhaps over one half of the populations of the United States and Europe did not enjoy the advantages of the universal project. They found the disappearance of good jobs not worth the upside of using Facebook to communicate across the world or downloading videos from abroad or buying cheaper sneakers assembled in China.

It was hard to see how someone in rural Michigan or in West Virginia benefitted from the assurance that most of the world's internet technologies were now American—especially when the tech products were assembled in China. The logic of bombing Libya in 2011 or intervening in Russian-controlled, Assad-ruled, and Hezbollah-infested Syria remained a hard sell to the middle classes who had experienced a decade of stagnant wages and lost seven thousand American soldiers killed in Afghanistan and Iraq. That the Forbes Fortune 400 now listed multibillionaires rather than multimillionaires did not mean that such exponential wealth creation was of much value to the American public.

The checkered record of those who tagged others as dense nativists and unthinking isolationists was ironic, at least in the sense of foreign policy. The globalist credentialed had by 2017 allowed North Korea to point likely nuclear-tipped ballistic missiles at the United States. The best and brightest had forged a deal with Iran that would have ensured it likely would become nuclear—and then jawboned banks to violate US law to allow Iran to convert its once embargoed currency into Western money. ISIS by 2017 was no "jayvee" organization, as nonchalantly described by the 2015 White House, or a ragtag tribe; it was a well-organized death cult that had swallowed much of Iraq with near impunity.

No one seemed to have any idea after nineteen years how to either stay in or depart from Afghanistan. So the US military and diplomatic corps just stayed mired there in what it called an endless path to victory. After placating Vladimir Putin's Russia for six years under the policy of "reset" led to Russian aggression and greater global influence, the bipartisan establishment, in part out of hatred of Donald Trump, simply reinvented itself as Russia-phobic and accused those who called for a balanced policy between appeasement and saber-rattling brinkmanship of being Putin's stooges.

Many of the globalized commandments so often canonized at international symposia such as at Davos, the Aspen Institute, or the Council on Foreign Relations turned out to be deeply flawed. In fact, events on the ground have overtaken these long-enshrined, yet never logical or commonsensical, canons. A trade-cheating ascendant China did not become democratic in its affluence, even when its elites sent their children to the Ivy League and bought property on Monterey's 17-Mile Drive or on Malibu's sands. After the Iran Deal, Iran still hated the Great Satan and had more money for its terrorist appendages in Lebanon, Syria, and Yemen—the more so, the more concessions it received.

The Palestinian question—and its veto power over all Arab-Israeli peace negotiations—proved no more central to Middle East calm than the Israeli-Palestinian conflict was central to world peace. There is no monolithic Islamic bloc. Israel is now likely to be counted more a friend to the Gulf monarchies than are the Palestinians, Hamas, Hezbollah, Syria, and Iran.

US oil and gas production meant that there was no economic need to intervene in the Middle East, unless the purpose was to secure for the Europeans and Chinese—usually opposed to US policy in the Persian Gulf—their imported fuel or the safety of their often-used commercial sea lanes. There is no such thing as having years ago reached "peak oil"—the point at which Americans have drawn more oil from their ground than is left beneath it—and there will not be at least for the foreseeable future. At least two-thirds of the NATO alliance members likely would not or could not come to the assistance of any tiny front-line NATO member threatened by neighboring Russia.

The foundations of the EU were essentially antidemocratic. Nations could easily vote to enter the redistributive bureaucracy but are not so easily released once their populations vote to leave the union. If Germany failed in 1914 and 1939 to achieve European hegemony by arms, it ironically succeeded by wealth in making Brussels synonymous with Berlin in the twenty-first century. NATO did not persist as a shared transcontinental post–Cold War stabilization force to protect the flanks of Europe and the West in general. Rather the alliance became a US-subsidized bureaucracy in which most European members did not pay what they had promised and resented the power and wealth of their American protector, but not quite to the point of wanting it gone.

In sum, globalization rests on a few poorly examined laws: those who draft globalized rules for others have the resources to navigate around them. Discussions of abstract cosmic challenges—achieving world peace, cooling the planet, lowering the seas, dismantling secure borders—are psychological ways to square the circle of failure to solve concrete problems at home from war to poverty. Wealthy tech workers in San Francisco hold frequent conferences and symposia about addressing water, sewage, and disease in Africa, but they have demonstrated no ability to address California's own fetid city streets, which are home to over three hundred thousand homeless and rife with medieval diseases, refuse, excrement, and rodents. In addressing such existential and age-old challenges, we are left where we started in Western civilization: the only means are transparent, decentralized local governments, audited by a free and disinterested press and acting under the aegis of a constitutional, consensual republic, serving only at the pleasure of a voting citizenry.

But if globalism has variously enriched, impoverished, and alienated the two respective halves of the United States, how in more particular ways has it posed a danger to the idea of everyone's citizenship?

In one sense, the global creed has destroyed the ancient idea of localism and regionalism as central to the human experience. It became popular in the twenty-first century to define global citizens as "anywheres," in contrast to those who saw themselves as "somewheres." That is, the citizen of the world can be at home anywhere there are like transcendent kind who share his tastes, language, aspirations, international experience, politics, class, and economic security. "Roots" are ossified concepts. If home is not the right neighborhood in London, then why not its clone in New York, and if not in New York, why not a simulacrum in Beijing?

Yet every human instinctively feels attached to the environs of his birth and residence. He is territorial and sees locale, family, friends, community, and familiar physical landscapes as essential to forming his persona and offering reassurances of belonging to, and being wanted by, someone, somewhere. The drafters of the US Constitution assumed that an independent and autonomous agrarian class, rooted in local communities and agricultural regions, was the model of constitutional government—given its innate loyalty to a particular place and long-held customs and beliefs.

But for the globalist, foreign is the idea of a permanent physical home that has unique traditions, ancestries, local histories—and differences. He sees no advantages or intrinsic worth in being rooted in a familiar local space, one that remains constant over generations and requires custodianship to preserve its survival and its role in creating stability for families and neighborhoods.

The globalist sees portable wealth as always preferable to fixed assets—homes, farms, stores, communities, neighborhoods—which are not transitory, their value uncomfortably hinging on the continuity, safety, health, and prosperity of the landscapes in which they exist. The globalist can simply pack up and leave when his environs are no longer to his liking or seem a bad investment; in contrast, those who cannot or will not flee must seek to improve their neighborhoods.[29]

It is no surprise that definitions of "citizen of the world" are always laudatory, such as that from Oxfam, a noted well-meaning confederation of global nonprofits and charities: "A global citizen is someone who is aware of and understands the wider world—and their [sic] place in it. They take an active role in their community, and work with others to make our planet more equal, fair and sustainable."

In other words, the duty of a Western citizen is to rally the assets of his local community and pledge them to the betterment of the wider world abroad. This would be a noble sentiment if Western communities could boast that they had first solved regional problems of crime, housing, and schooling. But when they fail first at home to create sustainable societies—and New York, Chicago, London, and Birmingham are American and British unsafe centers of unequal opportunity—why should they, at best, short their limited resources by expending them abroad or, at worst, spread their own failures in a global fashion?

Globalists also forget that one of the great worries of ancient participatory democracies was size. In antiquity it was feared that when the Greek city-state—such as imperial Athens—was no longer a face-to-face society, citizens would have less in common, become anonymous, and cease to recognize one another. Thus, as strangers they would find it more difficult to exercise self-governance.

As America grew from an agrarian society into a huge, largely urban and suburban transcontinental nation of 330 million people, citizens and their common bonds became more abstract and anonymous rather than concrete and familiar. Perhaps in times of national crisis, such as World Wars I and II and September 11, 2001, diverse people, scattered over three thousand miles, could reconnect as Americans with the aid of shared radio or, after 1950, continuous television news coverage. Yet, even now, in the age of more intrusive and ubiquitous social media, email, Zoom, and Skype, it is hard to imagine transnational or transcontinental democracies comprising hundreds of millions of people with different cultures and traditions normally trusting in a shared commonwealth of values.

Few dare to agree that citizens of the world so often are more insensitive to the needs of their own fellow citizens in their very midst. Do we ever consider that a nation's first critical need is to keep its own citizens secure and viable before it can extend such caring and attention to the unknown and unnamed abroad? Much less do citizens of the world contemplate that "equal, fair and sustainable" citizenship extended to eight billion people might well require a loss of individual liberty, lots of mandatory redistribution, political instability, and a considerable degree of coercion—starting first at home.[30]

Few today wish to describe themselves as nationalists, preferring to be praised as internationalists. International relations is a popular college major; "nationalist relations" would be an anathema on campus. Since antiquity's cosmopolitan Greek philosophers and intellectuals, who boasted that they did not deem themselves citizens of particular Greek city-states or, later, Hellenistic kingdoms, it has been a twenty-five-hundred-year noble tradition among Western intellectuals to identify with the common humanity of the world rather than exclusively with fellow citizens of their own nations or city-states—often in self-serving, agenda-driven, romantic, or abjectly naive ways. Indeed, for some globalism is a psychological condition that squares the circle of concrete impotence at home through romantic relevance abroad.

What is distant is seen as exotic and alluring; what is proximate becomes mundane and ordinary. Saving the world is a much more ambitious, ennobling, and ego-gratifying project than preserving the neighborhood. One aspect of the cynical genius of Alexander the Great was his applying a veneer of prior utopian and ecumenical traditions of Greek philosophy to his otherwise ruthless conquests. As Alexander was destroying the final vestiges of Greek democracy and the freedom of some fifteen hundred autonomous city-states, dismantling the Persian Empire, and killing tens of thousands of Greeks who opposed his autocratic agendas at home and abroad, he enlisted a host of paid philosophers and rhetoricians to help sell his new idea of a "brotherhood of man." Such ecumenicalism was a philosophical staple often fleshed out by the contemporary Stoic philosophers Diogenes and later Cleanthes in their respective utopian visions of one megalopolis of gods and men.

Macedonians would now equally kowtow to Alexander as Persians. In the spirit of non-judgmentalism, his Macedonian grandees would marry foreign wives, often in addition to their own. His army would incorporate elephants and Eastern horsemen to form a truly multi-cultural and more effective military. The companions might dress in Persian fashion, and Alexander himself might don the tiara and offer up a Davos-like prayer that all peoples and races under his new-world regime would be equal subjects. Hellenism, as Alexander understood it, would see the empowerment of Greek science and rationalism on a scale from Sicily to the Persian Gulf and from northern Afghanistan to the Nile, but properly shorn of such bothersome cargos as democracy, unfettered expression, and the idea of an autonomous city-state of free citizens.

Yet, when he died, Alexander left a chaotic Asia and Greece, stripped of democracy, to be fought over by his thuggish marshals until the "strongest" (in vain) might reconstitute his one-world dictatorship. All this is not to say that Alexander, like most megalomaniac globalists, from Julius Caesar to Napoleon, did not sometimes believe in his mission to better mankind by enslaving it.[31]

So often, abstract caring for those distant and unknown can purchase exemption for failure to solve problems in the immediate community. The clever globe-trotting fox learns many things about the world, the local burrowing hedgehog only one: the essential truth that people are people, and learning how to understand and serve them begins at home with those one sees and speaks with face to face.

Instead, we, of a new Victorian age, are adopting the "telescopic philanthropy" of Charles Dickens's bizarre character Mrs. Jellyby of *Bleak House* (1853). She is so consumed with worry about the poor and downtrodden abroad that she ignores her own family and friends and leaves her children unkempt and poorly educated. In the same manner, the late-nineteenth- and early-twentieth-century Fabian socialists sought world government through an eventual League of Nations that would end nationalism and usher in a globalist utopia abroad and a socialist paradise at home. Or perhaps the mentality of globalization is comparable to the partygoers at sophisticated Esther Jack's parlor in Thomas Wolfe's novel *You Can't Go Home Again* (1940). At elite get-togethers they enjoy artistic and cosmopolitan discussions of European intellectuals and artists, oblivious that during a fire in their own building the nobody, young service-elevator operators from the Bronx who ferry them to safety are killed by smoke inhalation.[32]

Intellectuals and the elite in general are especially prone to the globalist disconnect, most idealistically a concern for global well-being amid local intractable pathologies, most truthfully at worst an end-of-history, megalomaniac impulse to solve innate problems on a grand scale once and for all. The biographer and moralist Plutarch (ca. AD 100) claimed in his essay "On Exile" that Socrates had once asserted he was not just an Athenian but instead, like Diogenes, "a citizen of the cosmos"—a *kosmopolitês*. In later European thought, communist ideas of universal labor solidarity drew heavily on the idea of a world without borders. "Workers of the world, unite!" exhorted Karl Marx and Friedrich Engels. Or as Eugene V. Debbs, the American socialist, put it in 1915, "I have no country to fight for; my country is the earth; and I am a citizen of the world."

Wars broke out, in this thinking, only because of needless quarreling over obsolete state boundaries, when the real conflict was over wages, health, and safety, fought between uniform global elites and the world's collective and exploited underclass. The solution to this state of endless war, some argued, was to eliminate borders in favor of trans-national governance and policing. H. G. Wells's prewar science fiction novel *The Shape of Things to Come* (1933) envisioned borders eventually disappearing as elite transnational polymaths, in the manner of League of Nations grandees, enforced enlightened world governance. Norman Angell's earlier best-seller *The Great Illusion* (1909) argued that war between blinkered nationalist states had become so destructive and irrational in the Western industrialized world that it would gradually disappear, as transnational elites would certainly discover more civilized ways of resolving conflicts—as if they had ever done so in their own private or professional lives. I once watched twenty multilingual PhDs, many foreign-born and most well-established global travelers, squabble for an hour over the best way to divide up $2,000 in allotted Foreign Language Department travel money. Little did they know that the local meetings of the Fresno Lions or Elks Club did a much better of job of reconciling such conflicting egos and agendas.

On the urging of President Franklin Roosevelt, defeated 1940 Republican presidential candidate Wendell Willkie in 1942 went on a seven-week, thirty-one-thousand-mile tour of the world. He concluded from his travels and meeting with wartime allies that one world government was needed. His manifesto, *One World*, published in 1943, quickly hit the best-seller list. Indeed, the book sold 1.5 million copies in just four months, a record for nonfiction up to that time. Willkie met with Stalin and came home advocating more military aid to the Soviet Union. Had he not died at fifty-two, many would have considered Willkie for the first secretary-general of the United Nations.[33]

President Barack Obama may not have intended to deprecate America when early in his first term he said at an April 2009 press conference, "I believe in American exceptionalism, just as I suspect that the Brits believe in British exceptionalism and the Greeks believe in Greek exceptionalism." To Obama, to suggest that his own country was like every other in thinking itself exceptional, rather than its actually being so by some disinterested standard, was not controversial. America was, in fact, demonstrably "exceptional" by any metric, but to Obama such recognition might have seemed parochial and chauvinistic—therefore counterproductive to his agenda.

As a candidate in 2008 Obama had gone to Berlin and declared himself both an American and a "world" citizen ("Tonight, I speak to you not as a candidate for President, but as a citizen—a proud citizen of the United States, and a fellow citizen of the world"). He added that the "burdens of global citizenship" united Germans and Americans. Obama seemed to suggest that borders, walls, and boundaries would fall and states be absorbed into a new enlightened transnationalism. Americans would recalibrate their norms to align with global standards, whose nature has never been quite spelled out. Indeed, US leaders' frequent, often clumsy emphasis on how they saw themselves as internationalists and their own Americanism as no big deal was quite striking.

Or as Vice President Joe Biden put it to a questioner during a 2014 town hall at Harvard University, "America's strength ultimately lies in its people. There's nothing special about being an American. None of you can define for me what an American is. You can't define it based on religion, ethnicity, race, culture." Biden may have been trying to define, correctly, Americanism as more of an idea than a status rooted in blood and soil, but for that very rare reason there *is* something special about the American system that is not found abroad.

Citizenship by definition imposes certain responsibilities in exchange for delineated rights. But who or what would dispense such *global* gifts? And what do citizens of the world ask in return? How do eight billion get along as a global commonwealth under a shared protocol of values, when no message of ecumenicalism would dare to transcend race, religion, and gender, especially not one akin to the Western tradition of personal freedom, consensual government, and human rights? In the current relativist mindset, no leader would claim values such as democracy or the equality of women are in any way intrinsically superior to their antitheses. And even those Western nations that might hold themselves up as models for others less wealthy, safe, and free can no longer claim a common core of values among their growing diverse populations at home. Indeed, in the globalist West, regressive tribal identities are most in ascendence.

American voters elect national leaders, not utopian philosophers. An allegiance to the world, in the zero-sum game of fidelity and time, implies some diminishment of commitment to one's particular homeland. During the COVID-19 outbreak, both former First Ladies Michelle Obama and Laura Bush spoke at an international symposium titled "One World: Together at Home," a well-meaning global-citizen effort designed to support and help fund the World Health Organization. But WHO is a United Nations–affiliated health group that from the beginning of the coronavirus pandemic mouthed Chinese propaganda that the virus was not transmissible between humans, that China had already contained it, and that national travel bans were unnecessary. Those falsehoods may well have led to hundreds of thousands of deaths and should have advised Western liberals that subsidizing, or at least trusting in, such an unaccountable transnational organization was illiberal.[34]

Being willfully blind to such global fictions leads to one-world fads in the real world, such as in H. G. Wells's time the League of Nations or the current United Nations. Such visions, similar to those of Wells and Willkie, have always failed. One-worldism requires the subordination of ancient local cultures, the creation of an all-knowing, all-powerful, all-coercive unelected executive elite, and the use of force to implement such visions—things that are incompatible with the professed pacifism and humanitarianism of the very architects of such projects. Indeed, ultimately the only theoretical solution to ending national differences for good is global war that seeks to absorb nations into a few imperial blocs.

Such coerced consolidation is the stuff of George Orwell's *1984*. More recent arguments that wars are ultimately and innately good hinge on their supposed aggregation of warring tribes into larger and more uniform peoples, whose differences central and transnational governments can at last check. But who is the constituency for the United Nations or world government, given the billions who now live under autocratic governments?[35]

Implicit in the mind of the world citizen is a transference of his national allegiance to a global commonwealth, roughly half of whose member states are currently not democratic or constitutional. Would global citizenship, then, under the tenets of contemporary diversity, be a fair and equitable potpourri—proportionately borrowing and incorporating ideas equally from all the world's constitutions, including, to be fair, Chinese, Russian, Iranian, Somalian, and Venezuelan protocols? Or is globalized citizenship again a synonym for magnanimous and condescending westernization, as if the rest of the world will accept either the American Declaration of Independence (1776) or the French Declaration of the Rights of Man and of the Citizen (1789)—or else should be politely nudged to do so?

Many would-be citizens of the world might not agree with the idea of a Western model for the world. Increasingly, disheartened Westerners themselves now look abroad, not at home, for sometimes non-Western constitutional inspiration. In this age of globalization, Americans also seek global moral instruction overseas—having been taught about the United States' flawed founding in racism, sexism, and endemic white privilege bias. The nonparliamentary US Constitution, its ossified tripartite separations of power, the odd-ball Bill of Rights, and the anachronistic Electoral College are likewise all considered aberrant. In 2008, Supreme Court justice Ruth Bader Ginsburg suggested that US judges could benefit by seeking guidance from foreign jurisprudence, even informally voiced on blogs, when interpreting the now apparently passé US Constitution:

> Judges in the United States, after all, are free to consult all manner of commentary—Restatements, treatises, what law professors or even

law students write copiously in law reviews, and, in the internet age, any number of legal blogs. If we can consult those sources, why not the analysis of a question similar to the one we confront contained, for example, in an opinion of the Supreme Court of Canada, the Constitutional Court of South Africa, the German Constitutional Court, or the European Court of Human Rights?[36]

In answer to "why not," one might answer that there is not really a living First, Second, or Fourth Amendment in such constitutions or a comparable record of republican stability.

The result of such indoctrination is that the last two generations of Americans do not especially believe in American exceptionalism. They seem to feel that other less democratic and free systems of government abroad somehow can legitimately claim a higher moral standing than the United States—if not offer America instruction on human rights, race and gender relations, climate change, and enlightened social policy. The West has had a long history of providing material bounty and personal freedom—but also, thereby, a history of spiraling popular demands for perfection. Being good rather than divine is unacceptable, the more a population is freed from worries about its elemental safety and sustenance.

Another good example of the dangers of globalization is the internationalist and never-ending expansive idea of "human rights." The 1948 United Nations Universal Declaration of Human Rights is often cited as the biblical canon of globalization. But the treatise is not designed to protect the human rights and liberties of the individual. Rather, it demands that the state intervene to provide all-encompassing *material* security for the individual without much worry over the level of political coercion and forced redistribution needed. Or, as the lofty declaration puts it, everyone has a "right" to "a standard of living adequate for the health and well-being of himself and of his family, including food, clothing, housing and medical care and necessary social services, and the right to security in the event of unemployment, sickness, disability, widowhood, old age or other lack of livelihood in circumstances beyond his control."

Yet, by 2015, a new addendum (seven times longer than the original UN declaration)—"Transforming Our World: The 2030 Agenda for Sustainable Development"—pledged that all planetary dwellers would enjoy in just fifteen years guarantees to seventeen sorts of universal rights centered around guaranteed economic equality, social and cultural equity, and environmental transformation; it then detailed ninety-one approaches to achieving such entitlements—all predicated on some sort of unstated mandatory redistribution and implied use of enlightened force.

The Anglo-American drafters of the original postwar declaration in many ways were updating the New Deal's thematic "Four Freedoms." The goals, as Franklin Delano Roosevelt eleven months before the start of World War II brilliantly and eruditely condensed them, encompassed supposedly innate human aspirations. Indeed, they were popularized in Norman Rockwell's iconic paintings.

In turn FDR's 1944 State of the Union address expanded the "Four Freedoms" under a new, more ambitious banner of a "Second Bill of Rights." This recalibration would guarantee every American inalienable rights to jobs, housing, sustenance, education, health care, and pensions. Lyndon Johnson's "Great Society" later took up such entitlements, which are today difficult to provide without huge government outlays, a great degree of state coercion, and individual initiative, discipline, and ambition.

Still, little did the postwar architects of the UN charter know that most communist governments would soon justify their denials of private property, free commerce, and the right of dissent on grounds that the state must first provide for the greater welfare of the proletariat. Nor did they reckon that those governments that screamed the loudest for such inclusive rights were innately the most incapable of delivering them, given their absorption or outright destruction of the free market.

In contrast, who in such a climate would have talked of guaranteeing "rights" by ensuring protection of the traditional creators of wealth, such as private property, free market economics, and stable, predictable, and fair government?[37]

The naïveté of the internationalists was even more shocking because the national socialist instigators of World War II in Adolf Hitler's Germany and Benito Mussolini's Italy had recently railed against corporatists, merchants of wealth, capitalists, and other dark forces that had allegedly denied the working classes fulfillment of basic human needs and rights. Thus, the only way to address these tragic lapses was to give an idealist and national socialist like Hitler or Mussolini the power to ensure cradle-to-grave entitlements, to protect the environment, to rein in capitalism, and to provide a worker's paradise on earth. In that context, curtailment of free expression and dissent was, and often is today, seen as a small price to pay.[38]

Nowhere are the results of world citizenship more apparent than in the global intersections of profits and values, given that the former usually drive the latter. In the larger sum of things, basketball might seem irrelevant. But its latest incarnation offers a so-called teachable moment about the hypocrisies and contradictions of American globalists. As such it deserves some further illustration of the realities behind the platitudes. In October 2018 an American general manager of professional basketball's Houston Rockets, Daryl Morey, offhandedly expressed sympathy with democratic protesters in Hong Kong. That should have been a routine, noncontroversial, and free assertion for an American citizen.

Instead the Chinese government immediately ordered the National Basketball Association (NBA) to silence any player or staffer who further criticized Beijing's repression in Hong Kong—although most players had always willingly refrained from criticizing China in contrast to their frequent attacks on their own country. To make its threat credible, China began dialing back its cooperation with the NBA, to the great consternation of the league's accountants.

The intimidation worked like a charm. Former globalists were now exposed as rank communist apologists. Hip, elite, and suddenly toady-ish athletes were all too eager to give up their First Amendment rights *inside their own country*. The Chinese viewership of American basket-ball is believed to approach eight hundred million, a larger—and far more profitable—source of income than the domestic market, which for a variety of supposedly inexplicable reasons is either static or shrink-ing. In truth, the NBA had experienced sharp declines in viewership in 2019 and again in previrus 2020. Yet it had been jacking average player salaries to near $8 million per year—overhead leveraged by some $6 bil-lion in franchising fees, endorsements, merchandising, and advertising in China.

Outspoken players and coaches who had variously boycotted the state of North Carolina for its insistence that there would be only male and female public restrooms in state facilities, who damned the Second Amendment as culpable for mass shootings, and who boycotted events at the White House in their collective loathing of legally elected pres-ident Donald J. Trump suddenly went mute in obedience to Beijing's orders. They turned from radical critics of their own democratic govern-ment into obsequious encomiasts of the Chinese communist autocracy.

Or as San Francisco Warriors coach Steven Kerr put it, "You know, things that our country needs to look at and resolve, that hasn't come up either. So none [of] us are perfect and we all have different issues that we have to get to. People in China didn't ask me about, you know, people owning AR-15s and mowing each other down in a mall. I wasn't asked that question." In other words, in terror over Chinese threats to withdraw sponsorship and promotion of US professional basket-ball, the NBA's vocal critics of the United States began offering moral equivalencies between a democratic United States and a communist dictatorship in China.

If the citizen wondered why NBA players were not standing for their own country's pregame national anthem, Kerr offered insight. Indeed, he simplistically framed his own moral symmetries: "So we can play this game all we want and go all over the map and you know, there's this issue and that issue and that world is a complex place and there's more gray than black and white." Note how the desire for global moral homogeneity—again fueled by enormous transnational profit—trumped both common sense and the truth. Note how "black and white" absolutism selectively fuels the NBA's own criticism of US history and traditions. For global citizen Kerr, who sees "gray" instead of black and white, the crimes of a small number of unhinged private American individuals become a referendum on the entire United States system—in a way not true of the policies officially set by the Chinse Communist Party for a nation of 1.4 billion people. The globalist Kerr, who counts on the cosmopolitanizing of basketball, suddenly wants no part in applying supposedly Western ecumenical standards to dictatorial China.[39]

As for the silliness of Kerr's apologetic assertions: in 2018, about forty thousand Americans died of gun-related injuries, including suicides, accidents, law enforcement shootings, private citizens exercising self-defense, and homicides. Of the roughly 14,500 murders by firearms, *just 373 people in a nation of nearly 330 million* died in mass shootings and tragedies such as "mowing each other down in a mall," as Kerr phrased it. About 4 percent of all homicides were committed with rifles, some of them so-called assault weapons. More specifically, in the decade between 2007 and 2017, semiautomatic rifles or "assault weapons" in mass shootings counted for just 253 deaths out of some 150,000 homicides.

In contrast, the Chinese communist government currently detains about 1.5 million to 3 million of its citizens in "reeducation camps" on the basis of unorthodox religion or thought. It is a communist government with a direct lineage to Mao Tse-tung's Communist Party, which was responsible for between 50 million and 70 million deaths of Chinese citizens. In Kerr's mind, the toll of 373 deaths due to supposed US government laxity was the moral equivalent of 70 million deaths at the hands of the Chinese Communist Party.

Kerr may see himself as a former athlete and coach of the world, eager to blend fact with fiction. Yet he is instructive of globalism because his affinities are one with transnational corporate profit making, itself a driver of much of the virtue-signaling citizen-of-the-one-world rhetoric. Had China been a small autocratic country without much financial clout, where the NBA occasionally played a demonstration game, Kerr might well *never* have spoken out in its defense. The catalyst for his candor was money and hope of more money, not principle. The National Basketball Association is really an International Basketball Profit-Making Association, with ever diminishing identification with a unique United States. Its NBA China franchise is said to be worth over $6 billion. Its growing Chinese profits are estimated at anywhere from $500 million to $4 billion at a time of static domestic viewership.[40]

But the NBA should be careful. The Chinese, unlike Americans, are only globalists in the sense of being neoimperial mercantilists. They don't tolerate dissent. They are racially obsessed and are not comfortable with the African American descent of over 75 percent of NBA players. The Chinese have little interest in the cultural tapestry of diversity that the NBA so often, at least rhetorically, champions. But most of all, they are harsh Belt and Road taskmasters who demand a Faustian bargain from all they make rich in the short term. Chinese courting of American industries over the last half century has been a story of luring them in with promises of big money, copartnering with them, rigging the arrangement, xeroxing their expertise, and then absorbing their markets. The same paradigm applies to American universities who partner with Chinese institutions, themselves almost always deeply enmeshed within the Chinese Communist Party's apparatus.

Bookending the NBA illustration of globalized, and particularly Chinese, influence upon American life was 2020's strange, brief $1 billion Democratic primary candidacy of former New York mayor Mike Bloomberg. Reportedly worth over $60 billion, Bloomberg tapped his unlimited funds to conduct his campaign, while deeply involved in leveraging Western capital to fund Chinese start-up companies. That profitable multi-billion-dollar effort helped the Chinese Communist Party find liquidity for some of its own business ventures. In reductionist terms, Bloomberg, who had a long history of contextualizing and apologizing for Chinese autocracy and censoring criticism of the Chinese Communist Party by his own reporters at *Bloomberg News*, was deeply compromised by his lucrative business deals, which were synonymous with unquestioned transnational profiteering.[41]

So, in the end, what real dangers to American citizenship do globalization and "citizen-of-the-world" pieties pose?

A chief worry is an insidious surrender of sovereignty. The United States either legally or de facto will tend to follow international rather than its own norms. Under the notions of international diversity and inclusion, all the members of the United Nations General Assembly are equal, as are the large powers of the Security Council. There is no requirement that those who vote at the United Nations must at home hold fair and open elections or protect human rights.

To require such requisites for UN membership would be considered noninclusive, judgmental, and arbitrary. So, by its very nature, transnationalism is illiberal. The requirement of any subject of an authoritarian regime is to further the state's interest, whether serving in an international capacity or not. Given that most antidemocratic regimes dislike most democratic regimes, and given the nonjudgmental nature of the United Nations, international bodies are by definition inherently hostile to tolerant regimes.

But why object if such global standards and values abroad are superior to our own? Because there is no evidence that any place on earth protects individual liberty in the fashion of the American Bill of Rights.

What, then, are some conceivable examples of the outsourcing of national sovereignty to transnational organizations, all at the expense of the US citizen? Might an Iranian judge of an Islamist sharia court, assigned to a term on the International Criminal Court, adjudicate the wartime morality of a US soldier in Afghanistan? Or would a Nevada polling booth meet the standards of a Saudi election judge tasked by the Organization for Security and Cooperation in Europe? Or would a Ugandan serving as a United Nations special rapporteur, inspecting American border hot spots, intervene to protect the supposed human rights of migrants illegally crossing the US border? Should we consult the United Nations Human Rights Council, a body whose current membership includes China, Pakistan, the Russian Federation, and Venezuela, for help in investigating police excesses in Seattle or Minneapolis?

In all these proposed scenarios, subjects of authoritarian regimes, some of them hostile to the United States, would be auditing Americans already subject to the jurisdiction of US federal and state courts. The rationales for such international intrusion are, first, that auditors from nondemocratic states have a perfect right to censure the behavior of democratic nations. And, second, their presence, in the view of the American globalist and progressive Left, is a check upon its own purportedly backward domestic political opponents.

It is no accident that with the advent of globalism came a new flurry of old putdowns—isolationist, xenophobe, nativist, racist—as if the most interventionist, pluralistic, open-borders democracy in the world should be found wanting. Yet note, for example, that no one from the American Left—which, unlike the Right, believes in transnational organizations and an eventual trajectory to world government—has appealed to any United Nations human rights group to investigate whether Carter Page was illegally surveilled by the US government through the doctoring of written evidence by the FBI to mislead a Foreign Intelligence Surveillance Act court or whether the Obama administration's intelligence and investigatory services illegally surveilled National Security Advisor–designate Michael Flynn. Few internationalists wish some high European commissions to investigate whether the US government restricts free speech on campuses or uses racial criteria to adjudicate government hiring and college admissions. Again, international ecumenicalism is predicated on shared progressivism.[42]

When Americans equate foreign products and customs with foreign political norms similar to their own, dangers arise. Hollywood, corporate America, and professional sports have all grown fabulously rich in tapping huge foreign consumer markets in Europe and Asia—often because their own proselytizing has alienated an increasing share of their domestic American markets even as they appeal to anti-Americanism abroad. Problems, however, arise when illiberal governments—the Chinese communists in particular—then attempt to censor US content by threats of boycotting, or curtailing access to markets for, any content they find incorrect.

Insidiously, the more film producers and sports franchises acquiesce to such demands, the more they censor themselves and promote values contrary to the spirit and letter of the Declaration of Independence and the US Constitution. Often professional athletes and actors—NBA star LeBron James is iconic in this regard—become far more critical of their own constitutional government than they are of foreign autocratic counterparts. The apparent logic is that attacking the United States resonates among an often youthful, hip domestic audience. It allows one, on the cheap, to appear the renegade and thus balances the image of obsequiousness and timidity when doing the bidding of a dictatorial foreign government.

No outspoken NBA star so far has objected that Nike—a large source of endorsement income for NBA players—employs indentured Uighur labor inside Chinese factories. Few refused to visit NBA-affiliated training camps in China where government coaches subject athletes to harsh physical punishment.[43]

On issues of apparent importance to actors and athletes—global warming, identity politics, minority rights, open borders, abortion on demand, matters of race, class, and gender—the Chinese government is certainly among the world's most repressive and reactionary, whether in terms of massive coal burning, reeducation camps for Muslims, mandated abortions and sterilizations, or annexations of neighboring land.

Recently Hollywood, in the wake of the death of George Floyd and subsequent protests, quite loudly instituted hiring quotas to ensure greater African American inclusion. Yet the film industry did not disclose that its own producers and directors had previously curtailed the presence of dark-skinned actors to ensure greater profitability by accommodating the on-screen aesthetic preferences of Chinese moviegoers.[44]

If we wonder why the United States by 2017 found itself a deer-in-the-headlights victim of long-standing Chinese patent and copyright infringements, technological appropriation, dumping, currency manipulation, and huge surpluses—topped off by systematic Chinese deceit in spreading the coronavirus—it may have been because so many celebrities, academics, and corporate interests were not just heavily invested in Chinese profiteering but quite willing to abide by Beijing's own requirements of censorship and obeisance. A certain arrogant fallacy exists among the American creators of globalization that they are naturally admired and envied—and thus their emulators would logically never seek to harm the font of their own commercial profiteering and psychological well-being.

The tech masters of the universe in Menlo Park and Sunnyvale are the kindred souls of their business counterparts in Shanghai, Seoul, and Tokyo, but not so much of the poor and lower middle classes of Bakersfield and Fresno a mere 150 miles away. The symbiosis between America's disparate regions is critical to the health of the country, especially in the sense of the duty to make sure not just that Silicon Valley's products enrich fellow Americans but also that foreign governments do not use them to harm the freedoms of US citizens—or indeed, in a military context, to threaten their very security.

Yet, if the shared referents of citizenship are not uniquely American—such as the Gettysburg Address, the speeches of Martin Luther King Jr., rock, jazz, and iconic Hollywood films—then the idea behind the melting pot erodes. With it wilts the power of assimilating and integrating legal immigrants. In reductionist terms, if we are all citizens of the world, why worry about "Americanizing" in speech, culture, law, and history the arriving immigrant? And why would he come to the aberrant United States if he really were a citizen of the world and thus could go almost anywhere else to find similar conditions?

Globalization, Americans are belatedly discovering, meant not that the citizens of the world would become Westerners but rather that the world would superficially look at times American. Such a world would more likely absorb Americans into something antithetical to their own foundations and freedoms—something akin to westernizing abroad while at home de-westernizing.

What arrogantly began as an Americanization of the globe has ended up as a globalization of America.

Epilogue

CITIZENSHIP, THE ANNUS HORRIBILIS, AND THE NOVEMBER 2020 ELECTION

U p until March 2020, many of the themes pertaining to the dangers to citizenship presented in this book's chapters had been hotly debated. But these issues were rarely argued over through revolutionary violence or in existential terms of life and death. After March 2020 they sometimes were.*

Many of these controversies concerning citizenship became central to the outsider Donald Trump's unforeseen capture of the Republican nomination and his subsequent 2016 defeat of Hillary Clinton in the November national election. It is almost impossible to separate any discussion of the decline of citizenship from the political fights of the 2016–2021 period, in which Donald Trump was often a central and controversial player.

---

* I wrote the great part of *The Dying Citizen* from 2018 to early 2020. This present epilogue updates a few of the events through March 6, 2021, during the final editing of the manuscript.

Trump, remember, had achieved both his primary and general election victories by campaigning on restoring the economic viability of the middle classes of the hollowed-out Midwest and especially on redressing the plight of the muscular workers in manufacturing and assembly. Few had thought such heterodoxy could result in a winning agenda. And it was not clear whether Trump himself in 2015–2016 was running consciously to restore elements of classical American citizenship or simply saw such issues as the most effective way to win states central to achieving 270 Electoral College votes.

But whether an idealistic populist, a rank cynic, a canny pragmatist, neither, or a combination of the three, Trump clearly sought to transform fundamentally the Republican Party's base of support. It must change, he argued despite his own billionaire status, from one run by financial and corporate elites to an envisioned populist workers' party concerned with jobs and viable middle-class wages. After his victory, most people eventually took him seriously, both supporters and critics. His unorthodox speech and demeanor and middle-class agendas certainly alienated Wall Street as much as he was already despised by Silicon Valley, academia, and the media.

If Trump brought the estranged voter back to the Republican Party, he also galvanized some of the richest and most powerful interests in America against him—as well as half the public, most of the traditional media establishment, and the wealthiest and most established of Republicans. The result was his chronic inability, despite his own wealthy status, to raise money to match the resources of his opponents, much less their corporate and cultural influence. He was unable to find many in the establishment willing to endure the social ostracism brought by allying with or working for him. And given his agendas and mercurial persona, he never enjoyed complete party unity to advance his political agendas.

Still, as part of his middle-class restoration agenda and appeals to the working poor and minorities, Trump sought to distinguish residency from citizenship by fortifying and thus securing the southern border, while enforcing laxly administered immigration laws.

The Trump administration deliberately attacked the orthodoxy of identity politics, sometimes bluntly and without refinement, in calls to return to the practice of the melting pot. Yet, paradoxically, it also sought to increase the previously anemic Republican appeal to minorities by emphasizing class commonalities rather than racial differences and by giving the worker greater leverage over the employer, mostly through achieving record low minority unemployment and near-record-low overall peacetime unemployment rates (3.5 percent).

As a result the Left, ironically, blasted Trump as both a racist and a dangerous conservative—but one with an ability to siphon off minority votes, which he did with more success than most recent Republican presidential candidates. No recent president has been called a racist more than Trump. And none has been more successful in lowering African American unemployment and cutting back the incarcerated black population by reducing sentencing for nonviolent drug crimes.

Trump's controversial 2016 "Make America Great Again" agenda, with mixed success, also targeted the "swamp," or the bipartisan Washington government, media, and bureaucratic nexus. The "unelected" were understandably quite hostile to his person and administration, despite his government's vast and sometimes reckless increases in federal expenditures and entitlements. The "deep" state, or so Trump railed, had, as soon as he took office, gone on the counterattack against him through its media surrogates and its own bureaucratic tentacles.

At his rallies, Trump quite presciently decried that such elites were continuously trying to recalibrate the Constitution as an agent of progressive change rather than as the citizen's shield of liberty. He mocked progressive attacks on the First and Second Amendments often to thunderous applause from raucous thousands—and openly caricatured the Washington bureaucracy and the hierarchy of the Federal Bureau of Investigation and Central Intelligence Agency. With each clap of the crowd, he gained a new enemy in Washington, even as he seemed oblivious of the growing number—and underappreciated and often silent wealth and power—of his various political opponents.

Finally, Trump took on globalization, especially after the outbreak of the COVID-19 pandemic. He focused in general on the practice of unfettered but asymmetrical transnational trade and in particular on the mercantilism of China, soon to be further suspect given the Wuhan, China, origins of COVID-19. When the pandemic hit, the United States and China were deadlocked in a trade war. The American pushback had both angered and surprised the Chinese, who had thought their imminent global hegemony a foregone conclusion.

The administration argued that transnational indifference, here and abroad, had allowed North Korea to test missiles in the air space of our allies. The globalist status quo had failed to achieve breakthroughs in the Middle East. Washington establishmentarians were flummoxed by affluent North Atlantic Treaty Organization allies who would not meet their promised defense expenditures. And the bipartisan apparatus had empowered Iran over America's traditional allies in the Middle East: Israel and moderate Arab regimes.

The twenty-two-month, $40 million Robert Mueller special counsel investigation found no actionable proof of Trump-Russian collusion. Trump, despite being impeached in December 2019 and acquitted by the Senate in January 2020, was impeached again in January 2021 and tried and acquitted in February 2021, when out of office and a private citizen during the Senate trial—the first such occurrence in American history. And despite a chronic inability to achieve a 50 percent approval rating in the major polls, by the beginning of 2020 Trump had crafted a resonant reelection theme of "Promises Made, Promises Kept."

In other words, had the national election taken place in January or February 2020, before the reemergence of Joe Biden and his successful nomination and the onslaught of the COVID-19 pandemic, Trump might well have won the Electoral College vote. The failed efforts of Mueller's special investigation to prove "collusion," the failed try to remove him from office after impeachment, and the failed auxiliary attempts of the media may have had the unexpected effect of making Trump stronger rather than weaker. In February 2020, on the eve of the COVID-19 lockdown, for example, Trump's approval rating in the Gallup poll had topped out at 49 percent.

So how well did Trump or his administration actually achieve his stated ambitious goals, among them the implicit restoration of traditional citizenship? For the first time in over a decade, in the three years before the onset of COVID-19, average middle-class income rose, especially for most minorities, reaching the highest level on record in July 2019. Record gas and oil production reduced commuting and home heating and cooling costs while adding tens of thousands of high-paying new energy jobs. Fracking also ensured that prior expeditionary engagements in the Middle East were now entirely optional, or at least not conditioned on the nation's perceived need for secure and affordable supplies of overseas gas and oil. Deregulation and tax incentives drew capital back to the United States and enticed new investors to focus on American companies.

By late 2020, a massive, imposing wall of reinforced concrete and electronic gadgetry had replaced over 450 miles of mostly old, porous southern border fence. Hard-ball trade negotiations had resulted in immigration concessions on the part of Mexico, which now began patrolling its own side of the southern border and not green-lighting Central American would-be entrants into the United States through their jurisdictions.

The Trump administration finally prevailed against nonstop lawsuits to overturn executive orders that had sought to restrict asylum laws while privileging legal over illegal entry into the United States. As a result, even by late 2018 illegal immigration into the United States had dipped to a near historic low—and political support for Trump's policies from various minority groups, while still modest, nonetheless inched up to new highs for a Republican, in direct relationship to the drop in unemployment and a rise in wages.[1]

Trump's efforts to bring back US jobs lost to unfair trade, capital lost to counterproductive tax policies, and good wages lost to unfair competition for entry-level employment from millions of illegal aliens had begun to resonate with even doctrinaire Republicans, independents, and swing voters. Despite his often off-putting behavior and his social media talk deemed "unprecedented" and "unpresidential," business groups and CEOs believed his economic plan was working and appealing to a majority of Americans.

In sum, by year's end in 2019, media pundits feared that despite Trump's high personal negatives, incessant and controversial tweeting, and nonstop media criticism, the president might well be reelected—especially given the hard-left turn of the Democratic Party and the strongest incumbent economy in nearly a half century, coupled with a general peace overseas.[2]

But then a series of unprecedented disasters unfolded. Most of them had nothing to do with either Democratic or Republican politics, at least initially. Yet most of the ensuing crises were leveraged to alter the president's once rosy chances in November 2020—in a fashion that Trump did not fully comprehend, or simply was unable to overcome, or even contributed to directly.

By February 2020, a respiratory flu-like disease (COVID-19), caused by a new coronavirus (SARS-CoV-2), had spread worldwide from its mysterious origins in Wuhan, China. The virus soon seeded terror and panic throughout the Western world in a fashion not seen since the H1N1 flu virus pandemic of 1918. COVID-19 certainly proved more infectious than even flu-like diseases—even if it eventually proved not necessarily more lethal to those under sixty than a severe flu strain (i.e., .02 to .05 percent of those infected under sixty died from the disease).

Yet, on rare occasions, it inexplicably killed even the middle-aged and healthy. Thus the nature of this new coronavirus for months remained mercurial and baffling—even as, by year's end 2020, over 350,000 Americans had died from the virus, followed by tens of thousands more during the January transition and the first weeks of the Joe Biden administration. Accurate data about rates of transmission, infectiousness, and lethality were impossible to come by due to the general chaos of the times and the politicization of the disease both in the United States and abroad.[3]

In stark terms, details about the pandemic were either deemphasized or exaggerated—depending upon the politics of the respective agency, media, or individual medical expert. Was Trump doing well in combatting the plague? After all, deaths per million in America for most of the pandemic were about on par with those in major European nations such as the United Kingdom, Spain, and Italy—while the US economy remained far stronger despite a national lockdown. Or was he doing poorly because the COVID-19 death rates were lower in Germany?

Did COVID-19 hit the United States like no other virus because it seemed to have killed more Americans than any infectious agent since the 1918 flu pandemic? Or were the definitions of deaths caused primarily, rather than secondarily, by the virus controversial and under constant dispute?

Was it a miracle that Trump had, as promised, galvanized government and industry to produce a safe and effective COVID-19 vaccine in 2020, less than ten months after the arrival of the virus on American shores—in a way the European Union, Russia, and China could not? Or was he to blame when states were initially slow to inoculate their populations, despite having plenty of vaccinations in stock? Did Trump's failure to articulate the full ramifications of the threat suggest that his actual reaction to the virus was accordingly flawed?

When weekly fatalities from all causes dipped below those of corresponding previrus periods in 2019, was that proof of presidential competency? Or whenever there were more deaths from flu in 2020 over the same week in the prior year, did that show Trump's incompetency? By August 2020, the United States had administered more COVID tests than any other major country. Was such massive testing the main reason why the United States had more confirmed cases than any other country? Or did the large number of cases by itself signify a defect in Trump's performance as president?

As a result of all these questions and controversies, strategies to combat COVID-19, as well as assessments of their efficacy, soon bifurcated along political lines in the election year 2020. At the outset, our globalist partner China terrified the world by suppressing key information about the nature, origins, lethality, and communicability of the virus. Beijing felt bound by no tie with the world community—and for some time barred foreign scientists from visiting Wuhan.

At best, the communist government lied about the virus to other nations to avoid damaging its commercial brand and aborting its lucrative export industries. At worst, China privately and early on sensed that the virus had become uncontrollable and probably had not entirely originated in its "wet" market, as alleged. So, in theory, Beijing may have shrugged that other nations might suffer from the accident and kept quiet about the potential for the inevitable early spread of the virus. In either case, China was quite willing to endanger millions worldwide.

The invisible virus easily hopped across borderless oceans and mountains, but now at the jet-engine speed of over five hundred miles per hour. Yet, for many critical days, it was considered xenophobic for the United States to issue a travel ban to and from China—as if worries about being either insensitive to Chinese concerns or at odds with international ecumenical platitudes outweighed the safety of American citizens.[4]

China had known of its first coronavirus case at least by mid-November 2019—and perhaps far earlier in August or September. Yet, until January 31, 2020, some tens of thousands of Chinese nationals had flown unhindered into US airports, the majority of them on the West Coast. The same easy entry into the United States was true of European Union nationals until March 11, 2020.

Furthermore, Europe's open-border policies meant that hundreds of thousands of Chinese nationals, some carriers, had flown into

European airports, then entered the quarantined United States on connecting flights, after the US travel ban on China. Remember: China had shut down *all* internal travel from and to Wuhan on January 23, *while allowing Chinese who had previously escaped from that ground zero city to travel all over the world.*[5]

The World Health Organization (WHO), an affiliate of the United Nations, assured worried countries that China was taking heroic measures to halt the spread. Yet the WHO initially declared that the virus was, as the Chinese also insisted, not transmissible between humans. A travel ban on flights to and from China was thus deemed unnecessary. Indeed, such a prohibition would indicate bias and prejudice. Almost all the early WHO assessments of the virus, based on either ignorance or Chinese pressure, proved wrong and thus further endangered millions worldwide. When, as a result, Trump later withdrew the United States from the WHO, outcry followed.[6]

In mid-March, the United States eventually began a nationwide shutdown. The ensuing and controversial blanket quarantine proved like none other in American history. Yet accurate information about the virus remained scant. Federal health bureaucracies such as the Food and Drug Administration, the National Institutes of Health, and the Centers for Disease Control and Prevention (CDC) still seemed both flummoxed and territorial. And their advice about quarantining and mask wearing, the nature of viral transmission, the level at which herd immunity kicked in, and the likely appearance of a vaccine were sometimes contradictory or subject to abrupt reassessment.

As a result, elected officials inevitably misled citizens. Medical experts, the president himself, House Speaker Nancy Pelosi, Senate Minority Leader Chuck Schumer, New York governor Andrew Cuomo, and expert statisticians at first variously downplayed the virus. But soon the opposite of exaggeration followed. Headlines now blared that the WHO or CDC claimed that out of every one hundred infected, two, three, or more patients would die from the disease. British epidemiologists warned that perhaps over two million Americans could die from the virus. It took a great deal of time, data, and reflection to concede that more likely two to five in a thousand of all those infected with the virus would die from it.

In such a year of plague, almost all the prior progress of the past three years in redressing the challenges to citizenship had fallen apart by December 2020. And the result was even further regression in all six of this book's chapter themes detailing long-standing pre- and postmodern threats to citizenship.

First, progress in remedying the plight of the middle class from 2017 to 2019, outlined in Chapter 1, suffered reversals. The nearly ten-month lockdown, beginning in early March, soon sent the economy into a tailspin. As millions stayed inside their homes and apartments, gross domestic product plummeted as unemployment soared.

The state quarantines fell most heavily on small businesses—and not just because they had less access to capital, savings, and liquidity to withstand the radical cessation of commerce. Americans quickly noticed an anomaly. Or rather, they sensed an arbitrary selectivity in state and local governments' determinations about which businesses were considered "essential" and could stay open and which were "nonessential" and could not. In my rural county, small florists, shoe stores, and gift shops were all closed. Yet *all* of their wares could easily be purchased at huge chain stores like Walmart or Target, into which hundreds of shoppers crowded in less safe conditions. A warehouse or chain store that sold essential food stuffs could sell anything else it wished under the same roof, from Christmas ornaments to video games. A store not purveying essential food stuffs—as is the case with most small, specialized businesses—could not. And if the shutdown of millions of businesses robbed consumers of products vital for life, then they could always order them on Amazon, a company that grew exponentially in 2020.

The overall consequence was that customers en masse shopped in conglomerate and outlet stores—and often with much less social distancing than if they had been widely dispersed in family-owned small businesses. In response to the virus, huge companies like Walmart and Amazon grabbed even more market share from tenuous family stores, thousands of which did not reopen after the end of the lockdowns and simply vanished. Jeff Bezos, founder of Amazon, in 2020 alone increased his net worth by over $75 billion after the start of the lockdown. No other event in recent American history has so grievously and so abruptly widened the gap between rich and poor, masses and elites, and large corporations and American small businesses.[7]

Second, in relation to the issues of Chapter 2, efforts to curb illegal immigration were likewise tabled. As the nation shut down, construction on the wall and the Mexican government's enforcement of its borders continued—in part over fears of transnational spreading of COVID-19. Yet the progressive effort to blend residency and citizenship would not waste such a serious crisis. Accordingly, state governments made no distinctions between citizens and illegal aliens in doling out cash relief in the wake of the recessionary lockdowns.

Moreover, in the election year 2020, Democratic presidential candidates promised blanket amnesties for some eleven to nineteen million illegal aliens and attacked the wall and the Trump administration's more rigid enforcement of the borders—to the delight of Mexico and Latin America. As a result, thousands began heading northward after November 3, in expectation of a porous border and amnesties. After the inauguration of Joe Biden, executive orders fast-tracked amnesties and weakened Trump border controls, resulting in a surge of illegal crossings, often by children unaccompanied by parents. Minors crossing the border without or separated from their parents had usually been housed in fenced-off areas without much notice under the Barack Obama administration. During the Trump years, these separated-minor detention areas were suddenly renamed "cages" and Trump declared a near criminal for using them—and yet, such facilities filled up again during the first months of the Biden administration to media yawns.[8]

Third, as far as the challenge of tribalism, racial acrimony increasingly permeated almost every aspect of American culture in the manner described in Chapter 3. Much of the healing brought about by the increased economic opportunity of the prior three years eroded. Somehow tribal tensions superseded even notions of public health in a time of pandemic. Over one thousand health care professionals nationwide offered an unapologetic defense of the seemingly selective enforcement of COVID-19 quarantines: "We created the letter in response to emerging narratives that seemed to malign demonstrations as risky for the public health because of COVID-19. Instead, we wanted to present a narrative that prioritizes opposition to racism as vital to the public health, including the pandemic response."

President-elect Joe Biden almost immediately announced he would be helping small businesses adversely affected by the pandemic and lockdown primarily on the basis of the race or ethnicity of their owners. Biden's choice to run the Civil Rights Division of the Department of Justice was Kristen Clarke, a noted civil rights activist who, however, had left a paper trail of racist obsessions that included arguments for the innate, genetic superiority of blacks over whites. Advisors to the CDC even suggested by December 2020 that initially scarce vaccinations be given first to various groups often prioritized by race, instead of simply focusing on all the elderly over seventy—despite the scientific data showing that the young of all races were relatively safe while the elderly of all races were not.[9]

Identity politics soon fueled protests that transcended those following the death of George Floyd. Protesters targeted the iconic Washington Monument, Jefferson Memorial, and Mount Rushmore as icons of white supremacy. In their frenzy of revolution, they often declared the United States racially cancerous at birth and thus deserving of toxic surgery that well might kill the host. That many of the architects of the radical protests, the creators of Black Lives Matter (BLM), the originators of the 1619 Project, and the Antifa protesters themselves had sometimes uttered racist or anti-Semitic slurs or vowed to overthrow the United States in their own pasts mattered little. Nikole Hannah-Jones, the *New York Times* journalist and the chief architect of the 1619 Project, declared she was honored that some had dubbed the 2020 summer riots, which caused forty deaths, injured seven hundred police officers, and led to billions of dollars in lost property and labor, the "1619 riots." And she explained that "destroying property, which can be replaced, is not violence. . . . Any reasonable person would say we shouldn't be destroying other people's property, but these are not reasonable times."[10]

Those calculating the effects on their own careers of cancel culture—either in fear of being outed as illiberal amid revolutionary turmoil or in anticipation of gaining favor with woke activists—began preempting the mob's wrath with the most bizarre array of virtue signaling seen in modern American history. University presidents and senior media editors promised to capitalize "black," as if new orthography alone might have a reparatory effect, or at least ease tensions, or perhaps preclude their own resignations. At a time of university financial crises, due to the lockdowns and forced closures of campuses, college administrators promised huge budget increases for segregated theme houses and new race-based programs. They agreed to hire far more diversity facilitators and coordinators, often on the basis of race. Faculty members were now to focus much more on the impact of race in America and enroll in accelerated and expanded mandatory diversity-reeducation workshops. Some English departments promised not to enforce traditional rules of English grammar in the grading of nonwhite student papers.

Retired generals who had spent their entire lives revolving in and out of Forts Benning and Bragg suddenly announced they too were suddenly woke to the prior racist messaging of the long-ago naming of US military bases after renegade Confederate generals. Once unaware of their own complicity in racism, they now opportunely asked the country to follow their lead in renaming these century-old bases.[11]

Corporate CEOs, fearful of boycotts and more looted stores, outdid each other in obsequiousness—none more so than Dan Cathy, CEO of the Chick-fil-A fast-food restaurant chain. He urged that white people shine the shoes of blacks in the manner that the disciples had washed the feet of Jesus. Indeed, Dan Cathy sort of did just that when, in a televised moment, he polished the sneakers of hip-hop artist Lecrae.[12]

Fourth, and perhaps most troubling, the year 2020 also saw the resurgence of the so-called administrative state and the powers of the unelected. The citizens' freedoms were further pruned in a variety of areas, as discussed in Chapter 4. Due to the national lockdown in early spring, an array of special interests galvanized to either change bureaucratic voting protocols or to sue in state courts to change current voting laws to facilitate mass mail-in and early voting. Either in panic over the virus or in expectation that changing existing voting rules would aid the progressive agenda, the entire nature of the 2020 election was irrevocably altered.

In many states, without a vote of the people or their elected officials, thousands of bureaucrats and state and local judges rewrote state voting laws, in contravention of the US Constitution, which allots to the legislatures the prime responsibility of crafting their own state voting procedures in national elections. As a result, over one hundred million citizens voted early or by mail in the November election—nearly 65 percent of the total vote—with far less audit of signatures, addresses, and deadlines. In contrast, in 2016—an election year that saw record rises in early and mail-in voting—about 60 percent of ballots were nevertheless cast in person on Election Day. That iconic day has now ceased to exist in a fashion that even the Left once warned was fraught with dangers of fraud and a general inability to authenticate voter eligibility and identification—at least in consistency with standards of the past.

Early voting even ensured that perhaps sixty to seventy million voters had cast their ballots well before the last presidential debate. Various Silicon Valley billionaires poured nearly $500 million into the race, focusing their gifts on targeted precincts felt to be vital for progressive candidates.[13]

The resulting conundrum led to immediate charges from the Trump camp of voter fraud—less than fifty thousand strategically placed votes had determined the election—and then countercharges against the

Trump campaign of insurrection, treason, and coups, especially when Trump demanded recounts and questioned the legitimacy of the electors and their vote all the way into January 2021.

After November 3, Trump sued in federal and state courts and demanded and achieved recounts. All for naught: he failed in almost all efforts to ask federal courts to overturn state ballot tallies on the rationale that unelected judges and bureaucrats had illegally voided state voting laws. His persistence in challenging the vote of the state electors of early December and his claims that he had actually won "in a landslide" soon proved increasingly polarizing and counterproductive to his own cause.

The constant promises to supporters of a new election or rejection of the November 3 decision sapped some of the lame-duck Trump's already eroding popularity and diminished sympathy for his grievances. And when a splinter group from an early Trump rally stormed the Capitol on January 6, 2021, while Congress was in session adjudicating the vote of the electors, the ensuing violence—five people died in the chaos, one violently—ended the Trump presidency on a sour note.

Yet even Trump's tumultuous final days of departure from office soon proved quite different from what was reported at the time. After the Senate impeachment trial had acquitted him as a private citizen, the entire media narrative discussed earlier of a January 6 "armed insurrection" that had caused the violent death of Capitol police officer Brian Sicknick only further disintegrated. There were still no "insurrection" leaders apprehended who were found to have organized what was in truth a mostly buffoonish, chaotic, and crackpot, albeit dangerous, Capitol assault. Officer Sicknick died of natural causes a day *after* the assault, not as sensationally reported at the hands of a violent Trump supporter. The circumstances around the one killing—that of unarmed fourteen-year Air Force veteran and small business owner Ashli Babbitt, who unlawfully entered the Capitol through a window—still remained shrouded in mystery. The details of an official inquest by the US Attorney's Office for the District of Columbia that exonerated the officer who shot her were mostly kept quiet. And the name, gender, age, and race of the officer in question were uncharacteristically not disclosed to the public—contrary to the custom of all other law enforcement officers nationwide involved in the lethal shootings of unarmed suspects.[14]

Unelected health care spokespeople, who, both inadvertently and knowingly, gave contradictory advice and were never subject to audit, prompted some of the hysteria that had green-lit massive quarantines and then, indirectly, the radical changes in election-year voting laws. Dr. Anthony Fauci, director of the National Institute of Allergy and Infectious Diseases (NIAID), a national icon, nonetheless confessed that he might have initially misled the nation about the irrelevance of protective masks. He ex post facto shrugged that his deception was designed to prevent mass demand for them and resulting shortages for key medical workers.

Fauci later further admitted that he had not relied on science per se when he changed the definition of "herd immunity" to make it a far more difficult proposition. He confessed that he wished to persuade citizens to keep wearing masks and to social distance in fear that the growing numbers of those with antibodies or who had been vaccinated might give the general public a false sense of security. Fauci seemed oblivious that he and federal health agencies generally were losing credibility. The public wondered whether each new Fauci pronouncement rested on sound medical evidence or was just another "noble lie" to serve his own interpretations of the greater good.[15]

Fifth, the more formal efforts to change long-standing American laws and customs outlined in Chapter 5 further eroded constitutionally protected freedoms amid the general chaos of 2020.

During the pandemic, state officials, by executive edicts, more or less abrogated some key elements of the Bill of Rights—at first to "flatten the curve" of infections but eventually without consistent or logical rationales. Governors, mostly in blue states, insisted on locking down businesses and events, even as the virus caseloads still rose under such stricter quarantines. Indifferent to evidence that suicides, missed health procedures and surgeries, substance abuse, familial and spousal abuse, and economic collapse may have been taking an even larger toll than the virus itself, governors only further doubled down. If a quarantine did not stop the spread of the virus, then surely laxity in quarantining was the fault and a greater lockdown the solution. Freedom of association, such as holding family Thanksgiving dinners, and of unfettered expression, such as questioning the science of quarantines or the lethality rate of the COVID-19 virus, was often curtailed by executive edict on grounds of public health.[16]

Even more draconian measures followed. In the Orwellian new world of governors and mayors as monarchs without parliaments, even small church services, with parishioners masked and socially distanced, were deemed dangers to public health. Meanwhile, thousands daily still crammed shoulder to shoulder into discount chain stores. Moreover, any slackness in public obedience to quarantine rules may have been fueled by the fact that many elected officials were often the most flagrant in violating them—be it House Speaker Nancy Pelosi (D-CA), or California governor Gavin Newsom, or San Francisco mayor London Breed.

The law was no longer equally applied. Some officials, after the George Floyd rioting and arson, simply invented new statutes and discarded old ones. Especially culpable were dozens of state, county, and city prosecuting attorneys elected between 2018 and 2020 by a national progressive funding effort headed by billionaire George Soros. In San Francisco and Los Angeles, newly elected district attorneys such as Chesa Boudin and George Gascón declared an entire assortment of laws inert and announced that crimes from resisting arrest to prostitution would no longer be prosecuted.[17]

While rioting, looting, and arson plagued big cities—many under quarantine lockdowns—from June to November, very few Black Lives Matter or Antifa lawbreakers were ever arrested, prosecuted, convicted, and jailed. Media efforts to distinguish mostly black "peaceful" BLM protests from often violent and mostly white Antifa demonstrations were usually unsuccessful in the eyes of the public—as even a sympathetic media broadcast scenes of mass looting and arson committed by participants of both groups. Ideology sometimes came to govern the degree to which elected prosecutors applied the law. In essence, public prosecuting attorneys now made, enforced, ignored, and judged statutes by bypassing state legislatures altogether. In February and March 2021, Harvard CAPS/Harris and USA Today/Ipsos polls revealed that sympathy for police had soared while support for Black Lives Matter in general had crashed and that most Americans had concluded that Antifa was a terrorist organization deserving far harsher punishment, that George Floyd was likely not murdered in first-degree fashion by the police, and that the aftermath of the January 6 riot was being used to punish conservative thought and expressions.[18]

In early January 2021, remember, not just Antifa and BLM were rioting and vandalizing the public domain; so were furious splinter groups of Trump supporters who either left or skipped a presidential rally to storm the Capitol in Washington, DC. Both Left and Right damned such violence, with each accusing the other of the greater hypocrisy in not restraining extremists. The Left claimed that law-and-order conservatives had insufficiently reined in their own. The Right answered that the Left had for months contextualized the mayhem of Antifa and BLM and therefore should not be surprised when others were emboldened to follow their violent example. The public was left with the general impression that, for political reasons, violence in the streets was being condoned and perpetrators not held to account for their illegal actions.[19]

In reaction to the storming of the Capitol on January 6 by a faction of Trump supporters, the 2020 defeat of Trump, the impending inauguration of President-elect Joe Biden, and the loss of Republican control of the Senate on January 5 in the two special elections in Georgia, the

Left became emboldened. One of the most disturbing threats to free expression in modern American history ensued. Progressives promised in 2020 to change not just the policies of the US government but the processes by which they are made, whether by ending the Senate filibuster, admitting new states, packing the Supreme Court, ending the Electoral College, or passing a national voting law. Whether all fifty Democratic senators would remain unified enough in efforts to end the filibuster—the key to enacting a subsequent radical reset of American institutions—became the political question of early 2021.

Not in doubt was that private companies judged the controversial end of the Trump administration would mean a free license to ban, deplatform, and censor both use of social media and the users themselves. Soon after, thousands of Trump followers had their social media accounts censored or frozen. Those who had posted evidence of attending a rally to support challenges to the acceptance of the Electoral College vote—and yet did not participate in violent protests with other splinter groups—were sometimes fired from their jobs, or banned from travel, or had their businesses boycotted.

Corporations threatened to withhold donations to any official who supported the Trump challenges to the November election. Former Trump administration officials were threatened with career cancellation. Employers were warned not to hire any of them. Whatever one thought about Trump's quixotic challenges to the November election vote count, he finally conceded defeat. No matter. Trump himself was banned for life from Twitter and Facebook for allegedly using social media to encourage protesters to assemble on January 6 in Washington, DC.[20]

Amazon, Google, and Apple—three of the top-five market-capitalized corporations in the world—in the same early hours of the same day, without warning and in a coordinated effort, blocked servers and apps used to access their upstart, conservative social media rival Parler. The latter had recently been flooded with millions of new users eager to follow Trump to an alternative platform after he was cancelled by Twitter and Facebook. Such suppression recalled the nineteenth-century cartels, whose monopolies had once spawned progressive muckraking opposition and the passage of antitrust legislation.

Twitter's new rival, Parler—summarily shut down for days and nearly ruined—filed antitrust suits against those who had sought to destroy it. No one could explain why the radical Iranian ayatollah Ali Khamenei could freely tweet about destroying Israel or Antifa could use social media to coordinate its often violent demonstrations, but the president of the United States and some of his supporters were banned from Facebook, Twitter, and a host of other social media platforms. And no one could quite figure out whether Silicon Valley had monopolistically coordinated its anti-Trump efforts after the surety of the Biden victory to destroy a rival who might, in theory, poach seventy million Trump Twitter followers, or because of political differences, or both.

The main problem with this furious reaction to Trump's objections to the vote counting was the abject asymmetry in the manner it threatened the free expression of citizens. And yet, many on the Left had challenged the legitimacy of the 2016 election with impunity well into December 2016. Defeated candidate Hillary Clinton had urged Joe Biden *never* to concede the 2020 election if it became apparent he had lost.

In summer 2020, elected officials who previously had supported the sometimes violent Antifa and Black Lives Matter demonstrations were not worried about repercussions. Vice President Kamala Harris had earlier, while still a senator, helped to organize bail funding for BLM and Antifa demonstrators arrested for violence or disobeying the law.[21]

Sixth, and finally, the baleful wages of globalism discussed in Chapter 6 were also illustrated as never before in 2020. Most analysts estimated that about 80 percent of the ingredients used in essential US pharmaceuticals were produced in China, as were an equal percentage of face masks and disposable gloves. The last penicillin plant in the

United States, for example, closed in 2004. Even more worrisome was that US authorities themselves seemed to have no idea what percentage of key drugs China produced, only that it was large and apparently seen in both countries as an American liability. One Communist Party organ, *Xinhua*, for example, at the height of the COVID crisis, warned that if an angry China interrupted its supply chain of drugs and medical supplies to the United States, then America might be overwhelmed and plunge into "the mighty sea of coronavirus."

China quickly began to limit exports of key medical supplies, including those produced by foreign companies inside China despite contracts that had allowed them to send their Chinese-produced drugs and medical wares first to their own countries of origin. In especially ironic fashion, given the birth of the virus on Chinese soil and its spread due to Chinese dissimulation and laxity, China at first received medical aid from abroad. Yet shortly thereafter, as the virus spread from its shores, Beijing became a donor and eventually an especially hard-bargaining exporter, jacking up the prices of masks, gloves, and other key medical supplies to ameliorate the infection it had spawned—and many of the products were not just overpriced but defective.[22]

Expert opinion about Sino-American relations turned on a dime. In the pre-coronavirus era, the call to keep industries inside the United States, especially those dismissed as drudgery or non-value-added manufacturing—such as producing simple N-95 face masks—was dismissed as low-tech know-nothingism at best and Trump's Neanderthal protectionism and nationalism at worst. In the era of the coronavirus, however, the same experts now lectured about the need to preserve "strategic industries" and "national assets" in times of emergencies. The about-face was not so much a recalibration in the heat of panic as an unknowing return to common sense and a realization of the limits of globalization.

As mentioned earlier, during the pandemic the reputations of transnational organizations and conglomerates took a beating, not just because there was plenty of previrus suspicion of their agendas but because they were inherently unaccountable and thus performed dismally in a crisis. The United Nations and the World Health Organization were slow to respond. When they initially did, they sent out not just false information but also data supplied by the Chinese government known to be inaccurate but useful for political purposes. American citizens began to grasp that their medical fates were not entirely in the hands of their own elected officials.

In 2018 and 2019, the United States—perhaps the nation most hurt by the WHO's initial obeisance to Chinese wishes to suppress the truth about the virus's infectiousness—contributed almost $900 million to the WHO budget. That sum was one-fifth of the organization's $4.4 billion budget over those two years. An even more unfortunate American investment, in a cost-to-benefit sense, was an indirect, largely symbolic contribution of at least $600,000 to the Wuhan Level 4 virology lab itself, the often-alleged ground zero of the plague. Ironically, the grant was in part due to the past recommendations of Dr. Anthony Fauci, the NIAID director and later the leader of the Trump administration's White House Coronavirus Task Force. The National Institutes of Health had approved two multiyear grants of some $3.4 million to the EcoHealth Alliance, which had partnered with a number of organizations, including many in China and in particular the Wuhan virology lab. One of the first orders of the Biden administration was to reinstate the United States as a major participant in and contributor to the WHO.[23]

China skillfully, throughout the year, both compromised American academics and sent some of its own operatives to American campuses in search of civilian and military expertise. Before the epidemic, no one would have questioned the loyalties of a number of foreign and native-born scientists and engineers at work at US universities and research centers who were either dual citizens or resident aliens or enjoyed shared appointments at Chinese universities that were often undisclosed to their American employers. To do so would earn one the slur of racist, xenophobe, or McCarthyite.

Yet, throughout the spring of 2020, larger numbers of high-profile researchers were arrested on charges of either engaging in espionage for China, or stealing US-patented technologies, or violating US national security laws, or improperly transferring American classified research to Chinese sources. The list of American universities and organizations that employed scientists stealthily working for the Chinese government, or held undisclosed joint appointments with China, or were secretly funded by China while enjoying US grants was diverse. The group included the nation's top universities and public and private research entities, such as Harvard University, Stanford University, the Cleveland Clinic, and NASA. Apparently the idea of global ecumenicalism or fear of being charged with xenophobia or racism trumped reasonable scrutiny of Chinese foreign nationals involved in important joint Chinese-American research projects.[24]

In sum, 2017 to 2019 had seen progress in restoring the sanctity of American citizenship, an effort rendered ever more controversial by the support and efforts of Donald Trump. During this period, there were some successful efforts to restore middle-class viability, secure the borders, return to the melting pot, rein in the deep state, reinvigorate the sanctity of the Constitution, and retreat from globalism. Yet many of those hard-won efforts were erased in 2020 by the pandemic, the recession, the national quarantine, the rioting, looting, and arson following the death of George Floyd, the radical alteration in the way Americans traditionally vote, the wild end of the 2020 election and its aftermath, the defeat and subsequent implosion of Donald Trump, and the increasing civil tensions between red and blue America.

What, then, did the future hold for the American citizen?

Perhaps the next few years would not be as bleak as 2020 might have suggested. If a figure as personally unpopular as Donald Trump had for three years often successfully reinvigorated citizenship, and if it took the annus horribilis to thwart the citizen's renewal, then the public wondered what might happen if another, perhaps less polarizing figure returned to promote a similar citizenship agenda and could do so without a black swan event such as 2020.

As 2021 began, the supporters of restoring the primacy of the American citizen were not so confident in their own powers of renovation as they were convinced that they had no other choice but to keep trying.

The stakes were no less than the preservation of the American republic itself.

NOTES

Introduction: Pre- and Post-American Citizens

1. According to Max Roser, "Democracy," Our World in Data, June 2019, https://ourworldindata.org/democracy, of the world's population of 7.35 billion in 2015, 4.10 billion lived in democracies. See Larry Diamond and Marc F. Plattner, eds., *Democracy in Decline?* (Baltimore: Johns Hopkins University Press, 2015). The number of democracies is shrinking: Charles Edel, "Democracy Is Fighting for Its Life," *Foreign Policy*, September 10, 2019, https://foreignpolicy.com/2019/09/10/democracy-is-fighting-for-its-life.

2. Kant, *Metaphysics of Morals*, 6:314.

3. True democracies: Richard Bellamy, *Citizenship: A Very Short Introduction* (Oxford: Oxford University Press, 2008), 13–14.

4. See Mogens Herman Hansen, *Polis: An Introduction to the Ancient Greek City-State* (New York: Oxford University Press, 2006), 31, 110–111.

5. On the self-criticisms of democracy in the ancient world, see Victor Davis Hanson and John Heath, *Who Killed Homer? The Demise of Classical Education and the Recovery of Greek Wisdom* (New York: Encounter Books, 2001), 101–115. For a different view, cf. Paul Cartledge, *The Greeks: A Portrait of Self and Others*, 2nd ed. (Oxford: Oxford University Press, 2002), esp. 8–104; for Alkidamas and Epaminondas, see Victor Davis Hanson, *The Soul of Battle* (New York: Free Press, 1999), 17–122; in general, see Victor Davis Hanson, *The End of Sparta: A Novel* (New York: Bloomsbury Press, 2011). Cf. Kostas Vlassopoulos,

"Greek Slavery: From Domination to Property and Back Again," *Journal of Hellenic Studies* 131 (2011): 115–130.

6. For property qualifications and the early Greek polis, as well as the frequent ironies of the percentages of free voting citizens in radical democracy compared to agrarian oligarchy, see Victor Davis Hanson, *The Other Greeks* (New York: Free Press, 1995), 126–178, 206–211.

7. See Aristotle, *Politics* (Jowett translation) 4.11 (1296a–c).

8. See Sandra R. Joshel and Sheila Murnaghan, eds., *Women and Slaves in Greco-Roman Culture: Differential Equations* (London: Routledge, 1998), 1–22. Cf. Susan Treggiari, *Roman Marriage* (Oxford: Oxford University Press, 1993), for a detailed discussion of the unique ways in the ancient Roman world that marriage affected women's social status and legal protections during the late republic and principate. Edmund Burke, *Reflections on the Revolution in France*, 89.

9. Plato's complaints that even the dogs, donkeys, and horses would enjoy too much freedom under democracy and other broadsides: cf. Plato, *Republic*, 8.557–563. On the long tradition of democracy's malcontents, beginning with classical antiquity, see Bruce S. Thornton, *Democracy's Dangers and Discontents: The Tyranny of the Majority from the Greeks to Obama* (Stanford: Hoover Institution Press, 2014), 9–54.

10. Joshua Bote, "92% of Americans Think Their Basic Rights Are Being Threatened, New Poll Shows," *USA Today*, December 16, 2019, www.usatoday .com/story/news/nation/2019/12/16/most-americans-think-their-basic-rights -threatened-new-poll-shows/4385967002.

11. Carroll Doherty, "Key Findings on Americans' Views of the U.S. Political System and Democracy," Pew Research Center, April 26, 2018, www .pewresearch.org/fact-tank/2018/04/26/key-findings-on-americans-views-of -the-u-s-political-system-and-democracy.

12. Ilya Somin, "Public Ignorance About the Constitution," *Washington Post*, September 15, 2017, www.washingtonpost.com/news/volokh-conspiracy/wp/2017 /09/15/public-ignorance-about-the-constitution; general ignorance of US history and customs: Patrick Riccards, "National Survey Finds Just 1 in 3 Americans Would Pass Citizenship Test," Woodrow Wilson National Fellowship Foundation, October 3, 2018, https://woodrow.org/news/national-survey-finds-just-1 -in-3-americans-would-pass-citizenship-test; statue toppling and defacing: Grant: Henry Olsen, "The Anti-statue Movement Has Taken a Turn into Absurdity," *Washington Post*, June 22, 2020, www.washingtonpost.com/opinions/2020/06/22 /anti-statue-movement-has-taken-turn-into-absurdity; Black Civil War veterans: Andrew Mark Miller, "George Floyd Rioters Deface 16 Boston Statues, Including Memorial Honoring Black Civil War Regiment," *Washington Examiner*, June 4, 2020, www.washingtonexaminer.com/news/george-floyd-rioters-deface

-16-boston-statues-including-memorial-honoring-black-civil-war-regiment; abolitionist: Lawrence Andrea, "Hans Christian Heg Was an Abolitionist Who Died Trying to End Slavery. What to Know About the Man Whose Statue Was Toppled in Madison," *Milwaukee Journal Sentinel*, June 24, 2020, www.jsonline.com /story/news/local/wisconsin/2020/06/24/hans-christian-hegs-abolitionist-statue -toppled-madison-what-know/3248692001. Lee statues: Mark Price, "Vandals Tried to Burn a Confederate Statue in NC—but It Was the Wrong General Lee," *Charlotte Observer*, February 20, 2019, www.charlotteobserver.com/news/local /article226506060.html.

13. Socrates's purported quote that he was not just an Athenian citizen ("But better still said Socrates, that he was not an Athenian or Greek, but a citizen of the world [as a man might say he was a Rhodian or Corinthian], for he did not confine himself to Sunium, or Taenarum, or the Ceraunian mountains") is found in Plutarch's *Moralia* (*On Exile*, 5) some five hundred years after the death of Socrates, and may refer mostly to his desire to travel beyond the confines of Attica. For the following centuries, J. J. Pollitt, *Art in the Hellenistic Age* (Cambridge: Cambridge University Press, 1986), identifies a "cosmopolitan outlook" as one of the five defining characteristics of this period of Greek art and philosophy.

Chapter One: Peasants

1. A variety of passages from Aristotle's *Politics* that offer theories about the rise of the city-state over four centuries before the philosopher's own time, as well as the military and agrarian ramifications of citizenship, are collected in Victor Davis Hanson, *The Other Greeks: The Family Farm and the Agrarian Roots of Western Civilization* (New York: Free Press, 1995), 216–235.

2. For the influence of the Greek *politês* of the city-state upon the Roman *civis*, cf. the essays in Lucia Cecchet and Anna Busetto, eds., *Citizens in the Graeco-Roman World: Aspects of Citizenship from the Archaic Period to AD 212* (Boston: Brill, 2017); on Rome, cf. the classic account of A. N. Sherwin-White, *The Roman Citizenship*, 2nd ed. (Oxford: Clarendon Press, 1980). On Phokylides and other similar passages trumpeting "middleness," see Hanson, *The Other Greeks*, 108–110.

3. Doyne Dawson, *Cities of the Gods: Communist Utopias in Greek Thought* (Oxford: Oxford University Press, 1998), 48–50; cf. Hans van Wees, "Conquerors and Serfs: Wars of Conquest and Forced Labour in Archaic Greece," in *Helots and Their Masters in Laconia and Messenia: Histories, Ideologies, Structures*, ed. Nino Luraghi and Susan E. Alcock (Washington, DC: Center for Hellenic Studies, 2003), 33–80.

4. Cicero, *Against Verres*, 2.5.157–162. On *civis Romanus sum* and its resonance in the modern era (from Lord Palmerston to John F. Kennedy), cf.

David Brown, "Lord Palmerston and the 'Civis Romanus Sum' Principle," *History of Government*, March 20, 2015, https://history.blog.gov.uk/2015/03/20/lord-palmerston-and-the-civis-romanus-sum-principle.

5. Juvenal, *Satires*, 10.77–81. On citizenship in the medieval and Renaissance world, see, especially, Keechang Kim, *Aliens in Medieval Law: The Origins of Modern Citizenship* (Cambridge: Cambridge University Press, 2000); on the strong civic traditions of eighteenth-century small European towns and communities, see Maarten Prak, *Citizens Without Nations: Urban Citizenship in Europe and the World, c. 1000–1789* (Cambridge: Cambridge University Press, 2018).

6. Scott A. Hodge, "60 Percent of Households Now Receive More in Transfer Income Than They Pay in Taxes," Tax Foundation, October 12, 2012, https://taxfoundation.org/60-percent-households-now-receive-more-transfer-income-they-pay-taxes. Less than $1,000 in bank savings accounts: Cameron Huddleston, "58% of Americans Have Less than $1,000 in Savings, Survey Finds," *Yahoo Finance*, May 15, 2019, https://finance.yahoo.com/news/58-americans-less-1-000-090000503.html; less than $10,000 at death: Andrea Coombes, "Half of Americans Die with Almost No Money," *MarketWatch*, August 29, 2012, www.marketwatch.com/story/half-of-americans-die-with-almost-no-money-2012-08-29; Peter Dizikes, "Study: Many Americans Die with 'Virtually No Financial Assets,'" *MIT News*, August 3, 2012, http://news.mit.edu/2012/end-of-life-financial-study-0803. Credit card debt: Bill Fay, "Key Figures Behind America's Consumer Debt," Debt.org, www.debt.org/faqs/americans-in-debt; Joe Resendiz, "Average Credit Card Debt in America: 2018," ValuePenguin, August 18, 2020, www.valuepenguin.com/average-credit-card-debt. Those on public assistance: "21.3 Percent of U.S. Population Participates in Government Assistance Programs Each Month," United States Census Bureau, May 28, 2015, www.census.gov/newsroom/press-releases/2015/cb15-97.html.

7. Allan Sloan, "The Fed Saved the Economy but Is Threatening Trillions of Dollars Worth of Middle-Class Retirement," *ProPublica*, October 21, 2020, www.propublica.org/article/the-fed-saved-the-economy-but-is-threatening-trillions-of-dollars-worth-of-middle-class-retirement.

8. See C. Bradley Thompson, *America's Revolutionary Mind: A Moral History of the American Revolution and the Declaration That Defined It* (New York: Encounter Books, 2019), 106; on the contradictions of American equality and slavery, see esp. 145–154.

9. For the Germantown document, see "Germantown Friends' Protest Against Slavery 1688," Library of Congress, www.loc.gov/resource/rbpe.14000200; on the paradoxes of early American citizenship, see David Azerrad, "What the Constitution Really Says About Race and Slavery," Heritage Foundation, December 28, 2015, www.heritage.org/the-constitution/commentary/what-the-constitution-really-says-about-race-and-slavery; on concepts of citizenship with reference to

the three-fifths clause of the Constitution, see Jan Ellen Lewis, "What Happened to the Three-Fifths Clause: The Relationship Between Women and Slaves in Constitutional Thought," *Journal of the Early Republic* 37, no. 1 (spring 2017): 1–46; cf., in general, Leonard L. Richards, *Who Freed the Slaves? The Fight over the Thirteenth Amendment* (Chicago: University of Chicago Press, 2015).

10. For the unique mindset of the peasant, which is antithetical to that of the agrarian, see Robert Redfield, *Peasant Society and Culture: An Anthropological Approach to Civilization* (Chicago: University of Chicago Press, 1956), 27.

11. For the idealization of the small farmer in early America and its precedents in the West, see, in general, James A. Montmarquet, *The Idea of Agrarianism: From Hunter-Gatherer to Agrarian Radical in Western Culture* (Moscow: University of Idaho Press, 1989). See also J. Hector St. John de Crèvecoeur, *Letters from an American Farmer and Other Essays*, ed. Dennis D. Moore (Cambridge, MA: Belknap Press of Harvard University Press, 2013).

12. Annie Nova, "Waiting Longer to Buy a House Could Hurt Millennials in Retirement," *CNBC*, October 25, 2018, www.cnbc.com/2018/10/25/the -homeownership-rate-is-falling-among-millennials-heres-why.html. Cf. "The Housing Non-crisis," *Wall Street Journal*, August 11, 2016, www.wsj.com/articles/the -housing-non-crisis-1470957926.

13. On the changing analytics of home ownership: "Historical Housing Data," United States Census Bureau, www.census.gov/history/www/reference /publications/historic_housing_data.html; PK, "Historical Homeownership Rate in the United States, 1980–Present," DQYDJ, https://dqydj.com/historical -homeownership-rate-in-the-united-states-1890-present; Patrick Sisson, "Why Buying a House Today Is So Much Harder Than in 1950," *Curbed*, April 10, 2018, www.curbed.com/2018/4/10/17219786/buying-a-house-mortgage-govern ment-gi-bill; cf. "Trends in Housing Costs: 1985–2005 and the 30-Percent -of-Income Standard," US Department of Housing and Urban Development, www.huduser.gov/portal/publications/Trends_hsg_costs_85-2005.pdf; see also Oren Cass, *The Once and Future Worker: A Vision for the Renewal of Work in America* (New York: Encounter Books, 2018), 185–190.

14. Nicholas Eberstadt, "2020 Irving Kristol Award Remarks," AEI, October 15, 2020, www.aei.org/research-products/speech/2020-irving-kristol-award -remarks. Mortgage squeeze: Congressional Research Service, "Real Wage Trends, 1979 to 2018," Federation of American Scientists, July 23, 2019, https://fas.org /sgp/crs/misc/R45090.pdf; "Wage Growth Tracker," Federal Reserve Bank of Atlanta, www.frbatlanta.org/chcs/wage-growth-tracker.aspx; "The Rise in Dual Income Households," Pew Research Center, June 18, 2015, www.pewresearch .org/ft_dual-income-households-1960-2012-2.

15. Tuition increases: Emmie Martin, "Here's How Much More Expensive It Is for You to Go to College Than It Was for Your Parents," *CNBC*, November

29, 2017, www.cnbc.com/2017/11/29/how-much-college-tuition-has-increased
-from-1988-to-2018.html; hypocrisies and contradictions of the modern university and its role in impoverishing indebted students: Richard K. Vedder,
Restoring the Promise: Higher Education in America (Oakland, CA: Independent
Institute, 2019), esp. 143–204. Endowments: Rick Seltzer, "Endowment Returns Slow; Survey Offers Peek at Sending," Inside Higher Ed, January 31, 2019,
www.insidehighered.com/news/2019/01/31/college-endowments-returned-82
-percent-2018-annual-survey-adds-some-insight-how. Part-time faculty: Caro-
line Fredrickson, "There Is No Excuse for How Universities Treat Adjuncts," *The
Atlantic*, September 15, 2015, www.theatlantic.com/business/archive/2015/09
/higher-education-college-adjunct-professor-salary/404461.

16. The social and cultural importance of marriage: Howard A. Husock, *Who
Killed Civil Society? The Rise of Big Government and Decline of Bourgeois Norms*
(New York: Encounter Books, 2019), 4–9.

17. Birth ages: Karen B. Guzzo and Krista K. Payne, "Average Age at First
Birth, 1970 & 2017," National Center for Family and Marriage Research at Bowl-
ing Green State University, 2018, www.bgsu.edu/content/dam/BGSU/college-of
-arts-and-sciences/NCFMR/documents/FP/guzzo-payne-age-birth-fp-18-25.pdf;
cf. Douglas Schoen and Jessica Tarlov, *America in the Age of Trump: Opportunities and Oppositions in an Unsettled World* (New York: Encounter Books, 2017),
71–72.

18. See Bruce S. Thornton, *Decline and Fall: Europe's Slow Motion Suicide*
(New York: Encounter Books, 2007), 76; Douglas Murray, *The Strange Death of
Europe: Immigration, Identity, Islam* (London: Bloomsbury Publishing, 2017), 23–
36; Erin Duffin, "Average Number of Own Children Under 18 in Families with
Children in the United States from 1960 to 2019," Statista, January 13, 2020,
www.statista.com/statistics/718084/average-number-of-own-children-per-family;
"Total Fertility Rate 2020," *World Population Review*, http://worldpopulation
review.com/countries/total-fertility-rate.

19. Radical changes in families, fertility, and parenting: cf. Andrew J. Cherlin,
Labor's Love Lost: The Rise and Fall of the Working-Class Family in America (New
York: Russell Sage Foundation, 2014), 192–195.

20. Sarah Harvard, "Alexandria Ocasio-Cortez Says It Is 'Legitimate' for
People to Not Want Children Because of Climate Change," *The Independent*,
February 26, 2019, www.independent.co.uk/news/world/americas/us-politics
/alexandria-ocasio-cortez-children-climate-change-aoc-instagram-young-people
-a8797806.html; "U.S. Energy-Related Carbon Dioxide Emissions 2019," EIA,
September 30, 2020, www.eia.gov/environment/emissions/carbon.

21. For the largely failed "moral" efforts of Augustus to restore Roman rural "virtue" and the Italian agrarian moral code by rewarding marriage and child
raising and by punishing sumptuary habits, see Michele George, ed., *The Roman*

Family in the Empire: Rome, Italy, and Beyond (Oxford: Oxford University Press, 2005), esp. 32–61; cf. the classic account of Augustus's moral reforms: Ronald Syme, *The Roman Revolution* (Oxford: Oxford University Press, 1939), 448–456.

22. Herodotus, 1.30.2–5.

23. For "Pajama Boy," see Rich Lowry, "Pajama Boy, an Insufferable Man-Child," *Politico*, December 18, 2013, www.politico.com/magazine/story/2013/12 /opinion-rich-lowry-obamacare-affordable-care-act-pajama-boy-an-insufferable -man-child-101304.

24. James Taranto, "The Lovely Life of Julia," *Wall Street Journal*, May 3, 2012, www.wsj.com/articles/SB1000142405270230474370457738217078917 9442; cf. Eugene Kiely, "'The Life of Julia,' Corrected," FactCheck.org, May 8, 2012, www.factcheck.org/2012/05/the-life-of-julia-corrected.

25. Alexis de Tocqueville, "What Sort of Despotism Democratic Nations Have to Fear," *Democracy in America*, Vol. II, Bk. 4, Chap. VI (translated by Henry Reeve).

26. Joel Kotkin, *The Coming of Neo-feudalism: A Warning to the Global Middle Class* (New York: Encounter Books, 2020), 49–50. Cherlin, *Labor's Love Lost*, esp. 121–147.

27. Coleridge and the clerisy: Deborah Elise White, "Introduction: Irony and Clerisy," Romantic Circles, https://romantic-circles.org/praxis/irony/white /ironyintro.html.

28. An entire industry, on both the Left and the Right, is devoted to the various ways globalization has hollowed out the American middle class: June Zaccone, "Has Globalization Destroyed the American Middle Class?," National Jobs for All Coalition, https://njfac.org/wp-content/uploads/2015/07/GloblMClass.pdf; Eric Shalyutin, "Globalization and the Demise of the American Middle Class," *Statesman*, September 10, 2012, www.sbstatesman.com/2012/09/10/globalization -and-the-demise-of-the-american-middle-class; Paul Craig Roberts, "Neoliberal Economics Has Destroyed the U.S. Economy and America's Middle Class," *GlobalResearch*, December 17, 2019, www.globalresearch.ca/neoliberal-economics -destroyed-economy-middle-class/5697972. On the bifurcation of the old middle class, see Joel Kotkin, "The Two Middle Classes," *Quillette*, February 27, 2020, https://quillette.com/2020/02/27/the-two-middle-classes.

29. Willow Run: Tim Trainor, "How Ford's Willow Run Assembly Plant Helped Win World War II," *Assembly Magazine*, January 3, 2019, www.assemblymag.com articles/94614-how-fords-willow-run-assembly-plant-helped-win-world-war-ii.

30. Barack Obama and "magic wand" and Krugman on jobs: Chuck De-Vore, "Trump's Policy 'Magic Wand' Boosts Manufacturing Jobs 399% in First 26 Months over Obama's Last 26," *Forbes*, March 11, 2019, www.forbes.com/sites /chuckdevore/2019/03/11/trumps-policy-magic-wand-boosts-manufacturing-jobs-399-in-first-26-months-over-obamas-last-26; Chuck DeVore, "The Trump

Manufacturing Jobs Boom: 10 Times Obama's over 21 Months," *Forbes*, October 16, 2018, www.forbes.com/sites/chuckdevore/2018/10/16/the-trump-manufacturing -jobs-boom-10-times-obamas-over-21-months/#7d2ca9205850. Larry Summers and "tooth fairies": Menzie Chinn, "Tooth Fairies and Ludicrous Supply-Side Economics," Econbrowser, May 23, 2017, https://econbrowser.com/archives/2017 /05/tooth-fairies-and-ludicrous-supply-side-economics. Paul Krugman and crashing stock market: Stephen Moore and Jonathan Decker, "And the Hits Just Keep Coming: The Greatest (False) Predictions of 2017," *Investor's Business Daily*, December 29, 2017, www.investors.com/politics/columnists/and-the-hits-just-kept -coming-the-greatest-false-predictions-of-2017. On the percentages of Americans invested in the stock market: Louis Jacobson, "What Percentage of Americans Own Stocks?," PolitiFact, September 18, 2018, www.politifact.com/factchecks /2018/sep/18/ro-khanna/what-percentage-americans-own-stocks. For the Summers quote, see Michael Sandel, *The Tyranny of Merit: What's Become of the Common Good?* (New York: Farrar, Straus and Giroux, 2020), 79.

31. Kevin D. Williamson, "Chaos in the Family, Chaos in the State: The White Working Class's Dysfunction," *National Review*, March 17, 2016, www .nationalreview.com/2016/03/donald-trump-white-working-class-dysfunction -real-opportunity-needed-not-trump.

32. See the statistics from U-Haul at "U-Haul Names Top Growth States of 2019, Florida Is New No. 1," U-Haul, January 6, 2020, www.uhaul.com /Articles/About/19965/U-Haul-Names-Top-Growth-States-Of-2019-Florida -Is-New-No-1.

33. Fred Siegel, *The Revolt of the Masses* (New York: Encounter Books, 2015), 126–127.

34. Michael R. Blood, "'Great Example for the Rest of This Country': Bloomberg Sees California as Model for U.S.," *Washington Times*, January 6, 2020, www .washingtontimes.com/news/2020/jan/6/michael-bloomberg-sees-california-model-us.

35. Gas: Nathan Bomey, "As You Head Out for Memorial Day, Watch Out for the 10 States Where Gas Prices Are Highest," *USA Today*, May 23, 2019, www.usatoday.com/story/money/2019/05/23/memorial-day-summer-gas-prices -travel/3768926002; electricity rates: "2020 Electricity Rates by State," Payless power.com, April 2020, https://paylesspower.com/blog/electric-rates-by-state; population living below poverty line: Evan Comen, "In States Such as California and Maryland, Poverty May Be Worse Than You Think," *USA Today*, November 12, 2019, www.usatoday.com/story/money/2019/11/12/15-states-where-poverty -is-worse-than-you-might-think/40569843.

36. Heat, fire, power outages: Tom Tapp, "California Governor Gavin Newsom Declares Statewide Emergency," *Deadline*, August 18, 2020, https://deadline .com/2020/08/governor-gavin-newsom-declares-statewide-emergency-fires-rolling

-power-outages-1203016958; high-speed rail: Susan Shelley, "Cancel the Bullet Train," *Orange County Register*, February 15, 2020, www.ocregister .com/2020/02/15/cancel-the-bullet-train; Hans Johnson and Sergio Sanchez, "Immigrants in California," Public Policy Institute of California, May 2019, www.ppic .org/publication/immigrants-in-california. The 99: Emma Goss, "Hwy 99 Ranked 'Deadliest' Road in America," *Bakersfield Now Eyewitness News*, May 7, 2018, https://bakersfieldnow.com/news/local/ca-99-ranked-deadliest-road-in-america.

37. Prep schools: Phil Beadle, "$40,500 for 8th Grade? Tuitions at Silicon Valley's Largest Private Schools," *Silicon Valley Business Journal*, December 2, 2014, www.bizjournals.com/sanjose/news/2014/12/02/40-500-for-8th-grade-tuitions -at-silicon-valleys.html; Morgan G. Ames, "The Smartest People in the Room? What Silicon Valley's Supposed Obsession with Tech-Free Private Schools Really Tells Us," *Los Angeles Review of Books*, October 18, 2019, https://lareviewofbooks .org/article/the-smartest-people-in-the-room-what-silicon-valleys-supposed -obsession-with-tech-free-private-schools-really-tells-us.

38. For the data, see Kotkin, *The Coming of Neo-feudalism*, 38–39, 43–44; see also Joel Kotkin and Marshall Toplansky, "California Feudalism: The Squeeze on the Middle Class," *New Geography*, October 19, 2018, www.newgeography.com /files/Feudalism_Web.pdf, 12–13.

39. California taxes and leaving California: Phillip Reese, "Roughly 5 Million People Left California in the Last Decade. See Where They Went," *Sacramento Bee*, August 28, 2015, www.sacbee.com/news/databases/article32679753 .html; California and business: Evan Harris, "California's Business Climate Continues to Receive Poor Scores," Pacific Research Institute, July 16, 2019, www .pacificresearch.org/californias-business-climate-continues-to-receive-poor -scores; California as forty-eighth of fifty states according to the Tax Foundation: Jared Walczak, "2020 State Business Tax Climate Index," Tax Foundation, October 22, 2019, https://taxfoundation.org/publications/state-business-tax-climate -index. Leaving California for Texas: Mark Calvey, "Latest Census Data Shows Californians Continue to Flock to Texas," *ABC8 WFAA*, November 9, 2019, www .wfaa.com/article/money/economy/latest-census-data-shows-californians -continue-to-flock-to-texas/287-8991ef8d-6184-4637-957f-313f25d1b724; Gordon Dickson and Luke Ranker, "If It Seems like More Californians Are Moving into Your Texas Neighborhood, Here's Why," *Fort Worth Star-Telegram*, January 23, 2020, www.star-telegram.com/news/business/growth/article239570433 .html; Dan Kopf, "The California Exodus Is Speeding Up," *Quartz*, April 18, 2019, https://qz.com/1599150/californias-population-could-start-shrinking-very-soon; "California Companies Flee Business-Hostile State in Droves," *Investor's Business Daily*, December 17, 2018, www.investors.com/politics/editorials/california -companies-leave-taxes; Middle- and lower-class flight: Kate Cimini, "'Not the

Golden State Anymore': Middle- and Low-Income People Leaving California," *CalMatters*, January 8, 2020, https://calmatters.org/california-divide/2020/01/not-the-golden-state-anymore-middle-and-low-income-people-leaving-california.

40. The idea of good riddance: Ian Schwartz, "Calexit Leader to Tucker Carlson: Export Middle Class to Make Room for Next 'Wave' of Immigrants," *RealClear Politics*, August 1, 2017, www.realclearpolitics.com/video/2017/08/01/calexit_proponent_to_tucker_carlson_were_exporting_middle_class_to_make_room_for_next_wave of_immigrants.html.

41. Outmigrants: Jeff Daniels, "More Californians Are Considering Fleeing the State as They Blame Sky-High Costs, Survey Finds," *CNBC*, February 13, 2019, www.cnbc.com/2019/02/12/growing-number-of-californians-considering-moving-from-state-survey.html; Brian Uhler, "California Losing Residents via Domestic Migration," Legislative Analyst's Office, February 21, 2018, https://lao.ca.gov/LAOEconTax/Article/Detail/265; Eric Escalante, "Nearly 700,000 People Left California Last Year," *ABC10*, November 5, 2019, www.abc10.com/article/news/local/california/691000-leave-california/103-e02662aa-dfae-46b2-b94a-f20158053e60.

42. Tax hikes: Joshua Rauh and Ryan J. Shyu, "Behavioral Responses to State Income Taxation of High Earners: Evidence from California," National Bureau of Economic Research, October 2019, www.nber.org/papers/w26349; cf. Orphe Divounguy, "California's 'Fair Tax' Hike Spurred Taxpayer Exodus, Hurt Middle Class and Went Mostly to Pensions," Illinois Policy, October 28, 2019, www.illinoispolicy.org/californias-fair-tax-hike-spurred-taxpayer-exodus-hurt-middle-class-and-went-mostly-to-pensions. On 16.8 percent: Robert W. Wood, "California 13.3% Tax Rate May Be Raised to 16.8% . . . Retroactively," *Forbes*, August 3, 2020, www.forbes.com/sites/robertwood/2020/08/03/california-133-tax-rate-may-be-raised-to-168retroactively/#22e6cd1bc026. See also Judy Lin, "The Open Secret About California's Taxes," *CalMatters*, September 17, 2020, https://calmatters.org/explainers/the-open-secret-about-california-taxes; California gas tax increases and commensurate shortage in road funding: Patrick McGreevy, "California Gas Tax Goes up July 1, but Leaders Say Road Repairs Need Even More Money," *Los Angeles Times*, June 20, 2019, www.latimes.com/politics/la-pol-ca-california-gas-tax-increase-road-repairs-20190620-story.html; Kevin Yamamura, "California's Fiscal Analyst Sees Smaller Deficit Than Newsom, but Still Up to $31B," *Politico*, May 8, 2020, www.politico.com/states/california/story/2020/05/08/californias-fiscal-analyst-sees-smaller-deficit-than-newsom-but-still-up-to-31b-9422928; "Gov. Newsom Says California Budget Deficit Is a Direct Result of COVID-19," *Fox40*, May 17, 2020, https://fox40.com/news/california-connection/gov-newsom-says-california-budget-deficit-is-a-direct-result-of-covid-19.

43. California's public schools in many ranks are listed among the worst in the nation: Dennis Romero, "California Is Home to Some of America's Worst

Public Schools," *LA Weekly*, August 2, 2016, www.laweekly.com/california
-is-home-to-some-of-americas-worst-public-schools; cf. John Fensterwald, "California at Bottom in Nationwide Ranking of Accountability Systems; State
Board President Disagrees," EdSource, November 14, 2017, https://edsource
.org/2017/california-at-bottom-in-nationwide-ranking-of-accountability
-systems-state-board-president-disagrees/590271. Property crimes in San Francisco highest in the nation among large municipalities: Megan Cassidy and Sarah
Ravani, "The Scanner: San Francisco Ranks No. 1 in US in Property Crime," *San
Francisco Chronicle*, October 1, 2018, www.sfchronicle.com/crime/article/The
-Scanner-San-Francisco-ranks-No-1-in-13267113.php. Rollback of high speed rail:
Romy Varghese, "California's Newsom Scales Back Plans for High-Speed Rail Line,"
Bloomberg, February 12, 2019, www.bloomberg.com/news/articles/2019-02-12
/california-governor-says-he-s-dropping-high-speed-rail-plan; last California res-
ervoir: Paul Rogers, "California Drought: Why Doesn't California Build Big Dams
Any More?," *Mercury News*, August 31, 2014, www.mercurynews.com/2014/08/31
/california-drought-why-doesnt-california-build-big-dams-any-more.

44. Ranking of inequality in California: "Income Inequality by State, 2021,"
World Economic Review, https://worldpopulationreview.com/state-rankings
/income-inequality-by-state. The Homeless: Jacob Passy, "Nearly Half of the
U.S.'s Homeless People Live in One State: California," *MarketWatch*, September 29, 2019, www.marketwatch.com/story/this-state-is-home-to-nearly-half
-of-all-people-living-on-the-streets-in-the-us-2019-09-18; California's percentage of the nation's poor: Kerry Jackson, "California, Poverty Capital," *City Journal*, winter 2018, www.city-journal.org/html/california-poverty-capital-15659
.html. One-third of Californians on Medi-Cal: Hattie Xu, "A Third of All Californians Depend on Medi-Cal. Here's Who They Are and Where They Live,"
Sacramento Bee, July 14, 2017, https://account.sacbee.com/paywall/stop?resume
=160786554; health issues: Teresa Wiltz, "Aging, Undocumented and Unin-
sured Immigrants Challenge Cities and States," Pew Charitable Trusts, January 3,
2018, www.pewtrusts.org/en/research-and-analysis/blogs/stateline/2018/01/03
/aging-undocumented-and-uninsured-immigrants-challenge-cities-and-states;
on the challenges of diabetes and dialysis: "Diabetes and Chronic Kidney Disease in Hispanic Americans," National Kidney Foundation, January 2016,
www.kidney.org/news/newsroom/factsheets/Diabetes-and-CKD-in-Hispanic
-Americans; 27 percent of Californians not born in the United States: Chris
Nichols, "TRUE: 27 Percent of Californians 'Were Born in a Foreign Land,'"
PolitiFact, January 24, 2017, www.politifact.com/factchecks/2017/jan/24/jerry
-brown/true-27-percent-californians-were-born-foreign-lan. Immigrants voting: Luis Noe-Bustamante and Abby Budiman, "Most of the 23 Million Immigrants Eligible to Vote in 2020 Election Live in Just Five States," Pew
Research Center, March 3, 2020, www.pewresearch.org/fact-tank/2020/03/03

/most-of-the-23-million-immigrants-eligible-to-vote-in-2020-election-live-in
-just-five-states.

45. I wrote about these cast changes in California agriculture in Victor Davis Hanson, *Fields Without Dreams: Defending the Agrarian Ideal* (New York: Free Press, 1996), and Victor Davis Hanson, *The Land Was Everything: Letters from an American Farmer* (New York: Free Press, 2000). Cf. Frank Bergon, "Here's Why the Central Valley Has the Most Productive Agricultural Land and Diverse Communities," *Visalia Times Delta*, August 15, 2019, www.visalia timesdelta.com/story/life/2019/08/15/california-agriculture-central-valley -productive-land-diverse-people/1989722001.

46. Over half of California births were paid for by Medi-Cal, and one in three in the state relied on the federal/state program: Len Finocchio et al., "2019 Edition—Medi-Cal Facts and Figures," California Health Care Foundation, February 25, 2019, www.chcf.org/publication/2019-medi-cal-facts-figures-crucial- -coverage; one-third of all births in California to undocumented mothers: Steven A. Camarota, Karen Zeigler, and Jason Richwine, "Births to Legal and Illegal Immigrants in the U.S.," Center for Immigration Studies, October 9, 2018, https:// cis.org/Report/Births-Legal-and-Illegal-Immigrants-US. Busiest border crossing in the world: Preeti Varathan, "The Busiest Land Border Crossing in the World Is Closed This Weekend," *Quartz*, September 22, 2017, https://qz.com/1085125 /san-ysidro-the-busiest-land-border-crossing-in-the-world-connecting-mexico-to -the-us-is-closed-from-sept-23-25.

Chapter Two: Residents

1. Emerson, journal entry, 1845, first published 1912 in *Journals of Ralph Waldo Emerson with Annotations*, Vol. IX, 119; cf. the now standard critique of such nineteenth-century melting-pot confidence as proof of white racism in Heike Paul, *The Myths That Made America: An Introduction to American Studies* (Bielefield, Germany: Transcript Verlag, 2014), 264. See also Alexander Hamilton in *Federalist Papers* Nos. 6 and 7.

2. Colin Woodard, *American Nations: A History of the Eleven Regional Cultures of North America* (New York: Penguin Books, 2012), 115–172; Mae M. Ngai and Jon Gjerde, eds., *Major Problems in American Immigration and Ethnic History: Documents and Essays* (Boston: Wadsworth/Cengage Learning, 2013).

3. Steven Hahn, *A Nation Without Borders: The United States and Its World in an Age of Civil Wars* (New York: Viking Press, 2016), 170–174, 347–349.

4. Ethnic incomes: Erin Duffin, "Median Household Income in the United States in 2018, by Race or Ethnic Group," Statista, November 12, 2019, www .statista.com/statistics/233324/median-household-income-in-the-united-states -by-race-or-ethnic-group; "Income and Wealth in the United States: An Overview

of Recent Data," Peter G. Peterson Foundation, October 4, 2019, www.pgpf.org /blog/2019/10/income-and-wealth-in-the-united-states-an-overview-of-data.

5. Kerby Miller, *Emigrants and Exiles: Ireland and the Irish Exodus to North America* (New York: Oxford University Press, 1985), 280–344 (esp. 291–293 and Appendix, Table 1, 569); cf. David M. Emmons, "Irish Catholics and Irish-Catholic Americans, to 1870," in *Immigrants in American History: Arrival, Adaptation, and Integration*, ed. Elliott Robert Barkan (Santa Barbara, CA: ABC-CLIO, 2013), 1:88, which increases the estimate to 1.7 million immigrants to the United States.

6. See Reihan Salam, *Melting Pot or Civil War? A Son of Immigrants Makes the Case Against Open Borders* (New York: Sentinel, 2018), 86–89.

7. "Letter from Theodore Roosevelt to Richard M. Hurd," January 3, 1919, Theodore Roosevelt Papers, Library of Congress Manuscript Division, Theodore Roosevelt Digital Library, Dickinson State University, www.theodoreroosevelt center.org/Research/Digital-Library/Record?libID=o265602.

8. Theodore H. White, *America in Search of Itself: The Making of the President, 1956–1980* (New York: Harper & Row, 1982), 363. On changing demography and the Great Society, Milton Friedman long ago warned, "You can have free immigration and a welfare state." Cf. Robert Rector, "Look to Milton: Open Borders and the Welfare State," Heritage Foundation, June 21, 2007, www.heritage.org /immigration/commentary/look-milton-open-borders-and-the-welfare-state.

9. Immigrant percentages: Office of Immigration Statistics, *Annual Flow Report: Lawful Permanent Residents*, US Department of Homeland Security, August 2018, www.dhs.gov/sites/default/files/publications/Lawful_Permanent_Residents _2017.pdf, esp. 5–7.

10. For the most recent data regarding lawful immigration, see "Yearbook of Immigration Statistics 2017," US Department of Homeland Security, www.dhs .gov/immigration-statistics/yearbook/2017.

11. On immigration legislation, see Jerry Kammer, "The Hart-Celler Immigration Act of 1965," Center for Immigration Studies, September 30, 2015, https:// cis.org/Report/HartCeller-Immigration-Act-1965; Dan Moffett, "The Immigration Reform and Control Act of 1986," ThoughtCo., August 26, 2020, https:// thoughtco.com/immigration-reform-and-control-act-1986-1951972; P. Schey, "Supply-Side Immigration Theory: Analysis of the Simpson/Mazzoli Bill," *In Defense of the Alien* 6 (1983): 53–77. On the explosion of illegal immigration in the years following the bill, see Brad Plumer, "Congress Tried to Fix Immigration Back in 1986. Why Did It Fail?," *Washington Post*, January 30, 2013, www.washington post.com/news/wonk/wp/2013/01/30/in-1986-congress-tried-to-solve-immi gration-why-didnt-it-work. On 19.6 million illegal aliens: E. Kaplan and S. Rodilitz, "Snapshots of Migrants in Mexico Suggest U.S. Undocumented Population Is Much Larger Than Previous Estimates," *Yale Insights*, January 13, 2021, https://

insights.som.yale.edu/insights/snapshots-of-migrants-in-mexico-suggest-us
-undocumented-population-is-much-larger-than.

12. Jerry Kammer, *Losing Control: How a Left-Right Coalition Blocked Immigration Reform and Provoked the Backlash That Elected Trump* (Washington, DC: Center for Immigration Studies, 2020), 10.

13. For the now popular idea that borders are constructs that artificially disrupt Latino peoples, see, in general, Josue David Cisneros, *The Border Crossed Us: Rhetorics of Borders, Citizenship, and Latina/o Identity* (Tuscaloosa: University of Alabama Press, 2013).

14. Presidents and immigration: William J. Clinton, "Address Before a Joint Session of the Congress on the State of the Union," American Presidency Project at UCSB, January 24, 1995, www.presidency.ucsb.edu/documents/address-before -joint-session-the-congress-the-state-the-union-11; Barack Obama, "Address Before a Joint Session of Congress on the State of the Union," American Presidency Project at UCSB, February 12, 2013, www.presidency.ucsb.edu/documents /address-before-joint-session-congress-the-state-the-union-2. On the unpopularity of illegal immigration in Mexico, cf. Kevin Sieff and Scott Clement, "Unauthorized Immigrants Face Public Backlash in Mexico, Survey Finds," *Washington Post*, July 17, 2019, www.washingtonpost.com/world/the_americas/unauthorized -immigrants-face-public-backlash-in-mexico-survey-finds/2019/07/16/f7fc5d12 -a75e-11e9-a3a6-ab670962db05_story.html. On American public opinion: Robert Draper, "The Democrats Have an Immigration Problem," *New York Times*, October 10, 2018, www.nytimes.com/2018/10/10/magazine/the-democrats-have-an -immigration-problem.html; "comprehensive immigration confusion": Peter Skerry, "Comprehensive Immigration Confusion," *National Affairs*, 2016, www.national affairs.com/publications/detail/comprehensive-immigration-confusion.

15. On the changing and politicized language of illegal immigration, see, e.g., Alex Nowrasteh, "'Illegal Alien' Is One of Many Correct Legal Terms for 'Illegal Immigrant,'" Cato Institute, October 14, 2019, www.cato.org/blog/illegal -alien-one-many-correct-legal-terms-illegal-immigrant; Jon Feere, "Language in the Immigration Debate," Center for Immigration Studies, October 26, 2012, https://cis.org/Language-Immigration-Debate.

16. For the Democrats' new acceptance of illegal immigration, see a synopsis of recent polls: Craig Kafura and Bettina Hammer, "Republicans and Democrats in Different Worlds on Immigration," Chicago Council on Global Affairs, October 8, 2019, www.thechicagocouncil.org/publication/lcc/republicans-and-democrats -different-worlds-immigration.

17. Costs of illegal immigration: Steven A. Camarota, "Welfare Use by Immigrant and Native Households: An Analysis of Medicaid, Cash, Food, and Housing Programs," Center for Immigration Studies, September 10, 2015, https://cis .org/Report/Welfare-Use-Immigrant-and-Native-Households; cf. Eddie Scarry,

"Center for American Progress Mistakenly Proves Why There Should Be Limits on Welfare for Immigrants," *Washington Examiner*, November 28, 2018, www.washingtonexaminer.com/opinion/columnists/center-for-american-progress-mistakenly-proves-why-there-should-be-limits-on-welfare-for-immigrants. See Samuel Huntington, *Who Are We? The Challenges to America's National Identity* (New York: Simon & Schuster, 2005), 218–219.

18. Primary candidates: Andrew Mark Miller, "Buttigieg Tells Illegal Immigrants That America Is 'Your Country Too' in Spanish," *Washington Examiner*, February 12, 2020, www.washingtonexaminer.com/news/buttigieg-tells-illegal-immigrants-that-america-is-your-country-too-in-spanish; cf. Jan Hoffman, "What Would Giving Health Care to Undocumented Immigrants Mean?," *New York Times*, July 3, 2019, www.nytimes.com/2019/07/03/health/undocumented-immigrants-health-care.html.

19. On the conflation of residency and citizenship in the twentieth-century West, see Huntington, *Who Are We?*, 214–220.

20. The relevant literature of eroding traditional Western citizenship in the age of globalization is reviewed in Christian Joppke, "The Inevitable Lightening of Citizenship," *European Journal of Sociology* 51 (2010): 9–32. For boasts in the Mexican media about easy vaccinations in the United States and concerns about an open border in times of a pandemic, see L. Bernstein and M. Sheridan, "Some Foreign Nationals Are Getting Coronavirus Vaccines in the United States," *Washington Post*, February 13, 2021, www.washingtonpost.com/health/covid-vaccine-foreign-nationals/2021/02/12/7d5edbb4-6d2f-11eb-ba56-d7e2c8defa31_story.html.

21. Cultural appropriation: D. Tortolini, "The Appropriation of Mythologies for Assimilation Through Media," *Perspectives on Global Development and Technology* 18 (January 18, 2019): 151–156. For a now common attack on the concept of the melting pot, see Alfredo Montalvo-Barbot, *Melting Pot, Multiculturalism, and Interculturalism: The Making of Majority-Minority Relations in the United States* (Lanham, MD: Lexington Books, 2019). See J. Hector St. John de Crèvecoeur, *Letters from an American Farmer and Other Essays*, ed. Dennis D. Moore (Cambridge, MA: Belknap Press of Harvard University Press, 2013).

22. See E. Aranda and E. Vaquera, "The Immigration Enforcement Regime, and the Implications for Racial Inequality in the Lives of Undocumented Young Adults," *Sociology of Race and Ethnicity* 1 (2015): 88–104.

23. A discussion of why Latin America did not "catch up" economically with Canada and the United States is found in Francis Fukuyama, ed., *Falling Behind: Explaining the Development Gap Between Latin America and the United States* (Oxford: Oxford University Press, 2008), 72–98. For Mexico's use of its expatriate community to interfere in the domestic politics of the United States, see Mark Krikorian, *The New Case Against Immigration: Both Legal and Illegal* (New York: Sentinel, 2008), 71–85.

24. On Mexico's exportation of its poor rather than its interest in providing structural reforms to keep its own within its borders, see Salam, *Melting Pot or Civil War?*, 134–136. Immigrant polls: "American Views of Mexico and Mexican Views of the U.S.," NumbersUSA, June 6, 2002, https://web.archive.org /web/20030813235933/www.numbersusa.com/text?ID=1149; Margaret Vice and Hanyu Chwe, "Dramatic Shifts in How Mexicans See the U.S.," Pew Research Center, September 14, 2017, www.pewresearch.org/global/2017/09/14 /dramatic-shifts-in-how-mexicans-see-the-u-s; one-third of Mexicans wish to immigrate to the United States: Rafael Romo, "Third of Mexicans Would Migrate to U.S., Survey Finds," *CNN*, August 27, 2014, www.cnn.com/2014/08/27/world /americas/mexico-immigration-survey. Cf. Krikorian, *The New Case Against Immigration*, 56–58.

25. See Lyndon Baines Johnson, "President Lyndon B. Johnson's Remarks at the Signing of the Immigration Bill, Liberty Island, New York," LBJ Presidential Library, October 3, 1965, www.lbjlibrary.org/lyndon-baines-johnson/timeline/lbj -on-immigration.

26. Former President Trump stated that the cost of illegal immigration (i.e., the cost of services received minus their tax contributions) is over $200 billion annually and perhaps as high as $275 billion. This amount exceeds most estimates across the political spectrum. Federation for American Immigration Reform (FAIR) report for 2017 of $116 billion annually: Matt O'Brien and Spencer Raley, "The Fiscal Burden of Illegal Immigration on United States Taxpayers," Federation for American Immigration Reform, September 27, 2017, www.fairus.org/issue /publications-resources/fiscal-burden-illegal-immigration-united-states-taxpayers. Heritage Foundation report for 2013 of $54 billion annually: Jason Richwine and Robert Rector, "The Fiscal Cost of Unlawful Immigrants and Amnesty to the U.S. Taxpayer," Heritage Foundation, May 6, 2013, www.heritage.org/immigration /report/the-fiscal-cost-unlawful-immigrants-and-amnesty-the-us-taxpayer. The National Academies of Sciences, Engineering, and Medicine estimates that illegal immigration actually benefits the economy: Francine D. Blau and Christopher Mackie, *The Economic and Fiscal Consequences of Immigration* (Washington, DC: National Academies of Sciences, Engineering, and Medicine, 2017).

27. Yale MIT study: Mohammad M. Fazel-Zarandi, Jonathan S. Feinstein, and Edward H. Kaplan, "The Number of Undocumented Immigrants in the United States: Estimates Based on Demographic Modeling with Data from 1990 to 2016," *PLoS ONE* 13, no. 9 (September 21, 2018), https://journals.plos.org /plosone/article?id=10.1371/journal.pone.0201193; border patrol apprehensions: Mike Guo and Ryan Baugh, "Immigration Enforcement Actions: 2018," US Department of Homeland Security, 2018, www.dhs.gov/sites/default/files/publications /immigration-statistics/yearbook/2018/enforcement_actions_2018.pdf.

28. On the relationship between illegal immigration and anemic entry-level wages for American workers, see Krikorian, *The New Case Against Immigration*, 148–153.

29. Voting: "Poll: Americans Overwhelmingly Reject Voting Rights for Undocumented Immigrants," *The Hill*, July 26, 2018, https://thehill.com/hilltv/what -americas-thinking/399016-poll-americans-overwhelmingly-reject-giving-voting -rights-to. Cf. various 2014 polls collated at "Public Opinion Polls on Immigration," Federation for American Immigration Reform, www.fairus.org/issue/public -opinion-polls-immigration; on health care for illegal immigrants, cf. John Gage, "Most Americans Reject Government Healthcare for Illegal Immigrants: Poll," *Washington Examiner*, July 1, 2019, www.washingtonexaminer.com/news/most -americans-reject-government-healthcare-for-illegal-immigrants-poll.

30. Polls about illegal immigration: Jeffrey M. Jones, "New High in U.S. Say Immigration Most Important Problem," *Gallup*, June 21, 2019, https://news .gallup.com/poll/259103/new-high-say-immigration-important-problem.aspx. Voting laxity: Lloyd Billingsley, "DMV Enables Massive Voter Fraud in the Golden State," *California Globe*, January 9, 2019, californiaglobe.com/legislature /dmv-enables-massive-voter-fraud-in-the-golden-state; Sophia Bollag, "California DMV Admits That Non-citizens Are Registered to Vote," *Washington Times*, October 8, 2018, www.washingtontimes.com/news/2018/oct/8/non-citizens-illegally -registered-vote-california-; same-day voting: "Same Day Voter Registration Allows Californians Who Missed Traditional Deadline Another Opportunity to Register and Vote," California Secretary of State Alex Padilla, www.sos.ca.gov /administration/news-releases-and-advisories/2020-news-releases-and-advisories /ap20018-same-day-voter-registration-allows-californians-who-missed-traditional -deadline-another-opportunity-register-and-vote.

31. Knowledge of US history and customs: Patrick Riccards, "National Survey Finds Just 1 in 3 Americans Would Pass Citizenship Test," Woodrow Wilson National Fellowship Foundation, October 3, 2018, woodrow.org/news /national-survey-finds-just-1-in-3-americans-would-pass-citizenship-test.

32. For a map of some 560 sanctuary cities, counties, and states, see Bryan Griffith and Jessica M. Vaughan, "Map: Sanctuary Cities, Counties, and States," Center for Immigration Studies, March 23, 2020, http://cis.org/Map-Sanctuary -Cities-Counties-and-States; "State Sanctuary Policies," Federation for American Immigration Reform, May 2018, www.fairus.org/issue/sanctuary-policies/state -sanctuary-policies.

33. For a list of Virginia's "sanctuary" jurisdictions that presume they are upholding federal law rather than nullifying it, see Jeff Williamson, "List of Second Amendment Sanctuaries in Virginia and Where It's Being Discussed," *WSLS 10 News*, January 23, 2020, www.wsls.com/news/local/2019/11/27 /list-of-second-amendment-sanctuaries-in-virginia-and-where-its-being-discussed.

34. On the extent of false documentations used by illegal immigrants, see R. Mortensen, "Illegal, but Not Undocumented: Identity Theft, Document Fraud, and Illegal Employment," Center for Immigration Studies, June 19, 2009, https://cis.org/Report/Illegal-Not-Undocumented.

35. Immigrant profiles: Jynnah Radford, "Key Findings About U.S. Immigrants," Pew Research Center, June 17, 2019, www.pewresearch.org/fact-tank/2019 /06/17/key-findings-about-u-s-immigrants. For more on the stark differences in the profiles of legal versus illegal immigrants, see also Steven A. Camarota and Karen Zeigler, "Better Educated, but Not Better Off," Center for Immigration Studies, April 17, 2018, http://cis.org/Report/Better-Educated-Not-Better.

36. Taxpayer costs: Matt O'Brien and Spencer Raley, "The Fiscal Burden of Illegal Immigration on United States Taxpayers," Federation for American Immigration Reform, September 27, 2017, www.fairus.org/issue/publications-resources /fiscal-burden-illegal-immigration-united-states-taxpayers.

37. Latino voters for Bernie: Lauren Gambino, "'He's Working for It': Why Latinos Are Rallying Behind Sanders," *The Guardian*, March 3, 2020, www.theguardian .com/us-news/2020/mar/02/bernie-sanders-latino-voters.; cf. esp. Wilhelm Urbina Meierling, "Latinos Know Bernie Sanders's Type," *Wall Street Journal*, March 5, 2020, www.wsj.com/articles/latinos-know-bernie-sanderss-type-11583447697.

38. Census: Steven A. Camarota and Karen Zeigler, "The Impact of Legal and Illegal Immigration on the Apportionment of Seats in the U.S. House of Representatives in 2020," Center for Immigration Studies, December 9, 2019, https://cis.org/Report/Impact-Legal-and-Illegal-Immigration-Apportionment -Seats-US-House-Representatives-2020; "Exit Polls 2016," *CNN*, November 23, 2016, https://edition.cnn.com/election/2016/results/exit-polls. Given that, in 2016, 64 percent of non-native-born voters favored the Democratic presidential candidate, immigration has become a potent way to alter political realities both in direct presidential elections and in congressional reapportionment.

39. Federal arrests: Cf. Paul Bedard, "Justice: 64% of Federal Arrests Are Noncitizens, with a 200% Increase," *Washington Examiner*, August 22, 2019, www .washingtonexaminer.com/washington-secrets/justice-64-of-federal-arrests-are -non-citizens-200-increase; cf. Preston Huennekens, "DOJ: 26% of Federal Prisoners Are Aliens," Center for Immigration Studies, June 12, 2018, https://cis.org /Huennekens/DOJ-26-Federal-Prisoners-Are-Aliens.

40. Crimes and illegal immigration: "US Immigration and Customs Enforcement Fiscal Year 2019 Enforcement and Removal Operations Report," US Immigration and Customs Enforcement, www.ice.gov/sites/default/files/documents /Document/2019/eroReportFY2019.pdf, 16.

41. On the use of illegal alien labor and its effect on wages, see George J. Borjas, "Yes, Immigration Hurts American Workers," *Politico Magazine*, September/October 2016, www.politico.com/magazine/story/2016/09/Trump-clinton

-immigration-economy-unemployment-jobs-214216; Steven Malanga, "How Unskilled Immigrants Hurt Our Economy," *City Journal*, 2006, www.city-journal.org /html/how-unskilled-immigrants-hurt-our-economy-12946.html. On percentages of illegal aliens involved in agriculture and the makeup of farming's total workforce, cf. "A Portrait of Unauthorized Immigrants in the United States," Pew Research Center: Hispanic Trends, April 14, 2009, www.pewresearch.org/hispanic/2009/04 /14/iv-social-and-economic-characteristics.

42. For the size and nature of remittances sent south of the border, see Niall McCarthy, "Immigrants in the U.S. Sent Over $148 Billion to Their Home Countries in 2017 [Infographic]," *Forbes*, April 8, 2019, www.forbes.com/sites /niallmccarthy/2019/04/08/immigrants-in-the-u-s-sent-over-148-billion-to -their-home-countries-in-2017-infographic/#2cc3238311f6; Manuel Orozco, Laura Porras, and Julia Yansura, "Remittances to Latin America and the Caribbean in 2018," *The Dialogue*, April 2019, www.thedialogue.org/wp-content/uploads /2019/04/2018-NumbersRemittances.pdf; cf. for 2016: Abby Buddiman and Phillip Connor, "Migrants from Latin America and the Caribbean Sent a Record Amount of Money to Their Home Countries in 2016," Pew Research Center, January 23, 2018, www.pewresearch.org/fact-tank/2018/01/23/migrants-from -latin-america-and-the-caribbean-sent-a-record-amount-of-money-to-their -home-countries-in-2016; Andrew R. Arthur, "Remittances Key to Central American Economies," Center for Immigration Studies, June 4, 2019, http://cis.org /Arthur/Remittances-Key-Central-American-Economies. Comic book manual to cross illegally into the United States from Mexico: Laurence Iliff, "Mexico Offers Tips for Crossing Border in Comic Book," *Seattle Times*, January 7, 2005, www .seattletimes.com/nation-world/mexico-offers-tips-for-crossing-border-in-comic -book. Mexican troops: Thomson Reuters, "Mexico Sends 15,000 Troops to Border in Unusual Move to Ward Off U.S. Trade Tariffs," *CBC*, June 19, 2019, www .cbc.ca/news/world/mexico-border-naitonal-guard-tariffs-us-1.5188487.

43. Malinowski quote: Joseph A. Wulfsohn, "Dem Rep. Tom Malinowski: We Need Illegal Immigrants to 'Mow Our Beautiful Lawns,'" *Fox News*, August 22, 2019, www.foxnews.com/politics/dem-rep-tom-malinowski-illegal-immigrants -to-mow-lawns.

44. Julián Castro: "People First Immigration," Julián Castro 2020, https:// issues.juliancastro.com/people-first-immigration.

45. La Raza: Jerry Kammer, "What's in a Name? The Meaning of 'La Raza,'" Center for Immigration Studies, January 7, 2015, http://cis.org/Kammer/Whats -Name-Meaning-La-Raza; cf. "El Plan Espiritual de Aztlan," University of Michigan, umich.edu/~mechaum/Aztlan.html.

46. Franco: Thomas Graham, "Raza: The Strange Story of Franco's 'Lost' Film," *BBC*, September 24, 2018, www.bbc.com/culture/article/20180921-raza-the -strange-film-that-franco-left-behind; Andras Lenart, "Ideology and Film in the

Spain of General Francisco Franco," Academia.edu, www.academia.edu/16565417 /Ideology_and_Film_in_the_Spain_of_General_Francisco_Franco; Mussolini on Razza: Martin Agronsky, "Racism in Italy," *Foreign Affairs*, January 1939, www .foreignaffairs.com/articles/italy/1939-01-01/racism-italy; Fabrizio De Donno, "La Razza Ario-Mediterranea," Taylor and Francis Online, February 17, 2007, www .tandfonline.com/doi/abs/10.1080/13698010600955958. On the use of Raza by Mexican American activists, see "El plan espiritual de Aztlan," MEChA Official National Website, www.chicanxdeaztlan.org; cf. Kammer, "What's in a Name"?

47. Those opposing illegal immigration in the 2000s: Perez: Ellie Bufkin, "'We're in a Different Era': Tom Perez Explains Democratic Flip-Flop on Healthcare for Illegal Immigrants," *Washington Examiner*, June 30, 2019, www.washington examiner.com/news/were-in-a-different-era-tom-perez-explains-democratic -flip-flop-on-healthcare-for-illegal-immigrants; Reid: Lukas Pleva, "Reid Bashes Republicans for a Position on Immigration That He Once Pushed," PolitiFact, August 25, 2010, www.politifact.com/factchecks/2010/aug/25/harry-reid/reid -bashes-republicans-position-immigration-he-on; Pelosi and Schumer: Daniel Horowitz, "Once upon a Time, When Schumer and Pelosi Supported Everything Trump Wants on Illegal Immigration," *Conservative Review*, January 3, 2019, www.conservativereview.com/news/once-upon-a-time-when-schumer-and-pelosi -supported-everything-trump-wants-on-illegal-immigration. See "1996 Demo-cratic Party Platform," American Presidency Project, www.presidency.ucsb.edu /documents/1996-democratic-party-platform.

Chapter Three: Tribes

1. See Plato, *Republic*, 1.329a.

2. Thucydides, *History of the Peloponnesian War*, 2.1.1, 3.10.

3. See, in general, John Boardman et al., *The Cambridge Ancient History*, vol. 4: *Persia, Greece, and the Western Mediterranean* (London: Cambridge University Press, 1970), esp. 303–332.

4. On the significance of tribes and Thracian pedigrees, see Plutarch, *Themist-ocles*, 1–2; for ancient references, see Anthony J. Podlecki, *The Life of Themistocles: A Critical Survey of the Literary and Archaeological Evidence* (Montreal: McGill–Queen's University Press, 1975).

5. Cf. Tacitus, *Germania*, 46; *Agricola*, 31, 33.

6. On diversity elsewhere: David Scott FitzGerald and David Cook-Martín, *Culling the Masses: The Democratic Origins of Racist Immigration Policy in the Americas* (Cambridge, MA: Harvard University Press, 2014), 220; "Mexico's Constitution of 1917 with Amendments Through 2007," Constitute Project, May 12, 2020, www.constituteproject.org/constitution/Mexico_2007.pdf; Laura V. González-Murphy and Rey Koslowski, "Understanding Mexico's Changing

Immigration Laws," Woodrow Wilson International Center for Scholars (Mexico Institute), March 2011, www.wilsoncenter.org/sites/default/files/media/documents /publication/GONZALEZ%20%2526%20KOSLOWSKI.pdf; Ronald Reagan, "Remarks at the Presentation Ceremony for the Presidential Medal of Freedom," Ronald Reagan Presidential Library and Museum, January 19, 1989, www.reagan library.gov/research/speeches/011989b. Peter W. Schramm quote: "Born American, but in the Wrong Place," *Claremont Review of Books* 6, no. 4 (fall 2006), https://claremontreviewofbooks.com/born-american-but-in-the-wrong-place.

7. On these various linguistic terms for the "other," cf. "Odar: The Omission of Identity," *Ianyan Mag*, www.ianyanmag.com/odar-the-omission-of-identity; Tomer Persico, "How the Jews Invented the Goy," *Haaretz*, November 9, 2019, www .haaretz.com/israel-news/.premium.MAGAZINE-how-the-jews-invented-the -goy-1.8093644; "Gaijin: Good or Bad?," *Japan Times*, October 26, 2004, www.japan times.co.jp/community/2004/10/26/issues/gaijin-good-or-bad; "Where Does the Word 'Gringo' Come From?," *Yucatan Times*, www.theyucatantimes.com/2018/04 /where-does-the-word-gringo-come-from.

8. Allen Lynch, "Woodrow Wilson and the Principle of 'National Self-Determination': A Reconsideration," *Review of International Studies* 28, no. 2 (2002): 419–436.

9. On Mexico's history of restrictive and ethnically based immigration laws, see Pablo Yankelevich, "Mexico for the Mexicans: Immigration, National Sovereignty and the Promotion of Mestizaje," *The Americas* 68, no. 3 (2012): 405–436.

10. See the official narrative of the Schengen agreement protocols: "Schengen Agreement," Schengen Visa Info, October 1, 2019, www.schengenvisainfo.com /schengen-agreement.

11. Stanley L. Engerman and Kenneth L. Sokoloff, *Economic Development in the Americas Since 1500: Endowments and Institutions* (Cambridge: Cambridge University Press, 2012), 222–224; Luis Martínez-Fernández, *Protestantism and Political Conflict in the Nineteenth-Century Hispanic Caribbean* (New Brunswick, NJ: Rutgers University Press, 2002), 24–26.

12. Sanders: Sarah Zimmerman, "Bernie's Journey Home," *The College*, April 12, 2016, https://college.uchicago.edu/news/student-stories/bernies-journey -home; cf. Emily Jacobs, "University of Chicago Only Accepting English Students Willing to Work in Black Studies," *New York Post*, September 15, 2020, https:// nypost.com/2020/09/15/uchicago-only-admitting-english-students-to-work-in -black-studies. Cf. Lydia Lum, "A Space of Their Own," *Diverse*, December 11, 2008, https://diverseeducation.com/article/12054.

13. On the CSU Fresno classics experiment, see Eric Adler, *Classics, the Culture Wars, and Beyond* (Ann Arbor: University of Michigan Press, 2016), 177.

14. Updating Marxism for race and gender considerations: Jean Ait Belkhir, "Marxism Without Apologies: Integrating Race, Gender, Class; a Working Class

Approach," *Race, Gender & Class* 8, no. 2 (2001): 142–171, www.jstor.org/stable /41674975.

15. Samuel Huntington, *Who Are We? The Challenges to America's National Identity* (New York: Simon & Schuster, 2005), 5.

16. David F. Epstein, *The Political Theory of* The Federalist (Chicago: University of Chicago Press, 1984), 59–110.

17. K. Boniello, "Colin Kaepernick Rips 4th of July as 'Celebration of White Supremacy,'" *New York Post*, July 4, 2020, https://nypost.com/2020/07/04/colin -kaepernick-rips-4th-of-july-as-celebration-of-white-supremacy. George Orwell, *1984* (New York: Signet, 1961), 34.

18. Great American novel idea: John William De Forest, "The Great American Novel," Uncle Tom's Cabin and American Culture, http://utc.iath.virginia.edu /articles/n2ar39at.html; cf. criticism of the idea: Cheryl Strayed, "Why Are We Obsessed with the Great American Novel?," *New York Times*, January 13, 2015, www.nytimes.com/2015/01/18/books/review/why-are-we-obsessed-with-the -great-american-novel.html.

19. Peter C. Rollins, *Hollywood's Indian: The Portrayal of the Native American in Film* (Lexington: University Press of Kentucky, 2003), 153–156.

20. Robert Nisbet, *Twilight of Authority* (New York: Oxford University Press, 1975), 69.

21. Irish were often considered "subhuman": Michael Harriot, "When the Irish Weren't White," *The Root*, March 17, 2018, www.theroot.com/when -the-irish-weren-t-white-1793358754.

22. Natalie Allison, "'This Country Was Founded on White Supremacy': Beto O'Rourke Speaks with Tennessee Immigrants," *Tennessean*, July 8, 2019, www.tennessean.com/story/news/politics/2019/07/08/beto-orourke-nashville -tennessee-visit-gathers-immigrants-white-supremacy-raids-detention-centers /1675044001.

23. "It's a black thing": "Mistaken for a Black Thing, Few Strive to Understand It," *Seattle Times*, July 4, 2007, www.seattletimes.com/opinion/mistaken-for-a-black -thing-few-strive-to-understand-it; Klan: Sarah Churchwell, "America's Original Identity Politics," *New York Review of Books*, February 7, 2019, www.nybooks.com /daily/2019/02/07/americas-original-identity-politics; Fukuyama: Francis Fukuyama, "Francis Fukuyama—Against Identity Politics," University of Pennsylvania, www.sas .upenn.edu/andrea-mitchell-center/francis-fukuyama-against-identity-politics.

24. On later embarrassments of Chicano racialist movements: Tim Rutten, "An Identity Issue for Bustamente," *Los Angeles Times*, September 6, 2003, www .latimes.com/archives/la-xpm-2003-sep-06-et-rutten6-story.html; Matea Gold, "Chicano Student Group Defended," *Los Angeles Times*, August 30, 2003, www .latimes.com/archives/la-xpm-2003-aug-30-me-mecha30-story.html. MEChA is the acronym for the Movimiento Estudiantil Chicano de Aztlan and translates

into English as "fuse." The organization's emblem is an eagle with dynamite and a machete-like weapon in its talons. Its agenda is often described as the "liberation of Aztlan"—Aztlan connoting the mythical homeland of the Aztecs that supposedly encompassed imperial land north of the current border with Mexico.

25. Objections to identifying criminal suspect by racial descriptions: B. Walker, "The Color of Crime: The Case Against Race-Based Suspect Descriptions," *Columbia Law Review* 103, no. 3 (2003): 662–688, www.jstor.org/stable/1123720?seq=1. "White Hispanic": Erik Wemple, "Why Did the New York Times Call George Zimmerman a 'White Hispanic'?," *Washington Post*, March 12, 2012, www .washingtonpost.com/blogs/erik-wemple/post/why-did-new-york-times -call-george-zimmerman-white-hispanic/2012/03/28/gIQAW6fngS_blog.html. California demography and changing majority/minority statuses: Hans Johnson, Eric McGhee, and Marisol Cuellar Mejia, "California's Population," Public Policy Institute of California, April 2020, www.ppic.org/publication/californias -population; minorities, majorities, race, and voting: Matthew Yglesias, "What Really Happened in 2016, in 7 Charts," *Vox*, September 18, 2017, www.vox.com/policy -and-politics/2017/9/18/16305486/what-really-happened-in-2016; Timothy Noah, "What We Didn't Overcome, Part 2," *Slate*, November 12, 2008, slate.com /news-and-politics/2008/11/what-we-didn-t-overcome-part-2.html; Alec Tyson and Shiva Maniam, "Behind Trump's Victory: Divisions by Race, Gender, Education," Pew Research Center, November 9, 2016, www.pewresearch.org/fact-tank /2016/11/09/behind-trumps-victory-divisions-by-race-gender-education; Euripides, *Phrixus*, fr. 970, in Euripides *Fragments* (Volume VIII), Loeb Classical Library 506 (Cambridge, MA: Harvard University Press, 2009).

26. Richard Alba, *The Great Demographic Illusion: Majority, Minority and Expanding American Mainstream* (Princeton, NJ: Princeton University Press, 2020), 4–5.

27. Problems of problematic and even contrived identity: Melissa Korn and Jennifer Levitz, "Students Were Advised to Claim to Be Minorities in College-Admissions Scandal," *Wall Street Journal*, May 19, 2019, www.wsj.com /articles/students-were-advised-to-claim-to-be-minorities-in-college-admissions -scandal-11558171800; Vijay Chokal-Ingam, "Why I Faked Being Black for Med School," *New York Post*, April 12, 2015, nypost.com/2015/04/12/mindy-kalings -brother-explains-why-he-pretended-to-be-black; Chris Bodenner, "Check Your Privilege, Kids, but Don't Check a Race Box," *The Atlantic*, December 17, 2015, www.theatlantic.com/notes/2015/12/check-your-privilege-kids-but-dont-check -a-race-box/421107.

28. DNA tests: C. Farr, "Consumer DNA Testing Has Hit a Lull—Here's How It Could Capture the Next Wave of Users," *CNBC*, August 25, 2019, www .cnbc.com/2019/08/25/dna-tests-from-companies-like-23andme-ancestry -see-sales-slowdown.html. Race and admissions: Douglas Belkin, "The Most

Agonizing Question on a College Application: What's Your Race?," *Wall Street Journal*, December 23, 2019, www.wsj.com/articles/the-most-agonizing-question -on-a-college-application-11577100370.

29. In fact, applicants are using DNA tests to find elements of nonwhite ancestry and thereby, in a nonsystematic fashion, to obtain some sort of advantage in hiring or admission—given that no federal guidelines establish the precise racial percentage that allows one to claim minority status: Sarah Zhang, "A Man Says His DNA Test Proves He's Black, and He's Suing," *The Atlantic*, September 19, 2018, www.theatlantic.com/science/archive/2018/09/dna-test-race-law suit/570250; Ashifa Kassam, "Users of Home DNA Tests 'Cherry Pick' Results Based on Race Biases, Study Says," *The Guardian*, July 1, 2018, www.theguardian .com/science/2018/jul/01/home-dna-test-kits-race-ethnicity-dna-ancestry.

30. George Hawley and Richard Hanania, "The Working-Class Party Myth, and What Really Motivates Voters," *National Review*, December 13, 2020, www.nationalreview.com/2020/12/the-working-class-party-myth-and-what -really-motivates-voters.

31. Kyle Smith, "Oscars' Woke Quota Will Backfire on Hollywood Spectacularly," *New York Post*, September 9, 2020, https://nypost.com/2020/09/09 /oscars-woke-quota-will-backfire-on-hollywood-spectacularly.

32. Kehinde Wiley Studio (kehindewiley.com); "Obama Portrait Artist's Past Work Depicted Black Women Decapitating White Women," *The Telegraph*, February 13, 2018, www.telegraph.co.uk/art/artists/obama-portrait-painterkehinde -wileys-past-work-depicted-black.

33. Testimony from McWilliams's lawsuit: Maxine Shen, "FDNY Diversity Official Defends Decision to Exclude Hero White Veteran Firefighter Who Was in Iconic 9/11 Photo from Ceremonial Color Guard So All Flag-Bearers Could Be Black," *Daily Mail*, July 25, 2020, www.dailymail.co.uk/news/article -8560689/FDNY-diversity-official-says-definitely-OK-exclude-white-firefighter -color-guard.html.

34. La Raza lawyers and Trump: La Raza Lawyers of California (larazalawyers .net); Garrett Epps, "The Problem with Calling Out Judges for Their Race," *The Atlantic*, June 5, 2016, www.theatlantic.com/politics/archive/2016/06/the -problem-with-calling-out-judges-for-their-race/485732.

35. Judge Sonia Sotomayor, "A Latina Judge's Voice," *UC Berkeley News*, May 26, 2009, www.berkeley.edu/news/media/releases/2009/05/26_sotomayor .shtml.

36. See Amy Chua, *Political Tribes: Group Instinct and the Fate of Nations* (London: Penguin Press, 2018), 171–172.

37. Asians and admissions: "Why Chinese and Asian Students Do So Much Better in School, or Do They?," Shout Out UK, June 3, 2018, www.shoutoutuk .org/2018/03/05/chinese-asian-students-much-better-school; Jane Kim, "How

Do Asian Students Get to the Top of the Class?," Great Schools, June 9, 2009, www.greatschools.org/gk/articles/parenting-students-to-the-top.

38. Indian American incomes: "Indian Americans Household Income Average USD120K Annually, Surpassing Other Ethnic Groups and White Americans," *Hindustan Times*, January 29, 2021, www.hindustantimes.com/india-news /indian-americans-household-income-average-usd120k-annually-surpassing-other -ethnic-groups-and-white-americans-report-101611909594788.html. See Peter W. Wood, *Diversity Rules* (New York: Encounter Books, 2020), 31–32.

39. "California Proposition 209, Affirmative Action Initiative (1996)," Ballotpedia, ballotpedia.org/California_Proposition_209,_Affirmative_Action_Initiative _(1996); cf. recent challenges: Alexei Koseff, "California's Affirmative Action Ban, Proposition 209, Targeted for Repeal," *San Francisco Chronicle*, March 10, 2020, www.sfchronicle.com/politics/article/California-s-affirmative-action-ban-1512 1025.php. Cf. the defeat of Proposition 16: David Lauter, "Failure to Bridge Divides of Age, Race Doomed Affirmative Action Proposition," *Los Angeles Times*, November 24, 2020, www.latimes.com/politics/story/2020-11-24/age-race-divides -doomed-affirmative-action-proposition.

40. Also most schools and universities now create administrators specifically to deal with diversity, and the number of job postings for "diversity coordinators" and the like is on the rise: Daniel Culbertson, "Diversity and Inclusion Jobs Grow Briskly," Indeed Hiring Lab, March 26, 2018, www.hiringlab.org/2018/03/26 /diversity-and-inclusion-grows-briskly; for racially segregated dorms and graduations, cf. Dion J. Pierre, "Demands for Segregated Housing at Williams College Are Not News," *National Review*, May 8, 2019, www.nationalreview.com /2019/05/american-colleges-segregated-housing-graduation-ceremonies. Claremont: E. Dordick, "Students at Claremont Colleges Refuse to Live with White People," *Claremont Independent*, August 9, 2016, https://claremontindependent.com /students-at-claremont-colleges-refuse-to-live-with-white-people.

41. Winfrey and other celebrities' dropping of diversity in preference for inclusion: Cady Lang, "Here's Why Oprah Winfrey Eliminated the Term 'Diversity' from Her Vocabulary, Thanks to Ava DuVernay," *Time*, August 17, 2016, https:// time.com/4455910/oprah-winfrey-ava-duvernay-diversity.

42. "Unearned" privilege and college presidents: Maggie Lit, "Univ. President: If You're 'Light Skinned,' You Have 'Unearned Privilege,'" *Campus Reform*, December 10, 2014, www.campusreform.org/?ID=6127; systemic racism: Lauren Camera, "Education Department Investigates Princeton After University Admits to Systemic Racism," *U.S. News & World Report*, September 18, 2020, www .usnews.com/news/education-news/articles/2020-09-18/education-department -investigates-princeton-after-university-admits-to-systemic-racism.

43. David S. Landes, *The Wealth and Poverty of Nations: Why Some Are So Rich and Some So Poor* (New York: W. W. Norton, 1999), 513–515.

44. Controversies over race, slavery, and the Middle East: B. Lewis, *Race and Slavery in the Middle East: An Historical Inquiry* (Oxford: Oxford University Press, 1995), 3–20; R. Segal, *Islam's Black Slaves: The Other Black Diaspora* (New York: Farrar, Straus and Giroux, 2001), 13–22; Yusuf Fadl Hasan, "Some Aspects of the Arab Slave Trade from the Sudan, 7th–19th Century," *Sudan Notes and Records* 58 (1977): 85–106, www.jstor.org/stable/44947358. Legacy of slavery in contemporary Middle East: S. Abulhawa, "Confronting Anti-Black Racism in the Arab World," *Al Jazeera*, July 17, 2013, www.aljazeera.com/opinions/2013/7/7/confronting-anti-black-racism-in-the-arab-world.

45. Edison: Casey Cep, "The Real Nature of Thomas Edison's Genius," *New Yorker*, October 21, 2019, www.newyorker.com/magazine/2019/10/28/the-real-nature-of-thomas-edisons-genius.

46. See Benedict Beckeld, "'Oikophobia': Our Western Self-Hatred," *Quillette*, October 7, 2019, quillette.com/2019/10/07/oikophobia-our-western-self-hatred; in general, see the same author's forthcoming *Oikophobia: Hatred of Home in the Decline of Civilizations*.

47. Wood, *Diversity Rules*, 61–62.

48. On hoax crimes: Wilfred Reilly, "Hate Crime Hoaxes, like Jussie Smollett's Alleged Attack, Are More Common Than You Think," *USA Today*, February 22, 2019, www.usatoday.com/story/opinion/2019/02/22/jussie-smollett-empire-attack-fired-cut-video-chicago-fox-column/2950146002; Tamar Lapin, "The List of Bogus 'Hate Crimes' in Trump Era Is Long," *New York Post*, February 21, 2019, https://nypost.com/2019/02/21/the-list-of-bogus-hate-crimes-in-trump-era-is-long. Both formal academic studies and popular websites have chronicled the growing phenomena of fake hate crimes: cf. popular accounts at Jason L. Riley, "Hate Crime Hoaxes Are More Common Than You Think," *Wall Street Journal*, June 25, 2019, www.wsj.com/articles/hate-crime-hoaxes-are-more-common-than-you-think-11561503352; cf., in general, Wilfred Riley, *Hate Crime Hoax: How the Left Is Selling a Fake Race War* (Washington, DC: Regnery Publishing, 2019).

49. Eric Bradner, Sarah Mucha, and Arlette Saenz, "Biden: 'If You Have a Problem Figuring Out Whether You're for Me or Trump, Then You Ain't Black,'" *CNN*, May 22, 2020, www.cnn.com/2020/05/22/politics/biden-charlamagne-tha-god-you-aint-black.

50. Foreign propaganda and support for identity politics: Lee Smith, "America's China Class Launches a New War Against Trump," *Tablet*, September 15, 2020, www.tabletmag.com/sections/news/articles/americas-china-class-fights-trump; Jake Novak, "China's Latest Tactic: Call America Racist," *CNBC*, November 29, 2019, www.cnbc.com/2019/11/29/chinas-latest-tactic-call-america-racist.html; cf. "Chinese and Russian State-Owned Media on the Coronavirus: United Against the West?," Alliance for Securing Democracy, February 27, 2020, https://

securingdemocracy.gmfus.org/chinese-and-russian-state-owned-media-on-the
-coronavirus-united-against-the-west.

51. Chinese espionage, particularly among Bay Area Democrats: Bethany Allen-Ebrahimian and Zach Dorfman, "Exclusive: Suspected Chinese Spy Targeted California Politicians," *Axios*, December 8, 2020, www.axios.com/china -spy-california-politicians-9d2dfb99-f839-4e00-8bd8-59dec0daf589.html; Tom O'Connor and Naveed Jamali, "Eric Swalwell Report Fits Bill of China Spy Pattern Identified by FBI," *Newsweek*, November, 11, 2020, www.newsweek.com/eric -swalwell-report-fits-bill-china-spy-pattern-fbi-1554281.

52. Inconveniences of multiculturalism: "Fact Sheets: Costs of Multilingualism," U.S. English, 2016, www.usenglish.org/official-english/fact-sheets-costs-of-multi lingualism; Paul Bedard, "Claim: Feds Spend Hidden 'Billions' Yearly for Non-English Translations," *Washington Examiner*, July 22, 2015, www.washington examiner.com/claim-feds-spend-hidden-billions-yearly-for-non-english-translations.

53. Opposition to race-based hiring and promotions: Juliana Menasce Horowitz, "Americans See Advantages and Challenges in Country's Growing Racial and Ethnic Diversity," Pew Research Center, May 8, 2019, www.pewsocialtrends .org/2019/05/08/americans-see-advantages-and-challenges-in-countrys-growing -racial-and-ethnic-diversity.

54. Pilots: Dan Peltier, "Government Report Highlights U.S. Airlines' Lack of Race and Gender Diversity," *Skift*, August 25, 2015, https://skift.com/2015/08/25 /government-report-highlights-u-s-airlines-lack-of-racial-and-gender-diversity.

55. Race and the NFL: Andrew Lawrence, "The NFL Is 70% Black, So Why Is Its TV Coverage So White?," *The Guardian*, January 31, 2019, www.theguardian .com/sport/2019/jan/31/nfl-tv-coverage-racial-demographics-super-bowl; "Only 4 NFL Coaches Are Minorities, While 70% of the Players Are," *MarketWatch*, January 8, 2020, www.marketwatch.com/story/nfl-hiring-of-black-coaches-remains -at-historic-low-2020-01-08; owners: Ahiza Garcia, "These Are the Only Two Owners of Color in the NFL," *CNN*, May 18, 2018, https://money.cnn.com /2018/05/18/news/nfl-nba-mlb-owners-diversity.

56. Race and the medical profession: "Diversity in Medicine: Facts and Figures 2019," AAMC, 2019, www.aamc.org/data-reports/workforce/interactive-data /figure-18-percentage-all-active-physicians-race/ethnicity-2018.

57. The Kaepernick controversies: "Bears DE: Kaepernick Used N-word," *ESPN*, September 23, 2014, www.espn.com/nfl/story/_/id/11574968/lamarr-houston -confirms-colin-kaepernick-used-n-word-chicago-bears-win-san-francisco-49ers; Liz Clarke and Mark Maske, "Tired of Politics, NFL Wants to Get Back to What It Does Best: Selling Football," *Washington Post*, April 6, 2018, www .washingtonpost.com/sports/tired-of-politics-nfl-wants-to-get-back-to-what -it-does-best-selling-football/2018/04/06/6d770e7e-3448-11e8-8abc-22a 366b72f2d_story.html; Michael McCarthy, "NFL TV Audience Numbers

Continue to Decline Early in 2017 Season," *SportingNews*, October 15, 2017, www.sportingnews.com/us/nfl/news/nfl-tv-television-ratings-down-numbers -national-anthem-protests/L2x7dhlkuubk1tbeftag9ttis; Maury Brown, "How the NFL Gained Back Viewers, but Lost Attendance," *Forbes*, January 7, 2019, www .forbes.com/sites/maurybrown/2019/01/07/how-the-nfl-gained-back-viewers -but-lost-attendance/#61e88ff55bb7; Valerie Richardson, "Survey: Main Reason for NFL's Ratings Slide Was Player Take-a-Knee Protests," *Washington Times*, February 6, 2018, www.washingtontimes.com/news/2018/feb/6/nfl-ratings-down -dueanthem-protests-survey.

Chapter Four: Unelected

1. For siblings, marriages, conflicts of interest, lobbyists, and long professional relationships between government officials and the proverbial mainstream media, see, in general, Mark Leibovich, *This Town: Two Parties and a Funeral—Plus Plenty of Valet Parking!—in America's Gilded Capital* (New York: Blue Rider Press, 2013).

2. On the limitations of "starve the beast" agendas, cf. Howard Gleckman, "Starving the Beast? The Tax Cuts and Jobs Act Seems to Be Feeding It," *Forbes*, February 6, 2018, www.forbes.com/sites/beltway/2018/02/06/starving-the-beast -the-tax-cuts-and-jobs-act-seems-to-be-feeding-it/#1bae7d0f3d64.

3. See the data of Charles J. Cooper: Charles J. Cooper, "Confronting the Administrative State," *National Affairs*, fall 2015, www.nationalaffairs.com /publications/detail/confronting-the-administrative-state.

4. Mogens Herman Hansen, *The Athenian Democracy in the Age of Demosthenes* (Oxford: Blackwell, 1991), 92–93, 232.

5. Robert Nisbet, *Twilight of Authority* (New York: Oxford University Press, 1975), 55.

6. On the Founders' worries about mass hysterias and mob rule, see Jeffrey Rosen, "America Is Living James Madison's Nightmare," *The Atlantic*, October 2018, www.theatlantic.com/magazine/archive/2018/10/james-madison -mob-rule/568351; Ryan Chung, "The Illusion of Mob Rule," *Harvard Political Review*, December 4, 2018, https://harvardpolitics.com/united-states/the-illusion -of-mob-rule.

7. Alexis de Tocqueville, *Democracy in America*, Vol. 2, Bk. 4, Chap. 4.

8. Aristotle, *Politics*, 5, 1 (1301a). See his long discussion that begins with "Democracy, for example, arises out of the notion that those who are equal in any respect are equal in all respects."

9. IRS apologies: Jake Miller, "IRS Official Apologizes to Tea Party Groups for 'Incorrect' Scrutiny During 2012 Election," *CBS News*, May 10, 2013, www .cbsnews.com/news/irs-official-apologizes-to-tea-party-groups-for-incorrect -scrutiny-during-2012-election; studies suggesting that the IRS's targeted focus

warped the 2012 election: Stan Veuger, "Do Political Protests Matter? Evidence from the Tea Party Movement," American Enterprise Institute, December 18, 2012, www.aei.org/research-products/working-paper/do-political-protests-matter -evidence-from-the-tea-party-movement.

10. For the raisin "crash," see Victor Davis Hanson, *Fields Without Dreams: Defending the Agrarian Ideal* (New York: Free Press, 1996), 61–86. In the 1980s, small farmers of, say, one hundred acres of Thompson seedless grapes produced two hundred tons of raisins, or about four hundred thousand pounds. So the idea of selling any sizable portion of such a crop at local markets was absurd but indicative of the desperation of the panic.

11. On the Raisin Administrative Committee, see Raisin Administrative Committee (www.raisins.org).

12. Raisin reserve tonnage: Hans A. von Spakovsky, "Stop the Farm Bill: FDR's Socialist Structure Still Violating Farmers," Heritage Foundation, June 15, 2013, www.heritage.org/agriculture/commentary/stop-the-farm-bill-fdrs-socialist -structure-still-violating-farmers; Jane Wells, "Farmers Raisin' Hell over the 'Raisin Reserve,'" *CNBC*, September 4, 2013, www.cnbc.com/id/101007496.

13. Clyde Wayne Crews Jr., "How Many Rules and Regulations Do Federal Agencies Issue?," *Forbes*, August 15, 2017, www.forbes.com/sites/wayne crews/2017/08/15/how-many-rules-and-regulations-do-federal-agencies -issue/#4954f36c1e64; cf. Clyde Wayne Crews Jr., "Ten Thousand Commandments 2019," Competitive Enterprise Institute, May 7, 2019, https://cei .org/10kc2019.

14. For the official version of the regulation and its consequences and modifications in 2020, see "Documents Associated with the 2015 Clean Water Rule," United States Environmental Protection Agency, www.epa.gov/cwa-404 /documents-associated-2015-clean-water-rule; cf. farmer anger: Ledyard King, "Trump's EPA Washes Away Obama-Era Clean Water Rule That Farmers, Manufacturers Hated," *USA Today*, September 12, 2019, www.usatoday.com/story /news/politics/2019/09/12/epa-repeals-obama-era-waters-u-s-rule-criticized -overreach/2301997001. In general, see James Copland, *The Unelected: How an Unaccountable Elite Is Governing America* (New York: Encounter Books, 2020), 52–54.

15. Oren Cass, *The Once and Future Worker: A Vision for the Renewal of Work in America* (New York: Encounter Books, 2018), 90–91.

16. Occasionally even left-wing critics acknowledged "deep state" interests in undermining the Trump presidency: Glenn Greenwald, "The Deep State Goes to War with President-Elect, Using Unverified Claims, as Democrats Cheer," *The Intercept*, January 11, 2017, https://theintercept.com/2017/01/11/the-deep-state -goes-to-war-with-president-elect-using-unverified-claims-as-dems-cheer. Cf. esp. Jefferson Morley, "The 'Deep State' Is a Political Party," *New Republic*, November 8, 2019, https://newrepublic.com/article/155629/deep-state-political-party.

17. The noble deep state: Michelle Cottle, "They Are Not the Resistance. They Are Not a Cabal. They Are Public Servants," *New York Times*, October 20, 2019, www.nytimes.com/2019/10/20/opinion/trump-impeachment-testimony.html; adults in the room: Quinta Jurecic, "Did the 'Adults in the Room' Make Any Difference with Trump?," *New York Times*, August 29, 2019, www.nytimes.com/2019/08/29/opinion/james-mattis-trump.html.

18. Jenna Curren, "New FBI Text Messages Reveal That Agents Purchased Liability Insurance over Russia Investigation," *Law Enforcement Today*, September 25, 2020, www.lawenforcementtoday.com/fbi-texts-reveal-agents-bought-liability-insurance-over-russia-investigation. On the destructive tactics of state prosecutors, see Sidney Powell and Harvey Silverglate, *Conviction Machine: Standing Up to Federal Prosecutorial Abuse* (New York: Encounter Books, 2020), 96–101.

19. See some examples of such "deep-state" resistance in Katrina Vanden Heuvel, "The Resistance to Trump Is Big, Diverse, and Ferocious," *Washington Post*, January 31, 2017, www.washingtonpost.com/opinions/the-resistance-to-trump-is-big-diverse-and-ferocious/2017/01/31/b0d89e52-e710-11e6-80c2-30e57e57e05d_story.html; Kimberley A. Strassel, "Whistleblowers and the Real Deep State," *Wall Street Journal*, October 11, 2019, www.wsj.com/articles/whistleblowers-and-the-real-deep-state-11570832622.

20. Jonathan Turley, "No Glory in James Comey Getting Away with His Abuse of FBI Power," *The Hill*, December 15, 2018, https://thehill.com/opinion/judiciary/421530-no-glory-in-james-comey-getting-away-with-his-abuse-of-fbi-power.

21. Schiff's distortions: "The IG, Nunes, and Schiff," *Wall Street Journal*, December 10, 2019, www.wsj.com/articles/the-ig-nunes-and-schiff-11576022741; cf. the concessions even from progressive sources: Matt Taibbi, "'Corroboration Zero': An Inspector General's Report Reveals the Steele Dossier Was Always a Joke," *Rolling Stone*, December 10, 2019, www.rollingstone.com/politics/political-commentary/horowitz-report-steele-dossier-collusion-news-media-924944.

22. The abuse of the FISA courts is outlined in detail in Lee Smith, *The Plot Against the President: The True Story of How Congressman Devin Nunes Uncovered the Biggest Political Scandal in U.S. History* (New York: Center Street, 2019), 10–11, 292–204. Steele's source: Rowan Scarborough, "Source for Steele Discredited Anti-Trump Dossier Outed," *Washington Times*, July 26, 2020, www.washingtontimes.com/news/2020/jul/26/igor-danchenko-outed-steele-dossier-source. Cf. Paul Sperry, "Meet the Dossier's Source: Troubled Russian at Dem Think Tank," *RealClear Politics*, July 25, 2020, www.realclearpolitics.com/2020/07/25/meet_the_dossiers_source_troubled_russian_at_dem_think_tank_518287.html.

23. FBI agents and lawyers investigating Trump, such as Lisa Page, Peter Strozk, Andrew McCabe, and Kevin Clinesmith, during the course of their investigations, all either wrote about their anti-Trump sentiments or were referred to by others as biased toward the object of their inquiries: Devlin Barrett et al., "Inspector General Blasts Comey and Also Says Others at FBI Showed 'Willingness to Take Official Action' to Hurt Trump," *Washington Post*, June 14, 2018, www .washingtonpost.com/world/national-security/trump-receiving-briefing-ahead -of-public-release-of-report-expected-to-criticize-fbi/2018/06/14/c08c6a5a-6fdf -11e8-bf86-a2351b5ece99_story.html; Sean Davis and Mollie Hemmingway, "IG Report: FBI Doctored Evidence to Falsely Paint Carter Page as Russian Spy," *The Federalist*, December 9, 2019, https://thefederalist.com/2019/12/09/ig-report -fbi-doctored-evidence-to-falsely-paint-carter-page-as-russian-spy. For subsequent FISA abuses, cf. "Management Advisory Memorandum for the Director of the Federal Bureau of Investigation Regarding the Execution of Woods Procedures for Applications Filed with the Foreign Intelligence Surveillance Court Relating to U.S. Persons," Office of the Inspector General, March 2020, https://oig.justice .gov/sites/default/files/reports/a20047.pdf; Eli Lake, "The FBI Can't Be Trusted with the Surveillance of Americans," *Bloomberg*, March 31, 2020, www.bloomberg .com/opinion/articles/2020-03-31/fbi-inspector-general-report-shows-agency -cannot-be-trusted. For admissions of the fictitious dossier, see Katelyn Polantz, "Steele Says He Used Unverified Information to Support Details About Web Company in Dossier," *CNN*, March 16, 2019, www.cnn.com/2019/03/16 /politics/steele-information-dossier; "The FBI's Dossier Deceit," *Wall Street Journal*, July 17, 2020, www.wsj.com/articles/the-fbis-dossier-deceit-11595027626.

24. Josh Gernstein, Kyle Cheney, and Natasha Bertrand, "Documents Show FBI Debated How to Handle Investigation of Michael Flynn," *Politico*, April 29, 2020, www.politico.com/news/2020/04/29/fbi-michael-flynn-224311; Kevin Johnson, Michael Collins, and Christal Hayes, "DOJ Drops Case Against Former Trump Adviser Michael Flynn in Boldest Step Yet to Undermine Mueller Probe," *USA Today*, May 7, 2020, www.usatoday.com/story/news/politics/2020/05/07 /trump-adviser-michael-flynn-has-case-dropped-justice-department/3090 071001.

25. Nisbet, *Twilight of Authority*, 31.

26. Deep/shallow state: Shalom Lipner, "Don't Fear the Deep State. It's the Shallow State That Will Destroy Us," *Foreign Policy*, February 4, 2019, https:// foreignpolicy.com/2019/02/04/dont-fear-the-deep-state-its-the-shallow-state -that-will-destroy-us-trump-theresa-may-netanyahu-brexit-israel-populism.

27. Dream-team ecstasies: Garrett M. Graff, "Robert Mueller Chooses His Investigatory Dream Team," *Wired*, June 14, 2017, www.wired.com/story/robert -mueller-special-counsel-investigation-team; Rebecca Tan and Alex Ward, "Meet

the All-Star Legal Team Who May Take Down Trump," *Vox*, August 2, 2017, www
.vox.com/policy-and-politics/2017/6/15/15783384/trump-mueller-team-russia
-investigation-dreeben-weissman-quarles-rhee-zebley; Max Boot, "You'd Be
Scared If You Were Donald Trump, Too," *Foreign Policy*, June 22, 2017, https://
foreignpolicy.com/2017/06/22/youd-be-scared-if-you-were-donald-trump-too.

28. Dream team versus nobodies: Tamara Keith, "Meet President Trump's
Outside Legal Team," *NPR*, June 24, 2017, www.npr.org/2017/06/24/533785914
/meet-president-trumps-outside-legal-team; cf. Kevin Breuninger, "Here Are
the Lawyers Who Quit or Declined to Represent Trump in the Mueller Probe,"
CNBC, March 27, 2018, www.cnbc.com/2018/03/27/all-the-lawyers-declining
-to-represent-trump-in-mueller-probe.html; Victor Davis Hanson, "The Dream
Team Loses to the Nobodies," *American Greatness*, August 4, 2019, https://
amgreatness.com/2019/08/04/the-dream-team-loses-to-the-nobodies.

29. Trump legal team: Michael Kranish, "Trump Needed New Lawyers for
Russia Probe. He Found Them at a Tiny Florida Firm," *Washington Post*, April 25,
2018, www.washingtonpost.com/politics/trump-needed-new-lawyers-for-russia
-probe-he-found-them-at-a-tiny-florida-firm/2018/04/25/7288a4f2-47cd-11e8
-9072-f6d4bc32f223_story.html; Tan and Ward, "Meet the All-Star Legal Team
Who May Take Down Trump." Mueller investigation: Gregg Re, "Flynn Bomb-
shells Cast Doubt on Mueller Prosecutor Brandon Van Grack's Compliance with
Court Order," *Fox News*, May 6, 2020, www.foxnews.com/politics/flynn-evidence
-calls-into-question-statements-by-former-special-counsel-brandon-van-grack;
testimony: "Full Transcript: Mueller Testimony Before House Judiciary, Intelligence Committees," *NBC News*, July 25, 2019, www.nbcnews.com/politics
/congress/full-transcript-robert-mueller-house-committee-testimony-n1033216.

30. Erased phones: Mark Moore, "Action Must Be Taken Against Mueller's
Team for 'Wiping Phones,'" *New York Post*, September 14, 2020, https://nypost
.com/2020/09/14/trump-action-must-be-taken-against-muellers-team-for-wiping
-phones; DOJ mandate: see the official order of the Office of the Deputy Attorney General of May 17, 2017, found at www.politico.com/f/?id=00000171-ebc4
-d2fd-a9f5-efe5ebf00000. Trump lawyer's assessment of Mueller: Gregg Jarrett,
"Trump Attorney Accuses Mueller of 'Monstrous Lie and Scheme to Defraud,'"
Fox News, May 27, 2020, www.foxnews.com/opinion/trump-attorney-accuses
-mueller-lie-defraud-gregg-jarrett. Mueller's congressional team: B. Singman,
"Mueller Says He Is Not Familiar with Fusion GPS," *Fox News*, July 24, 2019,
www.foxnews.com/politics/mueller-says-he-is-not-familiar-with-fusion-gps-the
-firm-behind-the-steele-dossier.

31. Mueller's team: Allan Smith, "Robert Mueller's 'Pit Bull' Is Coming Under
Intense Scrutiny over Perceived Anti-Trump Bias," *Business Insider*, December 9,
2017, www.businessinsider.com/who-is-andrew-weissman-mueller-trump-clinton
-russia-investigation-fbi-2017-12.

32. Andrew C. McCarthy, *Ball of Collusion: The Plot to Rig an Election and Destroy a Presidency* (New York: Encounter Books, 2019), 350.

33. For anonymous, see "I Am Part of the Resistance Inside the Trump Administration," *New York Times*, September 5, 2018, www.nytimes.com/2018/09/05 /opinion/trump-white-house-anonymous-resistance.html.

34. Anonymous revealed: J. Concha, "Critics Blast 'Two-Faced Liar' Miles Taylor After Revelation as NYT 'Anonymous' Author," *The Hill*, October 28, 2020, https://thehill.com/homenews/media/523250-critics-blast-two-faced-liar -miles-taylor-after-revelation-as-nyt-anonymous.

35. Praise of the deep state: Alexander Naumov, "'Thank God for the Deep State': Hayden Center Launches New Series with Lively Panel of Former Intel Leaders Discussing the 2020 Election and More," Michael V. Hayden Center for Intelligence, Policy, and International Security, https://haydencenter.gmu.edu news/%E2%80%9Cthank-god-deep-state%E2%80%9D-hayden-center-launches -new-series-lively-panel-former-intel-leaders; cf. esp. Tom Elliott (@tomselliott), "@JohnBrennan on the whistleblower coming from the intel community: They're '[f]ighting in the trenches here and overseas. . . . I'm just pleased every day that my former colleagues in the intelligence community continue to do their duties,'" *Twitter*, October 31, 2019, 4:01 p.m., https://twitter.com/tomselliott/status /1190041236318642176.

36. See also the tweets of Mark Zaid: Victor Morton, "Whistleblower Attorney Tweeted of Trump 'Coup,' Rebellion," *Washington Times*, November 6, 2019, www.washingtontimes.com/news/2019/nov/6/mark-zaid-whistleblower-attorney -tweeted-trump-cou; Tristan Justice, "Anti-Trump Whistleblower's Attorney: 'Coup Has Started,' 'We Will Get Rid' of Trump," *The Federalist*, November 7, 2019, https://thefederalist.com/2019/11/07/anti-trump-whistleblowers-attorney -coup-has-started-we-will-get-rid-of-trump. Kristol: Bill Kristol (@BillKristol), "Obviously strongly prefer normal democratic and constitutional politics. But if it comes to it, prefer the deep state to the Trump state," *Twitter*, February 14, 2017, 5:36 a.m., https://twitter.com/billkristol/status/831497364661747712. Mattis: Bob Woodward, *Rage* (New York: Simon & Schuster, 2020), 66–67; Tal Axelroad, "Mattis Told Coats Trump Is 'Dangerous,' 'Unfit': Woodward Book," *The Hill*, September 9, 2020, https://thehill.com/homenews/administration/515673 -mattis-told-coats-trump-is-dangerous-unfit-woodward-book.

37. "Wise men": Citizens for Responsibility and Ethics in Washington, "CREW: Department of Defense: Regarding Ethics Opinions Database: 7/31/2013—Crew Database Spreadsheet," Scribd, 2013, www.scribd.com /document/172539789/CREW-Department-of-Defense-Regarding-Ethics- Opinions-Database-7-31-2013-Crew-Database-Spreadsheet; Charles S. Clark, "Latest Count of 'Revolving Door' Defense Contractors Names Names," *Government Executive*, November 14, 2018, www.govexec.com/management/2018/11

/latest-count-revolving-door-defense-contractors-names-names/152836; CREW Staff, "Military Contractors Open the Revolving Door for Former Pentagon Officials," Citizens for Responsibility and Ethics in Washington, October 24, 2013, www.citizensforethics.org/military-contractors-open-the-revolving-door-for-for mer-pentagon-official; the locus classicus of "wise men" hagiography is Walter Isaacson and Evan Thomas, *The Wise Men: Six Friends and the World They Made* (New York: Simon & Schuster, 1986).

38. For post–Cold War failures, see John M. Diamond, *The CIA and the Culture of Failure: U.S. Intelligence from the End of the Cold War to the Invasion of Iraq* (Stanford, CA: Stanford University Press, 2008), 3–16; cf. some examples at Uri Friedman, "The Ten Biggest American Intelligence Failures," *Foreign Policy*, January 3, 2012, https://foreignpolicy.com/2012/01/03/the-ten-biggest-american -intelligence-failures. For liberal and conservative criticisms of the politicization and weaponization of the intelligence and investigatory agencies: Andrew C. McCarthy, "The Case for Repealing FISA and Reforming the FBI and CIA," *Washington Examiner*, February 20, 2020, www.washingtonexaminer.com /opinion/fixing-the-fbi-and-cia; Jonathan Bowman, "Former CIA Directors Just Politicized the Intelligence Community," *The Hill*, August 22, 2018, https://thehill .com/opinion/white-house/402891-former-cia-directors-just-politicized-the -intelligence-community; Rachel Kleinfeld, "The Politicization of Our Security Institutions," *Just Security*, April 25, 2018, www.justsecurity.org/55383 /politicization-security-institutions.

39. See, in general, Loch K. Johnson, *A Season of Inquiry Revisited: The Church Committee Confronts America's Spy Agencies* (Lawrence: University Press of Kansas, 2015), xiii–xix; cf. the Church Committee's official report, *Intelligence Activities and the Rights of Americans: 1976 U.S. Senate Report on Illegal Wiretaps and Domestic Spying by the FBI, CIA and NSA* (St. Petersburg, FL: Red and Black Publishers, 2007).

40. Comey/Mueller friendship: Peter Holley, "'Brothers in Arms': The Long Friendship Between Mueller and Comey," *Washington Post*, May 17, 2017, www .washingtonpost.com/politics/2017/live-updates/trump-white-house/trump -comey-and-russia-how-key-washington-players-are-reacting/brothers-in-arms -the-long-friendship-between-mueller-and-comey.

41. Comey: Daniel Chaitin, "'I Would Be a Coward if I Didn't Speak Out': Comey Blasts Mattis for Silence on Trump," *Washington Examiner*, December 6, 2019, www.washingtonexaminer.com/news/i-would-be-a-coward-if-i-didnt -speak-out-comey-blasts-mattis-for-silence-on-trump; "Can't remember": Adriana Cohen, "James Comey 'Can't Recall' Squat," *Boston Herald*, December 9, 2018, www.bostonherald.com/2018/12/09/comey-cant-recall-squat; cf. Paulina Dedaj, "Comey Transcript Released: Ex-FBI Boss Claims Not to Know, Remember

Key Details in Russia Case," *Fox News*, December 8, 2018, www.foxnews.com /politics/comey-transcript-released-ex-fbi-boss-claims-not-to-know-remember -key-details-in-russia-case.

42. Liberal sympathies for the military and intelligence services: Jeet Heer, "Trump's War on the CIA Has Deep, Right-Wing Roots," *New Republic*, December 15, 2016, https://newrepublic.com/article/139348/trumps-war-cia-deep -right-wing-roots; Elaine Kamarck, "The US Military's Integration of Transgender Troops: Another Milestone in Social Change," Brookings Institution, July 16, 2015, www.brookings.edu/blog/fixgov/2015/07/16/the-us-militarys-in tegration-of-transgender-troops-another-milestone-in-social-change.

43. Brooks: Rosa Brooks, "3 Ways to Get Rid of President Trump Before 2020," *Foreign Policy*, January 30, 2017, https://foreignpolicy.com/2017/01/30/3-ways -to-get-rid-of-president-trump-before-2020-impeach-25th-amendment-coup.

44. Impeachable crimes: Ebony Bowden, "Alan Dershowitz Tells Senate 'Abuse of Power' Is Not an Impeachable Offense," *New York Post*, January 27, 2020, https://nypost.com/2020/01/27/alan-dershowitz-tells-senate-abuse-of-power -is-not-an-impeachable-offense; Tim Hains, "Jonathan Turley: 'You Could Impeach Every Living President' by the Standards of Trump Impeachment," *Real-Clear Politics*, December 18, 2019, www.realclearpolitics.com/video/2019/12/18 /jonathan_turley_you_could_impeach_every_living_president_by_the_standards -of_trump_impeachment.html.

45. "Transcript of the Duty to Warn Conference, Yale School of Medicine, April 20, 2017," Macmillan Publishers, https://static.macmillan.com/static /duty-to-warn-conference-transcript.pdf; Dr. Lee: Bandy X. Lee, "At Your Request, a Mental Health Report on Joe Biden," *Medium*, March 5, 2020, https://medium.com/@bandyxlee/at-your-request-a-mental-health-report-on -joe-biden-608ed43a54a0.

46. On the use of the media to brand presidents non compos mentis, see Mark R. Levin, *Unfreedom of the Press* (New York: Threshold Editions, an imprint of Simon & Schuster, 2019), 82–87. On the psychiatrists' efforts to destroy the Goldwater candidacy, see H. Stein, "The Goldwater Takedown," *City Journal*, August 2016, www.city-journal.org/html/goldwater-takedown-14787.html.

47. Trump test: Bryan Resnick, "Trump Aced the Montreal Cognitive Assessment. Here's What That Means," *Vox*, January 17, 2018, www.vox.com /science-and-health/2018/1/16/16899150/trump-montreal-cognitive -assement-ronny-jackson; Twenty-Fifth Amendment: Avery Anapol, "McCabe Says DOJ Talked 25th Amendment, Rosenstein Offer to Wear Wire Around Trump Was Serious: Report," *The Hill*, February 4, 2019, https:// thehill.com/homenews/administration/429960-mccabe-said-justice-dept -discussed-25th-amendment-confirms-rosenstein; history: Scott Bomboy, "How

JFK's Assassination Led to a Constitutional Amendment," National Constitution Center, November 22, 2019, https://constitutioncenter.org/blog/how-jfks-assassination-led-to-a-constitutional-amendment.

48. For retired military and their notions of a military intercession, see John Nagl and Paul Yingling, "'. . . All Enemies, Foreign and Domestic': An Open Letter to Gen. Milley," *Defense One*, August 11, 2020, www.defenseone.com/ideas/2020/08/all-enemies-foreign-and-domestic-open-letter-gen-milley/167625; "coup porn": Byron York, "Coup Porn: Resistance Sees Military Removing Trump from Office," *Washington Examiner*, August 13, 2020, www.washingtonexaminer.com/opinion/columnists/coup-porn-resistance-sees-military-removing-trump-from-office. For Rosa Brooks's gaming exercise, see Jess Bidgood, "A Bipartisan Group Secretly Gathered to Game Out a Contested Trump-Biden Election. It Wasn't Pretty," *Boston Globe*, July 26, 2020, www.bostonglobe.com/2020/07/25/nation/bipartisan-group-secretly-gathered-game-out-contested-trump-biden-election-it-wasnt-pretty.

49. Cf. criticisms of Farkas, who left federal service to work for the Clinton campaign but still apparently had influence with "former colleagues": Politick Dick, "Time to Decide. Was President Donald J. Trump Correct?," *Medium*, May 17, 2017, https://medium.com/@PolitickDick/time-to-decide-was-president-donald-j-trump-correct-348aaa559350; cf. Sean Davis, "Obama Defense Official Evelyn Farkas Admitted She Lied on MSNBC About Having Evidence of Collusion," *The Federalist*, May 8, 2020, https://thefederalist.com/2020/05/08/obama-defense-official-evelyn-farkas-admitted-she-lied-on-msnbc-about-having-evidence-of-collusion; Obama widens intelligence and sixteen agencies: Kate Tummarello, "Obama Expands Surveillance Powers on His Way Out," Electronic Frontier Foundation, January 12, 2017, www.eff.org/deeplinks/2017/01/obama-expands-surveillance-powers-his-way-out.

50. Retired officer codes: "10 U.S. Code § 888—Art. 88. Contempt Toward Officials," Legal Information Institute at Cornell University, www.law.cornell.edu/uscode/text/10/888; cf. Rick Houghton, "The Law of Retired Military Officers and Political Endorsements: A Primer," *Lawfare*, October 3, 2016, www.lawfareblog.com/law-retired-military-officers-and-political-endorsements-primer.

51. Retired officers' criticism of Trump: "Obama 'Angry' After Reading McChrystal's Remarks," *CNN*, June 22, 2010, www.cnn.com/2010/POLITICS/06/22/general.mcchrystal.obama.apology; Brett Samuels, "Retired Gen. McChrystal: I Think Trump Is Immoral," *The Hill*, December 30, 2018, https://thehill.com/homenews/sunday-talk-shows/423227-mcchrystal-i-think-trump-is-immoral; "Former CIA Head Compares US Immigration Policies to Nazi Germany," *Times of Israel*, June 17, 2018, www.timesofisrael.com/former-cia-head-compares-us-immigration-policies-to-nazi-germany.

52. Allen quotes: Paul LeBlanc and Jake Tapper, "Retired Marine Gen. John Allen: 'There Is Blood on Trump's Hands for Abandoning Our Kurdish Allies,'" *CNN*, October 13, 2019, www.cnn.com/2019/10/13/politics/syria-marine -general-john-allen-trump; cf. J. Allen, "A Moment of National Shame and Peril— and Hope," *Foreign Policy*, June 3, 2020, https://foreignpolicy.com/2020/06/03 /trump-military-george-floyd-protests; McRaven: Josh Rogin, "McRaven to OPSEC: Zip It," *Foreign Policy*, August 24, 2012, https://foreignpolicy.com/2012/08/24 /mcraven-to-opsec-zip-it; William H. McRaven, "Opinion: Our Republic Is Un- der Attack from the President," *New York Times*, October 17, 2019, www.nytimes .com/2019/10/17/opinion/trump-mcraven-syria-military.html.

53. Mattis: Jeffrey Goldberg, "James Mattis Denounces President Trump, Describes Him as a Threat to the Constitution," *The Atlantic*, June 3, 2020, www.theatlantic.com/politics/archive/2020/06/james-mattis-denounces -trump-protests-militarization/612640. Cf. T. Ricks, "The Obama Administration's Inexplicable Mishandling of Marine General James Mattis," *Foreign Policy*, Janu- ary 28, 2013, https://foreignpolicy.com/2013/01/18/the-obama-administrations -inexplicable-mishandling-of-marine-gen-james-mattis-2.

54. Biden and the generals: Jason Silverstein, "Biden 'Convinced' Military Will Escort Trump from White House if He Loses Election and Doesn't Leave," *CBS News*, June 11, 2020, www.cbsnews.com/news/biden-trump-election-military -escort-office.

55. Milley: Helene Cooper, "Milley Apologizes for Role in Trump Photo Op: 'I Should Not Have Been There,'" *New York Times*, June 11, 2020, www.nytimes .com/2020/06/11/us/politics/trump-milley-military-protests-lafayette-square html.

56. Bush and Powell: Natalie Ermann Russell, "Riots in the City of Angels," Miller Center at University of Virginia, April 24, 2017, https://millercenter.org /riots-city-angels.

57. Underwear bomber: Joe Concha, "CNN Issues Correction After Comey Statement Contradicts Reporting," *The Hill*, June 7, 2017, https://thehill.com blogs/blog-briefing-room/336871-cnn-issues-correction-after-comey-statement -contradicts-reporting; jihad: "John Brennan: 'Jihad Is a Holy Struggle,'" Middle East Forum, 2010, www.meforum.org/2949/john-brennan-jihad-holy-struggle; Bin Laden raid: Mark Landler and Helene Cooper, "New U.S. Account Says Bin Laden Was Unarmed During Raid," *New York Times*, May 3, 2011, www .nytimes.com/2011/05/04/world/asia/04raid.html; Alex Pappas, Catherine Her- ridge, and Brooke Singman, "House Memo States Disputed Dossier Was Key to FBI's FISA Warrant to Surveil Members of Team Trump," *Fox News*, February 2, 2018, www.foxnews.com/politics/house-memo-states-disputed-dossier-was-key -to-fbis-fisa-warrant-to-surveil-members-of-team-trump. Brennan's record of

lying under oath to US elected officials: Debra Heine, "Did Brennan Lie to Congress About Gang of 8 Briefings?," *RealClear Politics*, July 30, 2019, www.realclear politics.com/2019/07/30/did_brennan_lie_to_congress_about_gang_of_8 _briefings_481774.html; Trevor Timm, "CIA Director John Brennan Lied to You and to the Senate. Fire Him," *The Guardian*, July 31, 2014, www.theguardian .com/commentisfree/2014/jul/31/cia-director-john-brennan-lied-senate; Daniel Chaitin, "Trump Spy Chief Declassifying Documents Showing CIA Director John Brennan 'Suppressed' Russia Intelligence: Report," *Washington Examiner*, May 12, 2020, www.washingtonexaminer.com/news/trump-spy-chief-declassifying -documents-showing-ex-cia-director-john-brennan-suppressed-russia-intelli gence-report. For the Russian surprise at the Clinton ruse, see Andrew C. McCarthy, "Not Treason, Not a Crime, but Definitely a Gross Abuse of Power," *The Hill*, October 8, 2020, https://thehill.com/opinion/white-house/520153-not-treason -not-a-crime-but-definitely-a-gross-abuse-of-power.

58. The dossier and Brennan: Aaron Maté, "The Brennan Dossier: All About a Prime Mover of Russiagate," *RealClear Investigations*, November 15, 2019, www.realclearinvestigations.com/articles/2019/11/15/the_brennan_dossier_all _about_a_prime_mover_of_russiagate_121098.html.

59. John O. Brennan (@JohnBrennan), "When the full extent of your venality, moral turpitude, and political corruption becomes known, you will take your rightful place as a disgraced demagogue in the dustbin of history. You may scapegoat Andy McCabe, but you will not destroy America . . . America will triumph over you," Twitter, March 17, 2018, 5:00 a.m., https://twitter.com/john brennan/status/974978856997224448; Lance Perriman, "'Your Kakistocracy Is Collapsing': John Brennan Burns Trump with Epic Word That Is Breaking the Dictionary," *PoliticalDig*, April 14, 2018, https://politicaldig.com/your -kakistocracy-is-collapsing-john-brennan-burns-trump-with-epic-word-that-is -breaking-the-dictionary; Margot Cleveland, "Schumer: Intelligence Agencies 'Have Six Ways from Sunday of Getting Back at You,'" *The Federalist*, September 27, 2019, https://thefederalist.com/2019/09/27/schumer-intelligence-agencies -have-six-ways-from-sunday-of-getting-back-at-you. Brennan under investigation: Jerry Dunleavy, "Durham Investigation Intensifies Focus on Brennan," *RealClear Politics*, April 4, 2020, www.realclearpolitics.com/2020/04/03/durham_investi gation_intensifies_focus_on_brennan_506794.html.

60. Kucinich quote: Ian Schwartz, "Kucinich: 'Deep State' Trying to Take Down Trump, 'Our Country Is Under Attack Within,'" *RealClear Politics*, May 18, 2017, www.realclearpolitics.com/video/2017/05/18/kucinich_deep_state_trying _to_take_down_trump_our_country_is_under_attack_within.html.

61. Clapper: Logan Newman, "Did Obama's Director of National Intelligence Say There Is No Evidence of Trump-Russian Collusion?," *Arizona Republic*, June 7, 2017, www.azcentral.com/story/news/politics/fact-check/2017/06/07

/fact-check-andy-biggs-james-clapper-donald-trump-russia-collusion/3469
93001; cf. Sean Davis, "Declassified Congressional Report: James Clapper Lied
About Dossier Leaks to CNN," *The Federalist*, April 27, 2018, https://thefederalist
.com/2018/04/27/house-intel-report-james-clapper-lied-dossier-leaks-cnn.

62. Confessions of media bias: James Taranto, "The Post-Trump Media,"
Wall Street Journal, October 18, 2016, www.wsj.com/articles/the-post-trump
-media-1476813699; "Christiane Amanpour Drops Truth Bomb on Trump
Era Press: 'I Believe in Being Truthful, Not Neutral,'" *Daily Kos*, November 26,
2016, www.dailykos.com/stories/2016/11/26/1604306/-Christiane-Amanpour
-Drops-Truth-Bomb-on-Trump-Era-Press-I-Believe-in-Being-Truthful-Not
-Neutral; cf. Joseph A. Wulfsohn, "Liberal Media Teamed Up for 'Smear Campaign'
to Dismiss the Post's Hunter Biden Story," *New York Post*, December 11, 2020,
https://nypost.com/2020/12/11/liberal-medias-smear-campaign-against-the
-posts-hunter-biden-story; Jim Rutenberg, "Criticism of the News Media Takes
on a More Sinister Tone," *New York Times*, October 16, 2016, www.nytimes
.com/2016/10/17/business/media/criticism-of-the-news-media-takes-on-a-more
-sinister-tone.html; "Jorge Ramos: We Can't 'Be Neutral' with a President like
Trump," *The World*, May 4, 2018, www.pri.org/stories/2018-05-04/jorge-ramos
-we-cant-be-neutral-president-trump.

63. Noose: David Close, "This Is the Noose That Was Found in Bubba Wallace's Garage Stall at the Talladega Superspeedway," *CNN*, June 26, 2020, www
.cnn.com/2020/06/25/us/nascar-noose-investigation-complete-trnd; cf. David
Close and Jill Martin, "FBI Says Bubba Wallace Not a Target of a Hate Crime,"
CNN, June 23, 2020, www.cnn.com/2020/06/23/us/nascar-noose-not-hate
-crime-bubba-wallace. Taliban bounties: "Russia Offered Bounties to Afghan Militants to Kill US Troops," *CNN*, June 28, 2020, https://www.cnn.com/videos/politics
/2020/06/27/russia-us-troops-afghan-militants-sot-vpx-nr.cnn; Ryan Brown and
Paul LeBlanc, "Top US General Says Russian Bounty Intelligence 'Wasn't Proved'
but 'Proved Enough to Worry Me,'" *CNN*, July 8, 2020, www.cnn.com/2020/07/07
/politics/us-russia-afghanistan-bounty-intelligence. Story completely debunked:
B. Adams, "The Russian Bounties Story Was Apparently Fake News All Along,"
Washington Examiner, April 17, 2021, www.msn.com/en-us/news/world/the
-russian-bounties-story-was-apparently-fake-news-all-along/ar-BB1fGUwy.
Mount Rushmore speech: Michael D'Antonio, "Trump's Powerful Message of
Rage," *CNN*, July 5, 2020, www.cnn.com/2020/07/04/opinions/trump-moun
t-rushmore-speech-monuments-rhetoric-dantonio; cf. Rich Lowry, "Patriotism Is
Becoming 'White Supremacy,'" *National Review*, July 6, 2020, www.nationalreview
.com/2020/07/president-trump-mount-rushmore-speech-distorted-by-media.

64. Raju: Oliver Darcy, "CNN Corrects Story on Email to Trumps About
Wikileaks," *CNN*, December 8, 2017, https://money.cnn.com/2017/12/08/media
/cnn-correction-email-story.

65. Davis: Allan Smith, "Lanny Davis's Walk-Back of His Bombshell Claim to CNN Is More Complicated Than It Looks. And Experts Say It Causes Michael Cohen Some New Problems," *Business Insider*, August 28, 2018, www.business insider.com/lanny-davis-cnn-claim-hurt-michael-cohen-2018-8.

66. CNN inaccuracies: "3 Journalists Resign from CNN After Network Retracts Russia-Related Story," *CBS News*, June 26, 2017, www.cbsnews.com/news /cnn-journalists-resign-story-retraction-anthony-scaramucci; Concha, "CNN Issues Correction After Comey Statement Contradicts Reporting."

67. More CNN false reporting: Jeff Zeleny (@jeffzeleny), "The Twitter accounts of @JusticeGorsuch and @JusticeHardiman were not set up by the White House, I've been told," Twitter, January 31, 2017, 2:13 p.m., https://twitter.com /jeffzeleny/status/826553951323553796; Michael Harthorne, "Anderson Cooper Is Sorry for That Trump Poop Joke," *Newser*, May 20, 2017, www.newser .com/story/243076/anderson-cooper-is-sorry-for-that-trump-poop-joke.html; "CNN Severs Ties with Reza Aslan After He Called Trump a Piece of Poop on Twitter," *The Federalist*, June 11, 2017, https://thefederalist.com/2017/06/11 /cnn-severs-ties-reza-aslan; Joe Concha, "CNN Host Bourdain Jokes About Poisoning Trump," *The Hill*, September 15, 2017, https://thehill.com/homenews /media/350857-cnn-host-bourdain-jokes-about-poisoning-trump; Sam Adams, "Kathy Griffin Poses with Donald Trump's Severed 'Head,' Which Is a Bad Idea on Several Levels," *Slate*, May 30, 2017, www.slate.com/blogs/browbeat/2017/05/30 /kathy_griffin_poses_with_trump_s_severed_head_which_is_a_bad_idea.html.

68. Gruber: "GRUBER: 'Lack of Transparency Is a Huge Political Advantage,'" video posted to YouTube by American Commitment, November 7, 2014, www.youtube.com/watch?v=G790p0LcgbI.

69. Rhodes: Larry O'Connor, "D.C. Reporters Can't Get Enough of Ben Rhodes' Echo Chamber," *Washington Times*, December 22, 2017, www.washingtontimes .com/news/2017/dec/22/dc-reporters-cant-get-enough-of-ben-rhodes-echo-ch.

70. Media bias: Erik Wemple, "Study: 91 Percent of Recent Network Trump Coverage Has Been Negative," *Washington Post*, September 12, 2017, www .washingtonpost.com/blogs/erik-wemple/wp/2017/09/12/study-91-percent-of -recent-network-trump-coverage-has-been-negative. Ferguson: Josh Levs, "One Challenge for Ferguson Grand Jury: Some Witnesses' Credibility," *CNN*, December 14, 2014, www.cnn.com/2014/12/14/justice/ferguson-witnesses-credibility; Hans A. von Spakovsky, "What the Ferguson Report Really Exposed," Heritage Foundation, March 16, 2015, www.heritage.org/crime-and-justice/commentary /what-the-ferguson-report-really-exposed. For the Shorenstein study, see T. Patterson, "News Coverage of Donald Trump's First 100 Days," Shorenstein Center on Media, Politics, and Public Policy, May 18, 2017, https://shorensteincenter .org/news-coverage-donald-trumps-first-100-days.

Chapter Five: Evolutionaries

1. See, in general, Thomas N. Mitchell, *Democracy's Beginning: The Athenian Story* (New Haven, CT: Yale University Press, 2015); S. Bokobza, "Liberty Versus Equality: The Marquis De La Fayette and France," *French Review* 83, no. 1 (2009): 114–131, www.jstor.org/stable/25613910.

2. T. Moe, "Our Outdated Constitution," *Defining Ideas*, June 2, 2016, www.hoover.org/research/our-outdated-constitution. L. Diamond, "Can American Democracy Recover After Trump?," *American Purpose*, November 18, 2020, www.americanpurpose.com/articles/can-american-democracy-recover-after-trump. On an evolutionary and fluid Constitution, see the interview with University of California, Berkeley, law dean Erwin Chemerinsky: A. Cohen, "Constitution's Biggest Flaw? Protecting Slavery," *Berkeley News*, September 17, 2019, https://news.berkeley.edu/2019/09/17/constitutions-biggest-flaw-protecting-slavery.

3. Charles Murray, *Losing Ground: American Social Policy, 1950–1980* (New York: Basic Books, 1994), 43; Alexis de Tocqueville, *Democracy in America*.

4. Undeclared wars: Jennifer K. Elsea and Matthew C. Weed, "Declarations of War and Authorizations for the Use of Military Force: Historical Background and Legal Implications," Congressional Research Service Report, Federation of American Scientists, April 18, 2014, https://fas.org/sgp/crs/natsec/RL31133.pdf; Philip Marshall Brown, "Undeclared Wars," *American Journal of International Law* 33, no. 3 (July 1939): 538–541.

5. Bypassing Congress: Matthew Fleming, "Iran Deal: Treaty or Not?," *Roll Call*, July 21, 2015, www.rollcall.com/2015/07/21/iran-deal-treaty-or-not-2; Arthur Milikh, "The Obama Constitution," Heritage Foundation, April 16, 2015, www.heritage.org/political-process/commentary/the-obama-constitution.

6. Warren and Electoral College: John Daniel Davidson, "Warren: I'll Be 'Last American President Elected by the Electoral College,'" *The Federalist*, December 3, 2019, https://thefederalist.com/2019/12/03/warren-ill-be-last-american-president-elected-by-the-electoral-college; cf. "Get Rid of the Electoral College," ElizabethWarren.com, https://elizabethwarren.com/plans/electoral-college.

7. "Faithless electors": Ariane de Vogue and Chandelis Duster, "Supreme Court Says States Can Punish Electoral College Voters," *CNN*, July 6, 2020, www.cnn.com/2020/07/06/politics/faithless-electors-supreme-court.

8. Unconstitutional compact: Andrew C. McCarthy, "Supremes Signal a Brave New World of Popular Presidential Elections," *National Review*, July 11, 2020, www.nationalreview.com/2020/07/supremes-signal-a-brave-new-world-of-popular-presidential-elections; The compact: "Agreement Among the States to Elect the President by National Popular Vote," National Popular Vote, www.nationalpopularvote.com/written-explanation.

9. Harvard proposal: "Pack the Union: A Proposal to Admit New States for the Purpose of Amending the Constitution to Ensure Equal Representation," *Harvard Law Review*, January 10, 2020, https://harvardlawreview.org/2020/01 /pack-the-union-a-proposal-to-admit-new-states-for-the-purpose-of-amending -the-constitution-to-ensure-equal-representation.

10. On the sometimes bizarre politics of opposition to or support for the Electoral College, see Ben Adler, "Would the National Popular Vote Advantage Red-State Republicans?," *American Prospect*, January 9, 2009, https://prospect.org /article/national-popular-vote-advantage-red-state-republicans.

11. Electoral College trends: Nate Silver, "Will the Electoral College Doom the Democrats Again?," *FiveThirtyEight*, November 14, 2016, https://fivethirtyeight .com/features/will-the-electoral-college-doom-the-democrats-again.

12. On the simplicity of the Electoral College in comparison to electoral systems in Europe: Allen Guelzo, "In Defense of the Electoral College," *National Affairs,* no. 34 (winter 2018), www.nationalaffairs.com/publications/detail /in-defense-of-the-electoral-college.

13. For the Founders' idea of the Senate balancing the House, see Emmet McGroarty, Jane Robbins, and Erin Tuttle, *Deconstructing the Administrative State* (Maitland, FL: Liberty Hill Publishing, 2017), 36–41. For Roman checks and balances, see Barry Strauss, "Populares and Populists," in *Vox Populi*, ed. R. Kimball (New York: Encounter Books, 2017), 36–40. In the same volume, see, especially, Roger Scruton, "Representation and the People," 120–125. Pros and cons of repealing the Seventeenth Amendment: John York, "Would Repealing the 17th Amendment Revive Federalism?," Heritage Foundation, July 19, 2018, www.heritage.org/the -constitution/report/would-repealing-the-17th-amendment-revive-federalism. For characteristic criticism of the Senate, see Hans Noel, "The Senate Represents States, Not People. That's the Problem," *Vox*, October 13, 2018, www.vox .com/2018/10/13/17971340/the-senate-represents-states-not-people-constitution -kavanaugh-supreme-court.

14. For various recent progressive arguments for radically changing the election of senators and the makeup of the Senate, see Eric W. Orts, "The Path to Give California 12 Senators, and Vermont Just One," *The Atlantic*, January 2, 2019, www.theatlantic.com/ideas/archive/2019/01/heres-how-fix-senate/579172.

15. See Michael Barone, *How America's Political Parties Change (and How They Don't)* (New York: Encounter Books, 2019), 89–90.

16. On changing the House: "America Needs a Bigger House," *New York Times*, November 13, 2018, www.nytimes.com/interactive/2018/11/09/opinion /expanded-house-representatives-size.html; Dylan Matthews, "The Case for Massively Expanding the US House of Representatives, in One Chart," *Vox*, June 4, 2018, www.vox.com/2018/6/4/17417452/congress-representation-ratio-district -size-chart-graph. Cf. Chris Wilson, "How to Fix the House of Representatives

in One Easy, Radical Step," *Time Magazine*, October 15, 2018, https://time
.com/5423623/house-representatives-number-seats.

17. Statehood for Puerto Rico and Washington, DC: Nolan D. McCaskill,
"In Lewis Eulogy, Obama Issues Forceful Call to Action on Voting Rights, Racial
Equality," *Politico*, July 30, 2020, www.politico.com/news/2020/07/30/clinton
-bush-obama-john-lewis-funeral-388050.

18. Cf. David Harsanyi, "Barack Obama's Filibuster's Hypocrisy," *Detroit
News*, August 12, 2020, www.detroitnews.com/story/opinion/2020/08/13/opinion
-barack-obamas-filibuster-hypocrisy/3353317001.

19. Nuclear option: Mahita Gajanan, "Why Republicans Are Suddenly
Thanking Harry Reid for a 2013 Tweet About Filibuster Reform," *Time*, June 28,
2018, https://time.com/5324365/harry-reid-filibuster-reform-supreme-court.
"Jim Crow relic": Max Cohen, "Obama Calls for End of 'Jim Crow Relic' Filibuster if It Blocks Voting Reforms," *Politico*, July 30, 2020, www.politico.com
/news/2020/07/30/barack-obama-john-lewis-filibuster-388600.

20. Makeup of the Supreme Court: Jean Edward Smith, "Stacking the
Court," *New York Times*, July 26, 2007, www.nytimes.com/2007/07/26/opinion
/26smith.html.

21. Conservative justices becoming liberal: Adrian Vermeule, "Why Conservative Justices Are More Likely to Defect," *Washington Post*, July 8, 2020,
www.washingtonpost.com/opinions/2020/07/08/why-is-it-always-conservative
-justices-who-seem-defect-disappoint.

22. Court packing: Michael Scherer, "'Court Packing' Ideas Get Attention
from Democrats," *Washington Post*, March 11, 2019, www.washingtonpost
.com/politics/court-packing-ideas-get-attention-from-democrats/2019/03/10
/d05e549e-41c0-11e9-a0d3-1210e58a94cf_story.html; cf. Pema Levy, "How
Court-Packing Went from a Fringe Idea to a Serious Democratic Proposal,"
Mother Jones, March 22, 2019, www.motherjones.com/politics/2019/03/court
-packing-2020.

23. The Pack the Court movement: Moira Donegan, "Enough Playing Nice.
It's Time to Pack the Courts," *The Guardian*, April 19, 2019, www.theguardian
.com/commentisfree/2019/apr/19/pack-the-courts-democrats-2020.

24. Candidates and court packing: Russell Wheeler, "Pack the Court? Putting a Popular Imprint on the Federal Judiciary," Brookings Institution, April
3, 2019, www.brookings.edu/blog/fixgov/2019/04/03/pack-the-court-putting-a
-popular-imprint-on-the-federal-judiciary.

25. The modern argument for speech restrictions is discussed in Robert
Shibley, "What Provosts Get Wrong: A Failed Case for Campus Speech Restrictions," James G. Martin Center for Academic Renewal, April 24, 2020,
www.jamesgmartin.center/2020/04/what-provosts-get-wrong-a-failed-case
-for-campus-speech-restrictions.

26. Speech restrictions on campus: "Fire's Guide to Free Speech on Campus—Full Text," *The Fire*, www.thefire.org/research/publications/fire-guides/fires-guide-to-free-speech-on-campus-3/fires-guide-to-free-speech-on-campus-full-text-2.

27. For a few minor examples, see Victor Davis Hanson, "Slurs Replace Seasoned Debate," Victor Davis Hanson Private Papers, October 15, 2010, http://victorhanson.com/wordpress/slurs-replace-reasoned-debate; Victor Davis Hanson, "Politics Upside Down," *PJ Media*, October 9, 2010, https://pjmedia.com/victordavishanson/2010/10/09/politics-upside-down-n118087; "The Blogosphere Responds to The Stanford Daily's Attack on Hoover Scholar Victor Davis Hanson," *Stanford Review*, 2010, https://stanfordreview.org/the-blogosphere-responds-to-the-stanford-dailys-attack-on-hoover-scholar-victor-davis-hanson; "Letters to the Editor," *Stanford Daily*, October 11, 2010, www.stanforddaily.com/2010/10/11/letters-responses-to-editorial-on-victor-davis-hanson; Victor Davis Hanson, "Denigrating Hoover," *Stanford Daily*, December 2, 2020, www.stanforddaily.com/2020/12/02/denigrating-hoover; S. Atlas, N. Ferguson, and V. Hanson, "Atlas, Ferguson, and Hanson: On Free Speech at Stanford," *Stanford Review*, February 23, 2021, https://stanfordreview.org/atlas-ferguson-hanson-stanford-free-speech; cf. Emily Ekins, "Poll: 62% of Americans Say They Have Political Views They're Afraid to Share," Cato Institute, July 22, 2020, www.cato.org/publications/survey-reports/poll-62-americans-say-they-have-political-views-theyre-afraid-share; Emily Ekins, "Poll: 71% of Americans Say Political Correctness Has Silenced Discussions Society Needs to Have, 58% Have Political Views They're Afraid to Share," Cato Institute, October 31, 2017, www.cato.org/blog/poll-71-americans-say-political-correctness-has-silenced-discussions-society-needs-have-58-have.

28. On the defense of exercising social media censorship (before the banning of Trump), see A. Sewer, "Trump's Warped Definition of Free Speech," *The Atlantic*, May 29, 2020, www.theatlantic.com/ideas/archive/2020/05/trumps-warped-definition-free-speech/612316. On the monopolies of Silicon Valley and the attack on Parler, see the interview of A. Kantrowitz and S. Burch, "How Parler Crackdown Could Make 'Life Miserable' for Amazon, Google," *The Wrap*, January 12, 2021, www.thewrap.com/tech-talk-parler-crackdown-amazon-google-antitrust. Cf. S. Frier, "Bans on Parler and Trump Show Big Tech's Power over Web Conversation," *Bloomberg*, January 10, 2021, www.bloomberg.com/news/articles/2021-01-11/parler-trump-bans-show-big-tech-s-power-over-web-conversation.

29. Diversity statements: Brian Leiter, "The Legal Problem with Diversity Statements," *Chronicle of Higher Education*, March 13, 2020, www.chronicle.com/article/the-legal-problem-with-diversity-statements; Colleen Flaherty, "Diversity Statements as 'Litmus Tests,'" *Inside Higher Ed*, November 19, 2019, www.insidehighered

.com/news/2019/11/19/mathematician-comes-out-against-mandatory-diversity-statements-while-others-say-they.

30. ACLU: Robby Soave, "Leaked Internal Memo Reveals the ACLU Is Wavering on Free Speech," *Reason*, June 21, 2018, https://reason.com/2018/06/21/aclu-leaked-memo-free-speech; Joe Lieberman, "The ACLU's Regrettable Turn to Partisan Politics," *RealClear Politics*, February 8, 2018, www.realclearpolitics.com articles/2018/02/08/the_aclus_regrettable_turn_to_partisan_politics_136220.html; Marin Cogan, "The Twilight of Free Speech Liberalism," *New Republic*, July 16, 2018, https://newrepublic.com/article/148873/free-speech-liberalism-aclu.html; David E. Weisberg, "ACLU Proves Yet Again It's a Guardian of Left-Wing Agenda," *The Hill*, August 21, 2017, https://thehill.com/blogs/pundits-blog civil-rights/347375-aclu-proves-yet-again-its-a-guardian-of-left-wing-movement.

31. The new ACLU: Marin Cogan, "The Twilight of Free Speech Liberalism," *New Republic*, July 16, 2018, https://newrepublic.com/article/148873/free-speech-liberalism-aclu.html. The new First Amendment: Dale Maharidge, "Can the ACLU Remake Itself as a Mass Movement for Progressive Change?," *The Nation*, May 21, 2018, www.thenation.com/article/archive/can-the-aclu-remake-itself-as-a-mass-movement-for-progressive-change.

32. Gun confiscation: Todd J. Gillman, "'Hell, Yes,' Beto O'Rourke's Call to Confiscate AR-15s Pushes Gun Debate to New Level," *Dallas Morning News*, September 13, 2019, www.dallasnews.com/news/politics/2019/09/13/hell-yes-beto-o-rourke-s-call-to-confiscate-ar-15s-pushes-gun-debate-to-new-level; Beto: Mark Moore, "Joe Biden Promises to Put Beto O'Rourke in Charge of Gun Control," *New York Post*, March 3, 2020, https://nypost.com/2020/03/03/joe-biden-promises-to-put-beto-orourke-in-charge-of-gun-control.

33. Closure of gun stores: "LA County Sheriff Closes Gun Stores in 42 Cities Due to Coronavirus Outbreak," *NBC Los Angeles*, March 26, 2020, www.nbclosangeles.com/news/local/la-county-sheriff-closes-gun-stores-in-42-cities-due-to-coronavirus-outbreak/2336094; cf. Alexandra Meeks and Leah Asmelash, "Los Angeles Sheriff Orders Gun Stores Shut Down Due to Coronavirus Restrictions," *CNN*, March 24, 2020, www.cnn.com/2020/03/24/us/los-angeles-gun-store-close-coronavirus-trnd; Justin Carissimo, "1,700 Inmates Released from Los Angeles County in Response to Coronavirus Outbreak," *CBS News*, March 24, 2020, www.cbsnews.com/news/inmates-released-los-angeles-county-coronavirus-response-2020-03-24. Armed store owners: Jack Shea, "Owners of Corbo's Bakery Arm Themselves with Guns as Violent Protesters Try to Get Inside," *Fox8 News Cleveland*, May 31, 2020, https://fox8.com/news/owners-of-corbos-bakery-arm-themselves-with-guns-as-violent-protesters-try-to-get-inside.

34. "Black Victims of Violent Crime," US Department of Justice Special Report, Bureau of Justice Statistics, August 2007, www.bjs.gov/content

/pub/pdf/bvvc.pdf. Assault-weapons ban: "Attn. Gun Control Advocates: We Banned Assault Weapons Before . . . and It Didn't Work," *Investor's Business Daily*, March 1, 2018, www.investors.com/politics/editorials/we-banned -assault-weapons-before-and-it-didnt-work.

35. First-time gun buyers: "First-Time Gun Buyers Grow to Nearly 5 Million in 2020," National Shooting Sports Foundation, August, 24, 2020, www.nssf .org/first-time-gun-buyers-grow-to-nearly-5-million-in-2020; so-called red-flag laws: Timothy Williams, "What Are 'Red Flag' Gun Laws, and How Do They Work?," *New York Times*, August 6, 2019, www.nytimes.com/2019/08/06/us /red-flag-laws.html.

36. Data on gun deaths: John Gramlich, "What the Data Says About Gun Deaths in the U.S.," Pew Research Center, August 16, 2019, www.pewresearch .org/fact-tank/2019/08/16/what-the-data-says-about-gun-deaths-in-the-u-s. On the original constitutional debates on gun ownership and the Bill of Rights, see Stephen P. Halbrook, *The Founders' Second Amendment: Origins of the Right to Bear Arms* (Lanham, MD: Rowman & Littlefield, 2019), 182–188.

37. Jackson: Andrew Jackson, "January 16, 1833: Message Regarding South Carolina Nullification of Federal Legislation," Miller Center at University of Virginia, https://millercenter.org/the-presidency/presidential-speeches/january-16-1833 -message-regarding-south-carolina-nullification.

38. Don E. Fehrenbacher, *The Dred Scott Case: Its Significance in American Law and Politics* (New York: Oxford University Press, 1978), 209–238.

39. Sending in military troops to override nullifying state governance: Jonathon Berlin and Kori Rumore, "12 Times the President Called in the Military Domestically," *Chicago Tribune*, June 1, 2020, www.chicagotribune.com/news /ct-national-guard-deployments-timeline-htmlstory.html.

40. Sanctuary cities: Hans A. von Spakovsky, "Sanctuary Cities? That's a Constitutional 'Hell No,'" Heritage Foundation, April 18, 2017, www.heritage.org /immigration/commentary/sanctuary-cities-thats-constitutional-hell-no; cf. Lorraine Marie A. Simonis, "Sanctuary Cities: A Study in Modern Nullification?," *British Journal of American Legal Studies* 8, no. 1 (April 16, 2016), https://content .sciendo.com/view/journals/bjals/8/1/article-p37.xml.

41. Illegal alien crime and Steinle case: Christina Maxouris, "Kate Steinle's Parents Can't Sue 'Sanctuary City' for Failing to Tell ICE About Shooter's Release," *CNN*, March 26, 2019, www.cnn.com/2019/03/26/us/kate-steinle-family -cannot-sue-city; Larry Neumeister, "Court Sides with Trump in 'Sanctuary Cities' Grant Fight," *Washington Times*, February 26, 2020, www.washingtontimes.com /news/2020/feb/26/court-sides-with-trump-in-sanctuary-cities-grant-f; Shikha Dalmia, "Undocumented Aliens May Be Safe in Sanctuary Cities, Thanks to Conservative Justices," *Reason*, February 2, 2017, https://reason.com/2017/02/02 /undocumented-aliens-may-be-safe-in-sanct.

42. Illegal immigration and crime: Heather Mac Donald, "The Illegal-Alien Crime Wave," *City Journal*, winter 2004, www.city-journal.org/html/illegal-alien-crime-wave-12492.html. Cf. Editorial Board, "Steinle Case—a Complete Miscarriage of Justice," *Pleasanton Weekly*, January 16, 2020, www.pleasantonweekly.com/news/2020/01/16/editorial-steinle-case---a-complete-miscarriage-of-justice.

43. Utah and the Second Amendment: Allison Schuster, "Sanctuary Cities for Guns? This Utah County Is Trying It Out," *National Interest*, February 22, 2020, https://nationalinterest.org/blog/buzz/sanctuary-cities-guns-utah-county-trying-it-out-125661.

44. Dangers of nullification of gay marriage ruling: David A. Graham, "Can States Ignore the Supreme Court on Gay Marriage?," *The Atlantic*, July 1, 2015, www.theatlantic.com/politics/archive/2015/07/nullification-again/397373.

45. John Temple, *Up in Arms: How the Bundy Family Hijacked Public Lands, Outfoxed the Federal Government, and Ignited America's Patriot Militia Movement* (Dallas: BenBella Books, 2019), 303–342.

46. Second Amendment sanctuaries: Peter Galuzska, "The Disturbing 'Second Amendment Sanctuary' Trend in Virginia," *Washington Post*, January 3, 2020, www.washingtonpost.com/opinions/local-opinions/the-disturbing-second-amendment-sanctuary-trend-in-virginia/2020/01/03/21a442b2-2c0f-11ea-bcb3-ac6482c4a92f_story.html.

47. Nonsanctuary jurisdictions: Tatiana Sanchez, "California Cities Are Rebelling Against State Sanctuary Law, but How Far Can They Go?," *Mercury News*, April 23, 2018, www.mercurynews.com/2018/04/23/california-cities-are-rebelling-against-state-sanctuary-law-but-how-far-can-they-go.

48. Summer of love: Andrew Gleeson, "Seattle's Summer of Love," *Quillette*, June 16, 2020, https://quillette.com/2020/06/16/seattles-summer-of-love. State-federal tensions over use of federal marshals: Scott Neuman, "Governors Push Back on Trump's Threat to Deploy Federal Troops to Quell Unrest," *NPR*, June 2, 2020, www.npr.org/2020/06/02/867565338/governors-push-back-on-trumps-threat-to-deploy-federal-troops-to-quell-unrest.

49. Baltimore mayor: "Baltimore Mayor: 'Gave Those Who Wished to Destroy Space to Do That,'" *CBS Baltimore*, April 25, 2015, https://baltimore.cbslocal.com/2015/04/25/baltimore-mayor-gave-those-who-wished-to-destroy-space-to-do-that. Minneapolis mayor: Ian Schwartz, "Minneapolis Mayor Jacob Frey Defends Riot Response: 'Brick and Mortar Is Not as Important as Life,'" *RealClear Politics*, May 29, 2020, www.realclearpolitics.com/video/2020/05/29/minneapolis_mayor_jacob_frey_defends_riot_response_brick_and_mortar_is_not_as_important_as_life.html. Tim Walz and "space": "Minnesota Gov. Walz Stresses Importance of 'Creating Space' for Peaceful Protesters," *NBC*, May 31, 2020, https://news.yahoo.com/minnesota-gov-walz-stresses-importance-035633142.html.

50. Liberals and states' rights: Heather Gerken, "We're About to See States' Rights Used Defensively Against Trump," *Vox*, January 20, 2017, www.vox.com /the-big-idea/2016/12/12/13915990/federalism-trump-progressive-uncooperative. Murder rates soar in 2020: S. Pagones, "America's Murder Rate Increase in 2020 Has 'No Modern Precedent,'" *New York Post*, February 1, 2021, https://nypost .com/2021/02/01/americas-murder-rate-increase-in-2020-has-no-modern -precedent; Stephen Green, "Video of NYC Mob Taking Over Street, Attacking Car, as Murder Rate Skyrockets," *PJ Media*, December 30, 2020, https://pjmedia.com /vodkapundit/2020/12/30/insanity-wrap-115-video-of-nyc-mob-taking -over-street-attacking-car-as-murder-rate-skyrockets-n1292379.

51. For the constitutional description, see "List of Individuals Impeached by the House of Representatives," History, Art, & Archives: US House of Representatives, https://history.house.gov/Institution/Impeachment/Impeachment-List.

52. On Hamilton and impeachment, see Alexander Hamilton, *Federalist Papers* No. 65; cf. Alan M. Dershowitz, "Hamilton Wouldn't Impeach Trump," *Wall Street Journal*, October 9, 2019, www.wsj.com/articles/hamilton-wouldnt -impeach-trump-11570661260; Michael Stokes Paulsen, "Alexander Hamilton, *The Federalist*, and the Power of Impeachment," *Law and Liberty*, August 15, 2018, https:// lawliberty.org/alexander-hamilton-the-federalist-and-the-power-of-impeachment.

53. On the politics of impeachment and especially the case of 1998, see Ronald Brownstein, "Democrats Learned the Wrong Lesson from Clinton's Impeachment," *The Atlantic*, June 6, 2019, www.theatlantic.com/politics/archive/2019/06 /did-clintons-impeachment-actually-hurt-republicans/591175; David Leonhardt, "The Clinton Legacy: Impeachment Hurts the President," *New York Times*, October 13, 2019, www.nytimes.com/2019/10/13/opinion/impeachment-clinton .html. David M. Drucker, "Redistricting Gives GOP a Built-In Edge to Win House Majority in 2022," *Washington Examiner*, December 17, 2020, www.washington examiner.com/news/campaigns/redistricting-house-gop-edge-win-house-majority -2022.

54. On the second Trump impeachment and trial and the January 6, 2021, violence at the Capitol, see, e.g., G. Greenwald, "The False and Exaggerated Claims Still Being Spread About the Capitol Riot," *Substack*, February 15, 2021, https://greenwald.substack.com/p/the-false-and-exaggerated-claims; J. Kelly, "No Proof January 6 Was an 'Armed Insurrection,'" *American Greatness*, February 19, 2021, https://amgreatness.com/2021/02/19/no-proof-january-6-was-an-armed -insurrection; A. McCarthy, "The Times Corrects the Record on Officer Sicknick's Death, Sort Of," *National Review*, February 15, 2021, www.nationalreview .com/2021/02/the-times-corrects-the-record-on-officer-sicknicks-death-sort-of.

Chapter Six: Globalists

1. On Caracalla's edict, see Cassius Dio 78.9; cf. "Edicts of Caracalla on Citizenship, on Amnesty, and on Expulsion from Alexandria (AD 212–215)," Université Grenoble Alpes, https://droitromain.univ-grenoble-alpes.fr/Anglica/Antoniniana_johnson.html. On ancient Roman globalization, see, e.g., Geraldine Djament-Tran, "Rome and the Process of Globalization," *Annales de géographie* 670, no. 6 (2009): 590–608, www.cairn-int.info/article-E_AG_670_0590--rome-and-the-process-of-globalization.htm; Ryan M. Geraghty, "The Impact of Globalization in the Roman Empire, 200 BC–AD 100," *Journal of Economic History* 67, no. 4 (December 2007): 1036–1061, www.jstor.org/stable/40056408?seq=1.

2. On the adolescence and senescence of the Greek state, see, in general, Jacqueline de Romilly, *The Rise and Fall of States According to Greek Authors* (Ann Arbor: University of Michigan Press, 1977). Costs of globalism in the West: D. Thompson, "How Globalization Saved the World and Damned the West," *The Atlantic*, February 7, 2019, www.theatlantic.com/ideas/archive/2019/02/new-american-populism-needed-save-west/582202.

3. Samuel P. Huntington, "Dead Souls: The Denationalization of the American Elite," *National Interest*, March 1, 2004, https://nationalinterest.org/article/dead-souls-the-denationalization-of-the-american-elite-620.

4. Walter Russell Mead, "All Aboard the Crazy Train," *Wall Street Journal*, January 20, 2020, www.wsj.com/articles/all-aboard-the-crazy-train-11579554512.

5. Tobias Hoonhout, "Bill Gates Dismisses Chinese Coronavirus Coverup: 'It's Not Even Time for That Discussion,'" *National Review*, April 27, 2020, www.nationalreview.com/news/bill-gates-dismisses-chinese-coronavirus-coverup-its-not-even-time-for-that-discussion; Ariel Zilber, "Bill Gates Defends China's Coronavirus Response: Billionaire Says Beijing 'Did a Lot of Things Right' at the Start of the Pandemic and Claims Criticism of the Communist Party Is a 'Distraction,'" *Daily Mail*, April 26, 2020, www.dailymail.co.uk/news/article-8259591/Now-not-time-Bill-Gates-defends-China-coronavirus-response.html.

6. Jack Goldsmith and Andrew Keane Woods, "Internet Speech Will Never Go Back to Normal," *The Atlantic*, April 25, 2020, www.theatlantic.com/ideas/archive/2020/04/what-covid-revealed-about-internet/610549.

7. For globalized "fast fashion," see Victoria Ledezma, "Globalization and Fashion: Too Fast, Too Furious," *Semantic Scholar*, 2017, www.semanticscholar.org/paper/Globalization-and-Fashion%3A-Too-Fast%2C-Too-Furious-Ledezma/fca5ba60509e4bc821b97082a1b8996c857c0baf?p2df.

8. Global language: Richard Nordquist, "Definition and Examples of Linguistic Americanization," ThoughtCo., July 3, 2019, www.thoughtco.com/what-is-americanization-linguistics-1688985.

NOTES TO CHAPTER SIX

9. Christian Schneider, "Stanford Likely Helped Develop Facial Recognition Tech Now Used Against Ethnic Minorities in China," *College Fix*, December 2, 2020, www.thecollegefix.com/stanford-likely-helped-develop-facial-recognition-tech-now-used-against-ethnic-minorities-in-china.

10. There remains controversy over how one defines a "democratic" nation: Max Roser, "Democracy," Our World in Data, June 2019, https://ourworld indata.org/democracy. See also the various approaches to understanding the health of democracy around the world in Larry Diamond and Marc F. Plattner, eds., *Democracy in Decline?* (Baltimore: Johns Hopkins University Press, 2015).

11. See Victor Davis Hanson, "Obama's Hazy Sense of History," *National Review*, August 28, 2014, www.nationalreview.com/2014/08/obamas-hazy-sense -history-victor-davis-hanson; David A. Graham, "The Wrong Side of 'the Right Side of History,'" *The Atlantic*, December 21, 2015, www.theatlantic.com/politics /archive/2015/12/obama-right-side-of-history/420462. Thomas L. Friedman, *The World Is Flat: A Brief History of the Twenty-First Century* (New York: Farrar, Straus and Giroux, 2005), 550.

12. Lawrence Wright, *The Looming Tower: Al-Qaeda and the Road to 9/11* (New York: Alfred A. Knopf, 2007), 376–407.

13. Tsarnaev: Janet Reitman, "Jahar's World," *Rolling Stone*, July 17, 2013, www.rollingstone.com/culture/culture-news/jahars-world-83856.

14. North Korea: "The Pyongyang Olympics," *Wall Street Journal*, February 11, 2018, www.wsj.com/articles/the-pyongyang-olympics-1518383959; "Media Bias: Hatred of Trump Brings Disgraceful Fawning over Kim Jong-un's Sister at Winter Olympics," *Investor's Business Daily*, February 13, 2018, www.investors.com /politics/editorials/media-bias-hatred-of-trump-brings-disgraceful-fawning-over -kim-jong-uns-sister-at-winter-olympics.

15. Rioter/demonstrator fashion: Robin Givhan, "The Protestors Are Dressed as Their Unique Selves—and That's Part of Their Power," *Washington Post*, June 2, 2020, www.washingtonpost.com/lifestyle/style/the-protesters-are-dressed-as -their-unique-selves--and-thats-part-of-their-power/2020/06/01/221b6fbc-a415 -11ea-bb20-ebf0921f3bbd_story.html.

16. Brian Reinbold and Yi Wen, "Historical U.S. Trade Deficits," Economic Synopses 2019, No. 3, Federal Reserve Bank of St. Louis, May 17, 2019, https://research.stlouisfed.org/publications/economic-synopses/2019/05/17 /historical-u-s-trade-deficits.

17. Douglas Ernst, "Bill Kristol Asks if 'Lazy' Pockets of White Working Class Should Be Replaced with 'New Americans,'" *Washington Times*, February 9, 2017, www.washingtontimes.com/news/2017/feb/9/bill-kristol-asks-if -lazy-pockets-of-white-working.

18. Steven A. Camarota and Karen Zeigler, "63% of Non-citizen Households Access Welfare Programs," Center for Immigration Studies, November 20, 2018, https://cis.org/Report/63-NonCitizen-Households-Access-Welfare-Programs.

19. See Nancy Rockwell, "Nativism v. Globalism," *Patheos*, July 17, 2016, www.patheos.com/blogs/biteintheapple/nativism-v-globalism.

20. See Friedman, *The World Is Flat*, 17.

21. Cf., e.g., J. D. Vance, *Hillbilly Elegy: A Memoir of a Family and Culture in Crisis* (New York: Harper, an imprint of HarperCollins Publishers, 2016), 5–7. See, e.g., Dabanjan Banerjee, Jagannatha Rao Kosagisharaf, and T. S. Sathyanarayana Rao, "'The Dual Pandemic' of Suicide and COVID-19: A Biopsychosocial Narrative of Risks and Prevention," *Psychiatry Research* 295 (January 2021): 113577, www.ncbi.nlm.nih.gov/pmc/articles/PMC7672361.

22. Recalibrating China: Seth J. Frantzman, "How to Avoid a China-Led World Order," *National Review*, May 25, 2020, www.nationalreview.com/2020/05/china-rise-what-american-history-can-teach-us/#slide-1; Matthew Continetti, "America Can't Face China Alone," *National Review*, April 25, 2020, www.nationalreview.com/2020/04/china-american-foreign-policy-facing-threat-requires-new-institutions-and-alliances.

23. Acceptance of decline: Jeff Cox, "Latest US-China Tensions Could Be the Trade Version of 'the End of the World as We Know It,'" *CNBC*, August 5, 2019, www.cnbc.com/2019/08/05/us-china-trade-tensions-could-be-the-end-of-the-world-as-we-know-it.html.

24. Managing decline: Kori Schake, "Managing American Decline," *The Atlantic*, November 24, 2018, www.theatlantic.com/ideas/archive/2018/11/how-bad-americas-decline-relative-china/576319; Gideon Rachman, "America Must Manage Its Decline," *Financial Times*, October 17, 2011, www.ft.com/content/0c73f10e-f8aa-11e0-ad8f-00144feab49a; Christopher A. Preble, "Adapting to American Decline," *New York Times*, April 21, 2018, www.nytimes.com/2018/04/21/opinion/sunday/adapting-to-american-decline.html.

25. The United States and immigration: "10 Countries That Take the Most Immigrants," *U.S. News & World Report*, December 18, 2019, www.usnews.com/news/best-countries/slideshows/10-countries-that-take-the-most-immigrants.

26. Troop realignment: Ryan Browne and Zachary Cohen, "US to Withdraw Nearly 12,000 Troops from Germany in Move That Will Cost Billions and Take Years," *CNN*, July 29, 2020, www.cnn.com/2020/07/29/politics/us-withdraw-troops-germany; cf. Ismay: "Lord Ismay," North Atlantic Treaty Organization (NATO), www.nato.int/cps/en/natohq/declassified_137930.htm.

27. US resources devoted to global presence: Amy Roberts, "By the Numbers: U.S. Diplomatic Presence," *CNN*, May 9, 2013, www.cnn.com/2013/05/09/politics/btn-diplomatic-presence; Niall McCarthy, "Trump Plans to Slash

U.S. Troop Numbers in Germany," Statista, June 8, 2020, www.statista.com /chart/17355/us-military-overseas; NATO Public Diplomacy Division, "Defence Expenditure of NATO Countries (2012–2019)," NATO, June 25, 2019, www.nato.int/nato_static_fl2014/assets/pdf/pdf_2019_06/20190625_PR2019 -069-EN.pdf; "Trump: What Does the US Contribute to Nato in Europe?," *BBC*, June 16, 2020, www.bbc.com/news/world-44717074.

28. Populists versus progressives: Richard Hofstadter, *The Age of Reform* (New York: Knopf, 1955), 60–93; cf. George Packer, "The Progressive and the Populist," *New Yorker*, March 10, 2010, www.newyorker.com/news/george-packer/the -progressive-and-the-populist.

29. David Goodhart, *The Road to Somewhere: The Populist Revolt and the Future of Politics* (New York: Oxford University Press, 2017), 19–48.

30. Global citizenship: "What Is Global Citizenship?," Oxfam Education, www.oxfam.org.uk/education/who-we-are/what-is-global-citizenship. On global democracies, see Richard Bellamy, *Citizenship: A Very Short Introduction* (Oxford: Oxford University Press, 2008), 84–86. On the controversies over whether Athens was a "face-to-face society," see Paul Cartledge, "Finley's Democracy: A Study in Reception (and Non-reception)," in *M. I. Finley: An Ancient Historian and His Impact*, ed. Daniel Jew, Robin Osborne, and Michael Scott (Cambridge: Cambridge University Press, 2016), 210–226.

31. The classic deconstruction of the romantic "Brotherhood of Man" propaganda remains Ernst Badian, "Alexander the Great and the Unity of Mankind," *Historia: Zeitschrift für Alte Geschichte*, B. 7, H. 4 (October 1958): 425–444. Cf. C. G. Thomas, "Alexander the Great and the Unity of Mankind," *Classical Journal* 63, no. 6 (March 1968): 258–260, http://132.74.10.54/images/2/22/Alex_and _the_Unity_of_Mankind_-_Thomas.pdf. On Alexander's ecumenical prayer at Opis, see Arrian 7.11.9. For Alexander's body count of Greeks abroad, see Victor Davis Hanson, "Alexander the Killer," *Military History Quarterly* 10, no. 3 (spring 1998): 8–19.

32. Jim Forest, "Mrs. Jellyby and the Domination of Causes," *In Communion*, February 19, 2006, https://incommunion.org/2006/02/19/mrs-jellyby-and-the -domination-of-causes. Cf. Russell L. Blaylock, "Managed Truth: The Great Danger to Our Republic," *Surgery Neurology International* 2 (2011): 179, www.ncbi .nlm.nih.gov/pmc/articles/PMC3263007.

33. Debbs quote: Eugene V. Debbs, "In Whose War Shall I Fight?" *Socialist Appeal*, April 2, 1938, www.marxists.org/history/etol/newspape/themilitant /socialist-appeal-1938/v02n14/debs.htm. See Samuel Zipp, *The Idealist: Wendell Willkie's Wartime Quest to Build One World* (Cambridge, MA: Belknap Press of Harvard University Press, 2020), 237–268.

34. "Citizen of the world": Kyle Smith, "Sure, Obama Loves America—Just Not the America We Live In," *New York Post*, February 21, 2015, https://nypost.com/2015/02/21/sure-obama-loves-america-just-not-the-america-we-live-in; "Barack Obama's Berlin Speech—Full Text," *The Guardian*, June 19, 2013, www.theguardian.com/world/2013/jun/19/barack-obama-berlin-speech-full-text; Kelly Mena and Kate Bennett, "Laura Bush and Michelle Obama Share Hopeful Message on Global Citizen Concert Special," *CNN*, April 18, 2020, www.cnn.com/2020/04/18/politics/michelle-obama-laura-bush-global-citizen-together-at-home. Biden: Natalie Winters, "Joe Biden Claims 'There's Nothing Special About Being an American," *National Pulse*, October 14, 2020, https://thenationalpulse.com/politics/biden-americans-arent-special.

35. War as a supposed eventual global unifier: Ian Morris, *War! What Is It Good For? Conflict and the Progress of Civilization from Primates to Robots* (New York: Farrar, Straus and Giroux, 2014), 332–394. The promise of global governance: Herbert George Wells, "The Idea of a League of Nations," *The Atlantic*, January 1919, www.theatlantic.com/magazine/archive/1919/01/the-idea-of-a-league-of-nations/306270.

36. Legal internationalism: Duncan B. Hollis, "Justice Ginsburg on Using Foreign and International Law in Constitutional Adjudication," *OpinioJuris*, February 8, 2010, http://opiniojuris.org/2010/08/02/justice-ginsburg-on-using-foreign-and-international-law-in-constitutional-adjudication.

37. On the original UN declaration of human rights, see "Universal Declaration of Human Rights," United Nations, www.un.org/en/about-us/universal-declaration-of-human-rights. For its 2015 codex, cf. "Transforming Our World: The 2030 Agenda for Sustainable Development," United Nations Department of Economic and Social Affairs, https://sdgs.un.org/2030agenda. Four freedoms: "Franklin Delano Roosevelt, 1941 State of the Union Address 'The Four Freedoms' (6 January 1941)," Voices of Democracy, http://voicesofdemocracy.umd.edu/fdr-the-four-freedoms-speech-text.

38. Cf. Bruce Bawer, "The 'Global Citizen' Fraud," *Commentary Magazine*, November 2019, www.commentarymagazine.com/articles/bruce-bawer/the-global-citizen-fraud; Bill Flax, "Obama, Hitler, and Exploding the Biggest Lie in History," *Forbes*, September 1, 2011, www.forbes.com/sites/billflax/2011/09/01/obama-hitler-and-exploding-the-biggest-lie-in-history/#4d215f4c47a6. On the striking occasional American affinities for an early Mussolini, see Jonah Goldberg, *Liberal Fascism: The Secret History of the American Left, from Mussolini to the Politics of Change* (New York: Broadway Books, 2009), 51–54.

39. Zachary Halaschak, "NBA Coach Steve Kerr Compares Gun Violence in US to Human Rights Abuses in China," *Washington Examiner*, October 11,

2019, www.washingtonexaminer.com/news/nba-coach-steve-kerr-compares-gun
-violence-in-us-to-human-rights-abuses-in-china.

40. Gun deaths: John Gramlich, "What the Data Says About Gun Deaths in the U.S," Pew Research Center, August 16, 2019, www.pewresearch.org/fact-tank/2019/08/16/what-the-data-says-about-gun-deaths-in-the-u-s; Jonah Blank, "China Bends Another American Institution to Its Will," *The Atlantic*, October 10, 2019, www.theatlantic.com/international/archive/2019/10/nba-victim-china-economic-might/599773.

41. China and democracy: Bloomberg: Leta Hong Fincher, "When Bloomberg News's Reporting on China Was Challenged, Bloomberg Tried to Ruin Me for Speaking Out," *The Intercept*, February 18, 2020, https://theintercept.com/2020/02/18/mike-bloomberg-lp-nda-china; Mark Moore, "Bloomberg: Xi Isn't a Dictator Because China Doesn't Want Democracy," *New York Post*, February 27, 2020, https://nypost.com/2020/02/27/bloomberg-xi-isnt-a-dictator-because-china-doesnt-want-democracy. On Chinese challenges to America, see Steven W. Mosher, *Bully of Asia: Why China's Dream Is the New Threat to World Order* (Washington, DC: Regnery Publishing, 2017), 235–260; in general, see Jonathan Ward, *China's Vision of Victory* (New York: Atlas Publishing, 2019).

42. International legal adjudication: Elian Peltier and Fatima Faizi, "I.C.C. Allows Afghanistan War Crimes Inquiry to Proceed, Angering U.S.," *New York Times*, March 5, 2020, www.nytimes.com/2020/03/05/world/europe/afghanistan-war-crimes-icc.html; Emily Deruy, "UN Affiliate Will Monitor U.S. Elections," *ABC News*, October 24, 2012, https://abcnews.go.com/ABC_Univision/Politics/election-monitors-free-countries-headed-us-election-day/story?id=17555988; Ed Pilkington, "US Halts Cooperation with UN on Potential Human Rights Violations," *The Guardian*, January 4, 2019, www.theguardian.com/law/2019/jan/04/trump-administration-un-human-rights-violations. See also, on the limitations of international courts, Bellamy, *Citizenship*, 85–92.

43. NBA and civil rights violations in China: Steven W. Mosher, "Nike Should Quit Lecturing on Social Justice—and Atone for Using Slave Labor in China," *New York Post*, July 25, 2020, https://nypost.com/2020/07/25/nike-should-quit-lecturing-on-social-justice-and-atone-for-using-slave-labor-in-china; Steve Fainaru and Mark Fainaru-Wada, "ESPN Investigation Finds Coaches at NBA China Academies Complained of Player Abuse, Lack of Schooling," *ESPN*, July 29, 2020, www.espn.com/nba/story/_/id/29553829/espn-investigation-finds-coaches-nba-china-academies-complained-player-abuse-lack-schooling.

44. Bethany Allen-Ebrahimian, "Study: Hollywood Casts More Light-Skinned Actors for Chinese Market," *Axios*, September 8, 2020, www.axios.com/hollywood-casting-china-colorism-light-skinned-df469d97-66c2-4b33-b41e-1feb29bf1f75.html.

Epilogue: Citizenship, the Annus Horribilis, and the November 2020 Election

1. Jeffrey Passel and D'Vera Cohn, "Radical Decline in Illegal Immigration: U.S. Unauthorized Immigrant Total Dips to Lowest Level in a Decade," Pew Research Center, November 27, 2018, www.pewresearch.org/hispanic/2018/11/27/u-s-unauthorized-immigrant-total-dips-to-lowest-level-in-a-decade.

2. Anthony Valastro, "Two-Thirds of Top Executives Say Trump Will Be Reelected in 2020, Business Survey Reveals," *CNBC*, September 13, 2019, www.cnbc.com/2019/09/13/trump-will-win-presidential-election-in-2020-business-survey-reveals.html.

3. Peng Zhou, et al., "A Pneumonia Outbreak Associated with a New Coronavirus of Probable Bat Origin," *Nature* 579 (2020): 270–273.

4. Joe Penney, "Racism, Rather Than Facts, Drove U.S. Coronavirus Bans," *The Intercept*, May 16, 2020, https://theintercept.com/2020/05/16/racism-coronavirus-china-europe.

5. A possible late summer appearance of the coronavirus: Shelby Lin Erdman, "Satellite Images of Wuhan May Suggest Coronavirus Was Spreading as Early as August," *CNN*, June 10, 2020, www.cnn.com/2020/06/08/health/satellite-pics-coronavirus-spread. Cissy Zhou, "China Coronavirus: As Travel Ban Is Issued for Wuhan, Many in City Rush to Escape," *South China Morning Post*, January 23, 2020, www.scmp.com/news/china/society/article/3047263/china-coronavirus-travel-ban-issued-residents-wuhan.

6. Hinnerk Feldwisch-Drentrup, "How WHO Became China's Coronavirus Accomplice," *Foreign Policy*, April 2, 2020, https://foreignpolicy.com/2020/04/02/china-coronavirus-who-health-soft-power.

7. Molly Kinder and Laura Stateler, "Amazon and Walmart Have Raked In Billions in Additional Profits During the Pandemic and Shared Almost None of It with Their Workers," Brookings Institution, December 22, 2020, www.brookings.edu/blog/the-avenue/2020/12/22/amazon-and-walmart-have-raked-in-billions-in-additional-profits-during-the-pandemic-and-shared-almost-none-of-it-with-their-workers.

8. Michael D. McDonald and Eric Martin, "Migrant Caravans Head to US Border Giving Biden an Early Test," *Bloomberg*, December 9, 2020, www.bloomberg.com/news/articles/2020-12-09/migrant-caravans-head-to-u-s-border-giving-biden-an-early-test. Cf. M. Krikorian, "The Biden Effect Continues at the Border," *National Review*, February 26, 2021, www.nationalreview.com/corner/the-biden-effect-continues-at-the-border. "Cages": M. Hackman and A. Caldwell, "Biden Administration Reopens Facility for Migrant Children: What to Know," *Wall Street Journal*, February 25, 2021, www.wsj.com/articles/biden

-administration-reopens-facility-for-migrant-children-what-to-know-116142 92613.

9. Health care workers: Mallory Simon, "Over 1,000 Health Professionals Sign a Letter Saying, Don't Shut Down Protests Using Coronavirus Concerns as an Excuse," *CNN*, June 5, 2020, www.cnn.com/2020/06/05/health/health -care-open-letter-protests-coronavirus-trnd. Clarke: "Biden Nominee for Justice Department Invited Anti-Semite to Harvard University," *Jewish News Syndicate*, January 12, 2021, www.jns.org/biden-nominee-for-justice-department-invited -anti-semite-to-harvard-university; vaccinations by race: Michael Graham, "Opinion: Are Some People 'Too White' to Get COVID-19 Vaccine?," *Detroit News*, December 21, 2020, www.detroitnews.com/story/opinion/2020/12/22 /opinion-some-people-too-white-get-covid-19-vaccine/3992869001.

10. J. Davidson, "In Racist Screed, New York Times 1619 Project Founder Calls White Race Barbaric 'Devils,' 'Bloodsuckers,' Columbus 'No Different Than Hitler,'" *The Federalist*, June 25, 2020, https://thefederalist.com/2020 /06/25/in-racist-screed-nyts-1619-project-founder-calls-white-race-barbaric -devils-bloodsuckers-no-different-than-hitler; M. Gonzalez, "To Destroy America," *City Journal*, September 1, 2020, www.city-journal.org/marxist-revolutionaries -black-lives-matter; K. Rahman, "Will Anti-Semitism Undermine the Black Lives Matter Movement?," *Newsweek*, July 24, 2020, www.newsweek.com /anti-semitism-derail-black-lives-matter-movement-1519728; J. Salo, "New York Times Reporter Says Destroying Property Is 'Not Violence,'" *New York Post*, June 3, 2020, https://nypost.com/2020/06/03/ny-times-reporter-says-destroying -property-is-not-violence.

11. N. Coleman, "Why We're Capitalizing Black," *New York Times*, July 5, 2020, www.nytimes.com/2020/07/05/insider/capitalized-black.html; A. Franks, "Rutgers English Department to Deemphasize Traditional Grammar 'in Sol- idarity with Black Lives Matter," *College Fix*, July 20, 2020, www.thecollege fix.com/rutgers-english-department-to-deemphasize-traditional-grammar-in -solidarity-with-black-lives-matter; cf. D. Petraeus, "Take the Confederate Names Off Our Army Bases," *The Atlantic*, June 9, 2020, www.theatlantic.com/ideas /archive/2020/06/take-confederate-names-off-our-army-bases/612832.

12. Shoshy Ciment, "People Are Slamming Chick-fil-A's CEO for Shining a Black Man's Shoes Onstage in a Bizarre Display of Repentance and Shame," *Busi- ness Insider*, June 22, 2020, www.businessinsider.com/chick-fil-a-ceo-criticized -shinin-black-mans-shoes-repent-2020-6.

13. Liberal worries over mail-in ballots: "Signature Verification and Mail Ballots: Guaranteeing Access While Preserving Integrity: A Case Study of California's Every Vote Counts Act," Policy Practicum: Every Vote Counts (Law 806Z), Stanford Law School Law and Policy Lab, May 15, 2020, www-cdn .law.stanford.edu/wp-content/uploads/2020/04/SLS_Signature_Verification

_Report-5-15-20-FINAL.pdf. Silicon Valley money and voting: C. Aguayo, "AMISTAT PROJECT Details FB CEO Mark Zuckerberg's $500 Million Influence on Election, in Recent Report," *NewsNet*, December 17, 2020, https://yournewsnet.com/amistat-project-details-fb-ceo-mark-zuckerbergs-500-million-influence-on-election-in-recent-report.

14. A. Viswanatha and S. Gurman, "Capitol Police Officer Brian Sicknick Died of Stroke, D.C. Medical Examiner Says," *Wall Street Journal*, April 19, 2021, www.wsj.com/articles/capitol-police-officer-brian-sicknick-died-of-stroke-d-c-medical-examiner-says-11618864840. Ashli Babbitt: S. Pagones, "Capitol Riot: Police Officer Won't Face Charges in Fatal Shooting of Ashli Babbitt, Prosecutors Say," *Fox News*, April 14, 2021, www.foxnews.com/us/capitol-riot-no-charges-officer-fatal-shooting-ashli-babbitt.

15. Fauci dissimulation: Mia Jankowicz, "Fauci Said US Government Held Off Promoting Face Masks Because It Knew Shortages Were So Bad That Even Doctors Couldn't Get Enough," *Business Insider*, June 15, 2020, www.businessinsider.com/fauci-mask-a[dvice-was-because-doctors-shortages-from-the-start-2020-6. COVID-19 testing incompetence and federal agencies: James Copland, *The Unelected: How an Unaccountable Elite Is Governing America* (New York: Encounter Books, 2020), 3–5. Cf. Peter Aitken, "Fauci Claims Herd Immunity Numbers Were 'Guestimates,'" *Fox News*, December 2020, www.foxnews.com/politics/fauci-herd-immunity-numbers-guestimates.

16. Doubts about lockdown costs to benefits: Greg Ip, "New Thinking on Covid Lockdowns: They're Overly Blunt and Costly," *Wall Street Journal*, August 23, 2020, www.wsj.com/articles/covid-lockdowns-economy-pandemic-recession-business-shutdown-sweden-coronavirus-11598281419; Jon Miltimore, "California Has the Strictest Lockdown in the US—and the Most Active COVID Cases (by Far)," Foundation for Economic Education, January 6, 2021, https://fee.org/articles/california-has-the-strictest-lockdown-in-the-us-and-the-most-active-covid-cases-by-far.

17. Jon Varney, "Crime Spikes as Soros-Funded DAs Take Charge: 'They're Not Progressive, They're Rogue," *Washington Times*, August 20, 2020, www.washingtontimes.com/news/2020/aug/20/george-soros-funded-das-oversee-big-cities-skyrock.

18. S. Hayward, "What Do the People Think?," *Powerline*, March 3, 2021, www.powerlineblog.com/archives/2021/03/what-do-the-people-think.php; S. Page, S. Elbeshbish, and M. Quarshie, "Exclusive: Stark Divide on Race, Policing Emerges Since George Floyd's Death, USA TODAY/Ipsos Poll Shows," *USA Today*, March 5, 2021, www.usatoday.com/story/news/politics/2021/03/05/americans-trust-black-lives-matter-declines-usa-today-ipsos-poll/6903470002.

19. Mayors' selective enforcement: Baltimore mayor: "Baltimore Mayor: 'Gave Those Who Wished to Destroy Space to Do That,'" *CBS Baltimore*,

April 25, 2015, https://baltimore.cbslocal.com/2015/04/25/baltimore-mayor
-gave-those-who-wished-to-destroy-space-to-do-that. Minneapolis mayor: Ian
Schwartz, "Minneapolis Mayor Jacob Frey Defends Riot Response: 'Brick and
Mortar Is Not as Important as Life,'" *RealClear Politics*, May 29, 2020, www
.realclearpolitics.com/video/2020/05/29/minneapolis_mayor_jacob_frey
_defends_riot_response_brick_and_mortar_is_not_as_important_as_life.html.
Tim Walz and "space": "Minnesota Gov. Walz Stresses Importance of 'Creating
Space' for Peaceful Protesters," *NBC*, May 31, 2020, https://news.yahoo.com
/minnesota-gov-walz-stresses-importance-035633142.html.

20. Trump banned: S. Fischer, "All the Platforms That Have Banned or
Restricted Trump So Far," *Axios*, January 11, 2021, www.axios.com/platforms
-social-media-ban-restrict-trump-d9e44f3c-8366-4ba9-a8a1-7f3114f920f1
.html; supporters banned: A. Martin, "Banned from Twitter and Facebook, Which
Sites Are the Pro-Trump Movement Using Now?," *Sky News*, January 1, 2021,
https://news.sky.com/story/banned-from-twitter-and-facebook-which-sites-are
-the-pro-trump-movement-using-now-12185181.

21. Parler: G. Turner, "Tech Under Attack After Parler Goes Dark, Twitter
Shares Drop," *Bloomberg*, January 12, 2020, www.bloombergquint.com/business
/tech-under-attack-after-parler-goes-dark-twitter-shares-drop. Clinton and no
concession: M. Choi, "Hillary Clinton to Biden: Don't Concede if the Election Is Close," *Politico*, August 25, 2020, www.politico.com/news/2020/08/25
/hillary-clinton-joe-biden-election-advice-401641; Harris and bail: D. Marcus,
"Meet the Rioting Criminals Kamala Harris Helped Bail Out of Jail," *The Federalist*, August 31, 2020, https://thefederalist.com/2020/08/31/meet-the-rioting
-criminals-kamala-harris-helped-bail-out-of-jail.

22. China and deceit about the virus: Josh Rogin, "How China Is Planning
to Use the Coronavirus Crisis to Its Advantage," *Washington Post*, March 16,
2020, www.washingtonpost.com/opinions/2020/03/16/how-china-is-planning
-use-coronavirus-crisis-its-advantage; Ana Swanson, "Coronavirus Spurs U.S. Efforts to End China's Chokehold on Drugs," *New York Times*, March 11, 2020,
www.nytimes.com/2020/03/11/business/economy/coronavirus-china-trump
-drugs.html; Mark Moore, "China Exporting Faulty Medical Equipment as
Manufacturing Rebounds: Report," *New York Post*, March 31, 2020, https://
nypost.com/2020/03/31/china-exporting-faulty-medical-equipment-as
-manufacturing-rebounds; Keith Bradsher, "China Delays Mask and Ventila-
tor Exports After Quality Complaints," *New York Times*, April 11, 2020, www
.nytimes.com/2020/04/11/business/china-mask-exports-coronavirus.html.

23. Director Tedros: World Health Organization (@WHO), "Preliminary
investigations conducted by the Chinese authorities have found no clear evidence of human-to-human transmission of the novel #coronavirus (2019-
nCoV) identified in #Wuhan, #China," Twitter, January 14, 2020, 3:18 a.m.,

https://twitter.com/who/status/1217043229427761152; "WHO Director -General's Opening Remarks at the Technical Briefing on 2019 Novel Coronavirus," World Health Organization, February 4, 2020, www.who.int/dg /speeches/detail/who-director-general-s-opening-remarks-at-the-technical -briefing-on-2019-novel-coronavirus; Grants to Wuhan: Dan Evon and Alex Kasprak, "Did Obama Admin Give Wuhan Laboratory a $3.7 Million Grant?," Snopes, April 24, 2020, www.snopes.com/fact-check/obama-admin -wuhan-lab-grant; Matthew Brown and Kim Hjelmgaard, "Fact Check: Obama Administration Did Not Send $3.7 Million to Wuhan Lab," *USA Today*, May 4, 2020, www.usatoday.com/story/news/factcheck/2020/05/04/fact-check-obama -administration-did-not-send-3-7-m-wuhan-lab/3061490001; Geoff Brumfiel, "Harvard Professor's Arrest Raises Questions About Scientific Openness," *NPR*, February 19, 2020, www.npr.org/2020/02/14/806128410/harvard-professors -arrest-raises-questions-about-scientific-openness.

24. Dual scientific duties: Hollie McKay, "China Ups Its Spy Game on US Soil as It Bids to Control Coronavirus Narrative," *Fox News*, April 21, 2020, www .foxnews.com/us/china-spying-us-soil-coronavirus-narrative; Josh Campbell, "FBI Arrests Researcher for NASA Who Allegedly Failed to Report Ties to China," *CNN*, May 12, 2020, www.cnn.com/2020/05/12/us/nasa-researcher-arrest-china. See, in general, Bill Gertz, *Deceiving the Sky: Inside Communist China's Drive for Global Supremacy* (New York: Encounter Books, 2019), 139–157; Sue Dremann, "Stanford Researcher and Others Allegedly Concealed Chinese Military Ties," *Palo Alto Online*, January 23, 2020, www.paloaltoonline.com/news/2020/07/23 /stanford-researcher-allegedly-concealed-chinese-military-ties.

INDEX

VICTOR DAVIS HANSON is the Martin and Illie Anderson Senior Fellow in military history and classics at the Hoover Institution at Stanford University and a professor emeritus of classics at California State University, Fresno. He is the author of over two dozen books, most recently *The Case for Trump*. He lives in Selma, California.